## Acknowledgments

Special thanks to these people for answering so many of our questions or helping us in other ways with this book: Jack and Adrienne Samuels, Kay Wanke, Shirley Harvey, Karen Ard, and Kymm Story. We are grateful to our daughters, Krista Jensen and Shelli Larson, for all the hours of help and editing. Krista also did the wonderful illustrations including the dragon, which represents the dangerous myth that MSG and other excitotoxins are safe, a myth that must be exposed and constantly battled. For a recent birthday, Krista presented me with a handmade mask and cape and thus, the MSG Avenger was born! A thank-you goes to our son, Michael, for his words of encouragement. It was out of our desperation to help him that we first discovered the truth about MSG. The biggest thanks goes to my husband, Mike, who patiently deciphered my often messy notes, entering and re-entering revised information into the computer, and organizing a readable book in the process. He is my quiet source of strength and support. Thanks, sweetheart!

Copyright 1997
Revised Edition Copyright 1999
by
Deborah L. Anglesey

All rights reserved

No part of this book may be reproduced or utilized in any form or by any means, electronic or mechanical, including photocopying and recording, or by any information storage and retrieval system, without permission in writing from the publisher.

ISBN 0-9670492-0-2

Disclaimer:
The writer, editors, publisher, and others referred to in this book are not responsible for any adverse reactions or results from the use of the recipes or information offered therein. The author has shared the information based on her own experiences, experiences shared by other MSG-sensitive individuals, and the resources referenced in the book.

Printed in the United States of America
Front Porch Productions
Kennewick, Washington

# Table of Contents

Acknowledgments . . . . . . . . . . . . . . . . . . . . . . . . . . . . . . . . . . . . . . . . . . . . . . . . . . . . . . . 1

The Discovery (Author's Story) . . . . . . . . . . . . . . . . . . . . . . . . . . . . . . . . . . . . . . . . . 5

An Introduction to Monosodium Glutamate . . . . . . . . . . . . . . . . . . . . . . . . . . . . . . . 9

Aspartame - Another Potent "Neurotoxin" . . . . . . . . . . . . . . . . . . . . . . . . . . . . . . . 12

Supportive and Interesting Articles . . . . . . . . . . . . . . . . . . . . . . . . . . . . . . . . . . . . . 15

Symptoms or Conditions Attributed to MSG Sensitivity . . . . . . . . . . . . . . . . . . . . 20

Common Names of MSG-Containing Ingredients Found on Food Labels . . . . . . . 22

Processed Foods Commonly Containing Some Glutamate . . . . . . . . . . . . . . . . . . . 24

Definitions and Helpful Information . . . . . . . . . . . . . . . . . . . . . . . . . . . . . . . . . . . . 25

Shopping Tips . . . . . . . . . . . . . . . . . . . . . . . . . . . . . . . . . . . . . . . . . . . . . . . . . . . . . 32

Brand Names of Products . . . . . . . . . . . . . . . . . . . . . . . . . . . . . . . . . . . . . . . . . . . . 39

Eating Out . . . . . . . . . . . . . . . . . . . . . . . . . . . . . . . . . . . . . . . . . . . . . . . . . . . . . . . . 42
     Fast Food Restaurants . . . . . . . . . . . . . . . . . . . . . . . . . . . . . . . . . . . . . . . . . 42
     Traveling . . . . . . . . . . . . . . . . . . . . . . . . . . . . . . . . . . . . . . . . . . . . . . . . . . . 43
     School Lunches . . . . . . . . . . . . . . . . . . . . . . . . . . . . . . . . . . . . . . . . . . . . . . 44

School Lunches and Snack Ideas . . . . . . . . . . . . . . . . . . . . . . . . . . . . . . . . . . . . . . 45

A Closer Look at Dairy Products . . . . . . . . . . . . . . . . . . . . . . . . . . . . . . . . . . . . . . 47

The Pitfalls of Corn . . . . . . . . . . . . . . . . . . . . . . . . . . . . . . . . . . . . . . . . . . . . . . . . . 49

Sulfites . . . . . . . . . . . . . . . . . . . . . . . . . . . . . . . . . . . . . . . . . . . . . . . . . . . . . . . . . . . 50

Remedies and Healthful Hints . . . . . . . . . . . . . . . . . . . . . . . . . . . . . . . . . . . . . . . . 53

Miscellaneous Information . . . . . . . . . . . . . . . . . . . . . . . . . . . . . . . . . . . . . . . . . . . 55
     The Glaucoma Connection . . . . . . . . . . . . . . . . . . . . . . . . . . . . . . . . . . . . . 57
     Fibromyalgia Report . . . . . . . . . . . . . . . . . . . . . . . . . . . . . . . . . . . . . . . . . . 58
     Fresh Produce and Meat Packaging Alert . . . . . . . . . . . . . . . . . . . . . . . . . 58
     Fruit and Vegetable Spray Alert . . . . . . . . . . . . . . . . . . . . . . . . . . . . . . . . . 59
     Lobby Groups for the Glutamate Industry . . . . . . . . . . . . . . . . . . . . . . . . . 60

Testimonials . . . . . . . . . . . . . . . . . . . . . . . . . . . . . . . . . . . . . . . . . . . . . . . . . . . . . . . 61

Excerpts from the 1997 Nomsg Conference . . . . . . . . . . . . . . . . . . . . . . . . . . . . . . . . . . . . . . . . . . 63

References and Suggested Reading . . . . . . . . . . . . . . . . . . . . . . . . . . . . . . . . . . . . . . . . . . . . . . . . 71

Scientific Studies and References Supporting the Fact that MSG Places Consumers at Risk . . . . . . . . 74

ATTENTION HYPERSENSITIVE INDIVIDUALS!! . . . . . . . . . . . . . . . . . . . . . . . . . . . . . . . . . . 79

Conclusion and Challenge . . . . . . . . . . . . . . . . . . . . . . . . . . . . . . . . . . . . . . . . . . . . . . . . . . . . . . 81

Recipes . . . . . . . . . . . . . . . . . . . . . . . . . . . . . . . . . . . . . . . . . . . . . . . . . . . . . . . . . . . . . . . . . . . . 82

# The Discovery (Author's Story)

This book is written first and foremost for our children, our good friends, and large extended family, all of whom make our lives worth living. It is also for their children, friends, and acquaintances and all those who would benefit from an MSG free diet - in our opinion, that includes all of us.

To explain more clearly how this simple food additive has affected my life, and many of those around me, I must go back a little in time, to the early part of 1975. My husband, Mike, and I were living in our first home in Seattle, Washington, with our three young children, Kris (four years), Shelli (two years), and baby Michael. It was an exciting and happy time in my life, filled with fun and work. I had great friends with whom I shared tole painting and Chinese cooking classes. I was full of energy, was still wearing the same size I wore when I got married, had a sweet and very helpful husband, and felt very busy but happy. Then suddenly I started experiencing chest pains. The first time it happened, the area around my heart hurt with knifelike pains and jabs whenever I tried to breathe in. Mike and I were terrified as I lay on the floor unable to get my breath. Mike was about to give me mouth to mouth resuscitation and call for an ambulance, when my normal breathing began to return. I felt so weak afterwards that I went to bed and later resumed life's normal demands. But a few days later, as I ironed, the same thing happened, and then again every three to five days. After a couple of weeks, I visited my doctor who gave me a complete physical and then declared my heart was "very strong" and everything else was very normal. He asked me if my life and marriage were "OK," if there were any problems. After all, I was reminded, I'd just had a baby and two other children and it was likely that stress was manifesting itself this way. I was shocked and embarrassed to think that I wasn't able to cope emotionally with the rigors of my chosen lifestyle. He suggested that I get out more with adults, take lots of restful baths, etc. I enrolled in a second Chinese cooking class with my sister and two other friends. It was great fun, but my symptoms continued. After a few months, I looked terrible. I'd lost some weight, my face was puffy, there were bags under my eyes and the girl who was nicknamed, "The roadrunner" in college, now walked around the house feeling like her arms and legs were dragging 50 pound weights. Getting the kids fed and dressed became huge chores. My idea of a successful day was when I could manage getting all three to nap at the same time so that I could rest, too. All I wanted to do was sleep. I put on a happy face at church, because it would have been embarrassing if anyone knew my secret: that I was unable to cope. I often had terrible headaches lasting two to three days. After a year, I confided in a close friend and she suggested a different doctor. Same tests, same results: "You're as strong as a horse - good heart. Try to relax more." The third doctor I saw told me, "It's all in your head, as far as I can tell." I felt humiliated. Three years and three more doctors later, I gave up. I then became acquainted with a nurse who eventually treated me like a big sister. One day, after an especially trying week, I blurted it all out to her. I felt like such a failure and hypocrite. My family and friends thought I had it "all together". I had always been labeled the "capable one", the lucky one, the one who could handle anything. In three years I had gone from a confident, cheerful mom and wife to a person I could barely understand or like very much. Cranky, tired, and always achy, my poor husband was at a loss as to how to help me. My friend listened and suggested another physician. I trusted her opinion and got an examination from this kind doctor. He told me my symptoms were very much like those of a young patient of his whose first attack happened on the football field during a game. Tests showed he had asthma and this doctor suspected the same of me. I saw an allergist and had the scratch tests done, which on a scale of 1-10, showed I was an 11, being mostly sensitive to mold, weeds, and dust. The immunization shots began. After a year I did feel somewhat better with fewer headaches and chest pains. However, I seemed to catch every viral or bacterial infection to come my way. Sore throats and bronchial infections plagued me often and the headaches I did get were still severe and sometimes debilitating. I learned to accept them and do the best I could on my better days.

Several years later, something new began to happen to me. I called them my stomach episodes. About five years ago, whenever Mike and I ate out, my stomach would feel full less than half way through the meal. Within half to one hour later, I'd be belching uncontrollably and racing to the nearest bathroom, suffering explosive and burning diarrhea. Following that, I'd have a terrible thirst and throbbing headache. For two or three days my stomach felt as though a tank had run over it. My mouth and tongue felt terribly dry and I'd be very thirsty. The whole time I'd be weak, headachy, and light headed, feeling chills or flushes and sometimes my fingers or toes felt numb. Another symptom appeared. The bones in my feet or hands would hurt if squeezed at all. My knees would sometimes ache. I wondered if it was arthritis. Also, I suffered from frequent urination, getting up two to four times at night. The episodes continued and often happened after I ate at home also. Mike bought me some electrolyte powder to help replace some of the minerals and liquids I often lost. Soon I was developing hemorrhoids due to the painful diarrhea. My doctor told me it was colitis or irritable bowel syndrome and suggested hemorrhoid surgery in the near future. Meanwhile, after suffering pain from a uterine fibroid tumor and heavy bleeding, I had a complete hysterectomy. While recuperating, I again developed terrible diarrhea. Mike kept trying to pump up my strength with canned chicken soup and lots of orange juice. It was a very slow recovery and I was convinced that I was a real wimp and poor health was my fate. A couple of months later, I developed a urinary tract infection. Resting at home, I faithfully took my prescribed medication, but only got worse. Again I suffered terrible burning diarrhea, and headaches that were worse than ever. After three days on the medicine, my husband took one look at me when he got home from work and said, "You look worse, not better" and ordered me to call the doctor's office. Fortunately, a nurse was put on the line. I told her of the problem. She told me to quit taking the medication immediately because I was obviously allergic to sulfa drugs. She herself was also, and consequently was the first person to give me insight into part of the cause of my health problems. She told me I was probably allergic to sulfites too. What were sulfites? She explained that a lot of processed foods contained sulfites, as preservatives, and that I should go to a health food store for resource books on food additives. This I did and was shocked at how many foods I often ate that contained sulfites, ie., dried apricots, fruit juice, fruit syrups, sauerkraut, soda pop, bottled lemon juice, dehydrated and french fried potatoes. Sulfites are even used to clean and disinfect commercial cooking equipment and storage bins. It was also sprayed on salad bars to keep the fruits, vegetables, and salads fresh appearing, although that practice is now prohibited. I cleaned out my cupboards and refrigerator of as much of the culprit as I could and noticed fewer stomach episodes, cramping, and headaches. I continued to read and send for more information from various sources. Then came the holiday season of 1994. I was trying to be so careful to avoid sulfites as I prepared all the family favorites during Thanksgiving, Christmas, and New Year's Eve. But my symptoms got worse and I became depressed. I told myself that perhaps it wasn't sulfites after all. Maybe IBS (Irritable Bowel Syndrome) would continue to plague me forever. But I didn't give up. I tried even harder after the holidays to eat healthy foods, read labels and memorize the various names of sulfite compounds on labels. Then my 20 year old son called from Miami where he was serving a church mission. He was suffering horrendous migraines. He was weak and getting outpatient treatment for a bronchial infection he couldn't shake. He had a battery of tests including an MRI and allergy tests. Since nothing organic could be found, the doctors felt he was just suffering from stress and allergies to the grasses that grew there. He suffered dizziness, an inability to concentrate or recall well, and after his bout with bronchitis, was sent home to see if he could recuperate here. What had happened to my usually strong, happy and healthy child? When we picked him up at the airport, I saw a different young man from the one that had left a year earlier. Something pricked my memory. I noticed the bags under his eyes, the tired look and the puffy face. It was like a mirror of me when I first started having health problems while in my twenties. Had he inherited my constitution? I never once believed he was suffering from stress. I knew my son. This was a kid to whom everything came easily. He'd even had his own lawn care business at age 16. Handsome, confident, athletic, intelligent. I could not shake the belief that there had to be something else going on here. I watched him closely. During his headaches, he'd hole himself up in a darkened room with a blanket covering him, chilled and in terrible pain, the strain showing in his hurting eyes. He said his arms would feel heavy and numb. He'd complain that he couldn't remember anything or speak clearly during and shortly after the episodes. He was becoming depressed and anxious about his future, which included college and a medical profession. How could he study with such debilitating headaches? He felt like a failure at 20. We took him to local doctors. He had a brain wave test, CAT scans and an MRI, visited a neurologist, allergist, and two other specialists. All said he was very healthy. One doctor, a psychologist (after all, it had to be in his mind since the tests were all negative) gave him a book about coping with stress. Even some relatives chose to believe it was his inability to handle a lot of demands or responsibility. This again was all too familiar with my own earlier experience. As for my condition, I was becoming very tired of unexplained headaches and sporadic diarrhea. I'd had all the unpleasant tests, including ultrasound and upper and lower gastro intestinal series and all were negative. I noticed my vision blurring, especially during and after headaches. I had learned all that I could about sulfites, was avoiding all the specified foods containing them and still I was not free of all the symptoms. I'd also gained 16 pounds in nine months, often had "blue" days when I felt a little black cloud hovered over only me and found my energy level fading. The word "depression" wasn't in my vocabulary. That happened to other people, not me.

Then one morning in February 1995, I woke up with a massive headache and felt the familiar nausea, accompanied by belching and some chest pains too. It had happened so many times in the last five years, but the memory of that particular morning is crystal clear in my mind. I was totally whipped and though people know me as an upbeat optimist, I finally felt beaten. For the first time I cried - for my son, and for myself. I'd often counted all my blessings to get me through hard times, but this morning, my Dad's words of "If you don't have your health, you don't have anything," ran through my mind. I slid from the bed to my knees and sought help and comfort from a higher source. Desperately pouring out my heart, I told God that I couldn't handle it anymore. I told Him that I would rather die than feel this rotten all the time and that I wanted to be able to enjoy my children and grandchildren and not be a burden. In essence, I turned it over to Him. Gradually calming down, I remained for several minutes at my bed side. Then soft, warm peace flowed over me. I felt a strong prompting to go over all my notes and information sent to me about sulfites one more time. I had done it several times before, but this time I had such a feeling of confidence and anticipation. I rushed to get my file and leafed through all the pages, pausing for a moment on a bulletin sent by the MSG Sensitivity Institute, about MSG. I'd never read it, believing sulfites to be the sole cause for my health problems. After reviewing everything I had, and flipping again through the pages, the article on MSG seemed to pop out at me, so I began to read it. Suddenly, I could feel an excitement growing inside of me. The article was describing all the symptoms that Mike and I had been experiencing, often using the exact same words that we often used to describe them! I immediately called my husband at work and told him I knew without a doubt what the culprit was and had been for years: Monosodium Glutamate. I, like most people, had assumed that MSG was found only in Chinese food. Little did I know it was in our cereal, catsup, crackers, mayonnaise, tuna, yogurt, diet food, soft drinks, salad dressings, poultry, most fast foods, and frozen snacks and meals, seasonings, canned soups and entrees, and even most ice creams. And many restaurants load their foods with this so-called safe flavor enhancer, often unaware of its hidden sources and names.

I sent for information from NOMSG (National Organization Mobilized to Stop Glutamate) and some other suggested resources in the article. Then I ordered two books through our local bookstore. I cleaned out half my cupboards and refrigerator. Using the information, I ate meals without MSG for the first time in years. Incredibly, all my symptoms disappeared, reappearing only after eating MSG by mistake usually at a restaurant or at parties. Unbelievably my post nasal drip, something I've endured since childhood, also disappeared.

I called my son the same day that I read the MSG article and sent him the information. He also improved. Away at college he finds it a struggle to avoid MSG since fast foods are mainstays of busy college students. Last semester I sent him boxes of homemade and bottled catsup, spaghetti sauce, and salsa. Incidentally, both of my daughters are now suffering early symptoms. Both are in their twenties like

I was when mine began. My sister, who is four years younger, is noticing symptoms.

It has been a few years since our discovery. But in that time I've been able to share the information that I've gleaned with many friends and relatives. One of my acquaintances has Parkinson's Disease. She has fewer symptoms as long as she avoids MSG and other toxic additives. My next door neighbor, Patsy Merriman, confided in me about her health problems. I gave her the information. In a couple of days she came over to ask for MSG free recipes and said she had thought she was dying but now knows her stomach problems and sometimes fuzzy memory are caused by MSG. Her mother had Alzheimer's. Dr. Russell L. Blaylock, the author of Excitotoxins: The Taste That Kills, believes that MSG, and other neurotoxins such as aspartame and L-Cysteine cause or exascerbate many neurodegenerative diseases. My husband's father is so sensitive to MSG, his throat closes off if he eats it and he must induce vomiting. His mother had Alzheimer's disease for several years before she passed away. The author also shows a link to attention deficit disorder, anxiety attacks, chronic fatigue syndrome, multiple sclerosis, glaucoma, depression, and asthma. Incidentally, after giving my findings to my own doctor, he suggested stopping my allergy shots to see if MSG was the cause for my asthma attacks and headaches. It was. After 20 years of injections, I no longer need them. I never did.

The FDA may call MSG safe, but independent researchers estimate at least 30% to 40% or more of the population may be MSG sensitive in varying degrees. Many are unaware of the reasons for their symptoms and are being misdiagnosed, mistreated, and are suffering needlessly. Some of those people are my friends, relatives, and my children. Man is slow to learn and change when it concerns food and money. Well-paid lobby groups funded by the multi-billion dollar food industry are constantly working to make MSG appear safe to the public. They send pamphlets to schools and health professionals and post websites to "educate" us about MSG's virtues (The International Food Information Council, Glutamate Association, International Glutamate Technical Committee). I believe change will eventually come, but until then, fellow sufferers, and the health conscious, this book is for you. I hope it will enlighten and help answer the question I hear most, "What can I eat, now?".

This book is dedicated to Mike, my supportive husband and "editor"; to Krista, Richelle, Michael, and Craig, our incredible children; to Kate, our granddaughter who came too early and left us too soon; to Chelsea, Rachel, Braeden, Tanner, and Jacob, our other sweet grandchildren and all those yet to come; to supportive family and friends; to my late father and his sister, whose last years we believe, were filled with needless suffering; and to the Lord above for His help and guidance. It was truly a miracle that led us to the answers we were seeking.

# An Introduction to Monosodium Glutamate

Glutamic acid is just one of many amino acids that are the building blocks of proteins. It occurs naturally in many foods such as tomatoes, milk, and mushrooms. It is also found in the cells of our bodies, including mother's milk, and involves a wide variety of brain functions since it functions as a neurotransmitter. This natural glutamate in plants and animals is known as L-glutamic acid.

Our normal digestive process slowly breaks down this natural or "bound" glutamic acid and it is then delivered to glutamate receptors in our body and brain. Broken down this way, it is harmless. In a factory, however, the bound glutamic acid in certain foods (corn, molasses, wheat) is broken down or made "free" by various processes (hydrolyzed, autolyzed, modified or fermented with strong chemicals, bacteria, or enzymes) and refined to a white crystal that resembles sugar. This substance is known as monosodium glutamate or MSG. It is 78.2% glutamate, 12.2% sodium, and 9.6% water. It is odorless and has no distinct flavor, although some describe a salty/sweet flavor. Its chemical formulation has been modified and it is technically known as D-glutamic acid. It also contains some L-glutamic acid, pyroglutamic acid, and other contaminants This factory made version causes sensitive individuals more serious reactions than any other form of glutamic acid. Keep in mind that there is no D-glutamic acid, pyroglutamic acid, or other contaminants in the protein found in plants and animals, only L-glutamic acid.

We are getting far too much MSG in the growing number of processed food items that we have come to rely on. Since free glutamate can be a component part of certain food additives, such as autolyzed yeast or hydrolyzed protein, the FDA allows it to go into food unlabeled as MSG. A label may say "yeast extract", "calcium caseinate", or "beef flavoring", but the product still contains varying amounts of "free" glutamic acid. This makes it very difficult for consumers who are trying to avoid it. It is also very dangerous for those who suffer severe reactions to it.

Monosodium glutamate in the form of a dried seaweed (Kombu) has been used for thousands of years in Oriental countries. Today, free glutamate or MSG is made from many different raw materials (mostly corn) using various chemical processes previously mentioned. Strong acids, alkalies, enzymes, bacteria, and heat are used to hydrolyze animal, vegetable, or milk products. Calcium and sodium caseinate are products of hydrolyzed milk protein. Maltodextrin comes from processed corn and although corn syrup and cornstarch are not as highly processed as maltodextrin is, they may not be totally free of glutamate as a result of their production. Yeast extract or autolyzed yeast is made by chemically processing natural yeast in a method similar to hydrolyzing. Barley malt and malt extract have small amounts of MSG because of an enzyme reaction used to produce them. Whey protein concentrate or protein isolate may contain MSG if hydrolyzed milk proteins are present or added. Soy protein isolate or soy protein concentrate is processed from soy beans and is often a component of textured protein. Most smoke flavor or smoke flavorings use hydrolyzed protein to intensify flavor. Some other "free" glutamate containing products are gelatins, which are highly processed by-products of animal protein that always contain MSG in varying amounts, and soy sauce, made from a fermentation process of soy beans. MSG can also be added to cheaper brands of soy sauce to enhance the flavor. Carrageenan is made from a type of seaweed known as Irish moss. It may contain MSG depending on its manufacturer. MSG or hydrolyzed milk protein is often added to it.

When I talk to people about MSG, most think it is a food preservative. Actually, MSG just makes food taste better. It stimulates the taste buds and eventually the brain receptors into perceiving salt and sweet sensations instead of bitter or sour. Food producers jumped on the flavor enhancing bandwagon as soon as WWII was over and Japan gave us our first taste. MSG can mask inferior or stale food, or tinny flavors in canned food, just as it enhances frozen or dry foods.

Dr. George Schwartz, a well-known physician and toxicologist, states in his book, In Bad Taste: The MSG Symptom Complex, that MSG is a neurotransmitter which is "a substance which stimulates brain-cell activity." He goes on to explain that the problem with this is that brain cells are being over excited and they burn themselves out, thus supporting his and other researchers' theories about the correlation of MSG to Alzheimer's Disease and other neurological disorders, such as Parkinson's and fibromyalgia.

We know the effect MSG has on brain cells, but I wanted to know why people suffer other adverse conditions, such as joint pain, stomach problems and vision problems. In his book, Dr. George Schwartz explains the mechanisms of MSG toxicity. Basically he describes the amino acid, glutamic acid, as being joined to other amino acids in a protein by peptide linkages. Normally, when we eat a protein rich food, the linkages are slowly broken apart during the digestive process. But when factory created MSG is consumed, it has no linkages to break down, since this has already been done in the production. It is now "free" glutamate and not bound to other amino acids. Consequently, the "free" glutamate is very rapidly absorbed into our system and the amount of glutamic acid absorbed in our blood stream can be eight to ten times the normal amount. It can even be absorbed through the membranes of the mouth and esophagus. Bound glutamic acid is naturally found in body cells as part of the protein composition. Remember, it's the "freed-up" form of glutamate (D-glutamate) produced in factories that can act as a powerful drug affecting not only brain cells, but also intestinal muscles, blood vessels, and any system the blood carries it to. We are discovering glutamate receptors in various parts of the body, not only in the brain. We know that in the lungs and organs, it can change normal breathing, heart rhythm, and hormone secretion. Settling in joints and muscles, it can cause "gout" or arthritis and tendinitis-like symptoms. I know several people who have put up with years of painful cortisone shots in the joints and powerful prescription drugs only to find out recently that MSG was the source of all their suffering. One woman needed a walker to get around prior to her MSG-sensitivity discovery. So before you put that tasty, flavor-enhanced morsel in your mouth, ask yourself, "Do I want toxins in my system, destroying the cells of my body?" The more MSG you can avoid, the less chance you will have of developing any number of terrible conditions and diseases.

Hydrolyzed vegetable protein, which is about 40% free glutamic acid, is made by boiling certain vegetables for hours in vats of sulfuric or other acids and water which is then neutralized with caustic soda. It is dried to form a powder which is high in "free" glutamate, aspartate and cysteic acid (excitotoxins). It also contains known carcinogens and dicarboxilic amino acid (safety unknown). MSG is often added to the hydrolyzed powder. Finally the product is bagged and shipped to food companies where it is added to many foods, including baby food.

Since MSG and hydrolyzed protein are produced by fermenting natural ingredients such as molasses, corn, wheat, soybeans, sugar beets, sugar cane, tapioca, and other vegetables, it would be easy to assume it has health benefits. But a growing number of people are finding the opposite to be true. The FDA says a "small" number of people are sensitive to MSG. Michael Taylor, then Deputy of Policy for the FDA in a Nov. 4, 1991 60 Minutes TV interview, stated that possibly 2% of the U.S. population are MSG reactive, about 5,000,000. But a chart called "Major Causes of Restaurant Syndrome" in the Jan-Feb 1987 NER Allergy Proc. Book, Vol 8, No 1, estimates that 15 to 20% of our population is sensitive, about 50,000,000. Dr. Blaylock, M.D. and Dr. Schwartz, M.D. both believe the numbers are much higher, perhaps 40% to 50%. Many people don't tie MSG to their health problems because reactions to MSG may occur anywhere from 10 minutes to 48 hours after eating a meal containing it.

An article in Science Magazine, Vol. 247, discussed a 1992 meeting of the Society for Neuroscience which debated the toxic effects on the brain of excitatory amino acids. Of glutamate it stated that besides stimulating some neurons to higher activity like other amino acids, glutamate "also acts as an excitotoxin: when present, it can actually stimulate nerve cells until they die."

For twenty years the New England Journal of Medicine has published research papers, citing the neurotoxicity of MSG.

There are no current limits on the amount of MSG that can be added to a food product and we have no way of knowing the amount we are consuming daily. Since most MSG is added as a component part of other ingredients, it is not recognizable or labeled as MSG and is therefore hidden from our view. Some brand names of MSG containing products follow: Accent, Glutacyl, Kombu Extract, Subu, Monopotassium glutamate, Ajinomoto, Glutavine, Lawry's Seasoning Salt, Vestin, Chinese Seasonings, Gourmet Powder, Mei-jing, Wei-jing, Zest, Glutamate, Spike, Torula Yeast.

Much of the above information was gleaned from the *MSG Healthline, Issue No 1, Jan 1993, in an article entitled, Introducing: Monosodium Glutamate. The title was ironic for me, for this was the article referred to in my story which first "introduced" me to MSG and resulted in the immediate discovery of the cause for all my suffering and that of my son.

By way of an update, Mike, who started my quest, was able to go on to chiropractic school and will soon (year 2000) dedicate some of his practice to helping other victims of MSG toxicity like himself. Originally, he considered traditional medical school, but decided to concentrate on causes for symptoms, versus treating them with drugs. He found chiropractors to be more aware of nutrition and food additives, including MSG, which is discussed at Palmer Chiropractic School. He's come a long way from that young man who thought his "life was over" just a few short years ago. To readers who are finding it difficult to find doctors sympathetic to MSG toxicity, you can call NoMSG at (800) BEAT MSG for a list of informed doctors that may be near you. Naturopathic and Osteopathic doctors are often educated about toxins, also.

*The MSG Healthline is issued by the MSG Sensitivity Institute in Concord, NH.

# Aspartame - Another Potent "Neurotoxin"

Recently, as I listened to a news report on TV, I was elated to hear research scientists, one of them Dr. John W. Olney, declare nationally that their studies showed aspartame caused brain tumors and cancer in lab animals. I naively thought that, surely, people will see the danger of artificial sweeteners and perhaps other factory produced neurotoxins, like MSG.

Soon after that announcement, we visited my husband's parents. Mom had suffered horrible migraines for many years and though she told me they aren't as diligent as we are to avoid MSG, that her headaches are now infrequent and not as severe. When I later opened their refrigerator to get something, I saw several cans of diet pop. I suppose my gaping mouth betrayed me but after considering whether to bite my tongue, I decided to ask Dad if he heard the recent "hoopla" about aspartame. He replied that he didn't buy into everything "they" say. I was concerned because his mother had Alzheimer's, his throat closes off when he ingests too much MSG, most of his children are reactive, and we all love him very much. But that experience was a reality check for me. Most people will prefer to believe what they want to believe. I, too, found it very difficult at first to give up some of my favorite foods and drinks. I've learned that if a person feels that by using sugar substitutes in foods and beverages, they will lose weight or prevent pounds, no one will have much influence. Besides, we've all been programmed to believe that our food is safe or "they" would have told us otherwise. I would like to inject my own opinions here in an attempt to provoke some consideration by people trapped in the world of aspartame consumption.

About five years ago, when I became tired all the time as a result of MSG, I began to stop at the local convenience store for a big diet cola. To me, it was the only defense I had against conking out before I could get all the day's demands accomplished. Drinking diet colas woke me up. I could tell when my body began to crash and needed more caffeine. I also popped Excedrin often to combat terrible headaches and fatigue. I had so many health problems, I figured that caffeine was the least of my worries, and it sometimes would raise my mood level, too. Then, when I learned about excitotoxins and gave up MSG, I decided to do the same with aspartame, which meant no more diet colas. At first it was difficult because in my mind, I truly believed that caffeine was the only thing keeping me going. But a very unexpected thing happened. After two weeks, I began to feel a new natural "high". Energy I hadn't felt in years returned and lasted all day. I was no longer on a mood roller coaster, and I began to lose weight. I believe that once the aspartame, caffeine, and MSG were not bombarding my system, it could function in a much more normal and efficient manner. My immune system was boosted, my muscles became stronger, I lost weight, and I could walk vigorously without the heavy dragging feeling I formerly experienced. Please reconsider the high aspartame, caffeine, MSG, or low fat diet you may be consuming in an attempt to lose weight or forestall it's gain.

The following information was taken from an article sent to me by Kaye Wanke, a NOMSG member, and was published by the Aspartame Consumer Safety Network, Inc., P.O. Box 780634, Dallas, TX 75378. It is entitled "Aspartame and Flying -- the Untold Story" by Mary Nash Stoddard and George Leighton. In it, the authors reveal that since the organization's hotline began in 1988, they have had over 600 pilot related calls. Pilots call to tell about their discovery that aspartame caused several of them to lose their licences to fly because they were unaware at the time that the diet shake, sodas, or aspartame sweetened coffee they had been consuming had any relation to symptoms that could have caused fatal results. They have described terrible in-flight incidents which involved seizures, vertigo, tremors, temporary black outs, visual problems, convulsions, disorientation, confusion, and loss of memory. One pilot said, since the FDA hasn't addressed the issue and declared it unsafe, the FAA can't recognize aspartame reactions in their regulations. He was able to retain his job by agreeing to go through an alcohol rehab center with his doctor using some syndrome name on his report. He had never had an alcohol problem, but he was forced to go through the motions just for the record. Another pilot, USAF Major Michael Collings, testified at the third Senate hearing on the safety of aspartame. He related that he remembered that he was free of tremors whenever he flew to remote areas where there was no access to diet soda or sugar-free Kool Aid. But his tremors eventually became so severe that a grand mal seizure finally hospitalized him and ended his flying career. He even had to turn down two invitations to join the prestigious Thunderbirds. He eventually learned of the cause of his seizures in 1985. Another pilot, willing to reveal his experiences, is George E. Leighton, one of the article's authors whose vision became so blurred that he could not read panel instruments and narrowly avoided an accident in landing. He said that even partial impairment to a pilot can have tragic results. Leighton now tries to spread the word to other pilots and he investigates suspicious flying incidents. After submitting a letter to the editor of the U.S. Air Force "Flying Safety" magazine, they printed an "Aspartame Alert" to all Air Force pilots. In his letter, he mentioned that certain individuals in government have used their power to misdirect the FDA, the FAA, and the DOD about the safety of aspartame because of special interests. He went so far as to say that if some of these people had not intervened, a grand jury would, more than likely, have indicted some of the producers of aspartame for fraud and criminal behavior in the concealment of the dangerous effects of aspartame from the FDA. It is pilot Leighton's opinion that lives and careers are being risked and that aspartame is just as dangerous to pilots and their flight crews, as a faulty flight instrument or other component. We applaud pilot Leighton's activism and courage as he battles indifference and ignorance.

Aspartame was discovered in the 60's and has enjoyed a rather controversial success, first being approved and then rescinded in the 70's due to a brain tumor issue. Over the objection of scientists it was again approved in 1981. Aspartame is composed of two synthetically created amino acids, phenylalanine and aspartic acid. It is in a methanol base (10% wood alcohol). It breaks down into formaldehyde, formic acid, and diketopiperazine, which has been shown to be a brain tumor causing agent. Aspartame will break down into its component parts at temperatures over 85° F. The article by Stoddard and Leighton went on to say that, for this reason, some researchers suspect that the Desert Storm or Gulf War Syndrome could actually be a serious reaction to aspartame. Large soft drink companies provided free diet drinks to rehydrate our soldiers during the Gulf War.

The FDA receives thousands of complaints about aspartame. Reports to the agency include symptoms of headache, nausea, balance problems, sleep disorders, numbness, depression, vision problems, memory loss, tinnitus, and even death. Aspartame has been often identified by doctors and researchers as an environmental trigger for several conditions:

Chronic Fatigue Syndrome
Post Polio Syndrome
Carpal Tunnel Syndrome
Anxiety/phobia Disorders
Multiple Sclerosis
Eosinophilia Myalgia Syndrome

Alzheimer's
Lyme Disease
Manic Depression
Epilepsy
Graves Disease
Heart Disease

So many of these conditions are the same as those caused or aggravated by MSG, which is not coincidence. Both contain a similar powerful chemistry to destroy our health. Both are powerful excitatory neurotransmitters created from amino acids. We ask everyone to consider the real consequences of a habit of ingesting aspartame and MSG laced foods and beverages. Please use your brain (while it can still function) to kick unhealthy and addictive eating and drinking habits now. Indifference can be deadly.

NOMSG members can help you start a MSG (and aspartame) awareness group if you call them. Kay Wanke places ads for meetings in local newspapers. She has met in churches, hospitals, and homes alerting consumers whenever and wherever she can.

We used the Internet to look up the Desert Storm Syndrome and received a summary of the report to the National Commander. The following symptoms that manifest this syndrome are: "fatigue, signs or symptoms involving skin (including hair loss), headache, joint and/or muscle pain, neurological signs or symptoms, signs or symptoms involving the upper or lower respiratory system, sleep disturbances, gastrointestinal signs or symptoms (including diarrhea and constipation), cardiovascular signs or symptoms, abnormal weight loss."

Veterans are seeking compensation for their mysterious syndrome. Doctors are having a hard time diagnosing the problem and many call it a "complex of ill-defined and often poorly characterized symptoms. It may not be one distinct illness, but several."

Is it possible that large amounts of aspartame they ingested in their sodas plus the amount of MSG in their meals along with other chemical assaults that they were subjected to are really the reasons why many of our soldiers might be victims of our own neurotoxic "friendly fire"? The aspartame/Desert Storm Syndrome connection is just a theory, one of many. However, we have to wonder how the government would handle a national health risk revelation considering how the FDA has chosen to minimize the effects of aspartame, MSG, and other so-called "safe" additives. It will be a costly mistake to ignore the mounting evidence.

Excellent books to read about aspartame:
Aspartame, Is It Safe? by H.J. Roberts, M.D.
The Deadly Deception by Mary Stoddard
The Bitter Truth About Artificial Sweeteners by Dennis Remington, M.D.
Bittersweet Aspartame by Barbara Mullarkey
Sweet Poison: How the World's Most Popular Artificial Sweetener is Killing Us by Janet Starr Hull

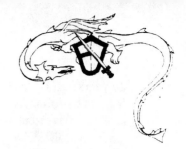

# Supportive and Interesting Articles

It's important to know that many doctors' and researchers' tests are showing a direct link of excitotoxins to neurodegenerative diseases, such as Parkinson's, diabetes, Huntington's Disease, Lou Goerig's Disease or ALS, and Alzheimer's. Important too, is that doctors are reporting growing cases of asthma, headaches, depression, and behavioral problems in children. Teachers and parents are alarmed at the growing number of attention deficient children and others with rage disorder or behavioral problems. Doctors are treating symptoms with drugs and more drugs. There are a number of diseases that have no known cause or cure, such as fibromyalgia which has joint pain, irritable bowel disorder and migraines among its major symptoms. How many people are being treated for ulcers and asthma or are being drugged for attention deficit disorder or neurotic behavior and are actually MSG reactive? What about the pregnant and nursing mothers and the babies who are the innocent victims? Often, I've mentioned to my husband how afraid I am of possibly ending up in a nursing home where all they serve is MSG laden food! A friend of mine said her mother developed severe stomach problems after her family put her in a nursing home. My heart aches for those who are in constant confusion about their health because I know first hand how little doctors know about MSG and other food additives. What painful tests must many people needlessly endure, and how many productive and happy days are lost forever? Think of young adults who never really reach their potentials because of chronic headaches, fatigue, and any number of "mysterious" symptoms. For many, the reason is because more and more MSG and similar additives are being used in this hurry-up world where busy people turn more and more to fast foods and prepared frozen and canned entrees. A NOMSG member told me it once took about 16 chickens to make a vat of commercial chicken soup. Now it takes a couple chickens and MSG!

We know that for some reason the barriers of the brain are broken down in MSG sensitive people. Too much glutamate gets into the brain cells and causes them to be stimulated so much that they literally burn themselves out. The neurons are like ricocheting bullets. The FDA (Food and Drug Administration) recently declared MSG safe in small amounts for the average person. But as the information in this book and others suggests, none of us is getting just a small amount of MSG. Ask the family of an Alzheimer's sufferer who has lost more than 80% of his or her brain neurons how devastating this disease can be. I personally know eight friends who are very sensitive to MSG and four of them also have relatives suffering from Alzheimer's. A good friend whose child had been diagnosed with Attention Deficit Disorder for four years excitedly told me just recently that the teachers in his special education class told her that they can't figure out why her son is in there. All she has done is change his diet and he no longer has the disorder. She's happy but mad that he's had such a struggle all this time. Childhoods are being robbed of joy.

There are more and more articles being published concerning MSG and the problems it is causing people. Here are just a few I've come across.

In the Nutrition Action Health Letter, May 1994 - Vol. 21/Number 4 - Center for Science in the Public Interest, by David Schardt, it reads that there have been few good studies done to test how MSG in small doses affects sensitive people.

In May of 1993, The New England Journal of Medicine reported that evidence is mounting that MSG is posing a serious health problem. Scientific awareness is growing.

In Sesame Street Parent's Magazine, Feb. 1996, a parent sent in a question to the "Your Child's Health" editor, Jo Martin. Answers were given by specialists of Johns Hopkins Children's Center. The parent was concerned if using a seasoning salt laced with MSG poses a danger to her children. The answer by Robin Henderson, Ph.D., a pediatric dietician, was a bit confusing. It stated that in a study done over

20 years ago large amounts of MSG fed to mice caused brain damage which prompted removal of MSG from baby food. This was the test done by Dr. Olney. However it also said that tests have shown it to be safe as a flavor enhancer in meats, vegetables, fish, etc. It went on to suggest that although moderate amounts of MSG were probably safe, parents should remember that it is high in sodium, so limiting MSG is a good idea. What this dietician probably isn't aware of is that MSG is still being put in baby food as a component of hydrolyzed food products that don't need labeling as MSG and that no tests have been done to test the effects of large or small amounts of MSG on human infants, children, or developing embryos. And although small amounts of MSG may be safe for children, what child today gets small amounts or even moderate amounts of MSG since most American diets depend on fast and processed foods more and more? And greater quantities of MSG are being poured into our food chain, mostly hidden.

The 700 Club Fact Sheet, "MSG: What You Really Need to Know," as featured on CBN's Newswatch Today, Nov. 3, 1995. In it, neurosurgeon Dr. Russell Blaylock accuses the FDA of tricking the public into believing MSG is safe and that it reports test findings in such a way that their reputation is protected if MSG is proven to be a toxic killer in the future. Jack Samuels, who has filed suit against the FDA for full disclosure of MSG on food labels, claims that the FDA has excluded volumes of research in its summary on the research report given by the Federation of American Societies for Experimental Biology (FASEB) after its latest study on MSG. He claims that one fact not included in the FDA summary of the report but in answer to question #13 in the study, was the FASEB research report that MSG was deadly to a certain section of the brain of every lab animal tested. As a neurologist, Dr. Blaylock warns that "humans would suffer worse trauma to that section of their brain." Samuels also said that the summary of the FASEB report totally neglected to address one of MSG's worse effects: migraine headaches, and that there are more than 40 other reported symptoms of MSG sensitivity. It merely suggested that only unstable asthmatics have attacks precipitated by MSG ingestion. Although the FDA insists MSG is safe at normal levels found in foods today, the FASEB says that three grams or one-ninth of an ounce is too much. Dr. Blaylock says that according to his research and studies on his own patients, he believes that most Americans are being affected by excitotoxins in one way or another. The article also discusses a lawsuit being filed by an asthmatic who almost died after eating soup at a restaurant that assured him it was MSG free. What is interesting is that the litigator has stable, controllable asthma and, according to the FDA report, he shouldn't react to MSG. His lawyer compares his case to the first tobacco or asbestos case and that it took 20 to 30 years for society to react and accept that certain toxins kill.

Woman's Day Magazine dated May 16, 1995, pp 99-101, "Asthma Unmasked", by Jacqueline Shannon, reveals recent statistics about asthma: (1) more than 5,000 Americans died in 1992 because of asthma. That's over twice as many as in 1978. (2) More than 12 million of us are asthmatic, over twice the number in 1980. (3) It's responsible for most hospitalization and absenteeism in children and three million lost work days for adults. (4) It's the reason for 15 million doctor visits and 30 million days each year of restricted activity.

This inflammatory lung disease which restricts breathing passages was a debilitating condition I suffered for more than twenty years. I relied on prescription and over-the-counter drugs and four allergy shots per month. When I pulled myself off of sulfites, also known to trigger attacks, and MSG, my symptoms totally disappeared. My chest pains, weakness, coughing, wheezing, and even post nasal drip and sinus problems were gone. Since I was young, I was the girl who carried a tissue box and cough drops in my purse to school. Little did I know that some of the ingredients in the cough drops were probably exacerbating the condition. Four years ago I remember, vividly, riding in the car with my husband and sighing, "I'd give anything to be able to know what it's like to breathe out of both nostrils deeply and to actually not have to continually gag on post-nasal drip." Besides not having to get poked with needles all the time, having a clear nose, throat, and chest is heaven! I used to get bronchitis at least once a year and several ear, nose, and throat infections all year long. Last year I went to the doctor two times, once for the flu and the other for a joint injury. It's nothing short of a miracle for me. And this winter I never got sick, not even a cold. That's never happened to me before.

The article went on to speculate on several causes of the incredible increase in asthma, all the things my allergist had told me about years ago. One reason that was particularly interesting was the author's suggestion that the number of children in our country who live in poverty has increased in the 1980's. Asthma cases, deaths, and hospitalizations, largely in inner-city populations also increased. The author wonders if this was because of over crowded, cockroach infested housing or lack of medical care. But Dr. A. Sonia Buist, M.D., head of the pulmonary and critical care division at Oregon Health Sciences University in Portland, said that the answers aren't that simple, that asthma cases are rising all over the world, even in countries that have little urban poverty. This statement really struck me: "Researchers are looking for missing pieces of the puzzle - perhaps some new allergen or environmental condition - that could explain asthma's global increase." (Page 100). The amount of MSG being added to our food is doubling every 10 years according to the reference books I've read by Dr. Blaylock and Dr. Schwartz. Surely cigarette smoke, pollen, mites, dander, and pollution all aggravate the lungs, but in my own case the trigger and the bullet, the "missing piece of the puzzle", was MSG. Consider the diet of an average child today, from MSG laden cereal, pastries, sweets, school lunches, processed snacks, coldcuts, flavored beverages, milk, sodas, prepackaged gelatin desserts, puddings, and yogurts, to trips to favorite fast food restaurants. These American establishments use MSG to enhance the flavor of dressings, french fries, and even the hamburgers. Then there are the ice cream treats, candy, flavored chips, crackers, and popcorn. Consider the glutamate-laced vitamins and toothpaste. And we haven't even discussed dinner yet! Most prepackaged, canned, frozen, and "bought-on-the-way-home-from-work meals" such as deli-chicken, salads, pizza, are all heavily "enhanced" with MSG, so you will come back for more of these "flavorful" and addicting foods. The way our society eats has changed dramatically since the 1940's. Children and their parents may be paying a higher price for convenience food than we ever dreamed of.

A review of the article, "Diabetes Danger in a Taste of Chinese", London Times, April 8, 1992, appears in the "NOMSG New Member Packet." It states that scientists have just discovered that glutamate affects insulin secretion by the pancreas. A team headed by Dr. Joel Bockaert at the Centre for Pharmacology and Endocrinology in Montpelier, France, has been working with other scientists at the Loubatieres Laboratory of Pharmacology and Pharmacodynamics, also in Montpelier. Their laboratory tests show that glutamate upsets the regulation of glucose blood levels by binding with receptors in the pancreas itself. A Hungarian scientist, Sandor Erdo, says that glutamate is interacting with other hormone secreting organs such as the adrenal and pineal glands, possibly causing other health problems. The French scientists conclude that they believe that glutamate will one day be accepted as a factor in sugar diabetes pathology.

In the May 1995 issue of Woman's Day Magazine, there was an article by Loraine Stern, M.D., called "My Head Hurts". It was about children's headaches. Migraines in children were described as running in families. They start often with blurred vision, pulsing on one side of the head, flashing lights, black spots, causing nausea, vomiting, and then the need for sleep. They can last two to 48 hours. Dare we ask if it's possible that some of these children are MSG reactive? My migraines and those of my son and many acquaintances were eliminated when MSG was eliminated.

Again, in Woman's Day, Feb. 18, 1997, in the "For Your Health" section by Flora Davis, the article described migraine symptoms and suggested avoiding cheese, MSG, chocolate, caffeine, and red wine. Drugs were suggested that might help, many of them causing serious side effects. Avoiding MSG is difficult, but well worth the effort and it beats drugs, if your migraines are caused by it. Masking symptoms with drugs is not a healthy treatment in my opinion. Your body is reacting to a poison. Listen to it, trust it. Find out if eliminating MSG for just a few days makes a difference.

According to the National Organization Mobilized to Stop Glutamate (NOMSG), many people who know their migraines are caused by MSG, report that most drugs have little effect on their headaches. Only by avoiding MSG can they be free of headaches. Many like my son, had to go through a battery of neurological tests for doctors and specialists who, after finding no evidence of tumor, disease, or other disorders as a cause for the suffering, suggested they learn to control the stress in their life or visit a psychotherapist. A specialist might be able to help them either deal with the pain or possible "psychological" causes for their migraines or other distressing symptoms. My son was so depressed as he bought into all the doctors' theories about his inability to cope with the stresses of life as the cause for his migraines, dizziness, inability to concentrate, fatigue, and numbness in his hands. Now he is free from headaches and other symptoms unless he cheats and buys a hamburger or other fast food. He's now well on his way toward fulfilling his dreams of a medical career. He would say to anyone who's had all the tests which come up negative, to test your tolerance for MSG and to not be intimidated by traditional doctors who know little or nothing about MSG sensitivity!

As I read the February 1996 issue of <u>Woman's Day</u> magazine, I found another article about an ailment considered to be on the rise and without a sure cause or cure. The article by Marie Savard, M.D. was about fibromyalgia. Major symptoms include painful muscles and joints. My antennae go up when I read things like, "I can't think of a medical problem that is more ignored and misunderstood. Some doctors don't even believe it exists." The article goes on to describe the other major symptoms: Fatigue, stiffness, sleep disorders, irritable bowel syndrome, migraine headaches, and poor circulation. All of these symptoms are classic examples of MSG and food chemical sensitivity. Exercise and drugs, and stress management were suggested therapies. I tried all of these for my so-called irritable bowel syndrome, but only when I started eliminating MSG and sulfite treated foods did my severe stomach problems disappear. Check the 1997 NoMSG conference report for Dr. Foster's comments on fibromyalgia. A clinical pharmacist has consulted with us by e-mail as he prepared a case report on four fibromyalgia patients whose symptoms improve significantly when MSG is removed from their diets. Not all medical problems can be explained away by MSG. But I am suggesting that there is a large segment of our population that could be suffering needlessly. My own doctor said he'd be the first to admit that doctors know very little about MSG and food additives. But he is very happy to see my complete health reversal and that of my son. He has written in my records that I am MSG and sulfite sensitive and is now more aware since he has witnessed for himself how MSG affects me and my son. He called to ask if he could refer his MSG sensitive and fibromyalgia patients to me. I was elated. A new physician in our area who works with fibromyalgia patients has ordered our book and another doctor has posted a copy of the front and back covers of our book on his waiting room bulletin board. More doctors need to be educated on this subject, so inform your doctor if you are sensitive.

"A Glimmer of Hope for People With ALS", is a September 1996, FDA Consumer Bulletin, which discusses a new drug called Rilotek which can help ALS patients. In the report, a suggested theory for the cause of ALS was given. It appears that a protein which normally removes excess glutamate from the brain does not function adequately and the resulting toxic build-up kills motor neurons. This leads to the devastating muscle wasting of ALS. Can't the FDA see the need for less glutamate in our diet instead of all the millions spent on new drugs? The article was discussed in the Spring 1997, <u>NOMSG Messenger</u>, page 4. Volume No. 2.

In the <u>Total Health</u> magazine, Jan. 1996 issue, 165 N. 100 E., Suite 2, St. George, Utah 84770, there is an eye opening article by Dr. Lendon H. Smith , entitled "Don't Be Cheated by Store Bought Food." Dr. Smith is a popular pediatrician. He has written many well-regarded books and articles and he lives in Portland, Oregon. He writes that even if you fill your pantry and refrigerator with fruits, vegetables, and good snacks, your child will get junk food anywhere he can. He tells us that there is no way to avoid the food manufacturers' influence in their diet. His feeling is that kids turn to drugs and a quick high because they don't feel good. He says if you notice kids today, many have circles under their eyes, are pale and generally don't feel great. He gives what he feels are two explanations: (1) Too much pollution and pesticides in the air, water, and food. (2) Impoverished foods for which he blames soil deficient in minerals in which products grow and high heavy metals like lead and arsenic. He believes there are reasons our kids are irritable and surly. He further states that our bodies were not designed for processed, chemically enhanced food but to eat whole foods cooked as little as possible. Our enzyme systems are not adapted to these hybrid and changed creations we call the latest new "food." And we can't handle all the preservatives in most of them. Dr. Smith cited a recent study done by Bob Smith of Doctor's Data, where certified organic produce was compared to supermarket produce in a lab. The organic food contained more nutrients besides being pesticide free. We are being cheated. Bob Smith also analyzed the

18

hair of violent criminals and found patterns of unacceptable amounts of lead arsenic and cadmium. When he analyzed hair of hyperactive children, the calcium and magnesium levels were exceptionally low, even though young people devour milk. Interestingly, Dr. Blaylock reports that MSG sensitive people show low levels of magnesium, calcium, and vitamin B6. Dr. Smith, in his article, suggests we eat foods that will rot if not eaten soon, eat more of them raw and eat lots of fruits, vegetables, and whole grain snacks, take a vitamin and mineral supplement daily, eat less meat, avoid aspartame, soft drinks, and caffeine. He believes that lifestyle and diet account for most sickness which includes cancer, cardiovascular diseases, allergies, repeated infections, insomnia, and most psychiatric conditions. More doctors should be as aware, since most just treat the symptoms.

Another such doctor is Richard R. Huntley, M.D. of Muskegon, Michigan. In the Spring 1997, issue of <u>NOMSG Messenger</u>, Volume 8, page 2, is a copy of a letter Dr. Huntly sent to the FDA. In it he states that he and his wife travel a lot and never get sick eating food in Turkey, Africa, South America, etc., but they always get sick eating in U.S. restaurants. Consequently, like us, they prepare and eat all their own food. He decided to consider MSG as a cause for some of his patient's illnesses and was amazed to see how many are affected by it and other similar chemicals. He went on to discuss in detail the typical tests doctors will prescribe in order to rule out more threatening conditions. For headaches, there are CAT scans, MRIs, full physicals, and trips to the neurologist. For patients with chest pain, doctors routinely do a cardiogram or a thallium exercise cardiogram, chest x-ray, blood work, and perhaps a visit to a heart specialist. If a patient complains of digestive problems, then gall bladder x-rays, stomach x-rays, a gastroscopy with a physical examination and blood work are often needed. A CAT scan or further consultation may be called for, from a gastroenterologist. His letter went on to say that he and other doctors should be glad about all the money they make because of MSG, not to mention drug companies, but instead, this doctor is trying to make a difference by calling the FDA to task. He challenges the government to ban MSG from our food immediately and calls it a crime that the FDA allows such adulteration to our food and fraud in its labeling. Realizing the clout that the multi-billion dollar food industry has, he ends his letter, by hoping the FDA will still do something and have a conscience. Please write the FDA and lend your appeal as this caring doctor has done.

The article, "Down's Syndrome", 1993 Grolier Electronic Publishing, is included because I personally know three mothers with Down's syndrome children, who also have severe MSG sensitivity in their family histories. Down's syndrome is caused by chromosomal abnormalities that take place during germ cell formation. If the resulting abnormal germ cell (ovum or sperm) takes part in fertilization, the resulting child will have the syndrome. What causes the germ cell to mutate? We don't know the answer, but we do know that most of the time the abnormal germ cell has an extra chromosome #21. In only 4% of the cases, the syndrome is the result of an inherited tendency of one chromosome (usually a third #21) to break off and join another chromosome (usually #14). Chromosome #21 is the smallest human chromosome. However, it is notable that its genes are being studied for their relationship to health problems ranging from Alzheimer's to vision problems. After the age of 35, almost all persons with the syndrome develop brain lesions and neuritic plagues like those persons with Alzheimer's disease. Thus, researchers are currently studying this shared pathology. Further research may help answer some perplexing questions.

In the book, <u>What to Expect When You're Expecting</u>, by Arlene Eisenberg, Heidi E. Murkoff, and Sandee E. Hathaway, expectant women are encouraged not to use MSG or flavor enhancers in cooking and to try to avoid it in restaurants. Also suggested is the avoidance of nitrates, nitrites, artificial color and flavors, and preservatives. Good advice for all of us!

I have to admit that before I was forced to revamp my eating habits, my family and I ate the typical high-in-junk and low-in-"whole"-foods diet. We are all creatures of habit. One of my friends who suffers from the MSG syndrome told me that at this time in her life she couldn't handle making herself a special diet when it was hard enough just to feed the kids. I told her that there is no special diet just for her. The change involves the whole family and it means changing bad habits, reeducation about what whole foods really are, making substitutions, and adapting favorite recipes to exclude MSG. This will benefit the sensitive person or persons, but it will also improve everyone's health and well being in the family and foster better future eating habits of children.

# Symptoms or Conditions Attributed to MSG Sensitivity

Based on books by Dr. Blaylock and Dr. Schwartz

Numbness or paralysis
Swelling of hands, feet, face
Mitral Valve Prolapse
Arrhythmias or paroxysmal atrial fibrillation (which can lead to stroke)
Rise or Drop in blood pressure (a fluctuation)
Tachycardia (rapid heartbeat)
Angina (pain in and around heart and ribs)
Heart palpitations (change in heart beat, or irregularities, such as atrial fibrillation)
Shuddering, shaking, chills
Tendinitis and joint pain
Arthritic-like pain
Muscle aches - legs, back, shoulders, neck
Flu-like symptoms
Stiffness - jaw, muscles
Heaviness of arms, legs
Mental dullness
Depression
Dizziness, light headedness
Disorientation and mental confusion (psychological disorders)
Anxiety or panic attacks
Hyperactivity, especially in children (A.D.D., A.D.H.D.)
Behavioral problems - delinquency, rage, and hostility
Feelings of inebriation
Slurred speech
Balance problems
Aching teeth
Seizures, tremors
Loss of memory
Lethargy
Sleeping disorders - Insomnia or drowsiness (chronic fatigue)
Migraine headaches - Facial or temporal
Eye symptoms - tired or burning eyes to blurry vision, Optic Neuritis
Neurological diseases: ALS, Parkinson's, M.S.
Prostate problems
Ear problems - tinnitus or Meniere's Disease

Mouth lesions, sores
Diarrhea
Nausea
Vomiting
Stomach cramps and gas
Irritable bowel, colitis, and/or constipation
Swelling of/or painful rectum
Spastic colon
Extreme thirst
Water retention and bloating (stomach swells)
Abdominal discomfort
Asthma symptoms
Shortness of breath
Chest pain
Tightness of chest
Runny nose and sneezing
Postnasal drip
Bronchitis-like symptoms
Hoarseness, sore throat
Chronic cough - sometimes a tickle cough
Gagging reflex
Skin rash - hives, itching, Rosacea-like reaction
Mouth lesions
Tingling numbness on face, ears, arms, legs, or feet
Flushing, tingling, burning sensation in face or chest
Extreme dryness of mouth, "cotton mouth", or irritated tongue
Dark circles or bags under eyes, face swelling
Urological problems, nocturia, uncontrollable bladder or swelling of prostate
Difficulty focusing
Pressure behind eyes
Seeing shiny lights
Burning sinuses, broken sinus capillaries
Gastro esophgeal reflux
Mitral valve prolapse
Cartilage, connective tissue damage
Gout-like condition (usually knees)
Gall bladder or gall bladder like problems
Kidney pain - Loin Pain Hematuria Syndrome

Some women have reported to NOMSG that they have experienced unusually heavy or delayed menstrual bleeding and early labor or miscarriage associated with MSG consumption. Some women had hysterectomies because of excessive bleeding that they believe was MSG caused. We have heard from people telling us that only after eliminating MSG were they able to conceive. National news reported that in recent years sperm count has dropped significantly in the U.S. There are probably other symptoms, but these are the most often cited. The books by Dr. Schwartz and Dr. Blaylock give more detailed explanations of symptoms.

Note to pet owners:

One man wrote to the "NOMSG Messenger Newsletter" that he had to change his dog food after his veterinarian told him that MSG was causing his pet's violent itching. A woman sent an e-mail to us about her dog finally losing his battle with seizures that, she learned too late, were MSG induced.

# Common Names of MSG-Containing Ingredients Found on Food Labels

These substances contain MSG in varying amounts. New flavor enhancers with new names are being developed all the time. Manufacturers may call them and MSG natural since MSG is found naturally in tomatoes, milk, and even in our bodies. But poisonous mushrooms and tobacco are "all natural" too. If you are suspicious of a label ingredient, call the manufacturer or avoid.

Foods <u>always</u> contain MSG when these words are on the label:

- MSG
- Monosodium glutamate
- Monopotassium glutamate
- Glutamate
- Glutamic acid
- Gelatin
- Hydrolyzed vegetable protein
- Hydrolyzed plant protein
- Autolyzed plant protein
- Sodium caseinate
- Calcium caseinate
- Textured protein
- Yeast extract
- Yeast food or nutrient
- Autolyzed yeast

Foods made with the following products <u>often</u> contain MSG (or are usually used in conjunction with it.):

- Malted barley (flavor)
- Barley malt
- Malt extract or flavoring
- Maltodextrin
- Caramel flavoring (coloring)
- Stock
- Broth
- Bouillon
- Carrageenan (if in a mixture of MSG but only labeled as carrageenan)
- Whey protein isolate or concentrate (if hydrolyzed milk proteins are present)
- Pectin
- Flavors, flavoring
- Natural chicken, beef, or pork, flavoring
- "Seasonings" (Most assume this means salt, pepper, or spices and herbs, which sometimes it is)
- Soy sauce or extract
- Soy protein
- Soy protein isolate or concentrate
- Cornstarch, dextrose, dextrin
- Flowing agents
- Corn, wheat, rice or oat protein
- Anything enriched or vitamin enriched
- Protein fortified "anything"
- Enzyme modified "anything"
- Ultra-pasteurized "anything"
- Fermented "anything"
- Modified food starch
- Rice syrup or brown rice syrup
- Lipolyzed butter fat
- "Low" or "no fat" items
- Citric acid (when processed from corn)
- Corn syrup and corn syrup solids (some companies use another process to make their product, saying it is MSG free, such as Karo Company)
- Milk powder
- Dry milk solids
- Protein fortified milk
- Annatto
- Spice (can mean MSG or a spice like pepper)
- Gums (guar, vegetable)
- Dough conditioners (some include lecithin, whey protein, L-cysteine)
- Lecithin (if from hydrolyzed soy products)

If these words are on the label, MSG is usually present since they are used to break down proteins:

Protease

Protease enzymes

Enzymes

Reaction flavors

Watch out for the following as they often contain MSG or other harmful ingredients, or are used in conjunction with MSG:

Gelcaps (if made from animal gelatin (which is over 11% free glutamic acid) or hydrolyzed vegetable protein), vitamin binders or fillers (some contain cornstarch and other protein rich formulas and amino acids created from milk, soy, etc.)

Poultry and meat injected with MSG containing substances and broth (some beef loins sold to restaurants have been injected.)

Phosphate rinses or basting materials - Some people report MSG-type reactions. (fish, shrimp, and poultry). Beef may be rinsed in phosphates to prevent infections. By law, it should be labeled as such. However, violations do occur and should be reported to the USDA. Much of the pork today is tenderized with basting injections containing phosphates and lactates (Hormel).

Candy, drinks, gums, and breath mints can contain MSG and aspartame.

Prewashed salads: some are rinsed in a citric acid solution.

Mouth wash and toothpaste that contain aspartame, natural flavor (even in some compounds dentists use to clean teeth).

Nutritional supplements for the elderly and dieters, binders and fillers for cough and other medications, prescription and OTC drugs, and children's medications and chewable vitamins (reports to NOMSG suggest that of all the supplement drinks, "Boost" seems to be the best tolerated).

Baby formula - often have soy protein and corn syrup, dry milk solids, and hydrolyzed proteins.

Enteral feeding materials and some fluids administered intravenously in hospital.

Cosmetics, cleaning agents, shampoos, hair mousses, gels, conditioners, lotions, soaps (lecithin, citric acid, citrates, hydrolyzed proteins).

Low fat milks - milk solids are added to pump up the protein content. In some states milk must contain a certain percent of protein. Milk solids assure the percentage.

Disodium guanylate and disodium inosinate additives (food additives often used to enhance MSG. If they are on label, MSG is usually present.

Aspartame - Another excitatory neurotoxin created from amino acids. Recently aspartame made national news when researchers announced test results that showed aspartame caused brain lesions and cancer in lab animals. Producers quickly tried to dispute the findings. It is found in candy, gum, toothpaste, beverages, diet foods, breath mints, mouthwash, medicines, and vitamins.

L-cysteine - Another amino acid exitotoxin used in some baked goods, breads, and flour tortillas. It's often in dough conditioners.

Stevia - This highly sweet herb is used as a sweetener in many parts of the world. By itself it is fine, however packets of Stevia in maltodextrin and other bases may contain MSG.

Many vitamin and mineral supplements including herbs, prescription drugs, and hormone replacement drugs contain MSG in the form of gel caps, dextrose, dextrates, and other hydrolyzed protein. I tried five thyroid medications before I found Nature Throid from Western Research Lab. (602) 482-9370, 12208 N. 32nd St., Phoenix, AZ 85032. So far it hasn't caused symptoms, but the starch in it may bother others. Also, the hormone replacement patch, Climara, contains only estridiol, and not other offending ingredients like lecithin and citric acid. Phyto or plant based estrogens are available, too. I can't recommended these products, as they may affect certain individuals differently. But in all the years we have been talking to people, we have learned that when they were still getting some kind of reaction after trying to eliminate MSG, the four main culprits were usually vitamins and medications, milk and/or dairy, corn by-products, and soy by-products.

This information was obtained from: (1) NOMSG hotline and educational material sent to me. (2) Books by Dr. Russell Blaylock and Dr. George Schwartz. (3) Jack Samuels of the Truth in Labeling Campaign.

# Processed Foods Commonly Containing Some Glutamate

Gelatin desserts
Skim, 1%, 2%, non-fat, or dry milk
Whipped cream topping substitutes
Evaporated milk
Half & Half
Buttermilk
Creamers (non-dairy)
Processed cheese and spreads
Yogurt
Chocolates
Candy bars
Low fat dairy & diet foods
Margarine and some butters
Ice cream
Flavored potato chips, snack chips
Cereal - dry and cooked
Breads
Baked Goods from bakeries
Frosting and fillings (baked goods)
Cured & processed meats - coldcuts, hams, sausages, and hot dogs
Catsup
Mayonnaise
Chili sauce
Mustards
Worcestershire sauce
Soy sauce
Pickles
Bottled spaghetti sauce
Oriental seasoning & sauces (oyster, teriyaki)
Canned tuna, oysters, clams, including smoked
Barbeque sauce
Canned, frozen or dry entrees and pot pies
Side dishes or sauces
Pizza - fresh or frozen
Flavored teas (often says natural flavors)
Seasoned crackers, chips, pretzels
Seasoned popcorn (microwave), theater popcorn
Seasoned, frozen, canned potatoes
Seasoned vegetables

Potato "tots" and french fries
Dry soup mixes and dips
Salad dressing and dry mixes
Some peanut butters
Canned soups, chili
Croutons, stuffing mixes
Boullion, canned stock (chicken, beef, vegetable)
Some bagged vegetables and salads
Bottled gravy
Dry gravy and seasoning mixes
Tomato sauce
Stewed tomatoes
Egg substitutes
Seasoning salts
Packaged puddings and pie mixes
Deli salads and chicken (fried or rotisserie)
Flour - if malted barley flour added
Some whipping creams
Cottage cheese, sour cream
Cream cheese
Some cheeses
Canned refried beans
Yogurt
Powdered or liquid whey, soy, or rice beverages including diet drinks, baby formulas, and supplemental beverages for body builders and the elderly.
Yeast (Most contain varying amounts of MSG though usually small as long as plain yeast is used, few or no additives. We like Red Star plain yeast.)
Gelatin and/or pectin candies (shaped worms, bears, dinasaurs, etc.)
Canned tomatoes, puree and paste
Nuts (especially flavored or seasoned)
Salt containing dextrose or corn starch
Tofu and other soy products (if fermented or hydrolyzed)
Table salts - Flowing agents and Iodine carriers may contain MSG (corn starch dextrose)

\* Don't despair. MSG free versions of many of these foods are available in most grocery stores. Joining NOMSG will help you network with others in your area who can help you find local products. Memorizing the MSG containing additives and reading labels will help also in locating safe versions of these foods. Some are impossible to find.

# Definitions and Helpful Information

**Ajinomoto** - Name of both the Japanese manufacturer and MSG product.

**Annatto** - Used to color butter, cheese, and other foods yellow. Some claim sensitivity to it. Perhaps the annatto bean, when processed, releases free glutamate. I have been informed by one butter producer that annato is sometimes "spiked" with MSG.

**Autolyzed Yeast and Yeast Extract** - This is a food additive, not bread yeast. Yeast is put through autolysis which is a lot like hydrolysis. Some MSG is released. Pure MSG may also be added to yeast extract without adding it on the food label.

**Baked goods** - When I experienced dizziness after eating some bagels from our grocery store's new bakery, I asked for a list of ingredients. Besides using the typical malted flour/wheat flour, I was informed that they also add liquid malt to enhance color and flavor to the bagels and to most of their pastries and bread products. Luckily a local bagel shop does not add liquid malt and they get our business now. Some severely sensitive people find that if they eat even small amounts of baked goods made with the flour that contains malted barley flour, they may not get a severe reaction but will often feel generally poor. Symptoms may be fatigue, congestion, or mild nausea, even itchy skin. Some baked goods contain whey and dough conditioners which may contain yeast nutrients such as lecithin, soy protein, or citirc acid. All contain glutamate. I make breads and baked goods often, and when I buy them, I look for whole wheat versions of baked goods, as whole wheat flour usually is not augmented with as much white or malted barley flour. Some flour tortillas now contain L-cysteine or other excitotoxins, as do many baked goods. Many very sensitive people avoid baked goods made with any yeast and eat those using baking powder or soda, instead.

**Barley Malt** - This is sprouted barley. It is dried and ground into flour and added to wheat flour. It adds a sweet flavor. It contains a small amount of free glutamic acid, but the problem is that the enzymes released in sprouting begin to break down the protein of the wheat flour it is added to, thus creating more MSG. It is only added to flour when the wheat quality that season is poor; however, the flour companies do not change the labels on their bag so there is no way to know if it has been added or not. Other by-products of malted barley or barley malt are coffee-free roasted grain beverages and liquid malt syrups, used in baked goods and cereals to improve color and flavor.

**Beverages** - Some frozen fruit juices are fine if they are 100% juice, though most contain preservatives and corn syrup which may contain glutamate residues. Juice drinks in cans, bottles or little boxes are often MSG flavor enhanced. And, for sulfite sensitive people, avoid white grape juice and a lot of bottled fruit juice mixes which use corn syrup which may contain sulfites too. Sulfites are often added to sodas and juice drinks as preservatives. Most carbonated beverages contain MSG, aspartame if diet, sulfites, and lots of artificial color and flavor. We drink lots of water. I keep my huge mug filled with it and take it everywhere. I called Seneca Company in N.Y. to ask about their concord grape juice since I started experiencing a sulfite type reaction after drinking two glasses. The plant manager said that I should avoid drinking it since they often dump leftover sulfur treated white grape juice into the concord juice. Now I add water and sugar it to make grape-ade and drink less of it. We plan to bottle more grape juice this year.

We do it the easy way. Put ¼ to ½ cup sugar in a quart bottle and pour about a cup of hot water in and swirl bottle to dissolve. Add 3 cups grapes and fill with hot water. Seal. Place in hot water bath and process 25-30 minutes. To use, simply drain juice into a pitcher and rub pulp through strainer with a wooden spoon or use a food strainer. Add water and sugar to taste. Delicious. Add a little pure fruit juice to mineral or carbonated water for a refreshing change.

**Bread yeast** - This type of yeast is produced by growing it on a nutritious base. This base often consists of some form of hydrolyzed protein. A Red Star spokesman told us that their plain dry yeast product contains a small amount of free glutamate. However, he said yeast extract contains anywhere from 7 to 24% glutamic acid, depending on its production by different companies. We'd suggest trying various brands to determine sensitivities. Or try our yeastless breads (tortillas, biscuits, muffins, yeastless bread).

**Butter** - Some brands contain annatto, added seasonally, which may cause a reaction in some individuals. Some of the salts added may also contain flowing agents that contain glutamate residues. Also, since many creams are being ultra-pasteurized, the high temperature may release some free glutamic acid. Lately we have noticed the words "natural flavoring" on unsalted butters. We have also been told that this means citric acid has been added. So please do your research with butter.

**Calcium Caseinate** - This is the calcium by-product of milk protein hydrolysis, which contains free glutamate. Often it is present in milk solids, milk powder, or dry milk products.

**Candy** - Many of the "gummy" candies are loaded with gelatin, not to mention artificial color, artificial flavor, and corn syrup. Candy bars are full of whey, milk solids, flavoring, pectin, vegetable gums, etc. Ingredients are often under a fold and the print is tiny, but read them carefully. Some MSG sensitive people say that pectin candies also bother them. Also, better quality and imported chocolates are better bets than the more commonly found cheaper ones. Some confection producers add sulfites to chocolates or it's in the coconut or dry fruits used. Sulfites are known to provoke asthma, stomach, or respiratory problems. Some sugar coated nuts are okay, too. We eat dried fruit like candy at our house so our dehydrator is often in use. Bananas, raisins, dates, prunes, peaches, and pears (unsulfured) from health and grocery stores are easy to find. Easy candy recipes are included in this book.

**Canned broth, Bouillon cubes** -Most canned broth, especially the inexpensive ones contain a lot of MSG. Some health food stores and grocery stores carry broth claiming it to be MSG free, but it may contain MSG in another ingredient such as autolyzed yeast. Read the labels. Bouillon cubes are tabu.

**Canned or frozen vegetables and fruit products** - If you suspect that you are reacting to any canned or frozen vegetables or fruits, you may be sensitive to citric acid or other preservatives. Also, some MSG may have been added for flavor and/or color enhancement, such as in some frozen peas. Corn syrup in commercial fruit products may also contain some glutamates and/or sulfites.

**Canned Tuna** - Most bargain tuna contains calcium caseinate and broth, which are two MSG containing products. I once wondered why tuna sandwiches made me so ill. Besides the tuna and mayonnaise, I would add MSG treated mustard and seasoning salt. There are low sodium versions without broth. Be sure to look on back label and be sure it says tuna and water only, or tuna, water, and salt. The low sodium versions are usually okay.

**Carmel or Caramel Coloring** - It is reported that this is sometimes a by-product of malted barley or corn (hydrolyzed) and can contain MSG residue.

**Carrageenan** - A seaweed derivative used to thicken products like ice cream, processed cheeses, toothpaste, cottage cheese, cream, eggnog, half and half, buttermilk, yogurt, etc.. It is often mixed with pure MSG or hydrolyzed milk protein, but the label will only state "carrageenan." This is confusing to the consumer, since it would probably be safe if used by itself.

**Catsup, Worcestershire Sauce** - Most catsups contain MSG. Some people claim that Muir Glen brand is okay (found in health food stores or sections). We always make our own catsup and skip the Worcestershire sauce in recipes.

**Chicken and Turkey** - Look for poultry with labels that say "No additives or preservatives". Often poultry is dipped in a broth solution containing MSG. "Naturally processed" or "all natural" ingredients can be misleading as MSG is a "natural" product. Turkey is often injected. We soak our poultry in salted water for an hour and rinse. It may not remove any additives, but it helps to clean it. Some people report being affected by the phosphate solutions added to some poultry. Read labels and clean poultry well. Call poultry plants and ask how they treat their product.

**Chocolate** - Some chocolate contains whole milk solids or whey, both sources of MSG. Sees informed us that when "milk" apears on the label, it means dry milk. Some chips and powdered mixes contain less of these products than others. Baking cocoa is okay to use. Lecithin may contain glutamate depending on how it is processed. It is often added to chocolate to make it smoother. If it is a hydrolyzed product, it will most likely contain MSG. Also, the caffeine in chocolate effects some people negatively. People who get frequent headaches are advised to avoid chocolate.

**Corn Products** - Many individuals who are "allergic" to corn may in fact be actually reacting to the free glutamate that is in many corn byproducts as a result of processing. Fresh corn on the cob is tolerated by most MSG sensitive individuals. However, they will probably react to corn syrup, dextrose, dextrin, maltodextrin, and all other products made by hydrolyzing or fermenting corn. Other examples are: alcohol, caramel color or flavor, and citric acid (rarely made from citrus fruits anymore). The following products may contain cornstarch: baking powder, confectioner's sugar, bleached flour, excipients which are binders and fillers in tablets (vitamins, medications).

**Croutons** - Most are seasoned with MSG. To make your own, stack buttered or oiled bread slices that are seasoned with garlic powder and any of your favorite spices or herbs. Cube and toss in fry pan on range or place in 350° oven and stir occasionally while they are toasting. Stale or dry bread cubes may be used plain or drizzle with oil or melted butter and sprinkle on the herbs and spices and toss. Toast in the oven until lightly golden. For weight watchers, toss plain toasted cubes over salad, soups, or casseroles. They add great texture.

**Disodium Guanylate/Disodium Inosinate** - Expensive flavor enhancers used in conjunction with less expensive MSG. If you see it on a label, chances are MSG is also present.

**Dough Conditioners** - Can contain MSG or L-cysteine. Used to improve texture of breads and pastries. "Yeast nutrients" may also be on labels and may contain MSG.

**Evaporated Milk** - Milk solids are often used and since it's heated, processed and concentrated, it contains glutamate. I use whole milk or cream instead.

**Fat Substitutes** - New ones are being developed continually. Beware!! A few on the market are: Guar Gum, hydrolyzed proteins (soy wheat, oat, gluten), modified food starch (made from soy, potatoes, whey, corn), xanthum gum, Appetize, Caprein, maltodextrin, and Olestra. Reports of stomach disorders are related to some of these products.

**Fresh Milk** - Milk processors sometimes add dry milk solids, dry whey, and occasionally gelatin, which contain glutamic acid, to milk to boost the protein content and bulk, especially in skimmed milk. Whole milk is a better choice. Dairy products are discussed in another chapter.

**Gelatin** - A natural, protein rich product derived from animal bones, tendons, skins, etc.. Besides the well known gelatin desserts, it is used to make gummy-type candies, many prepared foods, and vitamin and medicinal capsules. Sometimes it is added to skim milk to build it up. After eliminating my daily multivitamin and vitamin E gelcap, the chronic pain I experienced at the back of my neck, disappeared. Gelatin always contains MSG.

**Herbs and Spices** - We grow, dry, and use all kinds of them now. There are wonderful books available on their usage and great recipes to try. Beware of some spices. Some reports have been made that MSG is finding its way in some previously not using it. Garlic salt sometimes contains hydrolyzed protein as do many seasoning salt blends.

**Hydrolysis** - Process by which natural foods are broken down into component parts with the aid of heat, water, acids, and/or strong alkalies.

**Hydrolyzed Protein** - Foods high in protein are chemically treated and altered. The process breaks down the protein and glutamate is freed up. Hydrolyzed protein can have up to 40% MSG in it and still be labeled as just hydrolyzed protein. It's often used in meats to augment flavor and protein content.

**Instant and Special Bread Yeast** - Many contain yeast nutrients and L-cysteine which make the bread rise more quickly.

**Kombu Extract** - An MSG product extracted from seaweed. Seaweed was the original source of MSG in Japan many years ago. But this was originally a naturally dried product which probably contained a lot fewer free glutamates, compared to what is produced today. Our neighbor who is sensitive to MSG, recently toured China and said she didn't get sick once. But she does at Chinese restaurants here.

**Maltodextrin** - Made from hydrolyzed corn, either MSG is a residue left during it's manufacture, or MSG may be added to it and sold to food manufacturers that way. Other corn byproducts that may contain MSG depending on processes used: dextrose, dextrates, corn syrup, invert sugar, and fructose.

**Molasses** - Crude molasses is often used to produce MSG. Although it's important to avoid sulfured molasses, many individuals report that they can react to molasses and most brown sugars. You will have to judge any sensitivity yourself.

**Mayonnaise** - Most have "natural flavors" or MSG added. For those sensitive to sulfites, some contain sulfur-treated lemon juice or sulfites are added as a preservative more often than not. There are products that do not contain MSG. Some people report Saffola and Best Foods whole mayonnaise do not bother them as much as other products. A cup of whole sour cream or yogurt plus a couple of teaspoons of oil and vinegar make a good substitute. Sweeten to taste. This may be flavored with salt, pepper, and mustard.

**MSG** - Monosodium glutamate - A flavor enhancer most often produced from corn using bacteria and a fermentation process. The resulting salt-like substance contains approximately 78% pure free glutamic acid, thus making it the strongest of all free glutamate containing substances.

**Mustard** - There are MSG-free mustards, but many have it added. Wine mustards contain sulfites. We use some Hickory Farms mustards. We also make our own from dry mustard and water.

**Natural Flavors (flavorings)** - Can mean that autolyzed yeast or hydrolyzed protein is present since they are permitted by the FDA to use this designation on labels. This is very confusing since some ingredients designated as Natural Flavors, are just that, such as lemon oil.

**Oils** - We have been told that new oils obtained from genetically engineered soy beans are being added to regular oils. We have no such evidence. However, some oils contain sulfites. We use olive, safflower, and canola oils.

**Plain Dry Yeast** - May contain glutamate naturally, as a result of its production, some brands contain more than others. Natural compressed yeast is harder to find but is considered safer. Call a local bakery for a source if your grocery store doesn't stock it. Many MSG sensitive people have little or no problem with plain dry yeast. Try different brands and look for ones labeled "yeast" as the only ingredient

**Processed Meats** - Most are highly salted, MSG seasoned and nitrate treated. Many contain calcium caseinate and smoke flavoring, too. Sliced leftover meat loaf, chicken, turkey, and roast beef make great sandwiches.

**Red Meat** - Some roasts and steaks (beef and pork) are being injected with or dipped in glutamate containing solutions such as broth or hydrolyzed protein. Phosphates and chlorinated water can also be sprayed on cuts to prevent e-coli. I avoid "tenderized" pork.

**Seasoning Salts** - One brand claims to be MSG free, but it contains "spice" and "maltodextrin". Be wary. Make your own by adding your favorite herbs and spices to salt or sea salt. Many plain salts contain dextrose or cornstarch, which may contain glutamate residues.

**Sodium Caseinate** - A sodium salt of hydrolyzed milk protein, containing glutamate. Often present in milk solids, milk powder, or dry milk products.

**Soups** - Canned and dry packed versions are loaded with MSG. Check health food stores or grocery stores for safer versions. But even they fall short sometimes because their producers are unaware of hidden MSG. We make extra from scratch and freeze the leftovers. Avoid all cup and ramen style soups. It's even added to some of the dry noodles.

**Spaghetti Sauce** - The most commonly purchased brands contain MSG and corn syrup. We have seen some commercial brands, usually in health food stores, that claim to contain little or no MSG. But remember, many contain citric acid which affects some people. We often make our own sauce in large batches and freeze the extra for later. A food processor is a great aid in pureeing tomatoes, garlic, and onion.

**Spices/Seasonings** - The FDA doesn't allow pure MSG to use this designation on food labels, but the USDA does for some of its meat products such as sausage and cold cuts. MSG is in a lot of the spice and seasoning mixes used in the meat industry.

**Soy Protein Isolate and Soy Protein Concentrate** - Products they created from soy that can contain MSG depending on how it is produced. They are used for flavoring and increasing the amount of protein in a product.

**Smoke Flavors (flavoring)** - Can contain hydrolyzed protein or pure MSG to enhance the flavor. Added to hams, bacon, and even crackers and cheese.

**Soy Sauce** - Soy beans are very high in protein. When fermented, some glutamate is produced. There are some cheap brands that are made by adding hydrolyzed proteins and carmel coloring. Some sensitive people can handle small amounts of soy sauce. We avoid it. Tarmari sauce is said to conain less MSG. But sauces like oyster and teriyaki contain quite a bit.

**Soy Milk** - Some people use Pacific Original Soy Milk and can tolerate it. The fresh beans are ground, the liquid strained, then flash heated and packaged. The heat may free some glutamate, but not enough to bother some individuals. Vitamin D is added to some soy milk. I was told that it comes from torula yeast which contains free glutamate. Be sure to read the list of added ingredients. Most very sensitive individuals avoid all soy products.

**Stuffing Mixes** - Most are seasoned with MSG. Break up or cube old bread and rolls and place in a pan. Keep pan in the cold oven to dry. Just don't forget it's there when pre-heating! Or speed up the process by heating to lowest setting and dry. Turn off heat after half an hour and keep bread in oven. Bag when dry. Mix up with chopped onions, celery, seasonings (thyme, sage, tarragon, marjoram, salt, and pepper) and water to moisten when stuffing is needed. Place in processor or roll with rolling pin while in plastic bag to make fine bread crumbs.

**Table Salt** - Flowing agents and Iodine carriers may contain MSG (cornstarch, dextrose). Canning salt is chemical free. Some sea salts contain flowing agents, also. Also, people sensitive to phosphates should be aware that tri-calcium phosphate is an anti-caking substance used in many commercial salts. It is added to many butters, too. Whether these phosphates or these compounds affect phosphate sensitive individuals has not been tested, that we know of.

**Textured Protein** - Substance derived from processed soy products added to foods for flavoring and added bulk. May contain MSG depending on how it is derived. To speed up production, more companies are resorting to heat and chemicals (hydrolysis).

**Tomato Products** - Citric acid, most often a byproduct of hydrolyzed corn, not citrus fruit, can contain glutamate residues. It is used in most canned tomato products to raise the acidity to ensure canning safety. Many purees and pastes are citric acid free because they are so concentrated and consequently their acidic content is also. However, if tomatoes have been sitting too long, waiting to be strained, a natural fermentation process can occur, releasing glutamate. Sometimes to prevent fermentation, sulfite solutions are sprayed over them. Though rinsed, some residues may affect sulfite sensitive individuals. Try various brands to see how you react. Tomato puree can be made by pureeing peeled tomatoes and placing them in a cloth lined strainer over a bowl in the refrigerator. Freeze or use immediately.

**Tofu** - Made from strained soy milk, enzymes or other cultures are used to cure and solidify it. Soy beans are high in natural glutamate. Any fermentation process can create free glutamates. The amounts will be determined by the process used.

**Ultra-pasteurized** -Extra heat is used on some dairy products such as cream and milk. This may create more free glutamate in the product. Most dairy and non-dairy or rice beverage l cartons are ultra-pasteurized. Some sources say that boiling milk for long periods of time may release some glutamate.

**Vitamins** - Look for ones that do <u>not</u> contain cornstarch, dairy products, artificial sweeteners, gluten, or that do not contain minerals and vitamins chelated to amino acids. That means they are often bound to a rice or soy protein product. Oftentimes the fillers and binders used in vitamins contain glutamate as do the gel caps themselves. Look for vitamins that say "excipient free" or avoid them entirely and eat more fresh fruits and vegetables. We've talked to many people who, when they eliminated their vitamin pills, finally discovered they were the very things giving them problems. There are pure vitamin C crystals available and also calcium powders that may work for some. KAL and Nature's Life produce such products. Be advised that calcium from dolomite may contain lead in levels that the FDA considers safe. Since we are not too secure with that statement, we suggest that you do some research if calcium powder is a supplement that interests you. Crystal C is derived from corn. However, we have been told that there is no glutamic acid present.

**Whey** - When cheese is produced, milk is treated with enzymes and heated to separate the curds from the whey, which is a liquid high in protein. Some glutamate may be freed up by the heat and enzyme activity, but when whey is further processed and then dried to a powder, it may contain more glutamate. It is then bagged and sold as a food product to be used in the manufacture of many products such as ice cream, crackers, boxed macaroni and cheese, and candy. The more whey is processed, such as in whey protein or whey protein isolate, the more glutamate it will likely contain. Sometimes hydrolyzed milk solids are added, making it even higher in glutamate. When a label says "whey", it may contain any of the whey products.

**Yogurt** - Try to find plain or vanilla whole milk yogurt and add fruit or jam. Most contain carrageenan, gums, natural flavors, milk solids, and whey. Yogurt is easy to make without extra equipment, using our easy directions. Remember however, that the work of any culture on a protein product may create some free glutamic acid.

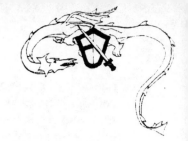

# Shopping Tips

Most people assume that food will be more expensive if they eliminate MSG. We found the opposite to be true since processed foods are the most costly. Instead, we can now afford some foods we thought too expensive before. Some products cost more because they use whole ingredients instead of using flavor enhancers, fillers, and thickeners.

You will need to take a day and systematically go through your cupboards, tossing away MSG laden foods using the information on its hidden sources given in this book. Be merciless! Your health benefits are worth it.

Make a shopping list, including ingredients you may need to make some of the recipes you'd like to try in this book or others.

Include:

**Fresh fruits and vegetables** - buy more than usual and try new ones. Include fresh garlic, onions, tomatoes, lettuce, cabbage, potatoes, carrots, and sweet potatoes.
**Canned diced, crushed, and pureed tomatoes** - Some highly sensitive people report reactions to citric acid, which is commonly added to tomatoes. Muir Glen tomato puree doesn't contain citric acid. We rely on fresh or our own frozen tomatoes primarily.
**Lemons and limes** - Use in drinks, salad dressing and marinades. Add a slice to your water.
**Whole sour cream** - Without carrageenan and additives
**Whole eggs** - Substitutes contain MSG.
**Fresh meats** - Exclude poultry injected with or dipped in a broth solution. Look for poultry labels that say no additives or preservatives. Some people are sensitive to phosphate solutions that are being used to kill E. coli and salmonella. Pork is being tenderized by phosphate containing ingredients. Avoid cold cuts, and sausages unless the butcher or grocery meat person can give a list of seasonings used. Call around to butcher shops and grocery stores to find specialty sausages and poultry without MSG. Ham and bacon: there are some brands that don't contain "natural flavoring" or "smoke flavoring", but most contain nitrites or nitrates which are known to cause headaches. I called a Washington chicken processing plant. They said that they do not treat the poultry sold in our state, only those sent distances. Check with your local meat processors.
**Cheese** - Most cheeses are made with low fat milk and enzymes. When low fat milk is used it often contains milk solids and/or whey solids, which contain MSG. The powerful enzymes used today probably break the milk protein into it's amino acids, one being glutamic acid. Most very sensitive people I talk to cannot handle cheese very well at all. Others can handle mild mozzarella, colby, and jack cheese. Some can tolerate a little Parmesan if imported, not domestic. Many Europeans still use the old cultures (bacteria), not our high tech enzymes. Go easy on hard or aged cheeses like Parmesan, aged cheddar, Romano, and blue cheeses. The protein is more broken down, is condensed, and is higher in glutamate, which is found naturally in milk. Most yellow cheeses contain annatto for coloring, which some people react to. We sometimes use jack, mozzarella, Swiss, provolone, and imported hard cheeses (sparingly). Avoid the soft processed cheese food in blocks or slices (the kind that needs no refrigeration), cheese spread, or cheese substitutes. NOMSG suggests buying regular cheese in blocks, not the pre-shredded kind, which can include some processed cheese mixed with regular cheese.
**Whole Milk and Whole cream** - Half & Half, frozen whipped cream substitutes, creamers, and most buttermilk contain carrageenan and/or vegetable gum, which usually are used in conjunction with milk protein products. Skim varieties contain milk solids. Make your own half cream & half milk. Sour your milk by adding one tablespoon vinegar or lemon juice to each cup of milk in

recipes calling for buttermilk. Remove one tablespoon milk first. Some people find better products from small dairies. One woman I talked to buys raw milk and purchased her own pasteurizer for $50.00. She's going to try cheese making next. I use plain varieties of rice milk.

**Canned Fruit, Vegetables, and Juices** - Many processors add some MSG to their canned products to hide the tinny flavor. Sulfites are often present but do not have to be labeled if under a certain parts per million.

**Frozen and Bottled Fruit Juices** - We prefer 100% grape juice, no sugar or corn syrup added. Because the flavor is stronger, up to 6 cans of water and some sugar can be added to make a great drink. We do this with orange juice, too. This is especially good to do if you are severely sulfite sensitive. A lot of fruit juices are laced with sulfites as a preservative. Grape juice is wonderful heated and spiced, the same way apple juice is done. Be aware that many bottled fruit beverages and soda pop contain MSG and sulfites. We buy pasteurized pure apple cider. We use frozen apple and orange juice concentrates that are preservative and corn syrup free. Many sensitive people have a reaction to the calcium and vitamin enriched orange juice. The binders for vitamins and minerals often contain MSG. Many people cannot handle the preservatives that are added to many juices.

**Dried peas, beans, rice, pasta** - Be adventurous! Some individuals report reactions to enriched pasta. The vitamin carrier can contain free glutamate. But it's difficult to locate un-enriched pasta. Stock up on dried lima, chili, black, navy, kidney, and garbanzo beans. If you are sulfite sensitive, be sure to read canned bean labels especially on light colored beans as sulfites are often used to prevent darkening. Since I am, I purchase dry garbanzos and limas. Rice comes in many varieties, too. There are brown, red, wild, and others. But avoid boxed flavored varieties. Some sensitive people react to white rice. Since the government requires the nutrients be put back into rice after the hull has been polished off, MSG may be present as part of the vitamin/mineral binder. Rinse the rice several times before using to remove the cornstarch or other binders.

**Ice cream** - Most contain carrageenan, corn syrup solids, and whey in various amounts. My daughter can tolerate plain vanilla but if she eats the same brand of french vanilla, she has a three day headache. We compared ingredients and the latter had three times as many additives. We stick to Breyers natural vanilla (not the new soft version or low fat) and home made. Some toppings have MSG. Fruit and chocolate toppings are easy to make. So are milk shakes, fruit juice popsicles, and fruit frappes of fruit, ice, water, and sugar.

**Seeds** - Sesame, poppy, sunflower, flax, and caraway seeds are great in breads and rolls. Fennel seeds are good in Italian sausage. Try sesame and sunflower seeds in granola. Sprout alfalfa and other seeds for great nutritional value and add to salads and sandwiches.

**Grains** - Old fashioned oat flakes and rolled wheat flakes are great cooked for breakfast or added to granola, cookies, and breads. Quinoa is high in protein and a good substitute for rice. Your local health food and grocery stores have a lot of grains to choose from.

**Cottage Cheese** - Most contain carrageenan, whey, and vegetable gum. If you must eat it, look for the brand with the least amount of ingredients and made from whole, not skim milk.

**Butter** - No more margarine! Fat is fat, no matter where it comes from. Now that we are eating better, our bodies are working more efficiently. But it is still important to cut out fat wherever possible. Moderation is the key. We do most of our baking with real butter, or canola oil and substitute some of the fats with applesauce in much of our baking. Olive oil is a favorite in our sauteed and Italian dishes now. Look for butter that has no annatto added if possible. Many varieties contain citric acid.

**Oil** - Olive and vegetable oils are good. They are very low in saturated fats. Doctor Andrew Weil, M.D., author of <u>Spontaneous Healing</u> and <u>8 Weeks to Optimum Health</u>, suggests that we only use canola oil that has been expeller pressed. We have found that type in health food stores.

**Flour** - Most flour contains some glutamate because of the malted barley flour which is added to enhance flavor. We use Gold Medal Organic white flour and grind our own whole wheat, but most grocery stores or health food stores carry many flour varieties.

**Crackers and chips** - Most of the popular ones and flavored ones have MSG. We have found most soda crackers are okay and some imported crackers are fine. But the very sensitive may react to the malted barley flour found in most. Look for ones with the least amount of ingredients. We make our own "wheat skinnies". They are delicious and fun to make. Plain Ry-Krisp and Ak-mak crackers are delicious with a little butter or almond or peanut butter on top. We like plain wheat type crackers, tortilla and corn chips without lime added, and potato chips (no preservatives or flavorings).

**Bakery goods** - Be careful of L-cysteine, a potent neurotoxin. It is now added to many baked goods. MSG is also in glazes and fillings, so be cautious. Scratch is always better anyway. Bake one day a week or less often and freeze lots.

**Tortillas** - Flour and corn. Great for quick burritos and Mexican dishes. Avoid those with L-cysteine on the label. When in doubt, call the company. The telephone number is on the label or call (800) 555-1212 to find the toll free number of most food companies. Again, very sensitive people may react if malted barley flour is present. Try our easy recipes.

**Catsup** - We haven't found any without MSG. We promise you will enjoy our easy recipes for catsup.

**Salsa** - Most fresh ones in refrigerated areas are okay. A lot of canned and bottled salsas are "flavor enhanced", so read labels. Some restaurants sell their own freshly made salsa. We have included recipes.

**Bottled Spaghetti Sauce** - The well known ones are loaded with MSG, corn syrup, and oil. We make our own and freeze or bottle it. But there are some safer ones on the market now, although most contain MSG or citric acid.

**Drinks** - As mentioned previously, most canned and bottled soft drinks contain sulfites and MSG, the former to preserve and the latter to enhance flavors. We drink water, and some fruit juices. Some brands of soft drinks contain more chemicals than others. Decaffeinated drinks and iced herb teas are okay. Since we avoid caffeine entirely (another headache causing chemical), fruit juices, water, and whole milk are good choices. Dilute whole milk to cut fat consumption and save money. Homemade lemonade or limeade is a treat. I always carry around a large plastic mug or sport bottle of ice water. A lemon slice or peppermint tea bag added now and then is refreshing. On the plus side, you will increase your water consumption which is healthier and decrease your sugar intake if you avoid pop. Some canned plain tomato and pineapple juices (no corn syrup) are okay. But the vegetable blended tomato drinks contain MSG and/or preservatives. A word of caution: Some herb teas now contain "natural flavors", citric acid or malt. Read the labels.

**Popcorn** - It's best to buy the dry natural kind. Most prepackaged popcorn contains "seasoned" salts and lots of fat. We found a brand of bagged microwave popcorn in the bulk section of our grocery store. It says it contains only oil and salt. Best to air pop. Try a little sugar or seasonings in your popcorn next time for variaty.

**Cereal** - There are so many and most contain some glutamate. We found the cheaper off brands to have less malt, whey and corn syrup added. We enjoy shredded mini wheats, farina, oatmeal (not the flavored packets), and most granolas. It's hard to beat hot oatmeal with brown sugar and cream or milk. It's great cooked up with a diced apple or peach, too. Un-sugared puffed wheat and rice are okay, too. We enjoy the rolled multi-grain cereals and cooked whole wheat. Look for cereals with the least artificial ingredients.

**Pickles and Olives** - Black olives are okay. A lot of oil and vinegar cured olives and green olives bother us. Some have sulfites which we can't tolerate. Sauerkraut often contains sulfites but is usually free of MSG. Most pickles contain MSG. We make our own, which is easier than we thought.

**Cocoa** - Dry powdered cocoa is fine and we've found Nestles Quick, the kind you mix with milk to be okay even though it says natural flavors. But it may bother others. However, some hot cocoa mixes contain glutamate, usually in the form of whey and milk solids. Mix 1 part cocoa powder to

2 parts sugar and store. Add to hot or cold milk to flavor. When adding to cold milk, dissolve first in small amount (2 tablespoons) of hot water.

**Mustard** - Most major brands have MSG but there are mustards that do not. We've found several brands to be MSG free.

**Yogurt** - Some contain carrageenan, whey and natural flavorings, especially low fat. Some of the fruit syrups contain sulfites. We make our own. Recipe is in this book. Easy!!!

**Fresh, Frozen, or Canned Fish** - Look for canned tuna without broth, calcium caseinate, or salt (water only). Some canned salmon are okay. Most fresh fish, if not breaded or seasoned, are fine. However, some frozen filets or steaks contain sulfites. Avoid tiny shrimp if sulfite sensitive. Large shrimp and shrimp raised in tanks are usually chemical free.

**Jams** - Highly sensitive people report reacting to pectin and/or corn syrup. We make ours seasonally by boiling 6 cups fruit with 6 cups sugar for 20 to 30 minutes or until thickened.

**Nuts** - Buy raw almonds, walnuts, pecans, and peanuts. Unsalted or salted, roasted or dry roasted nuts are fine. Just be sure they are preservative free, unseasoned, or contain just plain salt. Occasionally, carrageenan or hydrolyzed protein is sprayed on nuts to enable the salt to adhere.

**Dry Fruit** - Dry fruit snacks, unsulphured dates/raisins, and many others can be found at health food stores. When I crave a candy bar, I reach for dry pears.

**Vegetable Oil** - Olive, sunflower, and sesame (for flavoring Chinese dishes).

**Seasonings** - Try new herbs and spices, avoiding seasoned salts, blends, and dry soup or salad dressing preparations. Here are some of our standards: dry and fresh garlic, red, black, and cayenne peppers, Chinese Five Spice, oregano, garlic, cumin, basil, cilantro, ginger, dry mustard, paprika, thyme, chili powder, chili pods (pasilla, ancho). My daughter uses a teaspoon or two of cocoa powder to enhance chili, Mexican dishes, and stew.

**Vinegar** - Sulfur sensitive people may react to sulfites if present. White distilled vinegar is made from grain. The fermentation process may release some glutamates from the grain. We do best with some pure apple cider vinegar and even better substituting fresh lemon or lime juice in recipes. We have been told that glutamate can even be formed in the apple cider fermentation process.

**Salt** - Some salts, especially iodized salt, contain dextrose or cornstarch.

Read labels often, keeping a running list of foods that do not affect you, including brand names, and where purchased. At first you will be discouraged at how many products contain MSG, but the list of wholesome products will continue to grow. Bring your list of MSG containing food additives with you when food shopping. Soon you will have them memorized. One friend keeps a copy on the inside of her cupboard door for quick reference and one in her purse to show waiters. She keeps a list of safe products she has purchased and tried on her refrigerator attached with a magnet. She keeps adding to it, along with the stores where they were found.

Familiarize yourself with different grocery stores, including health food stores and farmer's markets to add variety to your diet. Beware of assuming that all health food products are MSG free. If you know the hidden sources for MSG, you will be safer. Look for farm products that are organic (pesticide free).

Remember to shop mostly the perimeter of the grocery store, which includes all of the fresh products: dairy, produce, and meat. I augment these foods each trip with canned diced tomatoes, canned kidney and black beans, bottled or frozen 100% apple juice, and other frozen juices. I also stock up on plain canned vegetables, canned salmon, canned fruits in water, MSG free tortilla chips, potato chips, and certain pretzels. We love frozen pretzels, also. Microwave them, and dip in sweet hot mustard for a fast snack. Some canned fruit products contain sulfites and citric acid to preserve color. They can cause reactions in some people.

For other snacks, especially for the grandchildren, I have boxed raisins, purchased dry fruit (no sulfur dioxide added), home dried bananas, prunes, whole almonds and other nuts, and fixings for homemade cakes, pies, cookies, and custards. Grandma knew best all along.

Search out small dairies, flour mills, bakeries, and cheese makers. The smaller family run businesses often do less processing. One sensitive friend who cannot drink any commercial milk, found a farm selling fresh goat milk and now she drinks that. She suggested checking out the operation for cleanliness.

Start a no MSG recipe file and file away successful menus for easy reference later. My daughter has a calendar form of 30 squares that she made up. At the beginning of each month, she fills each square with a menu. She posts that and a shopping list on her refrigerator. She even jots in comments and recipe references that will help her later.

Find a reputable butcher and ask for his help in locating non-MSG meat and poultry products. Suggest he make a MSG free sausage. He may have a new hit on his hands.

Avoid all fast food restaurants. All of us love the wonderful smells and strong tastes of these MSG traps, but they depend heavily on flavor enhancers to get our business. Bring water with you everywhere you go. In summer, fill a liter bottle ⅔ full and freeze. Enjoy it cold all day long. Remember to cook and bake in large batches and freeze in plastic zipper bags or containers. Be sure to label and date everything. Gravy looks a lot like soup stock once it is frozen. Don't be afraid to try new things like bread making or pickle making. Newer machines help make it fun and easier. If you don't already have one, invest in a freezer.

If you know you are MSG sensitive, it is important to let your doctor and anyone else who will listen know about your condition. The more they know, the more they can help others, maybe even themselves. In February 1997, I began suffering a bad toothache that would come and go. After a couple of weeks, I made an appointment to see my dentist of 15 years. The day before I had to go , I read in a NOMSG newsletter that medications are often in a protein base. So that day and on the day of my appointment I skipped my thyroid and estrogen pills. Amazingly, the toothache subsided. I had recently switched from an estrogen patch to a pill. I kept my appointment to be sure there wasn't a cavity, which he confirmed. I then explained what I had discovered and his assistant asked for more MSG information since her sister is very sensitive, but doesn't know what to avoid. After a few minutes discussing MSG sensitivity symptoms, I apologized for taking up the dentist's time. He exclaimed, "No, no, you're fine. In fact I think you've solved my medical problem!" He went on to explain that he had been to several clinics around the country, spending thousands of dollars. He suffers from chronic fatigue, headaches, and problems with his hands, his livelihood. He said "When I eat a can of "____" chili, I can feel the symptoms start soon after. Does that sound like its an MSG problem?" Well, I'm no trained professional, but I felt confident that it did. So the next day I took some information to him and hoped he and his family would see the need for a change in his diet. Incidentally, my doctor and pharmacist helped me find a thyroid hormone pill and estrogen patch that do not bother me. Your pharmacist will give you a list of all the inactive ingredients in any medication.

Remember, the more you share what you know with others, even when you sense a great reluctance to believe you, be confident and trust what your body knows without doubt: That MSG toxicity is no myth.

Write your congressmen and tell them your story, sending any information on MSG that you have. Ask them to find more information for you about other flavor enhancers, since the FDA has very little that they will send you. Who knows, one of them may be a sufferer and may use his/her position to further the cause!

The following suggested kitchen aids will make work and eating easier.

**Dehydrator** - Great for apples, bananas, and other fruits, meat jerky, fruit leather, red and green peppers, tomatoes, etc.
**Heavy duty mixer** - One that will knead bread. Bread makers are great, too. Avoid the flour mixes for them, as they contain malted barley flour and the special yeast often contains yeast nutrient (may contain MSG or L-cysteine).
**Vitorio Strainer** - Applesauce, tomato sauce, purees, and juices are a snap! We pureed currants last year.

It removed the seeds, skins, and stems in one step. Most health food stores carry them and the various sized strainers.

**Juice Extractor** - Get the benefit of fresh fruits and vegetables and fresh vitamins, enzymes, and minerals. However, eat whole fruit and vegetables often to get the fiber you need. Organically grown are best.

**Flour Grinder** - Enjoy whole wheat flour, without malt, and the nutritional benefits of unrefined cracked wheat and cereal, which are high in B vitamins and fiber.

**Ice Cream Maker** - All kinds and prices are available.

**Extra refrigerator or freezer** - We are planning to put an extra refrigerator next to our freezer in our garage to fill with fresh and frozen produce. Used ones are less expensive.

**Freezer Bags and Containers** - Invaluable to freeze leftover meals, soup stock, and garden produce. Quarter or slice tomatoes and microwave them for six minutes, cool, and package. Just before sealing, add a bunch of fresh basil leaves to some of the bags if desired. Great way to use up garden herbs.

**Yogurt Maker** - I found three for under $3.00 each in the thrift store. Recipes for yogurt are in this book and a yogurt maker is not necessary.

**Old-fashioned style citrus fruit reamer or juicer** - Look for these in antique stores and flea markets. I use my green tinted glass one continually. Also, I found an aluminum one that sits over a small bowl and catches the seeds at the local Goodwill Store.

**Aluminum foil** - Line cookie sheets and casserole dishes for easy cleanup when you are busy. Do this for roasted vegetables, turkey dressing and sticky dishes. Or make your own TV dinners by dabbing leftovers on single serving size pieces of aluminum. Top with second layer of foil and crimp edges closed. Freeze on cookie sheets for support and reheat (frozen) later at 425° for 25 to 35 minutes or until bubbly.

**Food Processor** - Great for slicing, shredding and chopping.

**Apple peeler, corer, and slicer, all in one** - A great tool found in health food stores along with cherry pitters and corn cutters.

**Blender** - Whip up fresh fruit or vegetable frappes.


Sources for food and food processing equipment:

1.  Leman's Hardware, P.O. Box 321, Kidron, Ohio 44636, (330) 857-5441. Their catalog offers all kinds of hard to find equipment for food preparation. The Amish use many of their products.

2.  Whole Foods Markets offers hormone free, untreated meats, pesticide free produce, and products free of artificial flavors and colors. However, some products that say "No MSG" still contain hydrolyzed protein, yeast extract, etc., so read all labels. Also available are environmentally safe cleaners. Stores are in 17 states and operate under four names: Whole Foods Market, Bread and Circus, Fresh Fields, and Well Spring Grocery. For more information, write, phone, or FAX:
    Whole Foods Corporate Office
    601 North Lamar, Suite 300
    Austin, TX 78703
    Voice: (512) 477-4455
    FAX: (512) 477-1069
    Internet Website at http://www.wholefoods.com

3.  Arrowhead Mills is a source for flour without malted barley flour. They no longer sell to indivdual consumers, but suggest asking your health food store to order for you.
    Arrowhead Mills
    Box 2059
    Hereford, TX 79845
    (800) 749-0730

4.  Walton Feed has many different grains in bulk, rolled flakes, beans, wheat grinders, juicers, and other products. Be careful of processed products such as the textured vegetable protein even

though "No MSG" is after the product name.  Send inquiries to:

Walton Feed, Inc.
P.O. Box 307
135 North 10th
Montpelier, ID 83254
Internet Website at http://www.waltonfeed.com

5.     Abundant Life collects and sells heirloom seeds.  My allergist told me that our bodies break down older varieties of vegetables and fruits more easily than the "high tech" hybrids.  For information call (360) 385-5660.

6.     Trader Joes has chemical free produce.  Lots of healthy canned and frozen items, but do read all labels.

# Brand Names of Products

I cannot recommend any products. It is a fact that a national product can have a different formulation in different parts of the country. Also, stores can give the same national product different names. Also, a producer may decide to add MSG or a glutamate containing ingredient to a product at any time. Consider too, that what may cause no reaction in some may send others to the hospital, since sensitivity varies with each person. This is just a list of what <u>we</u> or some friends find okay so far.

Carolina Natural Turkey (Albertson's) - Cooked and sold in the deli section for sandwiches. Ingredients include turkey, salt and spice. We called and were told the spice is pepper. (919) 658-6743.
Western Family apple cider vinegar
Hain Apple cider vinegar
Locally made ciders at the orchard where produced or at the Farmer's Market (pasteurized is safer)
Montana Territory Meats (Cottage Bacon) (406) 628-4822 (has nitrates, though)
Knudsen's Whole sour cream
Most whipping creams except those with carrageenan or additives. Some are being ultra pasteurized at a higher temperature. Some people report reacting to these products, perhaps because more glutamate is being released due to the higher temperatures. This is true for butter made with such cream.
Arrowhead Mills flour and other products
Tillamook mild and medium cheddar cheese
Most mozzarella and Monterey Jack cheeses do not bother us (used sparingly).
Ghiradelli <u>dark</u> chocolate chips (not milk chocolate) (the lecithin may bother some)
Most cocoa brands
Nabisco shredded wheat, spoon size and biscuit. Also Flavorite brand.
Flavorite mustard
Flavorite soda crackers, but they <u>do</u> have malted barley flour
Shoppers Value soda crackers, but they <u>do</u> have malted barley flour
"Valley Fresh" Premium Chunk White Turkey (or Chicken) in water (Costco)
Low sodium tuna, water only (Safeway brand Tongol, Tree of Life)
Safeway Select Verde Spaghetti sauce- mushroom and onion only
Safeway Select frozen Orange Juice (may contain some sulfites, under 1 part per million)
Safeway Select Mild Salsa
Townhouse Refried Beans - no fat variety
Cream of Wheat, farina
Adam's 100% All Natural peanut butter
Life cereal (original flavor)
Hain 100% pure expeller pressed canola oil. Found in health food stores. Look for any expeller pressed canola oil.
Red River cereal - needs to be cooked
Lay's plain potato chips (may contain sulfites, under 1 part per million)
Flavorite wheat Crackers
Panda All Natural Licorice
Aunt Patty's Blackstrap Molasses (unsulphured) at health food stores. Any unsulphured is good (some people may still react).
Malto Meal plain puffed wheat and rice

Some Matzo crackers (whole wheat). Eat with butter or use crumgs for breading.
ACT II Natural microwave popcorn
Unseasoned rice vinegar
Foster Farm Chicken (Washington)
Acme Natural Turkeys (Seattle)
Best Foods or Helman's mayonnaise - used moderately. Many people report they cannot use any brand.
Saffola mayonnaise - used moderately
Muir Glen tomato puree
Ak-mak crackers
Farman's pickles - A manager told me that their natural flavoring is a natural extract of dill in oil made in Utah. The vinegar may bother some individuals.
Pop Weaver gourmet popcorn - Natural microwave popcorn
Tree of Life toasted onion and cracked pepper crackers (Health food stores)
Cookie Lover's creme supremes - Chocolate sandwich style too (Health food stores)
Draper Farms Chicken - Food Pavillion, Templeman's Meat Market
Santitos Corn Chips
Select Harvest whole almonds and other nuts (Coscto)
Honeysuckle White Natural Turkey - Says "No MSG or Gluten" on label. I spoke with a registered dietitian from Cargill, Inc., producers of "Honeysuckle White Natural Turkeys" in Springdale, AR, (800) 532-5756. She assured me the ones that say, "No MSG or gluten", are not basted or injected with anything. They will soon offer a basted turkey that is basted with a pure meat broth that has no hydrolyzed product added. We discussed free glutamate and she said that they have had many calls from consumers with the same questions about MSG in their product. Interestingly she told me that I must react to tomatoes, too, since they are high in glutamate. We agreed that if the peptide links are broken, then the glutamate can cause more reactions. When she asked if I had to stay away from canned tomato products, we discussed how citric acid from corn added to tomatoes can cause problems. She was quite interested because she said they don't use any hydrolyzed corn products for the same reason, since they contain some MSG. I find a growing awareness in the industry. The ones that are aware and care about the effects of their product will probably fare better in the years to come.
Wisdom of the Ancients Stevia - White powder sugar substitute sold in health food stores. Avoid sugar packets in restaurants that contain fillers. An excellent book is Baking With Stevia by Rita De Puydt.
Whole Foods grapefruit seed extract cleaning products
Muir Glen Catsup
Domino brown and white sugar
Oscar-Myer center cut ham
Kava Kava - herb in health food stores that some use for MSG symptoms
Dr. Bronner's soaps and liquid castile for shampoo (the soap can be used to brush teeth)
Cherrios
Some Häagen-Dazs ice cream (not chocolate)
Breyers ice cream - not the new soft version. Jack Samuels says he received several calls from people who say they are starting to react to the original vanilla Breyers. He called the plant and found out they don't clean the equipment when they run a batch of the original after the soft version which is high in MSG. It's "cross contamination", he calls it.
S&W Baked Beans
Some Trader Joe Products (read labels)
Brown Cow yogurt
Organic free range chicken
Sucanat - raw sugar in health food stores
Amy's Frozen Entrees (but read labels first)
Dole Pineapple and raisins
Many Whole Foods private label products are okay (but read labels first)

Real Salt - no fillers, high in minerals

Canning Salt

Paul Neuman Picante Sauce

Johnson's Kids shampoo (blue liquid)

Whole Wheat and rye bread - several people said they handled them better than white

One woman mixes 2 to 3 tablespoons sugar to 1 cup water to make hair spray, since most contain irritants. More or less sugar can be added for various holds.

R.J. Ligits shampoo in a bar

Free and Clear All detergent

Erickson's Choice canned salmon

Raw sugar - Someone said some brown sugars are white refined sugar coated with sulfured molasses. I read the ingredients on one bulk brown sugar product. It said, "pure cane sugar, invert sugar, ASL, organic non-sugar." Your guess is as good as mine! Also, many so-called maple syrups are watered down and contain preservatives. We use honey often instead of sugar.

Some Sea Salts - fewer chemicals. Avoid salts containing dextrose, cornstarch or other flowing agents.

Some White Rain and Salon Selective hair products

Planters Dry Roasted, unsalted - we've been told that some salted peanuts are coated with hydrolyzed protein or carrageenan first to allow salt to stick.

Old Stone Mill Whole Wheat Wafers

Barbara's natural cereals

Tree of Life canned tuna

Clearly Natural unscented glycerine soap for skin and hair

Nature's Life 100% Vitamin C Crystals

I Want My Ya-Ya's popcorn (Fred Meyer health section)

Honey puffed Kashi (7 whole grain and sesame cereal - www.kashi.com)

Organic Valley butter (in blue box)

Pacific Foods of Oregon Organic Vegetable Broth

Stahlbush Island Farms frozen vegetables (sold at our Fred Meyer store)

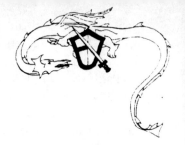

# Eating Out

A friend of mine who suffers from severe MSG sensitivity often begs me to open a restaurant so that "people like us" can enjoy eating out again. We know how she feels.

People who run restaurants, we've found, know very little about MSG and the amount they are actually using in their cooking. Asking the waiter is not enough. Asking them to ask the chef, cook, or manager is more helpful. First explain that MSG makes you very ill and you need to know the ingredients of a certain dish before you can order. Especially ask if seasoned salts; canned, packaged, or dry sauces; marinades; soy and other sauces; or canned soups have been used in the dish. Often, batter on fish has "seasoned' salt added, as do salad croutons. Most salad dressings contain MSG, so a good choice is to ask for oil and vinegar. I now carry my own little bottle with me since I've seen diet conscious people do the same. If you are sulfite sensitive, make sure the vinegar is not wine vinegar. Instead, ask for lemon or orange sections to squeeze over your salad. Add some sprinkles of oil if desired. I sometimes also sprinkle a tiny amount of sugar with salt and pepper to taste, over my salad. (We've included several tasty dressings in this book.) When ordering fish or meats, ask that no seasoned salts or sauces be added. Fish is wonderful grilled or sauteed with butter, lemon, salt, and pepper. Avoid all soups and chowders, unless made from scratch without seasoning salts and bouillon. Some cooks call their soups "made from scratch" but actually use a canned soup base or stock. Appetizers are often MSG seasoned, but never be afraid to ask what seasonings have been used. We, of course, are wary of most Chinese dishes, but some restaurants will prepare certain dishes without MSG or soy-based sauces (such as oyster sauce) if asked. We've often learned the hard way when it comes to oriental food, fast food, and many other restaurant foods. We've discovered that some Mexican dishes are safe, as long as they don't use prepackaged or canned sauces or add Accent or Adobo seasoning. When asked if they used seasoned salt in their pork verde burrito at a Mexican restaurant, they said "No". But they said they used it on the grilled meat dishes. I asked if the salt had MSG and they said, "Oh, no, never." When asked to see if hydrolyzed protein, etc, was in it, they checked and came back to tell us that ,"yes", it was and they were sorry. We felt pleased that they were made newly aware and we ordered the pork verde! Sometimes it is added to the rice and beans. Just ask!! We have included cards at the end of the this book section that can be taken with you and shown to waiters and cooks.

**Fast Food Restaurants**

Whether it's the fast hamburger or taco joint, most of these establishments load their meals with MSG products. There's a famous chicken franchise who's food is so tasty, you want to lick your fingers. Guess why it's so tasty? India closed them down after so many illness complaints of patrons, as reported in the "NOMSG Messenger". MSG is in everything from the chicken to the gravy. Ask any restaurant for a list of the ingredients or a nutrition chart. Most of the larger franchises like McDonald's, have them all printed up. They will make you very fast-food wise. We were shocked at how much MSG is in the typical hamburger and fries meal, including milk shakes and tasty chicken products. And we wonder why ADD, Attention Deficit Disorder, is on the rise, as is childhood asthma. I bought my three year old granddaughter fries and a shake at one of the most popular fast food places for two reasons. She wanted to play on the indoor playground and asked for a "nilla shake" with that look in her eyes. Besides, I thought it would be interesting to look for any changes in her (she is MSG reactive at certain amounts). Her cheeks flushed bright pink 10 minutes after finishing. Most notable, soon after we returned home, when she usually takes a nap and is very sleepy, she was twirling around, jumping on the bed, arguing with me, and being just plain contrary. The hyperactivity was out of character and I vowed never to experiment on her again! Her mother now avoids MSG religiously, thank goodness. An acquaintance, a single mom who works full time, has a three year old whose face and body are constantly covered with itchy hives. He's irritable and cries easily. They eat often at fast food places since she is so busy. Her problem is time. Don't assume high cost restaurants use less MSG. Most cooks use MSG, many unknowingly. Very few people are aware of its hidden sources. We've had great success picking the brains of chefs since most are very proud of their culinary skills and want to please their guests, not make them ill. Many appreciate a call ahead when making reservations informing them of your special needs. Most chefs will happily make substitutes or changes for you if forewarned.

When we are invited to friends homes, wedding receptions, parties, or potluck dinners, we now eat a little something at home first. It really helps. Otherwise we're really tempted to make some costly mistakes out of hunger. Our good friends know of our problem and will run the menu by us. Others feel less comfortable cooking for us and so we opt for dinner out or a movie together. My son recently called to say he went with friends to a restaurant and found nothing he could eat, but still enjoyed their company. Luckily he ate something at home. If you find yourself in a similar predicament, order a baked potato and butter, a mushroom omelet (ask them to use whole milk or water), or a bowl of steamed, unseasoned fresh vegetables and ask for a lemon slice and real butter. Most establishments will grill a 100% ground beef patty, steak, fish, or chicken breast without seasoning. I try to make my friends comfortable by telling them not to cook differently or I will tell them of a few items or ingredients that I can eat. I can usually find something to eat. After all, we don't want to alienate our friends and family. Our social life is already a challenge.

Christmas and other holidays are more difficult for avoidance. This is the time in the past when we have been headachy and sick from November to January. NO MORE!! We cannot enjoy these dinners anywhere else but home because most people cook with extra seasonings and MSG laden turkeys and hams at this time of year. My daughter had a hard time not eating her in-laws' meals, feeling rude if she didn't. Knowing they contained MSG ingredients, she hoped there wouldn't be enough in the meal to hurt her. Within half an hour she felt the familiar wooziness and flushing and headache beginning. Her husband threw his hands in the air and faced his family saying, "Well, you've poisoned my wife again!" They checked over labels as her husband pointed out ingredient after ingredient. They finally realized she'd be happier eating a peanut butter sandwich than nursing a 3-day migraine with little children to care for. Now they scramble to make sure there is something for her to eat. So don't be afraid to take care of yourself and speak up for yourself. Diabetics get respect and MSG sensitive people need to insist on it, too.

I have had the experience of not being taken seriously by people, even family, who themselves have become MSG sensitive since. Do not underestimate the influence you may have by sharing your story with others. The more the word is passed around, the more people will recognize their health problems or those of loved ones as possibly MSG related. Do we really think large food companies who count on flavor enhancers to compete with their rivals and reap high profits will remove MSG overnight? I would expect them to fight anyone who says MSG is dangerous. High priced lawyers and lobbyists have been hired to make courageous doctors and scientists who are trying to inform the government of the dangers of this dangerous toxin look like alarmists and fools. Few magazines or newspapers will publish articles about MSG because most of their paid advertisers come from the processed food industry. So the only way we can have any influence is to spread the word and educate as many as will listen. If you find the life style changes suggested in this book have helped you please pass on what you know and help others. As mentioned previously, Kaye Wanke in Florence, Montana, holds group meetings to inform others. She instructs church and other groups and advertises her services in the paper without charge. One person can make a difference.

**Traveling**

The ice cooler is a must! We pack ours with our favorite cheeses, cut up veggies in a plastic bag, cooked chicken, yogurt, nuts, fruit juice, mustard, homemade salad dressing, and butter. We often pack a coleslaw or pasta salad. We fill a gallon thermos with ice water and pack the MSG-free chips, cookies, trail mix, granola bars, crackers, and lots of fresh and dried fruit. Of course, the peanut butter and bread are always on hand. Boil, peel eggs, and place in zipper bag. Sprinkle with salt and pepper and seal. Cold sliced meat loaf, roast beef, and chicken make great sandwich fillings, as do egg and tuna salad, made with oil and vinegar if you cannot tolerate mayonnaise. Mashed avocado thickens egg or tuna fillings and is great in veggie sandwiches, or used as a spread instead of mayonnaise. The next chapter on school lunches contains additional ideas adaptable to traveling. If you must stop for a burger, my daughter says to make sure their beef is just that and has no protein filler added to the patties. She suggests asking that they leave out any seasoning salt or "special" sauces and only add fresh lettuce, tomato, and onion, if desired. She adds her own mustard and homemade catsup. (Burger King hamburgers don't bother her this way.) Many is the time that I have searched a menu to find a "safe" meal, only to find questionable offerings. In that case, I will order a plate of any steamed fresh vegetables (no seasoning salt) they have, with butter and a slice of lemon on the side. I have been rewarded with delightful surprises such as the time I received a heaping plate of steaming green beans, asparagus, new potatoes, huge mushrooms, onions, peppers, and corn on the cob (all for $2.50)! At Oriental restaurants, I often ask for mushroom or regular egg foo yung, but I ask that no MSG or seasonings of any kind be added to the vegetables or egg mixture and that the gravy be omitted. I salt and pepper it myself. If you order steak or fresh fish, ask that no seasonings be added. Pan fried is often better since the grill is often contaminated with seasoning salts and sauces. And remember, do bring your own salad dressings. A friend and her husband drove all the way to Alaska and back. They ate at restaurants often and by the end of the trip, knew they were both MSG sensitive. My husband and I used to travel around the country selling my doll and quilt patterns at wholesale trade shows. We had to quit because I would get so ill and didn't know why. We thought it was due to stress. So MSG can undermine one's income in addition to one's health.

**School Lunches**

Pack your children a lunch and warn them about processed snacks, especially in the middle and high schools. Often, they will run with a crowd and eat what they want, going to nearby fast food places even during school lunch breaks. Understandably, this will be the most difficult time for MSG-sensitive teens and their parents. But continue to encourage and educate even if they insist on eating the way they want. One day, when they are mature enough and perhaps sick enough, they will see the wisdom of your eating habits.

If you have young children, you will actually have a better influence over what they eat now and later. My granddaughter had a play date with a neighbor down the street and stayed through lunch time. When my son-in-law picked her up, he was told that she refused the hot dogs they grilled for lunch, so she was probably hungry. Later, when asked why she refused an offer for lunch, she simply said, "Because hot dogs are junk and we shouldn't eat them." Although her parents were mortified at the idea of their little girl refusing a generous meal with neighbors and referring to the offer as "junk" to their faces, they realized what influence they have over their young child's eating habits. They just needed to find a better word for the food we avoid!

Included is an entire section on school lunches with ideas and recipes. This book is the result of many requests, the largest single one being, "What can we eat?" We hope it helps.

# School Lunches and Snack Ideas

Dr. Russell Blaylock believes MSG to be one of the major causes of asthma and behavior disorders such as Attention Deficit Disorder, delinquency, rage disorder, and depression in children. All of my children but one are out of the public school system, so I'm not faced with the challenge of packing healthful lunches each day for youngsters. But since most lunches offered by schools are laced with MSG, here are some ideas we've gathered.

Roast whole natural turkeys and chickens and freeze meat in small portions. They can be taken frozen to school (or work) for lunch. Or defrost overnight and use in sandwiches.

Place some peanut butter in a small snap lid container or sturdy zipper bag. Core and cut an apple in sections or cut up celery and/or carrots for dipping and place in plastic baggies. Those little bags of precleaned and trimmed carrots from the grocery store are great! And they are not as costly as most convenience foods. Make sure they say "no preservatives". Since most cold cuts are out, use sandwich alternatives: Peanut butter with banana slices or honey or jam, non-MSG ham, non-MSG tuna or salmon mixed with non-MSG mayonnaise and/or sour cream, crackers and mild cheese chunks. Include fruits daily even if it's pitted prunes or raisins or other dried varieties. The health food stores have all kinds of unsulphured, dehydrated snacks. Some fruit rolls and fruit snacks contain MSG and sulfites. Place nuts and raisins in small zipper plastic bags and keep a supply handy to grab from the pantry. Kids love a few chocolate chips sprinkled in, too. Dark chocolate chips do not contain milk solids. Read labels of cookies, crackers, and chips before including in school lunches. Some newer baked potato chips and corn chips without fat have lots of MSG. Double batch on your baking days and keep extra cookies, brownies, and cakes in the freezer in bags or freezer containers. On cold days, leftover and heated soups and stews are great in a thermos or for after school. Some schools have microwaves for students today, so send cold or frozen leftovers. Mild cheddar sticks or mozzarella cheese sticks and crackers or unflavored potato chips are great with a thermos or bottle of fruit juice as are plain tortilla chips and salsa. Most processed fruit drinks in pouch, can or bottle, including soft drinks, contain MSG plus a lot of artificial color, flavor, preservatives and corn syrup. Kids get too many empty calories and sugar anyway. Send 100% fruit juices. Include money for one or two whole milks, not chocolate (contains carrageenan and other products). Ask the school to provide whole milk if they don't.

When my children were small and had difficulty peeling oranges, I cut the orange in four wheels and then cut through the skin on one width of each wheel to make peeling easier. Seal in zipper plastic bags. Any fruit can be cut and bagged this way. To prevent darkening, squeeze a little lemon juice in bag and shake. Also tasty is a good sprinkle of cinnamon/sugar in a bag of cut up apple. Sticky, but they will eat it. Fun too, are "ants on a log" celery pieces spread with peanut butter, dotted with raisins. Make "Noah's Ark" by using animal cookies instead.

Homemade granola bars make for a healthful lunch or snack. We have spread peanut butter between two bars. Granola bars freeze well, too. We have included recipes. Along with yogurt, they're very satisfying. Or make a mix of your child's favorite dry fruit, dry cereal, and nuts and keep it in a canister. Whole wheat bread or rolls are especially good spread with real butter or nut butters. Cut an apple in half crosswise, core and fill hole with banana chunks or raisins. Close apple and wrap. Spread natural peanut butter on an apple circle section and top with another circle for a fun sandwich. Children may balk at change, but when hungry enough will eat and even enjoy the change especially once they start feeling better.

Flour tortillas make easy and fun roll-up sandwiches. Many today contain L-cysteine and sulfites. Our favorite recipe is in the Breads and Baked Goods section of the this book. It is called "Tortillas I". I form the dough into 20 to 30 balls and place them on wax paper or a cookie sheet and freeze. Then I store them in the freezer in plastic zipper bags. To use, microwave about one minute before rolling it out then grilling in a pan. Spread with whole sour cream or butter and add jam or fruit or raisins. Also delicious is sour cream, butter, or mashed avocado topped with favorite fresh veggies: chopped bell peppers, olives, tomatoes, grated carrots. These can be seasoned with basil or oregano for an Italian taste or add salsa and cilantro for Mexican flavor. Just spread the toppings and roll up and wrap in plastic wrap. A friend of mine adds black beans to hers for more protein. Refried beans may be mixed with sour cream and salsa. Add a bag of tortilla chips for dipping. Also a pasta salad is delicious for lunch. Mix cooked pasta in fun shapes with sweet onions, olives, chopped tomato, and green pepper. Season with a light vinaigrette made of oil, vinegar, salt, pepper, sugar, and favorite spices. One of my teen's favorite snack or lunch is burritos. I spread ten flour tortillas out on my counter and divide a 1 lb. 14 oz. can of refried beans (Flavorite) between each one. Mild cheddar cheese chunks (or grated) are sprinkled on the beans. Mild chili powder, chopped onion, and diced canned green chilies can also be added if desired. Then I roll them up and wrap individually in plastic wrap. Place in a gallon zipper bag and freeze. They can be heated in the microwave and topped with sour cream and salsa for a quick meal. My husband has eaten them cold and they are great that way too. They are also good spread with butter, sprinkled with cinnamon sugar, rolled up, and heated.

Many of these lunches can be made in advance or frozen since most are not the typical soggy mayonnaise style sandwiches. The effort comes not in the food preparation, but in forming new habits. Change is challenging but very worthwhile.

Some other snack ideas are: Whole unsalted almonds, dates, dates stuffed with almonds, pistachio and peanuts in the shell, nut butters besides peanut (almond, cashew), home made skinny wheat crackers (recipe included) and cheese, fruit juices or shakes, MSG-free yogurt, MSG-free cookies, MSG-free potato chips. Jo Jos are easy to make. Just toss sliced potatoes lightly with oil and sprinkle with favorite herbs and spices, ie., garlic or onion powder, oregano, cayenne, basil, chili powder, salt, and pepper. Spread on cookie sheet or pan and bake until tender and brown at 425° for 15-20 minutes.

Try exotic fruits for a change such as mangos, papaya, pomegranate, and kiwi. Avocados are great to have on hand. Spread on sandwiches instead of mayonnaise. A dab of sour cream or yogurt on pineapple or strawberries with a sprinkling of brown sugar on top is delicious. Make fruit shish-kabobs with fresh strawberries, grapes, pineapple, and cheese chunks. Mash an avocado, then add salt and pepper, chili powder, salsa, chopped tomato, and use as dip for veggies or tortilla chips (guacamole). For sour cream and French onion chip dip, bake chopped onions at 350° on cookie sheet until brown and dry, stirring often. Store in refrigerator or freezer. To make chip dip, add 2 tablespoons onion to 1 cup sour cream. Season with salt, pepper, and dash of cayenne.

A delicious sandwich is made from whole wheat bread, sliced avocado, and tomatoes. Top with the overnight coleslaw (in the recipe section) or sprouts and sprinkle with raisins and nuts (peanuts, sunflower seeds, walnuts). Many children may not like nuts, so omit them. But if you can camouflage them by chopping finely, they will get extra protein. Don't forget fried egg or meatloaf sandwiches, both good with mustard and catsup. With the new cold pack lunch carriers (freeze the coolant overnight), children can now safely enjoy peeled hard-boiled eggs, left over chicken, and other perishables. Salmon or tuna patties are good eaten cold the next day or put on a bun with lettuce and homemade salad dressing.

# A Closer Look at Dairy Products

I had many questions, since I kept reacting to some milks and cheeses and not to others. For answers, I talked to dairy producers and with several NoMSG members, networking information. Unless milk is raw, the milk we consume has been pasteurized (heat treated), homogenized, had nutrients added, and in some cases with skim milk, has had some whey or milk solids or gelatin added. Since most cheeses, including cream cheese, cottage cheese, and dairy products such as yogurt, low fat sour cream, buttermilk, chocolate milk, and half and half are made from the same kind of milk, they will have ingredients that contain glutamate. Many will have stabilizers and gums, carrageenan, and whey added to make a thicker product. Some health food stores and "Ma and Pa" cheese makers offer cheese made the old fashioned way, whole milk, rennet, and bacteria, but they are few. I've seen cheese made from raw milk in our health food store, but some that I've tried still bother me. If you have questions, call the company and ask what is added to their cheeses. Many highly sensitive people avoid all cheeses.

I called the lab at the Tillamook cheese creamery in Tillamook, Oregon. They told me that most of their cheeses are made from low fat pasteurized milk which does have extra milk solids added "occasionally" to boost the protein content. They told me that their cheddar cheeses are made with whole raw milk that is heat shocked to kill bacteria. But they also use both enzymes and cultures. The problem with some enzymes used today is that they are very powerful and they break down the milk proteins, too much and too early, probably releasing glutamic acid. The milder the cheese, the less broken down by enzymes it is.

A Dairygold Consolidated milk producer told me that vitamins and sometimes milk solids are added to most of the skimmed milks to add body and protein and replace vitamins destroyed by heat. Vitamin D is often derived from Torula yeast, which contains glutamic acid. There may be residue present. High heat alone, especially as used in ultra-pasteurization, may free up glutamic acid. Milk and cream packaged in cartons are often ultra-pasteurized to lengthen shelf life. He told me that in California, milk solids are even added to whole milk because California law requires milk to contain at least 10% protein. Protein content varies due to several conditions; such as cow diet, seasonal changes, or the type of cow.

I asked another dairyman in Seattle, Washington about the base that the vitamins were in and he said the one they used had a soybean oil base used in minuscule amounts. When a lot of milk solids are added to skim milk, it is done to make it taste more like whole milk and they usually label it "protein fortified". We use whole milk and water it down to drink it. Undiluted, it makes wonderful thick mild yogurt that my grandchildren call pudding.

A local dairyman in Pasco, Washington educated me even more about milk production, explaining that homogenization obliterates the original natural structure of milk cells so that the fat will not separate and rise to the top. He personally feels that natural milk, especially that which comes from cows not systematically receiving antibiotics, hormones, and sulfa drugs is more healthy to our bodies. As he put it, for centuries our bodies were equipped to handle the natural form of foods and he questions the wisdom of processed foods. He is concerned about the bovine hormone given to dairy cows to increase their milk production. He explained that in our state, the largest dairy co-op includes hundreds of farmers who send their milk to processing plants where it is blended together. There is very little if any control over what farmers do to their animals, speculating it is possible for the hormone to find it's way into our milk. Since this hormone is found in cows naturally, it's addition is hard to detect. One problem with the use of bovine hormones he said, was as follows. Say a farmer's cows are averaging 65 pounds of milk. Since most cows average 85 pounds, he knows some of his are not producing well, but he does not know which ones they are. So he gives bovine hormones to all his cows, even ones that produce normal amounts of milk. Some experts predict that eventually what will happen will be the development of cows unable to produce unless they are given the hormone. There is a controversy about the effects of the bovine hormone on humans, too. Some scientists note that young girls are reaching puberty at earlier rates, some at the age of 8 and wonder if there is a correlation to hormones added to livestock feed. Estrogen is even added to some shampoos. Natural estrogen is found in soy products and, consequently, in soy baby formulas. Also, there is a report that cows treated with the hormone are developing more mastitis, for which more antibiotics are used. How are these residues affecting us? This dairyman said he was going to visit a highly successful dairy in Oregon which is now producing "cream top" milk and selling it in glass containers, which is environmentally friendly. They raise their own cows "organically", which means they cannot receive hormones or antibiotics. He said some scientists are questioning if the antibiotics cows get are interfering with the effectiveness of some antibiotics given to humans or if some people are allergic to the residues that may be in milk in addition to sulfa drug residues. The milk in the "organic" dairy is pasteurized but not homogenized and nothing is added. He would like to try a system like that, which was done for years before mass production and high technology, but he is afraid of the cost of change. I reminded him that we are already paying a high price.

Oh, the marvels of modern food processing! We can find almost any kind of food we desire in this country from nearby grocery stores, delicatessens, restaurants, fast food stores. But are we eating food or a close facsimile?

# The Pitfalls of Corn

We get lots of inquiries about corn and its by-products since things like cornstarch and syrup are in almost everything. The problem exists for MSG sensitive individuals because some of the protein naturally occurring in corn is broken down into free glutamic acid or MSG if it is highly processed. The following common items contain varying amounts of MSG:

Baking powder (cornstarch)
Caramel flavorings or coloring (when derived from corn syrup or other glutamate containing products)
Maltodextrin, dextrin, dextrose, dextrates
Tablets (used as the binder or excipient in vitamins and other medicines)
Table syrups (golden syrup, invert syrup or sugar, imitation maple syrup)
Mono and di-glycerides are found in shortening and margarine (although some are created from other vegetable or animal fats, some are derived from corn and may contain glutamate residue)
Sucrose and fructose (may also be derived from corn even though the word fructose suggests "fruit" derived)
Xanthan gum (corn sugar is often used as a base in the production)
Citric acid (once exclusively produced from citrus fruits, it is now commonly derived from corn)
Vanilla extract and other flavorings (corn syrup is often added along with alcohol. Some alcoholic beverages are also produced using corn by-products)
Corn syrup
Cornstarch and modified cornstarch
Flour (some bleached and pastry flours may contain cornstarch

# Sulfites

I've included information about sulfites because a large percentage of MSG-sensitive individuals are also sulfite sensitive. I am sensitive to sulfa drugs and sulfites as many of my family members are. Read symptom list to see if you too, may be unaware of a sulfite sensitivity. Sulphur is used in various compounds: Sulfur dioxide, sodium sulfite, potassium bisulfite, potassium sulfite, sodium bisulfite, potassium metabisulfite, sodium metabisulfite, sulfur dioxide, and sulfuric acid. They are used as antioxidants, anti-fermentatives, starch modifiers, food preservers, food color preservers, and bacterial inhibitors in wine. They are commonly found in table syrup, dried fruits, brined fruits and vegetables, glacéed fruits, maraschino cherries, in beverages, dehydrated potatoes, soups, condiments, some beers, sugar and corn syrup production, fruit juices, meat juices, vegetable juices, cut fresh fruit, frozen apples, prepared pie mixes, peeled fresh and frozen potatoes. They do not need to be labeled in some foods if under a certain amount is added.

Most often the following foods will contain sulfites in some form:

- Some ciders
- Fruit juice and drinks, bottled or frozen
- Soft drinks
- Beer
- Dried fruits
- Shrimp - sprayed on boat to prevent bacterial disease ("black spot")
- Wine
- Sauerkraut
- Pickles and Olives
- Mayonnaise
- Bottled lemon juice
- Salad dressings
- Dried vegetables
- Pickled products - onions, relish, pickles
- Tortillas, breads, dough conditioners
- Bread crumbs
- Vinegar, Balsamic, wine, distilled, or white
- Dijon mustard (wine)
- Yogurt and dairy products
- Potato chips and dry or frozen potatoes
- Bottled sauces containing wine or saki
- Corn syrup - may be as a residue of production or additive
- Light colored beans - garbanzo, canned lima and white beans
- Hot dogs, sausages, coldcuts
- Flaked coconut
- Processed cheese spread
- Frozen pizza
- Tomato puree, paste, and stewed
- Sulfa drugs*
- Some shelled nuts (roasted or raw)
- Some cooking oils including some imported olive oils
- Some brands of honey
- Some fish (ask at counter)
- Molasses
- Some brown sugars
- Some canned or smoked oysters, clams, etc.

* It is interesting to note that in emergency cases of extreme reaction to MSG, emergency room staff are advised not to administer any sulfa drugs or sulfites. Sulfite spraying on salad bars was recently outlawed in restaurants, finally, after several people, including a child, died as a result of sulfite toxicity.

According to Beatrice Trum Hunter, although sulfite use is under the jurisdiction of the FDA, they have never established an upper limit for its use, stating that the consumer will not eat a product if it has too much in it because it will taste bad. In other words, its use will regulate itself. But the author states that the toxic level of a substance can be reached before the tongue will be offended. She told the story of

Dr. Harvey W. Wiley, chief of the agency that later became the FDA. He showed through tests that sulfur dioxide caused harmful affects on humans, changed or destroyed the natural flavor of dried fruit and could be replaced with a harmless salt solution. He proposed a regulation that would ban its use on dried fruit, but fruit packers protested and while Wiley was temporarily overseas, their lobbyists killed the measure. The paper that Dr. Wiley's partner, Dr. W.D. Bigelow wrote following research, called, "Experiments Looking for Substitutes for Sulfur Dioxides in Drying Fruit", was denied publication in 1907 by the USDA. Europeans use much fewer sulfites in their food industry. Why are we so slow to learn?

A dairy farmer told me that sulfa drugs and antibiotics are given regularly to cows to prevent infections. Residues can end up in our milk and anyone sensitive to sulfur may experience symptoms. I always get a thickening of mucous in the mouth when I drink milk, but can't be sure if sulfa drugs or something else is the cause. One thing is certain. Most of us have very little idea of how many hidden chemicals are in the food that we take for granted is safe.

Sulfites are also particulates in the air often as a result of car exhaust, paper, lumber, and other factories' waste fumes. Sulfuric acid is often used in the production of paper. Scientists tell us the results of this acid mixed with rain (acid rain) could be catastrophic. Sulfur is poisoness to most life.

Some symptoms and conditions contributed to sulfites are:

Asthma trigger
Bronchial spasms
Belching of sulfur dioxide gas
Increased uric acid
Gastric distress and nausea
Albumin in the urine
Diarrhea
Anemia
Teeth on edge, sensitive
Thiamin deficiency - destroys vitamin B-1
Increased salivation

Backache
General malaise
Chills or feeling cold
Dull eyes
Listless
Inflammation of mouth's mucous membranes
and mouth lesions
Headache
Burning back and muscles .
Itchy skin

Dr. A.G. Corrado, M.D., Allergist, Richland, Washington, informed me that sulfites can trigger asthma and bronchial spasms as often as other allergens. One of his patients went into anaphylactic shock after eating some dried apricots treated with sulfur dioxide and had to be air lifted from her campsite to a hospital.

Read cleaning agent labels and avoid those containing acids made from sulfur. One such product gave me such terrible chest pains that I thought I was having a heart attack. We reached three chemical companies (Fluka, Sigma, and Aldrich) over the Internet and received frightening information about sulfamic acid which was in the product I used. They warned that sulfamic acid is corrosive, causes burns, and is harmful if inhaled or contacts skin. It gives off sulfur oxides so it can be very hazardous to health. My husband, who is not sulfite sensitive, later used the product outside to clean a shower door. He became nauseous and headachy. We replaced our sliding glass shower door with a shower curtain. Much easier to clean! Also, many people react to products that contain chemicals such as sodium lauryl sulfate, ammonium lauryl sulfate, sodium laureth sulfate, phosphoric acid, and phosphates. These substances can be found in shampoo, hair products, cosmetics, lotions, detergents, and other home care products. Reactions can vary from itchy skin to other MSG-like symptoms. I recently saw a TV program in which the following products were suggested over more toxic cleaners. They were Borax, baking soda, white distilled vinegar, hydrogen peroxide for bleaching, and abrasive cleaners without chlorine.

*Pure, 100% apple cider vinegar without preservatives can be found in health food stores as can dried fruits that are untreated. Look for potato chips that say "No Preservatives". Saffola and Best Foods

Company claim that their mayonnaise is MSG free and that the lemon juice they use contains no sulfites. However, I cannot use either product. Remember, a product can contain a certain amount of sulfites before it is required to be on the label. I have questioned companies who put "no preservatives" on their food labels, but they have informed me that there are sulfites added. They explain that the amount is low enough to go legally unlabeled. That seems very misleading to this consumer. Beatrice Hunter says sulfites can be added to mayonnaise without labeling, legally. Try using less or augment it with sour cream or homemade yogurt. Cooked egg yolks may be blended with oil, lemon juice and spices as a mayonnaise substitute.

*We now make homemade pickles and relishes the old-fashioned way using 100% apple cider vinegar. Read labels. I bought one brand of vinegar without doing that and got a reaction. My husband checked the label. It read "Apple Cider Flavored Distilled Vinegar". The ingredients were: Distilled vinegar, Natural flavor with caramel, and annatto). I was informed that one source of caramel coloring/flavoring is malted barley. The production of barley malt may release some glutamate. If you don't have time to make pickles or other food products, use the phone and track down pickle companies that don't use it. Ask for someone in charge of production. Most companies will ship cases. Start with local brands and move on to national brands. To find toll free company numbers, dial 800-555-1212. Many food producers are listed. The internet is also a great tool for tracking down healthful products.

I've discovered that I react with mouth sores and stomach distress after eating some corn tortilla chips and taco shells. I called a producer of corn chips in California. I was told that they soak the dry corn kernels in a solution of water and lime for several hours. He explained that it helps soften the corn and skins and assured me it was rinsed well. Some companies use sulfuric acid to do the same thing. Either way, after soaking in such products for so long, I am not assured that all of it gets neutralized or washed away. Also, I wonder if the soaking process along with the strong alkalies or acids doesn't hydrolyze the corn, forming MSG. Other companies are producing chips made "the old way", by cooking the dry corn all day slowly. Since corn is high in natural glutamic acid, this cooking or hydrolysis process most likely forms free or harmful glutamate. Also, we have read labels that say they have added "sprouted" corn to the cooked corn. We have heard reports from NOMSG that when sprouted, free glutamate is created in high protein grains like corn and wheat. I called Frito-Lay Company, whose plain "Santitos" chips do not bother me and was pleased to learn that they soak their corn in water only. So read labels and make your own decision.

Recently, my husband bought as a treat, a bottle of R.W. Knudsen papaya nectar, which says "no preservatives" on the bottle. I called to be sure, as I have been mislead before. I was told that the white grape juice added to this beverage was "tanked" in and "more than likely contains sulfites." She advised me not to drink it. When I asked why they still put "no preservatives" on the label, she hesitated. I suggested that the amount in there is below the amount the FDA allows without labeling. She answered with, "You're probably correct." So my warning is this. If a product says, "no preservatives", don't believe everything you are told. Knudsen's may be reached at (916) 899-5010.

References:
    Beatrice Trum Hunter's Additives Book: What You Need to Know, pages 108 -112.
    Dr. William E. Walsh, M.D., The Food Allergy Book: The Foods that Cause You Pain and Discomfort and How to Take Them Out of Your Diet.

# Remedies and Healthful Hints

Some people write to the "NOMSG Messenger" newsletter with some suggestions to minimize symptoms. Here are some of their ideas and those of friends. None are guaranteed to work, but they may be worth trying. Remember, there are no antidotes to MSG poisoning. Avoidance is the best medicine and immune system booster.

1. Taking magnesium and vitamin B6 supplements or eating more foods rich in these nutrients may help. Again, beware of MSG in tablets!
2. Drink lots of pure orange juice when symptoms begin until they stop.
3. Drink lots of water and take an over-the-counter high bulk laxative (without aspartame or "natural flavors"). Or take this natural laxative: Mix 1 tablespoon psyllium seed in ½ cup of water and drink quickly, or mix with applesauce and eat. May be repeated up to three times, an hour apart. Don't eat a lot until your system is rid of the offending foods. Rely on fruits, vegetables, rice, etc.
4. Relax in a hot bath adding ½ cup of sea salt and ½ cup baking soda. Some claim restorative powers, but it could just be soothing, too.
5. Take an enema to empty the bowel as soon as possible. There are many over-the-counter enemas.
6. Ask your doctor about new migraine medications that might be beneficial. Ask him to prescribe just one or two tablets or ask for a sample to see if it helps before paying for more.
7. Some people take one or two extra strength aspirin with caffeine (like Excedrin), at onset of first symptom and repeat every 3 to 4 hours of headache or symptom duration. Do not use for more than two days a week because rebound headaches can occur. Others use extra strength Bufferin or Ibuprofen.
8. One person claims Benedryl helps relieve her symptoms, taken once at onset and repeated once or twice or until symptoms leave. The liquid contains aspartame and other questionable ingredients. It does come in pills, however. One reaction we see from people who discover MSG is causing their migraines is that they want to find drugs to ease the pain instead of giving up certain foods. But if they understand that MSG is gradually destroying their health, perhaps setting them up for serious conditions in the future, and that brain cells are being devastated when too much glutamate gets to them, they might better consider their eating habits.
9. One reader takes 2 to 3 charcoal tablets (not capsules) just before ordering a meal out. She also takes them if she feels a reaction coming on. Since this depletes potassium, be sure to eat bananas, which are rich in this mineral.

Some suggestions that may improve health. Some are modern trends, others are tried and true.
1. Drink lots of water (filtered when possible). Recently, researchers have told us that chlorine causes cancer.
2. Use lots of raw garlic. Add minced garlic to spaghetti. Add to salad dressings, gazpacho, salsa, sauce, and pizza just before serving. I love raw garlic sliced on bread and butter. Garlic pills are also available, but read labels and avoid questionable fillers and gelcaps.
3. Eat lots of fruit and vegetables. Leafy yellow and green vegetables are high in beta carotene. Broccoli is very nutritional. Eat lots of raw carrots, peppers, cabbage, etc., and grab apples and bananas instead of fatty chips. There is growing evidence that enzymes from raw vegetables and fruits prevent disease.
4. Use oils low in saturated fat. Avoid hydrogenated fats. Eat fewer sugary desserts and beverages.

5. Avoid as many chemicals and additives as possible. A good reference book to read is Beatrice Hunter's Additives Book, which lists the most harmful ones such as: nitrates, nitrites, MSG, sulfites, food dyes, caffeine, calcium disodium, EDTA, calcium propionate, carrageenan, artificial food flavorings (France allows only seven synthetic ones. The U.S. allows over 1600, many poorly tested.), modified food starch, artificial sweeteners, and others.

6. Eat less red meat and more whole grains, fiber, beans, and nuts. Eat more fish and chicken. Certain fish, flax seeds, and flax seed oil are high in Omega-3, which may lower cholesterol levels.

7. Avoid processed foods wherever and whenever possible.

8. Eat foods high in vitamins A, B, C, E, and beta carotene or take safe supplements that contain important minerals and vitamins. From personal experience, safe supplements are hard to find. I eat foods rich in them and occasionally use vitamin C crystals and Dolomite Calcium powder, which contains calcuim, magnesium, and trace minerals.

9. Exercise regularly. Walking the mall with a friend is great.

10. If you feel sluggish or have eaten MSG by mistake or want to cleanse your system, you might want to try fasting for a day or two, augmenting with water and fruit and vegetable juices. In For Women First magazine, March 1997 issue, there is a step by step guide for a cleansing fast. It is found on page 16, and is called "You can bounce back from anything" by Barbara Cohn. Health food stores and bookstores also have information. There are also books on cleansing the colon.

11. Start a garden and enjoy organic fruits, berries, and vegetables.

12. Don't be angry. It is not your fault that you are getting too much MSG in the typical American diet. Be happy that you can look forward to better health and that you can help others achieve the same. True, the first few months will be frustrating as you try to change old eating impulses or give up favorite items. Remember substituting helps and you may discover new favorites. Fuller, healthier, and happier days will be yours.

13. Use dinner time and your new array of herbs and vegetables as a creative outlet, and come up with some mouth-watering recipes of your own. Practice is a great teacher.

14. Help and educate others. Little can compare to the happiness that you will feel when someone tells you that you have literally saved their life, or that of someone they love. Serving others gives important meaning to life and opens the door to joy and better health for both you and the recipient.

15. Eat foods closest to their natural forms as possible.

16. Take time to develop your viable, true inner soul. Pray, meditate, read, listen to the quiet whisperings from within and from our Creator, and then act upon those whisperings.

The September 1996 Ladies Home Journal article, "Super Foods for Kids", suggests these vitamin and mineral rich foods:

**Vitamin B6:** wheat germ, whole wheat bread and cereal, spinach, brown rice, sweet potatoes, brussels sprouts, barley, lentils, mangos, raisins, bananas, and watermelon.

**Magnesium:** acorn squash, almonds, beet greens, chard, walnuts, avacodos, bananas, barley, brown rice, pinto beans, raisins, dates, kiwi, white potaotes, spinach, and sunflower seeds.

**Calcium:** milk, kale, chard, collards, romaine, and molasses.

**Vitamin E:** nuts (hazelnuts, Brazil nuts, peanuts), kiwi, honey, prunes, sunflower seeds, wheat germ (keep fresh in refrigerator or freezer), wheat germ oil, olive oil, and salad oil.

**Vitamin A:** artichokes, honey, nectarines, brocolli, kale, apricots, peaches, cantaloupe, carrots, and dark green leafy vegetables.

**Vitamin C:** citrus fruits, peppers, papaya, kiwi, apricots, artichokes, blueberries, brocoli, brussel sprouts, cabbage, cauliflower, mangos, potatoes, pumpkin, raspberries, red bell peppers, strawberries, tomatoes, guava, white potatoes, and sweet potatoes..

**Folic Acid:** asparagus, peas, dark leafy greens (spinach), kidney beans, pinto beans, beets, brocoli, cauliflower, lima beans, kiwi, and chick peas.

**Omega-3 faty acids:** flax seed and oil, oily fish, and walnuts.

# Miscellaneous Information

The path of modern pioneers can be as riddled with obstacles along the way as those of early pioneers pushing a hand cart. They're just different obstacles. Jack Samuels and his wife, Adrienne, are just such pioneers, since they are leading the fight in the "Truth in Labeling" campaign to get the FDA to make food companies state "MSG" on all food labels containing any glutamate, including the quantity down to the third decimal, and a warning for sensitive people.

Whenever I have talked with Jack Samuels, he has patiently answered many of my questions. The following information is important, especially for severely sensitive people.

My daughter wanted to know about prenatal vitamins since she didn't want to take any chances when she was expecting. I had learned first hand how the gelatin in gelcaps and how hydrolyzed protein in my daily thyroid pill had affected me. He advised calling vitamin companies and asking for full disclosure of ingredients, including binders and fillers used. Every pill she tried bothered her. Finally her doctor told her to eat a balanced diet. She took folic acid the first three months. Her son is very healthy.

Many people debate the use of vitamins as many are hard to dissolve and if one eats a diet rich in fruits and vegetables, they are considered by many as unnecessary. The choice is the consumer's, considering life style and eating habits. But use caution when the following words are on vitamin supplement labels: "hydrolyzed" anything, citric acid or citrate (from corn), aspartic acid or aspartate, glutamic acid or glutamate. Some people react to cornstarch, gluten, rice, soy, and wheat "proteins," and "amino acids" to which some vitamins are attached. He explained that because glutamate is freed up when corn is hydrolyzed, cornstarch, corn syrup and maltodextrin are often "contaminated" with residual MSG. Maltodextrin is further processed than cornstarch and thus contains more MSG. The more a protein is processed, the chances are greater of it containing MSG. Look for vitamins without "excipients". Avoid gelcaps or just eat the contents. Do the same if medications are prescribed and eat in applesauce or with sugar and water. Other created sweeteners such as Manitol and Sorbitol give some people stomach problems and they are used often in liquid vitamins.

I had more questions about corn syrup, so I called Best Foods, the producers of Karo corn syrup. Their toll free number is (800) 338-8831. I was told that cornstarch is mixed with water. Enzymes and/or acid is added and the mixture is heated. This causes the large starch molecules to be broken down into sugars. The resulting product is filtered and evaporated to make corn syrup. Light corn syrup is composed of high fructose corn syrup and this is refined syrup. The darker varieties contain the refined syrup plus a cane syrup product that has a molasses taste. Salt, sodium benzoate, caramel coloring, and caramel flavoring are added. Sulfuric acid is one acid used in the process, so sulfur sensitive people may react to any possible residues. Caramel coloring and flavoring may contain glutamate depending on how they are processed.

Mr. Samuels told me that the pharmaceutical glaze that coats many medications for easier swallowing, can contain MSG in the form of hydrolyzed protein. He also quoted Dr. Blaylock as saying that 75% of the population is deficient in magnesium, which helps to prevent too much glutamate from entering the brain cells. His book, "Excitotoxins: The Taste That Kills," gives an in depth explanation of brain barriers, transmitters, and receptors and how calcium, magnesium and glutamate interact. If you decide to supplement your diet with magnesium, Jack Samuels says it takes at least six months to build up in the body. Those taking magnesium report that their symptoms don't go away, but that their magnitude and length lesson. Your pharmacist can order most vitamins for you. But always be cautious and check labels and ingredients. There are many vitamin companies so ask your pharmacist for help. Calcium powder by KAL also contains magnesium. But some people warn that calcium powder made from dolomite contains lead. Check with your doctor. My physician approves of calcium carbonate powder, but advises getting at least a few minutes of sunshine every day (for vitamin D production). Please read labels when trying any supplements, whether OTC or prescription.

Mr. Samuels also explained the problem with many vitamin fortified foods such as white rice. Since the hulls are polished off, so are the nutrients. The FDA requires that they be put back. So rice producers buy a vitamin product from a supplier. The product contains fillers and binders, which often include cornstarch or corn syrup. They help the vitamins stick to the rice. We rinse raw white rice now several times before cooking and use a lot of organic short brown rice most of the time. It is just as useful in dishes as white rice, has a wonderful texture, and takes a little more time to cook. It's never sticky and freezes well. Old habits can be broken and in regards to better health, are worth every effort. The body more readily uses vitamins derived from foods over those in a bottle.

Jack Samuels warned about the increased use of phosphates because many MSG sensitive people and those unaffected by MSG, are complaining of MSG-like reactions to phosphates. To prevent infections due to outbreaks of deadly diseases carried by meats, shrimp, poultry, they are being sprayed, dipped, and injected with phosphate solutions. He and his family react to phosphates in soaps and detergents also. We also discussed the report that some people react to tomatoes, whether fresh or canned. He gave a suggestion that it's possible that when tomatoes are cooked at high temperatures, for a long time, or are very ripe, some of the peptide links are broken down and glutamate is freed.

We wish the best of luck to Jack and Adrienne Samuels for their truly difficult fight on all our behalves. Their path is a truly altruistic and difficult venture, as anyone who has attempted to change FDA regulations knows. They continue to influence legislators with their hard work , which has included law suits, petitions, and initiatives.

Dr. W. John Olney is a world renown neuroscientist whose specialty is central nervous system research. He knows well the physiological effects of MSG and aspartame. His studies and testimony before Congress in 1969 prompted baby food manufacturers to pull MSG our of their products (though some remains in hidden forms). Recently, Dr. Olney was quoted in the March 1997, Parents Magazine, page 48, by Julie Walsh, R.D., in an article called, "Aspartame Alert". Dr. Olney reported that beginning in 1984, just three years after the FDA approved the wide spread use of aspartame, a 10% rise in brain tumors in older adults was reported. He believes that there is a direct relationship and warns of its use in everything from gelatin dessert to chewable vitamins. The article's author advised pregnant women not to use aspartame. It is our greatest hope that people will become alerted to the dangers lurking on those supermarket shelves, that they will demand change, and that they will see the importance of avoiding MSG and other excitatory neurotransmitters. Even if the FDA claims MSG is safe, it is the opinion of educated, unbiased, and concerned people that everyone can feel the effects of MSG if their dose threshold is reached. As more MSG infiltrates our foods, more and more people will find that they too will be victims of unnecessary suffering. Lab animals fed MSG displayed symptoms that became worse with successive generations, such as brain damage, retinal damage, brain cancer, obesity, and hyperactivity among other abnormalities. Jack Samuels agreed with me that this was a time bomb for society. In a booklet sent to me by the Glutamate Association, Monosodium Glutamate - A Look at the Facts, Suite 500 G, 5775 Peachtree-Dunwoody Road, Atlanta, Georgia 30342, (At the time I was unaware that this was a lobby group for food companies and MSG producers to promote the public's acceptance of glutamate's safety, and they have since moved to Washington, DC.) it says, "Research has shown that the placental barrier does not allow MSG to pass from a mother to her unborn child, so pregnant women need not be concerned about foods that contain MSG." If such claims are true, then why would the FDA disclose the following statement in its summary of the research done by the Federation of America Societies for Experimental Biology? Excerpt is taken from section 5B: Glutamic Acid. Safety of Amino Acids Used as Dietary Supplements, July 1992:

"The continuing controversy over the potential effects of glutamate on growth and development of neonatal animal models suggests that it is prudent to avoid the use of dietary supplements of L-glutamic acid by pregnant women, infants, and children. The existence of evidence of potential endocrine responses

. . . would suggest a neuroendocrine link and that supplemental L-glutamic acid should be avoided by women of child bearing age. . . . " When my daughters were expecting, their doctors never told them that. They probably never heard of the warning. Some might argue that most of us do not supplement our diets with glutamic acid, but consider the facts of the typical American diet. Unknowingly we supplement safe, naturally occurring MSG-containing foods with fast food entrees, frozen and canned meals, breakfast foods and convenience foods. Almost every box, can, and bottle in grocery freezers and shelves contains MSG. As baby boomers, my husband and I represent the generation first introduced to MSG in the 40's and 50's. My symptoms became very serious five years ago. My children are showing earlier signs of symptoms in their teens and early twenties. One son, 22, suffers heart fibrillations, migraines, and fatigue when MSG gets into his diet. Another son, a teenager, has developed a blind spot or retinal damage that specialists don't understand. One daughter suffers migraine and stomach problems when she eats it. My other daughter suffers depression, fuzziness of thought, migraines, and neck pain when she eats MSG. Before we knew to avoid MSG, both daughters lost babies, one in the first trimester, the other in the third, not common in our family until now. We now wonder if there is a link to MSG. They know it was in their prenatal pills. During her most recent pregnancy, my daughter took no supplements and ate lots of fresh foods, especially ones high in folic acid. We know that ingestion of certain drugs or alcohol, known excitatory chemicals, have devastating affects on forming fetuses. We need tests to at least eliminate the possibility that too much MSG may be harming our children yet to be born. Research on the effect of MSG on developing fetuses is being done in Canada. The NOMSG Messenger reports that women have written in believing that their early labor was induced by MSG consumption. What possible negative effects can the growing amount of MSG in food, including baby formula and supplements, have on the smallest and most innocent, our unborn and newborn babies whose blood-brain barriers have not yet fully developed? My heart aches for the parents of hyperactive, autistic, asthmatic, and delinquent children who may be unaware that MSG could be triggering or intensifying their children's problems. Based on personal experience and the reading and research that I have conducted, I feel confident in stating that monosodium glutamate created in processing plants is a toxic drug that is slowly injuring greater numbers of our population than we can imagine. Some people are only beginning to feel the symptoms and others have for years been believing in the misdiagnosis of unknowing or uninformed doctors and accepting their ailments as the effects of age, disease, or injury. Rats fed MSG and their offspring developed neuro-endocrine (vital glandular processes controlled or influenced by the brain including reproduction, and thyroxin and insulin production) problems later in their lives. Most animals developed obesity before they died. Just look at the numbers of obese children and adults in this country and the amount of diet foods and pills consumed. The FDA has allowed MSG to be added in greater and greater amounts without the right kinds or amount of testing. Jack Samuels and others claim some research tests, paid for by special interest food companies, whether knowingly or not, used aspartame in placebo pills. Testers came to the conclusion that since those who claimed to be MSG sensitive reacted to the placebo also, that there was no evidence MSG triggered their reaction. But aspartame, another neurotransmitter drug, precipitates MSG-like symptoms also, thus thwarting the legitimacy of those tests. People in influential positions need to wake up and become more interested in people than in power, popularity, money, or politics. Then positive change can begin.

I do not claim to be a scientist, nutritionist, or writer. I am only a concerned mother and friend. Fortunately, I have always enjoyed cooking, majoring in home economics and nutrition at college for 3 years. Mike and I only hope to help improve the health of family, friends, and anyone suffering as a result of the "MSG myth". Since our first book's printing, Mike and I have been invited to become members of the NoMSG Board of Directors. We love the work and are endeavoring to help spread the truth about MSG continually.

## The Glaucoma Connection

When I had my eyes examined last time, I was in the second day of an MSG reaction and my eye pressure measured quite high. My doctor was concerned about glaucoma. I explained how my sight was affected by MSG and the doctor decided to retest me in a week. He was amazed at the difference in my eye pressure. I told him how some researchers were linking glaucoma to a build-up of glutamic acid in the eye. Then the questions about MSG began. He looked as though a light bulb had gone on as he related the bad stomach episodes he suffered whenever he traveled and was forced to eat out a lot. He took our website address and, needless to say, others will benefit from his newly found knowledge.

Kaye Wanke, who mans the NoMSG hotline, has a neighbor, Dr. John Kupko, MD, PC, an ophthalmologist. He attended a medical conference in Chicago (Fall '97) and there learned that patients need to be warned to avoid MSG. Kaye also told me related information can be researched from the following magazines:
>"Ophthalmology Times"
>"Ocular Surgery News"
>American Academy of Ophthalmologists, who also publish, "The Blue Journal".

An issue of "American Health" as reported in the 1997 issue of the NoMSG Messenger referred to the work of a Harvard Medical School ophthalmologist who believes the blindness caused by glaucoma is caused by a buildup of glutamate in the nerve cells in the optic nerve. The cells die and release more glutamate into surrounding cells, causing them to die of overstimulation.

A "New York Times" article referred to another article published in the Archives of Ophthalmology by researchers at the Massachusetts Eye and Ear Infirmary. It reported that research suggests that the neurotransmitter, glutamate, could produce death in optic cells that closely resembled the cell death in glaucoma, and that the level of glutamate in the fluid of the eye is twice as high in people with glaucoma as in people with healthy eyes.

## Fibromyalgia Report

A clinical pharmacist from the University of Florida found our web site and contacted us for more information. He has written a case report on four fibromyalgia patients whose symptoms markedly improved after decreasing the MSG in their diets. With the help of their physicians, he submitted the report to the JAMA for publication in 1998. We can only hope that more doctors will become alerted to the real dangers of MSG, aspartame, and other excitotoxins as a result. More scientific studies and cold hard facts will eventually make a difference in this uphill battle. We increasingly hear from FMS patients who, after using the information in our book, are symptom free or notice a decrease in symptoms. Fibromyalgia support groups are beginning to share the information.

## Fresh Produce and Meat Packaging Alert

Think those beautiful strawberries are totally safe? Think again. A friend and I became ill after eating berries we bought separately from the same store. Not able to pin our reactions to excitotoxins, I called the California producer. Without describing our symptoms, he asked if we had experienced gas, belching, mouth sores, diarrhea, and headache. We had on all counts. He explained that strawberries that need to travel distances are stacked in boxes on pallets. They are wrapped in huge tectrol bags and sealed. A slit is made on the side, carbon dioxide is pumped inside to slow down oxidation, and the bag is resealed. Stores are instructed to remove the bags immediately upon arrival. If this is not done, the berries become anaerobic, meaning the acids become much more active. Eating them can cause some sensitive people's PH to be thrown off, causing the hyper acidic reactions as mentioned. He further went on to say that meats wrapped in cryovac plastic can result in similar reactions. He warned that prewashed salads in puffed or pillow bags cause problems for certain individuals, also. Be careful of similarly packaged products already high in natural glutamate, such as mushrooms and tomatoes. Nitrogen is added to the bag to regulate the respiration and deterioration. The product's $CO_2$ content is consequently increased, which changes its PH and prolongs its shelf life. But, again, this can affect the body's acidic balance and cause diarrhea, pain, and belching.

He suggested that I wait to buy strawberries until after Mother's Day, since they will be shipped from northern instead of southern California to Washington without the tectrol bag treatment. I think that I will plant more strawberries, also!

## Fruit and Vegetable Spray Alert

We received an e-mail from Adrienne and Jack Samuels warning us of a new agricultural spray used as a "growth enhancer". It contains about 30% MSG. This means that any fresh fruit or vegetable may have residues of MSG in them, including any processed foods containing them, such as baby foods. The U.S. Environmental Protection Agency (EPA) approved the use of Auxigro WP Plant Metabolic Primer (Auxigro), February 6, 1998. Jack Samuels has written to the EPA and the producers of Auxigro, Auxein Corporation, Lansing, Michigan, asking them to withdraw this product from the market immediately. But if they only hear from Mr. Samuels that we do not want MSG sprayed on our food, approval will not be rescinded. Please complain to your congressmen, farm companies, and especially to Carol Browner of the EPA. You can contact her at:

Carol Browner
Assistant Administrator for Prevention, Pesticides, and Toxic Substances
U.S. Environmental Protection Agency
401 M Street, SW
Washington, DC 20460

Phone: (202) 260-2902
Fax:     (202) 260-1847
E-mail: c/o Douglas Parsons
        parsons.douglas@epamail.epa.gov

For additional information concerning this issue, send e-mail to Jack Samuels at: adandjack@aol.com

Auxigro may be sprayed by airplane on crops such as snap beans, lettuce, peanuts, tomatoes, strawberries, cauliflower, broccoli, and potatoes. The product may also affect groundwater, drinking water, and ultimately endanger humans, farm animals, and wildlife. The EPA's action allows the amount of MSG residue on fruits and vegetables to be unlimited (Sec. 180.1187 - Code of Federal Regulations). Please lend your support if you do not want to be exposed to undeclared amounts of a toxic substance daily!

Update:
We are hearing from more and more individuals saying they are now reacting to some of their grocery store produce. Jack Samuels informed us that Auxigro is now being used on some products in central California. Since they use open irrigation ditches, contamination into other farms may be taking place. He told us that it is being used extensively on Idaho potatoes now. He personally has become severely ill after eating potatoes and lettuce sprayed with Auxigro.

# Lobby Groups for the Glutamate Industry

To see how the glutamate industry promotes the use and "safety" of MSG, you can find web sites for the Glutamate Association, The International Food Information Council (IFIC), and the International Glutamate Technical Committee. Often these lobby groups are mistaken for government agencies. They are organizations funded by the food industry, independent of the FDA. However, the FDA listens to them as do health and medical professionals. The Glutamate Association is a corporation created by Ajinomoto, a Japanese Company. Members include or used to include Ajinomoto U.S. A., Inc., Archer-Daniels-Midland Co., Campbell Soup Co., Corn Products Corp., Thomas J. Lipton, Inc., McCormick & Co., Inc., Pet Inc., Pfizer, Inc.,Takeda, and Tri-State Specialties Incorporated Seasonings. According to the Encyclopedia of Associations, IFIC represents the interests of the glutamate industry.

Warning!    Don't be fooled by their educational or scientific format. When browsing the Internet for MSG information, the mentioned organizations will likely respond to your search. They represent and are supported by the glutamate producers and the huge food industry. Their propaganda promotes MSG's safety, thus keeping food and glutamate companies "healthy" and us ill. I recently received an e-mail from a woman in Seattle. The food service director of the school district where she works brought her some pamphlets that she had received in the mail from the Glutamate Association. She assumed that these were being sent to all school districts across the nation. One is entitled, "A Look at the Facts", and the other is "Glutamate, Nature's Flavor Enhancer". The information blurs the lines between naturally occurring glutamate in foods and free, factory created glutamate, thus confusing the reader. It proclaims MSG's safety and includes endorsements by various organizations and clinics. It also makes the claim that MSG is always listed in the ingredient statement of any food unless it is a natural component of other foods such as cheese, tomatoes, or protein-based foods. What percentage of the country even knows that hydrolyzed protein has a large amount of MSG in it? If MSG were as safe as they propose, and people weren't complaining about it, would such a strong and expensive campaign, directed even at our public schools, have even been launched?!

Check their web sites to familiarize yourself with their tactics, but be cautious. They are well done. I am hearing from more and more physicians who want our information. Several doctors, nurses, and dieticians have ordered our book. They are putting 2+2 together and listening to patients. Trust your body. Trust your instincts.

Please check these web sites:
www.msgmyth.com.
www.nomsg.com.
www.truthinlabeling.org.
members.aol.com/_ht_a/adieonly/page/index.htm

# Testimonials

We've received some wonderful letters from people that we've been able to help. Here are excerpts from a couple of them.

... "I wanted to thank you for all the notes you gave us. They have really helped my mom out a lot. She tells me she feels <u>so</u> much better and she feels like she has much more energy." She goes on to ask for some recipes.

> Sarah Merrill
> Age 22
> American Fork, Utah

... "I began suffering from extreme migraines. I would become nauseous and would often vomit. The emergency room was the only relief quite a few times. I saw doctors at Johns Hopkins and spent $150 on different medicines, to no avail. Doctors said it was stress. I started getting sick a lot which was out of the ordinary. In three months I had strep throat and bronchitis, each twice, and the flu a number of times. I also had shortness of breath and light headedness. After five months of this, I had hit rock bottom. I received a call from home telling me about the effect MSG had on Debby and her family. It sounded so familiar so I immediately went off MSG products. Within a week, I felt like a new person. My headaches were gone and my throat, which was always sore, felt better. My ears no longer hurt and I actually began to sleep soundly for the first time in years. I used to wake up in the middle of the night and lay there for two to three hours before falling asleep again. I have so much more energy, and I can concentrate for longer periods of time. In college, my teachers would ask if I had an attention disorder because of my short attention span. I had suffered from water retention for years. No longer! I now lead a regular life as long as I watch what I eat." She goes on to ask me to hurry and finish the cookbook for her and others.

> Carrin Story
> Age 21
> Baltimore, MD
> Kennewick, WA

"I am so much more clear headed now and can concentrate. I used to get depressed, especially during the dark days of winter. But, I'm no longer bothered by that and I'm happier and upbeat. My headaches and dizziness are gone since eliminating MSG and aspartame. Your book has helped me immensely and it's not as difficult to eat as I thought it would be."

> Doug Larson
> Richland, WA

"If I could thank you every day for the rest of my life, it wouldn't be enough. You've given me and my children our lives back. Thank you."

> Gladys Reeder
> Kennewick, WA

"Your book is excellent. I'm telling many doctors about it."

> Dr. Stephen Collins
> Freemont, CA

"I can report that by 100% elimination of excitotoxins from my diet, I am 100% free from fibromyalgia. Glutamates in any form can put me right back down. I share your website with all who come to me for help. I can't thank you enough for your website and I love your cookbook."

A former FMS sufferer
Marcia

I got a call in Feb. 1999 from Robert Cupp. His story goes like this.

One and a half years ago he was slated for brain surgery to cut a nerve that his doctor told him would stop his spinning dizziness from Meniere's disease, a procedure that might leave him with a need to re-learn certain motor skills. He'd already suffered what doctors thought were heart attacks requiring de-fibrillation. But when his heart showed no damage from these attacks, he was tested for a brain tumor. After the horrible dizziness and nausea began, the next step was this serious surgery. Meanwhile his mother found our website, ordered the book and Robert gave MSG elimination a try. Well, his symptoms disappeared! A chiropractor friend tested him with a little bit of Accent under his tongue and had him lie on his stomach on the table. The chiropractor watched in amazement as three vertibrae moved out of place and his leg pulled into it's socket as muscles contracted (burning backache or sciatic conditions may often be a result of MSG). When Robert reported what he had learned to the surgeon and told him that he didn't need surgery after all, the surgeon told him that he was talking nonsense and that he had better be in for his scheduled surgery or not to bother coming back at all. Needless to say, Robert didn't. He called to thank me for saving him from an awful fate. He is telling everyone he knows and is responsible for his new doctor ordering our book and using it to help his patients in Kansas City, Missouri.

Dear Debby,
"Thanks so much for your quick response a few days ago. It really encouraged me. I have read your book and find your information to be so valuable. It is the most complete information I have on this subject (MSG). I don't think I would know what to do without the guidance you provide in your book. I was always taught that cooking was a chore - you just ate and got it over with. So you can imagine the sheer terror I felt at the thought of making everything by scratch for a family of 6! I am trying to find the silver-lining in this situation and am actually enjoying bread-making with my 4 year old and cooking meals with my 8 and 9 year olds. I am getting much joy when I watch my children ingest MSG-free food with me.... You are like an angel on earth to me. Because of your information, I think I caught this situation before it did some irreversible damage to my body (although I now wear glasses because my 20/20 vision was affected)."

Sincerely,
Natalie

We can't tell you what these letters mean to us. We have received over 100 of them. When others scoff, we have only to think of them to make us thankful that most people listen.

# Excerpts from the 1997 Nomsg Conference

Mike and I attended the NOMSG conference in October 1997 in Las Vegas, Nevada for the first time. It was a highly enjoyable and beneficial time. For two days, we listened to doctors and experts who generously shared their knowledge and answered our questions. It was a well organized, friendly, informal, sharing, nurturing, and educational experience. Here is a brief summary of our notes.

Kathleen Schwartz, president of NOMSG, did a wonderful job of conducting all of the conference meetings. She is a busy young mother who is very dedicated to the organization. She began by stating the goals of NOMSG.

The purpose of the National Organization Mobilized to Stop Glutamate (NOMSG) is to:
- A.    Be an emotional and practical support.
- B.    Make a lasting change, protect ourselves and others.
- C.    Educate others by reaching out and sharing information.
- D.    Ideally, get MSG declared a drug, get it better labeled on food products, and eventually get it banned.

One of the guest speakers was Dr. Arnold Mech, a child psychologist, addiction medical specialist, program developer at the Menninger Clinic, chemical dependency psychologist, eating disorder specialist and NOMSG member for three years. His theme was "Rage Reactions" caused by MSG. He had noticed that many of his patients seemed to be hypoglycemic. One of his patients was a young girl who had the habit of drinking three six-packs of diet cola per day. He gave her the glucose tolerance test and even though she was avoiding sugar, the test came back showing that she was hypoglycemic. He tested other patients and noticed a recurring pattern between aspartame, junk food, and hypoglycemia. He theorized that aspartame and other excitotoxins aggravate hypoglycemia. They cause people to crave more carbohydrates and sugar which sets the body up to release too much insulin which lowers glucose in the blood which in turn continues a cycle of craving more sweets and carbohydrates. But even if they aren't eating a lot of sugar or carbohydrates, excitotoxins like aspartame can still trick the body into releasing too much insulin, which sets up the hypoglycemia.

When the blood sugar crashes, people turn to caffeine and excitotoxins for an energy "kick" and they need more and more to get that "kick". Their lives begin to revolve around high carbohydrate and high excitotoxic addictive foods and it's big business to the companies that produce them. He called it the "craving and withdrawal" cycle. Kids constantly want cereals and other fast foods high in excitotoxins. First they may be diagnosed with ADD as youngsters, then as teens and young adults, they may develop rage reactions. Many children, and eventually adults, lose their ability to control their impulses. This has shown to have terrible results, not only in eating disorders, but in relationships with other people. Dr. Mech noted that schools send out warning notices to parents to feed their kids well during national standard testing time, suggesting they want to look good as a school district!

He said that from 1960 to 1980, 20% of us were overweight. From 1980 to 1991, 33% of us were overweight despite low fat products. He suggests that many of us are hypoglycemic and don't know it or may develop it. He suggests important lifestyle changes for all of us. He tells his patients to get off of MSG, wine, caffeine, sulfites, aspartates, citrus products, nitrates and nitrites, and dyes.

He discussed Explosive Rage Disorder: when a person loses control with very little provocation. It contributes to divorce, violence, child abuse, crime, destruction of family, and drug addiction. One man that he treated wasn't even aware of his rages and won his family back. We need to start early to make diet changes to avoid these problems for our children's sake.

Dr. Mech suggests that parents stop being "wimps" with their children's demands for junk food. He has treated children with seizures, depression, eating disorders, etc. whose symptoms completely disappeared when parents got tough about what they ate. He blames "unparented kids" and excitotoxins for delinquent, frustrated kids with "attitude". The lack of being models for "impulse control" by parents and culture, sets kids up for ADD and failure. Parents let other people and the media teach behavior which can sometimes reinforce disrespect for elders and the acceptance of violence. Add excitotoxins and you have explosive kids. How can we be examples of delayed gratification if we have lost touch with it?

He called MSG the first "gateway drug". This kind if drug leads to other drugs due to its ability to diminish impulse control at a very early age. Schools have caved in on fast foods for our children. Few serve untainted lunches anymore. He has little patience for parents and educators who say, "But it's the only thing they will eat" in reference to processed junk foods. He disdains what he labels "Toxic Food Manufacturers (TFM's) who say, "Snack foods are important to the American diet." He criticizes doctors who are so quick to use drugs to treat children and adults for conditions (often behavioral) caused by excitotoxins. He claims that funding by drug companies compels doctors to prescribe more and more medicines. After giving us amazing examples of the actual clinical success he's had with several of his patients ranging in ages from three years and up, he suggested the following to those who suspect they may be hypoglycemic:

1. You may try chromium supplementation. Start with 500 mcg for a couple of weeks, then reduce to 300 mcg, then reduce again to 200 mcg a day.
2. Eat fewer carbohydrates and drink 3 quarts of water a day.
3. Suggested food intake of 30% protein, 20% fat, and 50% carbohydrates; ideally, 40% from vegetables and 10% from fruit (less rice, grain, flour, and sugar).

A book that he recommends is, "The Zone" by Barry Sears, MD. However, avoid any excitatory amino acid-containing foods that the author may inadvertently recommend. One statement that Dr. Mech made brought applause, "Don't believe doctors who tell you that you or your child will probably always be on drugs."

Mark Davis spoke to us about the media and the MSG message. Mark works for NBC, writing and producing commercials.

Mark told us of his own struggle for good health, starting as an asthmatic child and then as a teen with a sleeping disorder. When he eliminated colas, he slept well for the first time in his life. He used to keep himself going with colas. He said we need to train people to crave the good way we feel after a good night's sleep and not after ingesting excitotoxins.

To publicize the message about excitotoxins, we need to be aware of the big walls or barriers:

1. People don't believe what you tell them about the caffeine and MSG-laden soft drinks or foods that they love and are conditioned to believe are safe by the media and others.
2. Magazines, TV shows, and newspapers are subsidized by selling ads to high paying clients, many of them processors of convenience and MSG-laden products.

He gave us suggestions for writing or calling our radio and TV companies. The government makes it mandatory that a certain amount of air time (locally and nationally) be given to do some public service announcing. Stations often do it at obscure times of the day or night (like Saturday at 4:00 or 5:00 a.m.). Even this time can reach insomniacs! Your letter to the station doesn't have to be wordy. A suggestion would be, "Suffering from migraine? Call 1-800-BEAT MSG" (or your number) for more information." When you call or write, direct your inquiry to the person in charge of public service announcements.

For writing to newspapers, he suggests that you "nag" in a nice way, send your article in telling them if they can't use it as a story to please use it in the editorial section. Tell them that it's an important health issue, "the scoop of the century", etc.

Other things that can be done are calling or writing health reporters of magazines, newspapers, radio, TV, and health periodicals. Write the local PTA, telling them about you or your children's experience with MSG. Advertize the next NOMSG conference in the newspaper. Run personal ads like, "Migraines, Irritable Bowel troubling you? Call _____ ."

Kay Wanke spoke to us next. She is the person at the other end of the NOMSG Hotline and truly is a gem. Dedicated to help others, she can barely keep up with the growing number of calls. She told us that every time a magazine article comes out mentioning the ills of MSG, she gets a ton of calls. She told us about a man who used to be a factory worker at a MSG production plant. He had complained for years about the terrible smell. His health is so bad that he has had strokes which he believes now were MSG induced. He is considering suing the company. Another caller's leg swelled so bad, the doctors were going to amputate. He saw an article on MSG and stopped eating it. His leg was saved. From March 1997 to October 1997 Kay had over 1200 calls. She said alternative health care professionals such as homeopaths and chiropractors know more about MSG than traditional doctors.

Erik Jaffe spoke to us about some of the interesting results of his survey of NOMSG members. He said that 10% of the respondents had been diagnosed by a physician with Fibromyalgia, 11% with Temporomandibular Dys., 19% with Irritable Bowel Syndrome, 18% with Reflux Esophagitis, Gastrocitis, Hiatal Hernia, 12% with Spastic colon, and 9% for both Chronic Fatigue Syndrome and PMS. Respondents averaged four reactions a month, took an average of 10.6 years to discover their sensitivity after their first reaction, and 77% diagnosed themselves. 45% react similarly to aspartame and 37% to sulfites. 45% react to a small quantity of MSG and 42% said any quantity. The average number of times medical help was sought for the more typical symptoms was 14 times.

Dr. Schwartz, M.D., author of the book, In Bad Taste, The MSG Syndrome, spoke to us about MSG as a drug. He gave us convincing reasons why MSG meets every requirement to be called a true drug. Only 1/10 gram swilled in the mouth with water will cause, in many people, immediate spreading excitation in the brain as cocaine will. It can immediately affect the lower esophagal sphincter muscle, and nerve cells in the mouth and tongue. When tested in vitro in the lab, MSG kills healthy cells. He said dosage amounts may have little to do with migraines, just the amount of direct contact to the MSG. He calls MSG the aphrodisiac of the mouth.

Beneficial drugs have a defined therapeutic potential (like Tagamet for stomach distress). He reasons that since MSG has no therapeutic potential, it fits the standard toxic drug profile, and since it is not a food, it should be banned according to the law.

He informed us that neurologists most commonly deal with people's headaches and anxieties. Often, when a patient complains of a heart that races a lot or of panic attacks, the doctor asks, "Why are you anxious?" Many will say, "Because my heart is racing!" They rarely see the connection to excitotoxins instead of stress. Neurologists have a great potential for helping people who are suffering the effects of MSG but the problem is that an industry has been created to hide MSG or make it appear safe. We need legal professionals involved to prove that MSG has direct toxic effects on people.

Jack Samuels filled us in about the Truth in Labeling campaign and gave us helpful information. He told us that laboratory created MSG has 78% glutamic acid. Although there are minute amounts of glutamic acid in tomatoes and mushrooms, there are chemical differences. In the factory, the glutamic acid that is produced is D-glutamic acid and pyroglutamic acid. Also created are mono and di-chloropropanols by acid hydrolysis and heterocyclic-amines by enzymes, which are all known carcinogenic substances. He said that some people are sensitive to food that is slow cooked for long periods of time, such as in a crock pot. Also he told us that until recently, it was believed that NMDA glutamate receptors were just found in the brain. But Dr. Said has found a NMDA glutamate receptor in the lung. Therefore it is possible that an MSG asthma reaction can be triggered in the lungs. He suggested the following to help our cause:

If you suspect that MSG is in a product that says "No MSG", call (800) BEAT MSG or the FDA at (800) 332-4010. For meat products, call the USDA at (800) 535-4555.

If you feel a company is lying to you about claims of no MSG in their product, call the Federal Trade Commission at (800) 872-8723.

In reporting about the FDA and his legal suit, Jack Samuels told us that the FDA now admits that bad placebos were used in the most recent testing of MSG (aspartame was used, another neurotoxin). He told us that the FDA says they are working on the regulation of MSG and encouraged us to write legislators. They are becoming more informed and concerned. Also, on a positive note, he said that Archer Daniels has decided to stop its production of MSG. He promises to keep the Truth in Labeling campaign going and insists that the FDA is on shaky ground and knows it.

The following information was given to us as a handout and was compiled by Adrienne Samuels who gave us permission for its printing.

SUPPLEMENTAL INFORMATION

MIGRAINE HEADACHE, HYPERACTIVITY IN CHILDREN, AND ALZHEIMER'S

THE COMMON DENOMINATOR MAY BE MSG

Evidence of risk posed by MSG[1] is straight forward:

Glutamate in the brain can be terribly destructive -- no matter where that brain glutamate comes from.[2]

The blood-brain barrier, once thought to rigorously restrict the flow of glutamic acid (glutamate) into the brain, is now understood to be "leaky" in places -- no matter what the age or physical condition of a person -- and is further understood to be susceptible to damage caused by high blood pressure, diabetes, hypoglycemia, trauma to the brain, and other pathological conditions.[3,4] It is also compromised by aging.

Review of the literature suggests that food additives that contain the three excitotoxic amino acids are implicated in neurodegenerative disease.[5]

Spencer, and others, have found evidence of a "slow toxin," a substance responsible for a pathological process which is expressed clinically years or decades after systemic exposure to the toxic substance.

Large numbers of consumers have complained to the FDA that when they ingest MSG, they experience reactions ranging from such things as simple skin rash, flushing of the face, extreme tiredness, and bloating, to hyperactivity in children, migraine headache, asthma attacks, irregular or pounding heartbeat, loss of consciousness, and/or severe depression -- reactions that they do not experience when they eat whole protein such as that found in unadulterated meat, tomatoes, and mushrooms.

All of the data presented by The Glutamate Association, the International Glutamate Technical Committee, and their sponsors, as "proving" that MSG is "safe" appear to be flawed. Some if not all, of those data appear to be fraudulent.

We are aware of no person, institution, or agency, that has claimed that MSG is "safe," that does not have close ties to the food and/or drug industries, or that has not been renumerated by them. The FDA has appointed both Andrew G. Ebert, chairman of the International Glutamate Technical Committee (IGTC), and Kristin McNutt, paid spokesperson for the IGTC, to the FDA Food Advisory Committee. Andrew G. Ebert is also an official "observer" at the World Health Organization. Dr. Steve Taylor who is (or was) The Institute for Food Technologists' communicator on the subject of MSG has been a paid spokesperson for the IGTC for years.

[1] The glutamic acid (glutamate) in MSG is one of three manufactured neurotoxic amino acids found in ever increasing amounts in food. Aspartic acid and L-cysteine are the others.

[2] Lipton, S.A., and Rosenberg, P.A. Excitatory amino acids as a final common pathway for neurologic disorders. N Engl J Med 1994;330:613-622.

[3] Evaluation of the Health Aspects of Certain glutamates as Food Ingredients. Prepared for the FDA Bureau of Foods by the federation of American Societies for Experimental Biology (FASEB) in 1978. Pages 18-19.

[4] Broadwell, R.D. and Sofroniew, M.V. Serum proteins bypass the blood-brain fluid barriers for extracellular entry to the central nervous system. Exp Neurol 1993;120:245-263.

[5] Blaylock, R.L. Excitotoxins: The Taste that Kills Santa Fe: Health press, 1994.

[6] Spencer, P.S. Western Pacific ALS-parkinsonism-dementia: a model of neuronal aging triggered by environmental toxins. In Parkinsonism and aging, ed DB Calne et al., pp 133-144. New York: Raven Press, 1989.

Our next speaker was Dr. Carol Foster, a neurologist practicing in Phoenix, Arizona at the Valley Neurological Headache and Research Center. She especially works with migraine sufferers. Statistics say that 18.84% of people have migraines. Many more suffer bad headaches regularly. She suggested that the percentage is probably higher because many statistics are based on information reported to doctors, and many go unreported, especially from male sufferers. Many children with epilepsy or seizures have migraines. She gave percentages of work days lost and what a serious growing problem it is. You never know when it's going to hit you. The pain causes irritability and disruption of family, work, and social life. The constant fear of future headaches drive many people to the use of drugs and alcohol. She told us that the headache is a symptom. The disease is migraine.

Migraines have been blamed on leaky and dilated blood vessels. But newer research proves the problem to be neurological related, not just vascular. This is obvious because many sufferers experience aura symptoms, and react to triggers and decreased amounts of serotonin. Research shows sufferer's brain cells are overly sensitive to certain stimuli and they easily short-circuit. The hypothalamus brain cells are especially sensitive. Triggers start an electrical storm which causes the migraine symptoms. The following migraine phases were given:

Prodromal phase - 12-24 hours before headache.

      (1)     Changes in appetite - either up or down
      (2)     Cravings (such as sugar, chocolate, or salty foods)
      (3)     Fatigue, yawning
      (4)     Irritability, mood changes

    (5)     Fluid retention

    (6)     Difficulty concentrating

Aura Phase - 20 to 30 minutes before headache (not all sufferers experience this).
    (1)     Vision or visual distortions (momentary spots of color, black spots, bright flashing lights, zigzag lines, or lost vision)
    (2)     Tingling sensations
    (3)     Vertigo, dizziness
    (4)     Speech disturbances
    (5)     One-sided weakness

Headache Phase
    (1)     Loss of appetite
    (2)     Drowsiness
    (3)     Sensitive to light, sound, smell
    (4)     Nausea or vomiting
    (5)     Deep sleep

Postdromal Phase 12-24 hours
    (1)     Limited food tolerance
    (2)     Fatigue
    (3)     Mood changes (depression or euphoria)
    (4)     Diuresis - frequent urination to get rid of body fluid build-up

The pathophysiology of migraines or the instability in brain cell sensitivity appears to be related to a possible inherited abnormal function of serotonin. Serotonin is the brain's "feel good juice". It helps us feel joy and peace. It also helps control blood insulin and glucose levels. It calms us after an adrenalin rush. It modulates the functions of the brain. She said that we are wasting this good natural drug when it is constantly combating the toxic effects of MSG. It is a neurotransmitter or brain chemical produced in the pineal gland and found in the area of the brain that controls many of our body's functions (the hypothalamus). The hypothalamus is the body's "stay alive software". It controls vital signs, hormones, blood sugar level, pain control, emotions, and sleep. To show us how important an influence this part of the brain has on our bodies, she told us that in women, for three days each month, it basically turns off the ovary's hormones and cuts back on serotonin, which can cause PMS headaches and the blue feelings. MSG ingestion forces us to release more adrenalin which in turn makes us use up our serotonin, since the two chemicals need to be in balance. Without enough serotonin, you get headaches and depression. Every time you eat glutamate or other excitatory drugs, you draw out adrenaline, which draws out more serotonin. Our reserves get lower and lower (and we feel lousy). Low serotonin is linked to low immunity. On days when your serotonin levels are high, you may notice fewer headaches even if you have some MSG.

She discussed analgesic rebound headaches which 75% of migraine patients suffer. These substances or drugs can/may cause them: Stadol, Fiorinal/Fioricet,caffeine containing foods or products, aspirin or acetametaphen with caffeine (She said that if you use Excedrin more than two days a week, you buy yourself a headache every day. She called recent sanctions by the FDA to allow it to be labeled "Migraine remedy" an "evil".), Anacin, Tylenol (She mentioned that people have used it to commit suicide since it destroys the liver. Since her comments, we have heard news reports linking Tylenol to children's liver problems.), Ergotamine, decongestants, antihistamines, muscle relaxants, and many other over-the-counter and prescription drugs

She said, "You don't have sinus headaches, you have a drug induced condition." She suggests that the best way to avoid headaches of any kind is a diet free of hyper-amino acids and excitatory substances. She called the following "food speed": glutamate, aspartate, and caffeine. Dr. Foster said that party food is party food because it actually makes people high. When eaten on an empty stomach, excitotoxins go to the brain even faster.

The following increase brain cell activity and use up serotonin also:
> Tyramine (found in citrus fruits, aged cheeses and meats, and fermented beverages)
> Nitrates and nitrites
> Glutamates
> Aspartates
> Caffeine
> Phenols
> Any other hyper-amino acids, such as L-cysteine

She assured us that "That headache isn't stress", as most doctors will argue, "it's low blood glucose and serotonin". She also suggests that we:
1. Avoid prolonged periods without eating.
2. Eat three regular meals a day plus three snacks.
3. Drink lots of water for adequate hydration.
4. Get adequate protein.
5. Limit carbohydrates. (She suggested eating desserts two times a week at the same time each week.) Don't over do on carbohydrates such as white rice and flour.
6. Exercise!! It's critical because it increases serotonin levels and endorphin levels in the brain. Start slow but be consistent. Your brain loves a regimen. Walk, walk, walk! Even if it's just a few minutes a day.
7. Have a menu plan.
8. Use soy free products.

Dr. Foster said that Imitrex may be okay, unless you have an underlying heart condition. However, NoMSG has received reports of severe reactions to Imitrex and other migraine medication. It's $15.00 per pill and shouldn't be used often. But as she put it, to keep the fire out you have to get rid of the kindling, the diet. Also, the more you take any drug, the less it will work. We need to put more time and space between headaches to make our brains less sensitive. Migrain cannot be cured, it can be managed. On a positive note, most MSG sensitive people have low blood pressure and suffer less hypertension, strokes, and less coronary disease.

*We would like to add that in 1998, we heard from two women who had suffered moderate heart attacks due to the migraine medication they were taking. They eventually learned through our website that MSG was the cause of their headaches.

She avoids vitamins, stating that most doctors agree they just create "expensive urine". She said that we get most of the necessary nutrients in a balanced diet.

New drugs are coming out that will help block glutamine nerve ending receptors. Merck is producing several. DHE, Zomig, and Maxalt are some new ones. She said we should try not to use them often, only for critical headaches. Besides, all drugs have side effects, many damaging. She warned against using muscle relaxants for more than three days.

Homeostasis is when the brain and system enjoy a normal rhythm and balance. It can be messed up by adding chemicals that shake up that balance. We need to maintain homeostasis in as many natural means as we can: proper diet, exercise, and sleep.

When asked about fibromyalgia, she told us that this was an "in-stage disease" of serotonin-related disorders and is just another manifestation of hyper-amino acid poisoning. She told us it is crucial for people with in-stage diseases to avoid MSG and other toxins (Parkinson's, ALS, MS, etc.). Dr. Foster got a lot of applause when she told us that nothing could have taken our country's health down so fast unless it was related to our food, and it goes across every sociological group. She called glutamate the "nicotine of food" since it gives food a kick by enhancing the flavor and addicting us to it.

For other questions regarding headaches, call The National Headache Foundation, (800) 843-2256 or (800) 255-ACHE and ask for a headache specialist.

Our next conference speaker was Jack Samuels. He told us that we should avoid sulfites and phosphates as most MSG sensitive people are sensitive to them. The government allows sulfites at 10 parts per million to go unlabeled in products (potato products, fruits, dried and canned fruit juices, vinegar, alcoholic beverages, syrups, and pop). We reacted to frozen Alaskan cod bought at our fresh seafood section and later learned that it had been sprayed in the factory. Since we can't read the box labels at the meat and fish market, it's wise to ask the butcher.

In conclusion, Mike and I were so glad we decided to attend. We were able to give new information to our family and friends and add the information to our cookbook. Since attending the conference, Mike and I were asked to be on the NoMSG board of directors and are able to man the NoMSG website, a job which puts us in touch with many fellow sufferers all over the world. As a result of a letter I wrote to Family Circle (June 22, 1999) that was printed, hundreds of readers called the NoMSG hotline or e-mailed the website. Many of them expressed surprise that their doctors never told them that MSG could be a migraine trigger. One person, a food science graduate of Cook College at Rutgers University, told us she had to quit working for the food industry (product research and development) due to conscience. She now wants to go public with some of the things she knows about MSG and food producers. We've heard from many angry educators and people who want to know why the government hasn't done more. The tide is changing. Kathleen Schwartz, NoMSG president, had her letter printed in Vogue magazine (June 1999) and Kaye Wanke of the NoMSG hotline was on the Mike Reagan talk show. The results have been wonderful for NoMSG.

We are thrilled with the results of our book as we get the feedback from those who have read it. Many have loaned their copy out and ordered several for other people. We have had orders from strangers who have called and become friends over the phone. The circle widens as we reach out to spread the word. Kathleen reminded us that we all come from different parts of the country with different lifestyles, but we all need to be united in our goal to help others and get the information out there. As Dr. Carol Foster told us, People Magazine quoted one of the Nobel Peace Prize winners as saying that they were just three people sitting in a room dreaming that they could ban land mines. We can make a difference, big or small. All we need to do is try.

# References and Suggested Reading

There is a wonderful poster available called "Chemical Cuisine", offered by The Center for Science in the Public Interest at 1875 Connecticut Ave. NW, #300, Washington DC, 2009. It's also available in a pocket-sized slide chart. It rates food additives by three colors:
Blue - Avoid
Yellow - Caution
Green - Safe.

<u>In Bad Taste, The MSG Symptom Complex</u> by George R. Schwartz, M.D., Health Press, PO Box 1388, Santa Fe, New Mexico 87504, Hlthprs@trail.com. To order, call (800) 643-book (2665), FAX (505) 988-1733, or visit their web site at www.healthpress.com. This book is great reading. Dr. Schwartz, M.D. is a toxicologist and visiting Associate Professor of Emergency Medicine at the Medical College of Pennsylvania who discusses migraines, nausea, stomach disorders, balance problems, asthma, arthritis, depression, hyperactivity in children, heart irregularities and other symptoms associated with MSG intolerance. He discusses misleading food labels, foods that contain MSG, and offers some good recipes for hard-to-find condiments. Dr. Schwartz has been featured on Good Morning America, The 700 Club, and 60 Minutes. In his book, the personal stories by several of MSG sensitive people are extremely enlightening and strangely comforting as the reader may discover he is not alone nor that his symptoms are "all in his head."

<u>Excitotoxins: The Taste That Kills</u> by Russell L. Blaylock, M.D. There is a new updated version of the original book available from Health Press, Santa Fe, New Mexico, (800) 643-2665. Dr. Russell Blaylock is an Associate Professor of Neurosurgery at the Medical University of Mississippi, who became aware of the devastating affects of MSG on many of his patients. Dr. Blaylock explains with words and diagrams how the brain functions normally and when it is affected by MSG. He goes into great depth about the reasons for the many symptoms associated with MSG including the disorders and diseases he believes MSG precipitates. He includes information about pharmaceuticals that can lesson the effects of MSG on the body. Some cited were glutamate blockers, such as MK801, and Parkinson's drugs such as ketamine, and Welcome Foundation's LTD-619-C89, which has fewer side effects and is used to treat people with strokes or other brain traumas. A highly informative book! Also available are audio tapes by Dr. Blaylock. Call Health Press or write the Truth in Labeling Campaign at PO Box 2532, Darien, IL 60561.

<u>Additives Book: What You Need to Know</u> by Beatrice Trum Hunter, in paper back, may be obtained through Keats Publishing, Inc. at 36 Grove St., Box 876, New Canaan, Connecticut, 06840. Look for it in health food stores. This book defines and describes the main additives used in our foods, including MSG, results of lab tests on them, and which foods contain them. She tells the reader that we each eat about 5 pounds of food additives every year and then describes most of the common ones in alphabetical order. Her insights into the history and workings of the FDA are very revealing, intelligent information. This author has also written many other informative books about the food we eat.

<u>NOMSG, National Organization Mobilized to Stop Glutamate</u>, PO Box 367, Santa Fe, New Mexico, 87504, (800) 232-8674. For information, send a self-addressed stamped envelope. You can join this non-profit organization for $25.00 a year. Donations are used to send informative mailings to thousands of physicians, HMO's, PTA's and other groups related to the MSG issue. You will receive the NOMSG "Messenger", a newsletter full of up-to-date information and support. Read reports that show correlations to sleeping disorders, artery constriction, chronic fatigue, and diabetes. NoMSG offers a telephone hot line for MSG related questions. They can put you in touch with other members in your area which can be very

helpful. Membership fees help pay for educational materials sent to doctors and groups related to the msg issue. You also won't feel alone anymore.

"MSG: The Truth and Consequences" by Jack L. Samuels and Adrienne Samuels, Ph.D., Search for Health magazine, Sept./Oct. Great article about MSG. For more information, write to: Truth In Labeling Campaign, P.O. Box 2523, Darien, IL 60561 or visit their website at www.truthinlabeling.org.

The Food and Drug Administration Office of Consumer Affairs, 5600 Fishers Lane, Room 1685, Rockville, MD 20857. Phone (301) 443-5006 or (301) 443-9767. When I first discovered my health problems were caused by MSG, I wrote the FDA for any information they might have concerning MSG. They sent a small article that basically said MSG has been used safely for hundreds of years. My husband then scanned the Internet and got 22 pages of information in one evening and most of it was condemning MSG. I wasn't reassured by the FDA, considering the amount of information they were willing to share with me, and it's sometimes questionable reputation for safeguarding our health over the years. We decided to consider other sources from then on. The Internet is a vast resource and NOMSG now has a web site. It is located at www.nomsg.com. Our own web site is at www.msgmyth.com.

We acquired results of MSG testing done on rats, gerbils, and chicken embryos over the Internet. The findings showed retinal damage, diabetes-like symptoms, changes in reproduction functions, endocrine abnormalities, damage to the brain, formation of brain lesions, behavioral abnormalities, learning disabilities in offspring, reduction in immune response, juvenile obesity, and reduced activity. How can the FDA claim MSG is a safe substance? How can they ignore the rise in depression, obesity, asthma, and hyperactivity in children. We are spending millions on drugs to treat these and the symptoms of ailments with unknown causes or cures like M.S. and Alzheimer's. Some people are making a lot of money because of it. We are spending millions on drugs and convenience foods at great profit to manufacturers and investors, but at what cost to millions of people? As one friend said to me, "I always took for granted that if something was dangerous or bad for me, the FDA would do something about it. So I just assumed that I was safe." I used to think the same way.

Monosodium Glutamate and the Chinese Restaurant Syndrome, by P.L. Morselli and S. Garattini in Nature Magazine, 1970; 227:611.

Late Endocrine Effects of Administering MSG to Neonat Rats, J.L. Blake, C.Y. Bower, N. Lawrence, J. Bennet, S. Robinson, Neuroendocrinology, 1978; 26:220.

Silent Spring, by Rachel Carson, Houghton Mifflin Company Boston, 1962. I've always chosen to ignore alarmists. But now I understand that some of the people we've called alarmists in the past were intelligent, educated, caring scientists fearful for the health of the world and its inhabitants. The amount of poisons, food additives, and chemicals are being created at such increasing rates, it's impossible to believe that there are safeguards and tests for all of them. Kay Wanke, a NOMSG member who lives in Montana recently told me that there's a controversy going on nearby about insecticides, pesticides, and herbicides being used that are hurting animals. She said of the 77 road-killed deer in her area, 70 have been found to have birth defects. Goats in ranches bordering mint farms using these poisons, are being born with birth defects from missing eyes to males growing breasts. Are these just exaggerations or should we become alarmed when our national news programs break stories about frogs with grotesque mutations in our ponds and streams?

Rachel Carson, writer and scientist, was a pioneer challenging us to protect ourselves and our environment. She warned of a silent spring, devoid of bees, birds, and blossoms if we are not careful with our lethal technology. She quotes Albert Schweitzer as saying, "Man has lost the capacity to foresee and to forestall. He will end by destroying the earth." Check your library for a copy of this enlightening book, written by a scientist ahead of her time, who loved nature and life.

Science Magazine, Volume 247.

MSG Healthline, MSG Sensitivity Institute, Concord, NH.

"Major Causes of Restaurant Syndrome", Jan-Feb 1987, NER Allergy Proc. Book, Volume 8, No. 1.

"Aspartame and Flying - The Untold Story", by Mary Nash Stoddard and George Leighton. Published by The Aspartame Consumer Safety Networks, Inc., P.O. Box 78064, Dallas, Texas 75378.

The New England Journal of Medicine, May 1993 publication.

Nutrition Action Health Letter, May 1994, Volume 21, No. 4, an article by David Schardt.

Sesame Street Parent's Magazine, Feb 1996, "Your Child's Health", by editor Jo Martin.

The 700 Club Fact Sheet, "What You Really Need to Know", featuring their CBN Newswatch Today on Nov. 3, 1995, with Dr. Russell Blaylock.

Women's Day Magazine, May 1995, pp 99-101, "Asthma Unmasked" by Jacqueline Shannon.

Women's Day, Magazine, May 1995, "My Head Hurts", by Loraine Stern, M.D.

Women's Day, Magazine Feb 1997, "For Your Health", by Flora Davis.

Women's Day, Magazine Feb 1996, an article about fibromyalgia, by Marie Savard.

Total Health Magazine, Jan 1996, St. George, Utah, :State of Your Health", by Dr. Lendon H. Smith.

Parent's Magazine, March 1997, "Aspartame Alert", by Julie Walsh, R.D.

What to Expect When You're Expecting, by Arlene Eisenbert, Heidi E. Markoff, and Sandee E. Hathaway.

NOMSG Messenger, Volume 8, No. 2, Spring issue, 1997. Page 4, "New ALS Treatment" refers to "A Glimmer of Hope for People With ALS", a FDA Consumer Report, Sept. 1996.

Spontaneous Healing and 8 Weeks to Optimum Health by Dr. Andrew Weil, M.D.

For Women First, March 1997, "You Can Bounce Back From Anything", page 16, by Barbara Cohn.

"Monosodium Glutamate - A Look at the Facts", by The Glutamate Association, Washington DC (Lobby Group).

FDA summary of a study by the FASEB, section 5B: "Glutamic Acid, Safety of Amino Acids Used as Dietary Supplements", July 1992.

"Diabetes Danger in a Taste of Chinese", London Times, April 8, 1992. A review of the article is in the NOMSG New Member Packet.

Aspartame: (Nutrasweet®) Is it Safe? by A.J. Roberts, M.D., Philadelphia Charles Press, 1990. 300 27th St., West Palm Beach, FL 33407, (407) 832-2408.

Bittersweet Aspartame, by Barbara Mullarkey, c/o NutruVoice, P.O. Box 946, Oak Hill, IL 60303. (708) 848-0116.

The Deadly Deception, (aspartame), by Mary Stoddard. Aspartame Consumer Safety Network, (214) 352-4268. Also has audio and video tapes.

Foods that Harm, Foods that Heal, Readers Digest 1996. ISBN 0-895577-912-9.

Why Can't My Child Behave?, Feingold Association, JH001, (516) 369-9340.

Why Your Child is Hyperactive, Feingold Association, RH734262, (516) 369-9340.

The Bitter Truth About Artificial Sweeteners by Dennis Remington, MD and Barbara Higa, RD, Vitality House International, Provo, Utah, c.1987.

From Fatugue to Fantastick by Jacob Teitelbaum, M.D., Avery Publishing Company. "A manual for moving beyond Chronic Fatigue Syndrome and Fibromalgia - a guide to overcome severe chronic fatigue, poor sleep, achiness, "brain fog", increased thirst, bowel distress, recurrent infections and exhaustion."

The Zone by Barry Sears, M.D. A dietary roadmap for weight loss. He advocates a high protein, low carbohydrate diet.

# Scientific Studies and References Supporting the Fact that MSG Places Consumers at Risk

Compiled by Adrienne Samuels, Ph.D.

Allen, D. H.,Delohery, J., & Baker, G. J. Monosodium L-glutamate-induced asthma. Journal of Allergy and Clinical Immunology. 80:No 4, 530-537, 1987.

Allen, D. H., and Baker, G. J. Chinese-restaurant asthma. N Engl JMed. 305: 1154-1155, 1981.

Anderson, S. A., and Raiten, D. J. Safety of amino acids used as dietary supplements. Prepared for the Food and Drug Administration under contract No FDA 223-88-2124 by the Life Sciences Research Office. FASEB. July, 1992. Available from: Special Publications, FASEB, Rockville, MD.

Asnes, R. S. Chinese restaurant syndrome in an infant. Clin Pediat. 19: 705706, 1980. Beal, M. F. Mechanisms of excitotoxicity in neurologic diseases. FASEB j. 6: 3338-3344; 1992.

Blaylock, R. L. Excitotoxins: The Taste that Kills Santa Fe, Health Press, 1994.

Broadwell, R. D., and Sofroniew, M. V. Serum proteins bypass the blood-brain fluid barriers for extracellular entry to the central nervous system. Exp Neurol. 120: 245-263, 1993.

Choi, D. W., and Rothman. S. M. The role of glutamate neurotoxicityin hypoxic-ischemic neuronal death. Annu Rev Neurosci. 13: 171-182, 1990.

Choi, D. W. Amyotrophic lateral sclerosis and glutamate-too much of a good thing? Letter. N Engl J Med. 326: 1493-1495, 1992.

Cochran, ]. W., and Cochran A. H. Monosodium glutamania: the Chinese Restaurant Syndrome revisited. JAMA. 252: 899, 1984.

Colman, A. D. Possible psychiatric reactions to monosodium glutamate. N EnglJ Med. 299: 902, 1999.

Droge, W., Betzler, M.; et al.: Plasma Glutamate Concentration and Lymphocyte Activity. J. Cancer Research Clinic Oncol. 114:124-128, 1988.

During, M. J., and Spencer, D. D. Extracellular hippocampal glutamate and spontaneous seizure in the conscious human brain. Lancet 341: 16071610, 1993.

Elman, R. The intravenous use of protein and protein hydrolysates. Ann New York Acad Sc. 47: 345-357, 1946.

Fisher, K. N.,Turner, R. A., Pineault, G., Kleim, J., and Saari,M. J. The post weaning housing environment determines expression of learning deficit associated with neonatal monosodium glutamate(M. S. G. ). Neurotoxicology and Teratology. 13(5):507-13, 1991.

Freed, D. L. J. and Carter, R. Neuropathy due to monosodium glutamate intolerance. Annals of Allergy. 48: 96-97, 1982.

Frieder, B. and Grimm, V. E. Prenatal monosodium glutamate (MSG) treatment given through the mother's diet causes behavioral deficits in rat offspring. Intern J Neurosci. 23: 117-126, 1984.

Frieder, B. and Grimm, V. E. Prenatal monosodium glutamate. Neurochem. 48: 1359-1365, 1987. Cann, D. Ventricular tachycardia in a patient with the; Chinese restaurant syndrome; Southern Medical J. 70: 879-880,1977.

Gao, J., Wu, J., Zhao, X. N., Zhang, W. N., Zhang, Y. Y., and Zhang,Z. X. [Transplacental neurotoxic effects of monosodium glutamateon structures and functions of specific brain areas of filialmice. ] Sheng Li Hsueh Pao Acta Physiologica Sinica. 46(1):44-51,1994.

Gordon, W. P. Neurotoxic theory of infantile autism. In: Neurobiology of infantile autism. Proceedings of the International Symposium on Neurobiology of Infantile Autism, Tokyo, 10-11 November 1990.

Eds H. Naruse and E. M. Ornitz. Amsterdam: Excerpta Medica, 1992. Gore, M. E., and Salmon, P. R. Chinese restaurant syndrome: fact or fiction. Lancet. 1(8162):251, 1980.

Kenney, R. A. The Chinese restaurant syndrome: an anecdote revisited. Fd ChemToxic. 24: 351-354, 1986.

Kenney, R. A. and Tidball, C. S. Human susceptibility to oral monosodium L-glutamate. Am J Clin Nutr. 25: 140-146, 1972.

Kubo, T. Kohira, R., Okano, T., and Ishikawa, K. Neonatal glutamate can destroy the hippocampal CAl structure and impair discrimination learning in rats. Brain Research. 61(1: 311-314,1993.

Levey, S., Harroun, J. E. and Smyth, C. I. Serum Glutamic acid levels and the occurrence of nausea and vomiting after intravenous administration of amino acid mixtures. J Lab ClinMed. 34: 1238-1248, 1949.

Iipton, S. A., and Rosenberg, PA. Excitatory amino acids as a final common pathway for neuroiogic disorders. N Engl J Med. 330: 613-622, 1994.

Lynch, J. E Jr., Lewis, L. M., Hove, E. L., and Adkins, J. S. Division of Nutrition, FDA, Washington, D. C. 20204. Effect of monosodium L-glutamate on development and reproduction in rats. Fed Proc. 29: 567Abs, 1970.

Lynch, J. E,Jr., Lewis, L. M., and Adkins, J. S. (Division of Nutrition, FDA, Washington, D. C. 20204). Monosodium glutamate-induced hypcrglycemia in weanling rats. J S Fed Proc. 31: 1477,1971.

Martinez, F, Castillo, J. Rodriguez, J. R., Leira, R.,and Noya,M. Neuroexcitatory amino acid levels in plasma and cerebro spinal fluid during migraine attacks. Cephalalgia 13(2):89-93, 1993.

Neumann, H.H. Soup? It may be hazardous to your health. Am Heart J. 92: 266, 1976.

Oliver. A. J., Rich, A. M., Reade, P. C.,Varigos, G. A., and Radden, B.G. Monosodium glutamate-related orofacial granulomatosis. Review and case report. Oral Surg Oral Med Oral Pathol. 71: 560-564, 1991.

Olney, J. W. Excitotoxin mediated neuron death in youth and old age. In: Progress in Brain Research, Vol 86, ed P. Coleman, G. Higgins, and C. Phelps, pp 37-51. New York: Elsevier, 1990.

Olney, J. W. Excitotoxic amino acids and neuropsychiatric disorders. Annu Rev Pharmacol Toxicol. 30:

47-71, 1990.

Olney, J. W. Excitatory amino acids and neuropsychiatric disorders. Biol Psychiatry 26:505-525,1989.

Olney, J. W., Ho, O. L., and Rhee, V. Brain-damaging potential of protein hydrolysates. N Eng] J Med. 289: 391-393, 1973.

Olney, J. W., Labruyere, I., and DeGubareff, T. Brain damage in mice from voluntary ingestion of glutamate and aspartate. Neurobehav Toxicol. 2: 125-129, 1980.

Olney, J. W., Ho, O. L. Brain damage in infant mice following oral intake of glutamate, aspartate or cysteine. Nature. (Lend) 227:609-611, 1970.

Olney, J. W. Glutamate-induced retinal degeneration in neonatal mice. Electron-microscopy of the acutely evolving lesion. J Neuropathol Exp Neurol. 28: 455-474, 1969.

Olney, J. W. Brain lesions, obesity. and other disturbances in mice treated with monosodium glutamate. Science. 164: 719-721,1969.

Pohl, R., Balon, R., and Berchou, R. Reaction to chicken nuggets in a patient taking an MAOl., Am J Psychiatry. 145: 651, 1988.

Pradhan, S. N., Lynch, J. F., Jr. Behavioral changes in adult rats treated with monosodium glutamate in the neonatal state. Arch Int Pharmacodyn Ther. 197: 301-304, 1972.

Price, M. T., Olney, J. W., Lowry, O. H. and Buchsbaum, S. Uptake of exogenous glutamate and aspartate by circumventricular organs but not other regions of brain. ] Neurochem. 36:2774-1990, 1981.

Raiten, D. J., Talbot, J. M., Fisher, K. D. Analysis of Adverse Reactions to Monosodium Glutamate (MSG), Bethesda, Md:American Institute of Nutrition; 1996.

Ratner, D., Esmel, E.,and Shoshani, E. Adverse effects of monosodium glutamate: a diagnostic problem. Israel J Med Sci. 20:252-253, 1984.

Reif-Lehrer, L. A questionnaire study of the prevalence of Chinese Restaurant Syndrome. Fed Proc. 3.1617-1623, 1977.

Reif-Lehrer, L. Possible significance of adverse reactions to glutamate in humans. Federation Proceedings. 35: 2205-2221, 1976.

Reif-Lehrer, L. and Stemmermann, M. B. Correspondence: Monosodium glutamate intolerance in children. N Engl J Med. 293: 1204-1205,1975.

Rothstein, J, D., Martin, L. J., and Kuncl, R. W. Decreased glutamate transport by the brain and spinal cord in amyotrophiclateral sclerosis. N Engl J Med. 326: 1464-14(18, 1992.

Said, S. I., Berisha, H.,and Pakbaz, H. NMDA receptors in the lung: activation triggers acute injury that is prevented by NO synthase inhibitor and by VIP. Society for Neuroscience Abstracts20:1994.

Samuels, A., Ph.D. Excitatory amino acids in neurologic disorders: letter to the editor. N Engl J Med. 331:

274-275, 1994.

Samuels, A. Ph.D. Monosodium L-glutamate: a double-blind study and review. Letter to the editor. Food and Chemical Toxicology. 31: 1019-1035.

Sathave, N. and Bodnar, R. J. Dissociation of opioid and nonopioid analgesic responses following adult monosodium glutamate pretreatment. Physiology and Behavior. 46: 217-222, 1989.

Sauber, W. J. What is Chinese restaurant syndrome? Lancet. 1(8170): 721-722, 1980.

Schainker, B., and Olney, J. W. Glutamate-type hypothalamic-pituitary syndrome in mice treated with aspartate or cysteate in infancy. J Neural Transmission. 35: 207-215, 1974.

Schaumburg, H. H.,Byck, R.,Gerstl, R.,and Mashman, J.H. Monosodium L-glutamate: its pharmacology and role in the Chinese Restaurant Syndrome. Science. 163: 826-828, 1969.

Scher, W., and Scher, B. M. A possible role for nitric oxide in glutamate (MSC)-induced Chinese restaurant syndrome, glutamate-induced asthma, 'Hot-dog headache', pugilistic Alzheimer's disease, and other disorders. Medicalhypothcses.38:185-188,1992.

Schinko, I. In: Cerebrospinàl flussigkeit-csf, ed D. Dommasch and H. G. Mertens, pp 66-99. Stuttgart: Thieme, 1980.

Schwartz, G. R. In Bad Taste: The MSC Syndrome. Santa Fe: HealthPress, 1988.

Scopp, A. L. MSC and hydrolyzed vegetable protein induced headache: review and case studies. Headache. 31:107-110, 1991.

Spencer, P. S. Guam ALS/ Parkinsonism-dementia: a long-laten cyneurotoxic disorder caused by slow toxin(s) in food? Can JNeurol Sci. 14:347-357, 1987.

Spencer, P.S. Environmental excitotoxins and human neurodegeneration. Conference on excitotoxic amino acids. London,November, 1991. (Peter S. Spencer, Center for research on occupational and environmental toxicology, Oregon Health Sciences University, Portland, Oregon 97201 USA)

Spencer, P. S. Western pacific ALS-Parkinsonism-dementia: A model of neuronal aging triggered by environmental toxins. In Parkinsonism and Aging, ed U. B. Calne, et al., pp 133-144. NewYork: Raven Press, 1989.

Spencer, P. S., Ross, S. M., Kisby, G., and Roy, D. N. Western Pacific ALS: putative role of cycad toxins. In: AmyotrophicLateral Sclerosis: Current Clinical and Pathophysiological Evidence for Differences in Etiology, ed J. A. Hudson. Toronto: University of Toronto Press, 1990.

Spencer, P. S. Linking cycad to the etiology of western pacifica myotrophic lateral sclerosis. In: ALS. New Advances in Toxicology and Epidemiology, ed E C. Rose and F. H. Norris. Smith-Gordon, 1990.

Spencer, P S. Amyotrophic lateral sclerosis and other motor neuron diseases. In: Advances in Neurology, Vol 56, ed L. P. Rowland. New York: Raven Press, 1991. Squire, E. N. Jr. Angio-oedema and monosodium glutamate. Lancet. 988, 1987.

As a note of interest, we recently caught a Channel TVW report on March 4, 1999. A Dr. Dane Wingerson was addressing the National Alliance for the Mentally Ill (NAMI) in Olympia, Washington. He stated that a vast amount of research was now being conducted on brain neurotransmitters, especially glutamate, as they relate to mental illness. Alzheimer's and schizophrenia were also discussed.

# ATTENTION HYPERSENSITIVE INDIVIDUALS!!

Before using any of the recipes in the next section, please realize that the ingredients called for do not affect our family, but depending on your own degree of sensitivity, some may bother you. Some hypersensitive people will not be able to use most processed foods. These individuals are wise to avoid most dairy products, most frozen or canned processed food (even processed juices, vegetables, and fruits), and most fermented products such as alcoholic beverages, most vinegars, and vinegar-containing products. We often use fresh lemon juice instead of vinegar. People with actual yeast* and/or mold allergies (not to be confused with MSG sensitivity) should avoid breads, baked goods, cheese, malt products, vitamin B (derived from yeast), milk that contains penicillin or antibiotics (look for organic milk at health food stores), and foods that develop mold even when refrigerated such as ham, bacon, jams, syrups and molasses. Yeast molds can be present in vinegar, spices like cinnamon and pepper, malt products and many canned or frozen vegetables and juices. Don't be discouraged. There are many foods that you can still eat! Be sure to read the 1997 NOMSG Conference report. It includes helpful information from guest doctors and experts. But be very cautious even if you are not hypersensitive to MSG and other food substances. If you react to all milk, try Pacific Original Rice Beverage (the one containing water, brown rice and oil only) or Rice Dream Original Rice Beverage.. Water may also be substituted for milk in many recipes. Rice milk works well in cream sauces, custards, puddings, and hot chocolate.

Many highly sensitive people report that they react to soups and other meat dishes that are cooked for long periods of time, such as in a crockpot or slow oven. When acidic ingredients such as lemon juice, vinegar, or tomatoes are added, there is even a greater risk of glutamate being freed up. We are actually using heat, water, and acid on a protein to recreate hydrolysis in our own kitchen. A suggestion is that meats be roasted or simmered in as little water as possible until cooked. Simmer vegetables in liquid separately and add cooked meat just before serving. Beans, barley, and lentils, if boiled too long can have their amino acids broken down into free glutamate also if it is present. Boil chicken rapidly for 30 minutes and check for doneness, or roast without water at 400° to 425° for one hour or until done. Fry hamburger and other meats separately for ten minutes, add to other ingredients, and roast on simmer together for an additional 15 to 20 minutes. Most of our recipes can be adapted to these methods.

Some highly sensitive individuals will need to avoid all processed corn products: chips, cornmeal, cornstarch, corn syrup, dextrose, maltodextrose, citric acid, mono- and di-glycerides. The only way to test one's sensitivity is by total elimination and re-entry of the item, one at a time. Corn is high in natural glutamate and eating it fresh is usually not a problem. But, depending on processes used to create its by-products, free glutamate can be created in varying degrees.

The recipes in this section have been adapted from old standards, are our own creations, or are those of friends and family. Using our substitution chart, you will be able to continue to enjoy most of your own favorite dishes or adjust new ones found in books or magazines. Feel free to experiment with these recipes and their ingredients according to your own needs and cooking techniques. Try adding or subtracting spices and herbs to your taste. Also, for those wanting to cut down on fats, try substituting half or most of the fats in baked goods with applesauce, pureed plums, stewed prunes, or bananas. Sugar amounts may be decreased in many dessert recipes and omitted in some main dishes. Honey can also be substituted for sugar, but use less in recipes than the sugar called for. Stevia, a white powder derived from an herb found at health food stores may be used in sugar restricted diets. It is a lot sweeter than sugar, so experiment with amounts in recipes. Avoid stevia products that contain fillers such as dextrose or maltodextrin.
Remember, the library is a wonderful resource. I have discovered recipes for skin lotions and cleaning solutions for the house, using safe and healthy ingredients.

All of us lead busy lives, so finding time to cook is a challenge. Hopefully, you will find many of these recipes fast and easy. Perhaps you could find another MSG sensitive person or persons (it's not hard) to share cooking chores, rotating nights and dividing preparation assignments. Someone who loves to make bread might make extra to share, while another person can make extra chili or salad dressing.

We hope that you will enjoy what we consider to be some of our best and favorite recipes. Please be sure to familiarize yourself with the substitution chart before using the recipes. It will help you to select and use safer ingredients in any recipe.

*Information about yeast was obtained from the Texas Agricultural Extension Service.

# Conclusion and Challenge

I've never intended to diminish the importance of the FDA, traditional doctors, or researchers by writing this book. I can't promise that MSG elimination will cure all a person's ills, but I have tried to share some of the insights that I have gained by reading and researching the few books available about this worldwide problem, known as the "MSG Symptom Complex" by the medical establishment. And I can say without a doubt that I know MSG was the cause for my failing health. I am a new person. People who haven't seen me in a few years always remark how much better I look and ask what I have done to myself. I've interjected a few of my own opinions throughout the book, based on my own experiences, hardly scientific, but honest. I do apologize if I have misinterpreted any of the information that I have researched and attempted to share with others. When I have been confused by some issues, I have called people who I consider to be experts for more clarifications. I realize that many readers will react by doubting that eliminating just one type of food additive when there are so many, will make such a dramatic difference. I don't know if I would believe it myself if someone approached me with such information. But truth is truth whether believed or not. *You* need to be the judge by how you are feeling now and how you feel after eliminating excitatory neurotoxins. Don't short change your health. We all need to examine our life styles. Are we working so hard at our jobs so that we can buy more wonderful things produced for our enjoyment and entertainment but at the same time, forfeiting the time to provide ourselves with good food? Many people refuse to or dislike to cook for many reasons. Some have never been taught the basics or feel too busy and rely heavily on fast food restaurants and convenience foods. The tragedy of this is not only the development of a society totally dependent on the processed food industry but one that is depriving itself of two joys: wholesome homemade meals, and good health. Like one friend said to me, "I'd rather be poor and feel like I feel now (after eliminating MSG) than have millions in the bank and feel like I used to". If you suspect in the least amount that you may be MSG sensitive, please try eliminating it from your diet for at least a week. Use some of our eating and recipe ideas or just boil up some brown rice, beans, potatoes, or pasta, and supplement these with plain water (sliced lemon can be added) and fresh vegetables, prepared any way you like (no seasoning salt, please!). Stop taking vitamin supplements or any unnecessary pills (Some OTC and prescribed medications may be giving you a reaction. Your pharmacist can give you a list of all the ingredients in any medication). Prepare ground beef or other meat yourself and season with salt and pepper only. Be sure pork, turkey or chicken is not basted or injected. Use only butter or oil and eat lots of fresh fruit. Omit bread or baked goods unless the yeast contains no additives (yeast nutrients) and the flour contains no malted barley flour or dough conditioners. Don't use any low fat products. When fat is removed, so is much of the flavor and often flavor enhancers are put back in . Avoid candy, gum, cookies, and other packaged processed food items. Remember, even your shampoo, toothpaste or breath mints may contain MSG or aspartame and may be giving you problems. Also read the chapters on sulfites and aspartame and test to see if they, too, are affecting you. Refer to our substitute information and recipes for help. Trust your body. It will not lie to you. Happy life and good health to all!

For the latest and most up-to-date information please visit our web site at www.msgmyth.com.

To help you shop and eat out, clip and carry one of these with you at all times. Share extras with friends.

---

I am severely sensitive to monosodium glutamate (MSG). Please check to see if any of these words are on food packaging and are used to make any dishes that I have ordered. When in doubt please show me the label.

Monosodium glutamate (MSG)
Glutamate or Glutamic acid
Hydrolyzed "anything"
Autolyzed "anything"
Gelatin
Bouillon/Broth/Stock
Flavor(s) or Flavoring(s)
Chicken, Pork, or Beef
Flavors, Natural Flavor(s)
Aspartame

Caseinate (sodium or calcium)
Carrageenan, L-cysteine
Yeast extract or nutrient
Seasonings, Spice
Prepared soup or sauce base
Textured or Soy protein
Whey protein or concentrate
Any seasoning salts
Soy sauce

---

I am severely sensitive to monosodium glutamate (MSG). Please check to see if any of these words are on food packaging and are used to make any dishes that I have ordered. When in doubt please show me the label.

Monosodium glutamate (MSG)
Glutamate or Glutamic acid
Hydrolyzed "anything"
Autolyzed "anything"
Gelatin
Bouillon/Broth/Stock
Flavor(s) or Flavoring(s)
Chicken, Pork, or Beef
Flavors, Natural Flavor(s)
Aspartame

Caseinate (sodium or calcium)
Carrageenan, L-cysteine
Yeast extract or nutrient
Seasonings, Spice
Prepared soup or sauce base
Textured or Soy protein
Whey protein or concentrate
Any seasoning salts
Soy sauce

---

I am severely sensitive to monosodium glutamate (MSG). Please check to see if any of these words are on food packaging and are used to make any dishes that I have ordered. When in doubt please show me the label.

Monosodium glutamate (MSG)
Glutamate or Glutamic acid
Hydrolyzed "anything"
Autolyzed "anything"
Gelatin
Bouillon/Broth/Stock
Flavor(s) or Flavoring(s)
Chicken, Pork, or Beef
Flavors, Natural Flavor(s)
Aspartame

Caseinate (sodium or calcium)
Carrageenan, L-cysteine
Yeast extract or nutrient
Seasonings, Spice
Prepared soup or sauce base
Textured or Soy protein
Whey protein or concentrate
Any seasoning salts
Soy sauce

---

I am severely sensitive to monosodium glutamate (MSG). Please check to see if any of these words are on food packaging and are used to make any dishes that I have ordered. When in doubt please show me the label.

Monosodium glutamate (MSG)
Glutamate or Glutamic acid
Hydrolyzed "anything"
Autolyzed "anything"
Gelatin
Bouillon/Broth/Stock
Flavor(s) or Flavoring(s)
Chicken, Pork, or Beef
Flavors, Natural Flavor(s)
Aspartame

Caseinate (sodium or calcium)
Carrageenan, L-cysteine
Yeast extract or nutrient
Seasonings, Spice
Prepared soup or sauce base
Textured or Soy protein
Whey protein or concentrate
Any seasoning salts
Soy sauce

---

I am severely sensitive to monosodium glutamate (MSG). Please check to see if any of these words are on food packaging and are used to make any dishes that I have ordered. When in doubt please show me the label.

Monosodium glutamate (MSG)
Glutamate or Glutamic acid
Hydrolyzed "anything"
Autolyzed "anything"
Gelatin
Bouillon/Broth/Stock
Flavor(s) or Flavoring(s)
Chicken, Pork, or Beef
Flavors, Natural Flavor(s)
Aspartame

Caseinate (sodium or calcium)
Carrageenan, L-cysteine
Yeast extract or nutrient
Seasonings, Spice
Prepared soup or sauce base
Textured or Soy protein
Whey protein or concentrate
Any seasoning salts
Soy sauce

---

I am severely sensitive to monosodium glutamate (MSG). Please check to see if any of these words are on food packaging and are used to make any dishes that I have ordered. When in doubt please show me the label.

Monosodium glutamate (MSG)
Glutamate or Glutamic acid
Hydrolyzed "anything"
Autolyzed "anything"
Gelatin
Bouillon/Broth/Stock
Flavor(s) or Flavoring(s)
Chicken, Pork, or Beef
Flavors, Natural Flavor(s)
Aspartame

Caseinate (sodium or calcium)
Carrageenan, L-cysteine
Yeast extract or nutrient
Seasonings, Spice
Prepared soup or sauce base
Textured or Soy protein
Whey protein or concentrate
Any seasoning salts
Soy sauce

# RECIPES

| | |
|---|---|
| SUBSTITUTION CHART | 83 |
| COOKING AND STORING GRAINS, BEANS, AND PASTA | 88 |
| APPETIZERS, SNACKS, AND DIPS | 89 |
| BEVERAGES | 93 |
| BREADS AND BAKED GOODS | 97 |
| BREAKFAST | 106 |
| CONDIMENTS, SAUCES, AND MARINADES | 111 |
| DESSERTS | 117 |
| DESSERT SAUCES AND SYRUPS | 136 |
| DRESSINGS | 138 |
| FREEZER OR CANNED GOODS | 144 |
| MAIN DISHES | 149 |
| MEATS, POULTRY, AND SEAFOOD | 171 |
| MIXES | 185 |
| SALADS | 187 |
| SANDWICHES | 196 |
| SOUPS | 199 |
| TREATS AND CANDY | 205 |
| VEGETABLES, BEANS, AND GRAINS | 212 |
| MISCELLANEOUS | 220 |

## Substitutions

| AVOID | USE INSTEAD |
|---|---|
| Cream of mushroom soup or other creamed soups called for in many casseroles | 1. Cream sauce<br>2. Sour cream<br>3. Whole whipping cream<br>4. Half cream/half milk<br>5. Half sour cream/half milk<br>6. Homemade Yogurt<br>7. Whole milk |
| Canned Tomato Soup and Tomato sauce | 1. Tomato puree watered down to sauce consistency. Look for puree without citric acid.<br>2. Pureed fresh, canned, or bottled tomatoes (whole or diced).<br>3. Recipe in book. |
| Tomato Paste | 1. Cut peeled fresh tomatoes in half. Squeeze out seeds and juice. Puree, then let drain in cloth lined strainer over a bowl for several hours in the refrigerator.<br>2. Use homemade catsup if only up to ⅓ cup is needed.<br>3. For pizza, use fresh or canned tomato puree, or diced, drained tomatoes.<br>4. For spaghetti or chili, use pureed, fresh diced, or frozen tomatoes.<br>5. Muir Glen Puree. |
| Sausage for pizza | Ground beef or pork spiced with basil, oregano, fennel seed, salt and pepper, garlic, and hot pepper flakes, if desired. Many meat markets will make up special orders of sausage. |
| Frozen Entrees | 1. Make extra large batches and freeze for other meals. Most commercial ones are MSG laden. |
| Cold Cuts | 1. Home boiled or roasted turkey or chicken (be sure it says "no additives").<br>2. Home roasted beef.<br>3. Nut butters.<br>4. Veggie sandwiches.<br>5. Fried egg sandwiches (great with butter and mustard).<br>6. Frozen (MSG free) ground beef burgers.<br>7. Cheese sandwiches unless you react to most cheeses.<br>8. Cold sliced meat loaf. |
| Cocoa Mixes | Hot chocolate from cocoa - Mix ¼ cup cocoa with ½ cup water and pinch salt. Bring to boil on medium heat. Simmer 1 minute. Add 5 - 6 cups milk, ⅓ cup sugar and heat. Add 1 teaspoon vanilla. Taste and add more sugar and milk to taste. Add more cocoa if a richer chocolate is desired.<br><br>For a mug of cocoa, place a heaping teaspoon and ¼ cup of water in mug. Microwave until it simmers 30 seconds. Add milk and 2 teaspoons sugar. Stir and heat. Add more sugar if desired. |

| AVOID | USE INSTEAD |
|---|---|
| Seasoning Salts | I prefer to make mine from sea salt.<br>1. My favorite: Creole salt<br>　　To ⅔ cup salt add:<br>　　　½ teaspoon cayenne pepper<br>　　　1 teaspoon garlic granules<br>　　　¼ teaspoon black pepper.<br>2. Lemon Pepper<br>　　⅔ cup salt<br>　　2 teaspoons black pepper<br>　　2 teaspoons lemon peel, ground, dry<br>　　pinch of tarragon, dill or thyme.<br>3. Experiment with herbs and spices. They really wake up meat, pasta, and vegetable dishes. |
| Oriental Seasoning, Soy Sauce, and other bottled Oriental style sauces | Some people can tolerate a small amount of soy sauce. I make a marinade using:<br>　　Juice of 1 lime or lemon<br>　　3 tablespoons oil<br>　　3 tablespoons water<br>　　1 teaspoon Oriental five spice powder<br>　　¼ teaspoon sesame seed oil<br>　　¼ cup brown or white sugar<br>　　¼ teaspoon dry powdered ginger (fresh can be used up to 1 teaspoon.)<br>　　⅛ teaspoon black pepper<br>　　¼ teaspoon red pepper flakes<br><br>This is good on beef, chicken, fish or pork. Can marinate 1 to 3 hours (1 to 2 pounds meat, sliced).<br>Drain meat (reserve marinade). Stir fry in 3 tablespoons oil and remove from pan. Set aside. Add vegetables to pan and stir fry until tender crisp. Stir 2 teaspoons flour into reserved marinade and add to vegetables, stirring until bubbly. Add meat. Heat and serve with rice, Chinese rice noodles, or spaghetti. Though many Oriental and vegetarian dishes call for soy sauce, just omit or decrease amount and add more salt and a pinch of sugar or brown sugar.<br><br>For a quicker, thinner oriental style sauce, simply sautee in oil, sliced meat and vegetables until the tender crisp. Sprinkle with the juice of half a lemon or lime and add 1 to 2 tablespoons white or brown sugar, dash of red pepper flakes, ½ teaspoon Chinese Five Spice, ¼ teaspoon garlic powder, and dash of ginger. Salt and pepper to taste. Stir and serve. |

| AVOID | USE INSTEAD |
|---|---|
| Mayonnaise in salads and sandwiches (Helman's, Best Foods, or Saffola brands don't bother some people. You will have to test for yourself). | 1. Mix:<br>    1 cup sour cream<br>    1 teaspoon oil<br>    1 to 2 teaspoons sugar<br>    salt and pepper to taste<br>    2 teaspoons lemon juice or vinegar<br>    ½ teaspoon mustard if desired<br>2. Plain sour cream<br>3. Homemade mayonnaise and dressings.<br>4. Plain homemade yogurt or seasoned as in #1.<br>5. Mashed avocado<br>6. Olive oil or butter spread on bread. |
| Evaporated Milk | 1. Whole milk<br>2. Cream<br>3. Sour cream diluted with water or milk<br>4. Homemade Yogurt |
| Fresh Buttermilk | 1. In baking:<br>    1 cup milk minus 1 tablespoon<br>    1 tablespoon vinegar or lemon juice.<br>    Let sit at room temperature 3 - 5 minutes.<br>2. In salad dressings:<br>    Dilute sour cream or plain yogurt with milk or water. |
| Non-Dairy Creamers | 1. Milk<br>2. Cream<br>3. Mixture of milk and cream |
| Non-Dairy Topping | 1. Real whipped cream<br>2. Sweetened homemade yogurt<br>3. Breyer's Original Vanilla ice cream<br>4. Meringue on pies instead<br>5. Try without a topping or serve hot fruit pies with ice cream. Pour cold fresh cream on top of hot fruit pies.<br>6. Serve with an old fashioned custard sauce or brown sugar sauce. |
| Sour Cream | We use Knudsen's Whole Sour Cream or make it using the recipe in the Miscellaneous section of this book. |
| Cornstarch | 2 tablespoons flour = 1 tablespoon cornstarch as thickener<br>1 tablespoon arrowroot = 2 tablespoons cornstarch = 4 tablespoons flour |

| AVOID | USE INSTEAD |
|---|---|
| Processed cheese slices, cheese spreads, cheese balls, cheese substitutes | Try cheeses made with whole milk, salt, and cultures. Mozzarella, or preferably any mild white cheese can be tolerated by some people. Many hard cheeses contain a lot of MSG. The enzymes break the protein into it's amino acids, one of which is glutamate. Since they are dryer, the product is denser and therefore higher in glutamate. Some people avoid all American made or aged cheeses. Modern enzymes are very powerful and break down milk protein. Some imported cheeses are better tolerated. |
| Ricotta and cottage cheese filling for lasagna or pasta shells | Make 2 cups thick white cream sauce. Slowly beat 1 cup of cream sauce into 1 beaten egg. Add to remaining sauce in pan, stirring constantly until cooked. Salt and pepper to taste. Add pinch of sugar and nutmeg. Parsley and/or 1 tablespoon parmesan cheese may be added. When cool, add grated mozzarella cheese (optional). |
| Artificial Sweeteners | 1. Sugar<br>2. Honey<br>3. Date sugar<br>4. Stevia - ⅓ to ½ teaspoon dry white powder = 1 cup sugar<br>  ½ to ¾ teaspoon liquid stevia = 1 cup sugar |
| Canned Tuna | Tuna with water or water and salt only added. Many low sodium tunas are MSG free. Canned salmon can be substituted in tuna recipes.<br>Rinse tuna in strainer before using. |
| Corn syrup | Honey, real maple syrup, homemade pancake syrup. |
| Pancake syrup | 1. Make syrup:<br>  1 cup brown sugar<br>  1 cup white sugar<br>  1 cup water<br>  Boil 1 minute and add a pinch of salt.<br>2. Real maple syrup (some contain sulfites)<br>3. Crush fruit, add water and sugar and boil 2 minutes or until thicker for fruit syrup. |
| Lotions, face creams, shampoo and conditioners that say words like: "protein enriched", " amino acids", "milk extracts", "hydrolyzed" anything, citric acid. | Plain white shortening makes great cream for dry hands and skin. Unscented glycerine soaps make gentle skin cleansers and shampoo (found in health food stores and many grocery and drug stores. We like Dr. Bronner's peppermint soap and liquid almond castile soap for shampoo. There are books available that teach how to make lotions and natural cosmetics. |
| Toothpaste | Plain baking soda works well. My dentist agrees it's very effective. A friend said that when she was growing up, her mother would shake together in a bottle, baking soda, mint oil, and a pinch of salt. Dr. Bronner's peppermint soap can also be used on teeth. It is very mild and minty. Use a tiny amount on tooth brush. |

| AVOID | USE INSTEAD |
|---|---|
| Breath mints | A colleague of my husband places a whole clove between his cheek and gum. I tried it and it works because my 4 year old granddaughter said that I "smelled like cookies". Essential oil of peppermint works well. |
| Canned tomatoes and canned tomato puree | Look for brands that use white lining in cans such as Muir Glen products. Avoid products with citric acid. Use fresh tomatoes, home canned or frozen tomatoes. |

*ATTENTION!     When canned tomatoes are called for in recipes, we use fresh tomatoes, our own bottled or frozen tomatoes, and Organic Muir Glen tomato puree. Some individuals tell us they even react to their own bottled tomatoes. While in the hot water bath, free glutamate may be created. Buy or use firm, not overripe tomatoes, and try not to cook too long.

When vinegar is called for in recipes, we use pure cider vinegar without preservatives or fresh lemon or lime juice.

When catsup is called for in recipes, we use homemade catsup (recipe included). Some individuals find they can use Muir Glen catsup. However it does contain white wine vinegar which usually contains sulfites.

When cheese is called for in recipes, you may omit it or decrease the amount. Some people cannot tolerate American cheeses at all. We use Kraft mozzarella (sparingly) and Tillamook cheddar. Remember, the milks used by cheese makers will vary all over the country. Some may contain whey and milk solids, or gelatin. Also, American cheeses are often made with fast acting, powerful enzymes which may break down the milk proteins too much, releasing free glutamate. That's why foreign cheeses are often better tolerated. I often use the substitute for Ricotta cheese, in the Substitutes charts, for casseroles. But we use cheese sparingly and not too often.

In some baking recipes, such as pancakes or muffins, water can be substituted for milk. Also, Rice Dream rice milk works well.

If you decide to substitute whole wheat flour in baking, 1 cup white flour is equivalent to 1 cup minus 2 tablespoons of whole wheat flour. Reduce any oil or shortening called for in the recipe by 1 tablespoon per cup of flour and increase liquid by 1 to 2 tablespoons per cup of flour.

Pastry whole wheat flour is preferred for baked goods such as pies, muffins, tortillas, and cookies. Hard whole wheat is best for bread making. Look for white flour without malted barley flour and that is not enriched, if possible. There is a "white" whole wheat that makes a great all purpose flour.

If you find that brown sugar or molasses bother you due to the chemicals used in their production, substitute raw sugar, white sugar, or honey.

Cooking and Storing Beans, Grains, and Pasta

**BEANS**

Start beans the evening before use. Wash and sort dry beans in a colander. Place about 6 cups in a large pot and fill with water to within 3" of top of pot. Bring to boil. Turn off heat, cover, and let stand over night. Drain water and refill pot with water a few inches above the beans. Bring to a boil, reduce heat, and simmer until tender, approximately 20 minutes to one hour or more. Do not let beans get mushy. Beans may be flavored while simmering with any of the following: chili powder, cilantro, oregano, chopped onion, salt, chopped celery, minced garlic or garlic powder, or cumin. This is especially good with pinto beans or beans to be used in Mexican dishes or as refried beans. Let cool and ladle beans including some liquid into 1 quart freezer bags. Use in chili, soups, refries, casseroles, and salads. Suggested beans: navy, pinto, lima, garbanzo, black, kidney, etc.. Beans may be cooked in larger batches than suggested. Beans may be started several hours before using. Just bring beans to a boil, turn off heat, cover, and let sit for one hour. Return to a simmer and cook gently until tender. Remember, too much cooking can create free glutamate.

**GRAINS**

Wheat

Wheat and other large hard grains may be cooked and stored the same way as beans. However, the wheat may be tender enough the next morning without the need for boiling. Salt may be added. Use in stews, breads, salads, casseroles, and as breakfast cereal.

*Barley, lentils, and other grains may be cooked as above or simply washed and added to boiling water or soup and simmered until tender.

Rice

Cook raw rice according to package directions. Cool and store in freezer bags. Use later in soups, casseroles, and puddings or as breakfast cereal. Try the many varieties available. Brown rice is high in fiber and is more nutritional. Rinse raw white rice well before cooking to remove corn starch.

Polenta

Combine 1 cup water with 1 ½ cups polenta (coarse corn meal). Bring 4 cups plus ½ teaspoon salt to boil. Reduce heat and whisk in polenta. Simmer on low, stirring often for about 10 minutes. Pour into buttered bread pans. Let cool and solidify. Remove from pan and place in freezer bags. Store in refrigerator or freezer for longer period of time. To use, defrost and slice cold polenta into half inch slices. Saute in oil or butter. Serve with honey or brown sugar syrup or use as a base for spaghetti sauce. May top with onions, mushrooms, and grated cheese.

**PASTA**

Left over pasta, especially if not over-cooked, freezes well. Simply place in freezer bags and label. Great to use in soups, and salads, sauted with onions and oil, or topped with sauces. Either defrost in refrigerator or place in strainer under running hot water. May also be defrosted in microwave oven, covered or kept in the bag. Kids love it simply tossed with butter.

# APPETIZERS, SNACKS, AND DIPS

### Chicken Paté

1 cup boneless raw chicken breast
2 egg whites
2 eggs
dash cayenne pepper
1 garlic clove
½ cup chopped red onion or 4 scallions cut in 1" lengths
2 tablespoons walnuts or pine nuts
1 tablespoon parmesan (optional)
2 tablespoons oil
dash pepper
1 teaspoon salt
⅓ cup cream or whole milk

Pulse and blend ingredients in processor or blender. Pour into small oiled loaf pan. Cover with foil. Place in another pan with water 1" deep. Bake at 325° for 1 hour plus 10 minutes. Cool in refrigerator. Invert and slice. Serve on bed of mixed salad greens and offer French dressing and Italian or toasted bread.

May use fresh raw salmon. Omit the parmesan and add 1 tablespoon lemon juice and 1 teaspoon dry dill.

### French Onion Dip for Chips and Crackers

Chop up 1 large onion.

Place in single layer on glass or metal pan and place in 375° oven. Roast, stirring occasionally until medium brown. Let cool.

Mix 2 to 3 tablespoons onions with a pint of sour cream. Add salt and pepper to taste. Dash of cayenne pepper may be added. *Try to find whole sour cream without additional thickeners.

### Fritters

1 egg
1 ¼ cup water or milk
1 cup flour
¼ teaspoon salt
½ teaspoon baking powder
1 cup favorite fruit or vegetable, grated or chopped (corn, zucchini, onion, apples, berries, etc.)

Whisk ingredients together, folding fruit in last. May be deep fried or fried like pan cakes in a small amount of oil. Sprinkle fruit fritters with confectioners sugar or cinnamon sugar.

## Stuffed Baked Green Chilies

Wash several green peppers (Anaheim, jalapeno, or small bell). Slice off top. Wash out seeds slitting along one side if necessary. Stuff with mild cheese cut in ½" thick sticks. Jack or Mozzarella are good. Beat 1 egg with 2 tablespoons water. In a bowl, mix 1 cup flour, ½ cup corn meal, a dash of garlic powder, and salt and pepper to season. Oil a cookie sheet liberally. Heat oven to 400°. Dip each pepper in egg mixture, shaking off excess. Roll in flour mixture and place on pan. Bake 15 minutes. Any vegetables may be oven fried this way. Omit the cheese. Try sliced onions, green tomato circles, green pepper slices, or whole mushrooms.

## Olive Spread

1 can black olives (rinse and drain)
dash salt
2 tablespoons olive oil
1 teaspoon vinegar
1 clove garlic
dash pepper, black or cayenne

Process together but not completely smooth. Use as a spread on sandwiches, crackers, or on toasted french bread. Top with sliced tomatoes and sweet onion for a tasty Italian sandwich. Fresh or dry basil may be added to puree for a pesto flavor.

## Quesadillas

Flour or corn tortillas
sliced cheese (jack, mozzarella, cheddar)
toppings (sliced tomatoes, chopped onions, chopped green peppers or chilies, salsa, or black olives.)

Place a tortilla in a small fry pan. Cover ½ or entire surface with favorite toppings. Cook over medium-low heat until tortilla softens and can be folded over in half. Saute until golden then flip over. Brown other side.

## Steam Buns

1 lb. boneless lean pork, cut in chunks
1 package wonton wrappers (can use 1 recipe of flour tortillas. Roll out in 3 to 5" circles about ⅛" thick or less, but do not bake).
1 bok choy cabbage, cut up coarsely
10 mushrooms
3 cloves garlic
2 tablespoons fresh ginger root, peeled or 1 teaspoon dry
1 teaspoon toasted sesame seed oil
salt and pepper
4 green onions, cut in 1" pieces or 2 tablespoons onion, chopped
1 small can water chestnuts, rinse and drain (or ½ cup chopped fresh bean sprouts)

1 teaspoon sugar
1 teaspoon vinegar or lemon juice

Put all but water chestnuts and wanton wrappers in processor and blend. Add chestnuts and pulse, leaving some crunchy pieces.

Fill each wrapper with a mound of filling (about 1 to 2 tablespoons or more) in center. Then push wrapper up around filling, pinching ½" from top to make a "waist". Filling should reach top. Dip top in some grated carrot. Place in a steamer basket and steam covered 25 to 30 minutes.

*Oil basket before placing buns inside.

## Steamed Vegetables

Simply steam a medley of favorite vegetables cut into chunks. Steam tender crisp and serve with drawn butter, and/or lemon juice for dipping (or other homemade dip).

Suggestions: little potatoes cut in half, 2" chunks of corn on cob, broccoli, cauliflower, onions, carrots, mushrooms, etc.

## Baked Tortilla Chips

Cut flour or corn tortillas like a pie in sixths or eighths. Place on a cookie sheet. Sprinkle with salt or a mixture of salt and chili powder. Bake at 350° for 10 to 15 minutes or until crisp. Watch closely to prevent burning. Eat with salsa or refried beans and sour cream.

## Roasted Onion and Garlic Spread

2 onions
1 tablespoon oil
1 teaspoon honey or sugar
6 large cloves garlic, peeled
dash salt

Peel and quarter onions. Place in baking dish with whole peeled garlic, oil, honey, and salt. Stir well to coat onions. Roast uncovered at 350° for 35 minutes or until tender. Blend or process. While processing, add 4 tablespoons of butter or oil. Serve as a spread for crackers or French bread. Cracker recipes are found in the Bread and Baked Goods chapter.

## Grilled Vegetables

whole mushrooms

Slice into ½" slices:
zucchini
eggplant
onions
green tomatoes
green peppers

Mix together:
⅓ cup cider vinegar or fresh lemon juice
¼ cup olive oil

¼ cup chopped fresh herbs (basil, oregano, parsley)
⅛ teaspoon black pepper
1 garlic clove, sliced

Place vegetables in a bowl and pour marinade over all. Gently mix with hands. Let marinade for 2 hours. Grill over coals or broil until tender crisp. These are great made into sandwiches. Simply fill bread slices, tortillas, or rolls with a mixture of the grilled vegetables and serve. Butter bread or drizzle with olive oil to moisten. Offer salt and pepper.

## Stuffed Mushrooms
### (Great for New Year's Eve)

24 large mushrooms, washed, stems removed and set aside
2 ½ cups fresh bread crumbs
1 small onion, minced
2 cloves garlic, minced
1 tablespoon imported Parmesan cheese, grated (optional)
½ cup butter, melted (may use part oil)
1 teaspoon dried parsley
⅛ teaspoon dry thyme
dash of cayenne pepper
½ cup shredded cheese (optional)
½ teaspoon sugar (optional)
salt and pepper to taste

Butter two 9" x 13" pans and place caps upside down evenly in pans. Set aside.
A processor works well for chopping mushroom stems and mincing garlic, onions and bread crumbs. Process bread crumbs separately until fine. Melt butter in saute pan. Add onions, garlic, and minced mushroom stems. Stir and cook until tender. In a large bowl, place bread crumbs, remaining ingredients and sauted mushroom mixture. Stir well. Moisten with water if too dry. Taste and adjust seasonings. Fill each mushroom with stuffing. Bake covered 15 minutes at 375°. Uncover and bake at 350° for 10 minutes.

# BEVERAGES

### Banana Smoothy

Mix in blender:
2 cups whole milk (or rice milk)
2 bananas
6 to 8 ice cubes
1 to 2 tablespoons
sugar or honey to taste

### Boston Cooler
### (For 1 serving)

Fill a third of a tall glass with milk. Stir in 3 tablespoons sugar and ⅛ teaspoon ginger (powdered or fresh) until dissolved. Fill glass with plain seltzer water. Add ice and enjoy. My husband omits the ginger and adds a little vanilla. Often he'll use homemade pancake syrup for a sweetener. The grandkids love pancake syrup stirred into whole milk. Add a couple of ice cubes. Some bottled water may contain sulfites.

### Breakfast Shake

⅔ cup whole milk, rice milk, or water and cream
½ cup fruit, fresh or frozen (strawberries, bananas, peaches)
2 to 3 tablespoons quick oats
4 ice cubes
2 to 3 tablespoons sugar or honey

Place milk and oats in blender. Let sit for 5 minutes. Blend until smooth. Add remaining ingredients and blend again. Add more sugar if needed.

*More fruit may be added for fruitier drink. Increase sugar if fruit is tart.

### Chocolate Frappe

Puree in blender:
2 cups whole milk
1 cup water
6 ice cubes
⅓ cup sugar
dash salt

2 tablespoons cocoa

Use all milk for a richer drink. For a soda, whirl all but water and add 1 cup seltzer water just before serving.

### Punch for a Crowd

2 large cans (1 qt. 14 oz. each) pineapple juice
3 large cans frozen orange juice concentrate plus water to reconstitute
1 teaspoon dry ginger
2 qts. water

1 to 2 qts. carbonated water (seltzer)
1 cup sugar
1 cup fresh lemon juice
dash salt
vanilla ice cream (Breyer's Original)

Many canned juices contain sulfites so use caution. Mix all but carbonated water and ice cream. Add ice, carbonated water, and scoops of vanilla ice cream on top.

If you can't find a pineapple juice that doesn't bother you, use more reconstituted orange juice or other fruit juice instead. Pureed pineapple or strawberies diluted with water work well, too.

## Protein Fruit Drink

1 mango, peeled and diced
6 strawberries
1 cup water or milk
5 ice cubes
sugar to taste (start with 2 tablespoons)
¼ to ½ cup cooked beans (garbanzo, pinto, navy)

Puree and enjoy with a squeeze of lime if desired.

Variations:
Vary fruit used such as banana, pineapple, or other berries.

## Cooked Egg Nog
### (Not for the dairy sensitive)

1. Heat 3 ½ cups whole milk, pinch of salt, and ½ cup sugar in heavy bottomed sauce pan. Add ½ teaspoon nutmeg and ½ teaspoon cinnamon.

2. Separate 4 eggs. Beat yolks with ½ cup milk in large heat proof bowl.

3. When milk is steamy hot, slowly pour into egg yolks, whisking quickly. Return to pot and on medium low heat cook, stirring until it comes to low boil. Remove from heat.

4. Pour custard into large serving bowl. While whisking, add 2 cups cream, 2 cups milk, and 2 teaspoons vanilla (or omit cream and use all milk).

5. Taste and add more spices and sugar to taste. Chill before serving.

## Cooked Egg Nog for a Crowd

8 eggs
1 gallon whole milk
¼ teaspoon salt
½ teaspoon nutmeg
⅔ cup sugar
¼ teaspoon cinnamon (optional)
2 teaspoons pure vanilla
1 pint whipping cream
milk to thin

Beat together in a large heavy bottomed pot, eggs and milk. Add salt, sugar, and spices. Stirring constantly over medium heat, bring just to boil. Remove from heat and chill. Taste for sweetness and add more sugar if desired. Add vanilla and more nutmeg to taste. Beat 1 pint whipping cream with 2 teaspoons sugar and fold in. Add more milk to desired thickness. Garnish with grated nutmeg. Cream may be omitted. Add more milk if desired.

## Fruit Blitz
### Great for hot summer days!  Fewer calories than traditional milk shakes.

Partially freeze 2 bananas and 8 whole strawberries. Fill a 6 cup capacity blender with bananas and 2 cups milk or water and ⅓ cup sugar and dash of salt (optional). Pulse to blend smooth. Add the strawberries and enough milk or water to fill 6 cups. Pulse just enough to blend strawberries and retain thickness of shake. I use ½ cup sugar, especially if berries are tart.

Variation:
Use any berries and fruit that are partially frozen or use fresh fruit and ice cubes for some of the liquid.

A squeeze of lemon or lime in an all water blitz is delicious. Honey or stevia may also be used as the sweetener.

## Gazepacho
### (A cold vegetable soup or beverage high in antioxidants)

½ sliced cucumber, scrape off wax or skin.  If unwaxed and tender, may leave skins on.
5 large fresh tomatoes, cut into chunks
1 clove garlic
1 teaspoon olive oil
¼ to ½ cup onion, chopped
salt to taste

Quarter tomatoes and place with other ingredients in food processor or blender. Blend until smooth. Best to drink immediately.

*Bell peppers or mild chilies are also good in this but drink won't be as smooth. A dash of cayenne pepper is good.

## Easy Grape Juice

Place 2 to 3 cups concord grapes in clean canning jar. Add ½ cup sugar. Fill jar with hot or boiling water, leaving ¼" head space. Place cap on and process quarts for 15 minutes in water bath. Let sit 2 weeks. Strain to use. More water may be added. We push the pulp with a wooden spoon through a strainer.

## German Switchel
### Old thirst quenching recipe for hot days or after workouts.

1 cup pure apple cider vinegar or fresh lemon juice
2 cups sugar
1 teaspoon powdered ginger or 2 teaspoons grated fresh
1 gallon water

up to 1 cup molasses (unsulphured) or brown sugar (if these bother you, use more white sugar)
up to ½ teaspoon salt

Mix vinegar, sugar, ginger, and molasses (start with ½ cup). Add to the water, stir and chill well. May be diluted with mineral water or carbonated water.

## Mulled Cider

½ gallon cider or apple juice
10 cloves
3 cinnamon sticks
juice of 1 lemon or 2 oranges
1 orange
4 cups water
½ cup sugar (may decrease)

Cut orange into 3 circles and stud with the cloves. Since some producers are spraying their oranges with a coating of hydrolyzed protein product, omit this step if desired and just place the cloves in cheese cloth or a tea strainer or let float in cider. Simmer ingredients for 20 to 30 minutes. Grape juice may be substituted for cider.

## Orange Smoothie

1 - 6 oz. can frozen orange juice concentrate
1 cup milk
1 cup water
¼ to ⅓ cup sugar
½ teaspoon vanilla
10 ice cubes

Puree in blender and enjoy.

## Slush

Cube and puree 4 cups of any fruit or mixture of fruit with 1 cup water and ⅔ cup sugar. Pour into a 9" x 5" pan and let freeze. Stir once per hour until it is frozen. To serve, let sit at room temperature for 20 minutes, then scoop into glasses and dilute with plain seltzer water. Offer spoons.

Suggested fruits: bananas, strawberries, mangos, kiwis, and peaches.

## Hot Winter Punch

3 qts. apple cider
2 to 3 cinnamon sticks
½ teaspoon nutmeg
½ cup honey or brown sugar
⅓ cup fresh lemon juice

5 cups pineapple juice (or any favorite juice)
1 orange studded with 10 cloves

Place ingredients in large pot and simmer for 10 minutes.

## Sun Tea

Place 8 to 10 herb or decaffeinated tea bags in a gallon jar of water. Allow to steep in the sun at least 3 hours. Remove bags, sweeten to taste, and chill or serve over ice. The juice of a lemon or lime added with sugar is wonderful. Green tea is high in antioxidants and also comes decaffeinated.

Variation:
If you grow mint, rinse a bunch and add to the jar.

## BREADS AND BAKED GOODS

For best breads, use a hard wheat flour. Our favorite is Wheat Montana Natural White unbleached flour. It does not contain malted barley flour nor is it enriched. The carrier agent for vitamins in many flours and other "enriched" foods can contain MSG. For more information write: Wheat Montana Farms and Bakery, P.O. Box 647, Three Forks, MT 59752, or visit their web site at www.wheatmt.com. Gold Medal offers an organic flour now.

The yeast amount may be reduced in most of these bread recipes to approximately 2 teaspoons per loaf yield. Avoid yeasts containing nutrients, instant yeasts, and flour containing yeast or nutrients. We use Red Star regular plain yeast. A yeast free bread recipe is included in this section for yeast sensitive individuals.

### Favorite French Bread

Mix together and let sit for 5 minutes:

2 ½ cups warm water
2 tablespoons sugar
2 tablespoons yeast

Add in 4 cups flour and mix. Add 1 teaspoon salt and 2 ½ more cups flour. Knead 10 minutes until smooth. Let raise until double. Punch down and shape into 4 long baguettes. Grease 2 large pans and sprinkle with corn meal. Place 2 loaves on each pan. Let raise until double in size. May slit tops with sharp knife or kitchen shears. Bake at 375° for 20-25 minutes. A pan of boiling water placed on the bottom oven rack helps make a chewier crust.

Variations:

For a richer dough, add an egg, 2 tablespoon oil, and more sugar. Add more flour if sticky.

May substitute whole wheat flour, oatmeal, or wheat flakes for part of the white flour. May be shaped into traditional loaves or into 4 round loaves. This also makes a great pizza crust.

### Multi-grain Bread with Flax Seed

Mix and let set 10 minutes:
2 tablespoons yeast
3 cups warm water
3 cups flour, can mix half white and half wheat
1 cup oat bran or oatmeal
½ cup honey, sugar, brown sugar, or applesauce
¼ cup flax seed

Add: ¼ cup oil (optional)

2 to 3 ½ cups more flour (until not sticky, but not hard and tough)
2 ½ teaspoons salt

Knead until smooth and elastic. Let raise until doubled, then punch down and form into 2 large or 3 medium loaves. Let double in size and bake at 350° for 30 minutes or until tapping on top sounds hollow.

97

## Johnny Cake
### (A very moist corn bread)
### We have it with chili every Christmas.

1 cup sugar
½ cup butter
2 eggs
2 cups flour
2 teaspoons baking powder
½ teaspoon salt
1 teaspoon baking soda
2 cups milk soured with 2 tablespoons vinegar
1 cup yellow corn meal

1. Cream butter and sugar well. Add eggs and mix well.

2. Mix dry ingredients and add alternately with sour milk. Stir in corn meal.

3. Pour into a greased and floured 9" x 13" pan. Bake at 375° for 25 to 30 minutes or until done.


## Corn Bread
### (Low sugar, low fat)

Mix:
½ cup sugar
¼ teaspoon stevia
2 eggs
¼ cup oil
¼ cup applesauce

Add and mix:
2½ cups flour
2 teaspoons baking powder

½ teaspoon salt
1 ½ teaspoons baking soda
2 cups rice milk minus 2 tablespoons
2 tablespoons vinegar or fresh lemon juice
1 cup corn meal

Pour in greased 9" x 13" pan. Bake at 375° for 20 to 25 minutes.


## Bran Muffins

1 cup unprocessed wheat bran
1 ¼ cup whole milk
¼ cup honey or unsulfured molasses
¼ cup sugar
¾ cup whole wheat flour
¾ cup white flour
2 teaspoons baking powder
½ teaspoon baking soda
1 teaspoon salt
½ cup oil
1 egg

May use 1 ½ cups of either whole wheat flour or white flour.

Blend egg, sugar, honey, and oil. Add milk. Blend dry ingredients including bran. Mix with liquid ingredients until just barely blended. Fold in any favorite chopped dry fruits and nuts. Raisins or dates are good. Bake at 400° for 15 to 20 minutes.

Variations:
Substitute apple or orange juice for the milk. Add spices such as cinnamon or nutmeg. Substitute oat bran for wheat bran. Substitute applesauce for part or all of oil. Add lemon or orange zest.

## Large Batch Muffins for Freezing

4 cups flour
¾ cup oat bran, wheat bran, or whole wheat flour
8 teaspoons baking powder (2 tablespoons plus 2 teaspoons)
1 to 2 teaspoons cinnamon (optional)
2 teaspoons salt
2 cups sugar
4 eggs
1 cup oil or melted butter (may use part applesauce
2 cups whole milk
zest of a lemon or orange (optional)
4 to 5 cups berries or cut up fruit

Mix dry ingredients, except sugar. In other bowl, beat eggs, sugar, and oil. Beat in milk.

Stir gently together with dry ingredients and fold in fruit. Fill greased muffin tins ⅔ full. Sprinkle with sugar. Bake at 400° for 16 to 20 minutes. Makes 20 to 24 extra large muffins or 40 to 48 smaller ones. Cool and freeze in plastic freezer bags.

*If using frozen berries, don't defrost totally or they will get mashed when added to batter.

Suggested fruit:
berries, apples (good topped with cinnamon sugar), peaches, nectarines, rhubarb (top with a little extra sugar), cherries (add 1 teaspoon almond extract).

## Crescent Rolls
### (Make ahead and freeze unbaked rolls)

Mix together:
4 tablespoons yeast
1 tablespoon sugar
1 cup warm water

1.  Beat 4 eggs.
2.  Add 1 cup oil and 1 cup sugar.
3,  Add 4 cups soured whole milk (4 tablespoons vinegar mixed with 3 ¾ cups milk).
4.  Add yeast mixture.
5.  Add 6 cups flour, 2 tablespoons salt, and 2 tablespoons baking powder.

6.  Mix/beat really well, then add 1 to 2 cups more flour.
7.  Dump 6 cups flour on table. Scoop dough onto flour and knead into dough. May not need all of the flour.
8.  Divide into 4 pieces.
9.  Roll out each piece into circle like a pizza. Butter top. Using pizza cutter, cut into 16 "slices". Roll up starting at wide end.
10. Place on greased cookie sheet and freeze. Store in freezer containers.
11. On day of baking, let raise for 5 hours. Bake at 350° for 15 minutes or until golden.

## Soft Whole Wheat Rolls
### So moist, they don't need butter!

Mix:
½ cup sugar or honey
4 cups warm water
3 tablespoons yeast

Add and beat well:
6 cups flour (can be part whole wheat and white)
1 tablespoon salt

⅔ cup oil or melted butter
3 eggs (an extra egg makes dough richer)

Knead in enough more flour (up to 4 cups) until no longer sticky. Knead 8 minutes. Let rise in covered bowl until doubled (about 30 minutes). Punch down and shape into 2" balls. Divide between two 9" x 13" greased pans. Let rise until almost doubled and bake at 350° for 18 to 20 minutes.

Can put in 3 large or 4 medium bread pans for loaves. Bake 25 to 30 minutes.

These rolls freeze well in gallon freezer bags.

## Sticky Pecan Rolls and Cinnamon Rolls
### (General directions)

Use a rich yeast recipe such as Betty Crocker's "traditional sweet roll dough". Roll out to a 10" x 15" rectangle and spread with butter. Sprinkle with some cinnamon and sugar. Roll up, along wide side and pinch to seal.

In a 9" x 13" pan, melt together, ⅓ cup butter, dash of salt, ½ to ⅔ cup brown or white sugar, and 2 tablespoons honey in a warm oven. Add a little water if brown sugar looks dry. Should be a thick syrup consistency. Stir and sprinkle ½ cup pecans evenly over syrup. Slice rolls with a serrated knife into ¾" thick slices (12 to 15). Lay evenly over syrup. Let rise until doubled. Bake at 350° to 375° for 25 to 35 minutes. Quickly invert onto a large pan.

Variations:
1. For cinnamon rolls, omit syrup and nuts. With rolls still warm in pan, spread with a butter cream frosting. There are lower fat versions using less butter, but they don't make my children happy! Besides, we reserve these for special occasions.
2. For Danish-style rolls, place rolls on a floured towel, cut side up, roll to ⅛" to ¼" thickness. Twist in center if desired. Place on buttered cookie sheet and let rise for 15 minutes. Bake at 375° for 15 minutes or until golden. Frost with glaze of confectioners sugar, milk, and almond extract if desired. Fruit jam or filling may be spread on rectangle instead of cinnamon and sugar.

## Yeast Free Bread

2 ½ cups flour (may be part whole wheat)
½ cup quick oats or oat bran
2 tablespoons sugar or honey
2 teaspoons baking powder
1 teaspoon soda
½ teaspoon salt
¼ cup flax or sunflower seeds (optional)
1 egg (optional)
1 ¾ cup sour milk (1 ¾ tablespoon vinegar or lemon juice plus milk to make 1 ¾ cups liquid) (may use water or rice milk)

2 tablespoons to ¼ cup oil (may use part applesauce)

Combine dry ingredients. Mix egg, oil, and milk and add to dry ingredients. Stir until just moistened. Pour into greased bread pan. Let stand for 10 minutes. Bake at 350° for 40 to 50 minutes. Makes great toast.

*Up to ⅓ cup sugar or honey may be used. Oats may be omitted, but decrease sour milk to 1 ½ cups. Vinegar amount may be reduced to 1 tablespoon.

## Whole Wheat Bread

Beat together and let sit 10 minutes:
2 tablespoons yeast

2 ¾ cups warm water
4 cups whole wheat flour

1 tablespoon sugar

Add:
2 cups white flour (or all whole wheat)
2 eggs
2 teaspoons salt
⅓ cup honey

Knead until smooth, adding more flour if necessary, 8 to 10 minutes. Should be soft, not stiff. Let rise for 30 minutes and knead again for 1 minute. Shape and place in 2 greased pans, then raise until double. Bake for 25 minutes at 375° to 400°.

## Barbara Randolph's Best Biscuits

5 cups flour
10 teaspoons baking powder (3 tablespoons + 1 teaspoon)
2 teaspoons salt
1 tablespoon sugar (optional)
10 tablespoons butter
1 egg
1 to 1½ cups milk or water plus some cream

Mix dry ingredients. Cut in butter. Beat egg and liquid. Add to dry ingredients and stir gently to moisten until it resembles course cornmeal. Can rub with fingers to blend. Pat to ½" thick, cut out, and bake at 350° for 15 to 20 minutes.

## Date and Nut Bread
### (No butter or oil used)

1 ½ cup snipped dates (½ lb.)
1 teaspoon baking soda
1 cup boiling water
1 egg, beaten
1 cup sugar
2 cups flour
1 teaspoon baking powder
½ teaspoon salt
1 cup chopped walnuts

Sprinkle dates with soda. Stir in boiling water and let stand. In large bowl, combine egg and sugar. Stir together dry ingredients and add all at once along with date mixture to egg mixture. Mix well. Spoon into 9" x 5" x 3" pan. Bake at 350° for 1 ¼ hours or until toothpick inserted in center comes out clean. Cool before slicing. This cake is moist even without shortening. It's more moist the next day.

## Pumpkin Bread

3 cups sugar
1 cup oil (can use part applesauce)
2 eggs
1 cup water
1 cup pumpkin
3 ½ cups flour
½ teaspoon baking powder
2 teaspoons soda
1 teaspoon salt

½ teaspoon cinnamon
½ teaspoon nutmeg
1 teaspoon vanilla
½ cup walnuts, chopped

Mix dry ingredients together. Mix liquid ingredients and pumpkin together. Blend and add nuts. Pour into 2 greased and floured loaf pans. Bake at 325° for 1 to 1 ½ hours.

## Bread for a Week

7 cups very warm water
½ cup applesauce
¼ cup honey
3 tablespoons dry yeast
⅔ cup oil
2 teaspoons salt
15 to 17 cups whole wheat flour or mixture of white and wheat

Mix all but flour in a large bowl. Add 8 cups flour and blend well. Let set for 10 minutes. Add 7 to 9 more cups flour and mix thoroughly.

Dough should be soft and a little sticky. Knead for 10 to 15 minutes. Let rest for 5 minutes and then knead for 1 more minute. Oil bread pans (4 large or 5 medium) and divide dough into quarters. Shape into loaves and place in pans. Let rise until doubled. Bake at 350° for 30 minutes. Freeze some loaves for later in the week.

Variation:
Instead of using ½ cup applesauce and ¼ cup honey, ¾ cup of either may be used.

## Flour Tortillas I

9 cups flour (I use soft white whole wheat flour and they roll out easily)
1 ½ teaspoons salt
2 teaspoons baking powder
⅔ cup oil
3 to 3½ cups warm water

Mix dry ingredients. Pour warm water and oil over ingredients and mix with hands. Cut off small portions and roll into 6" to 7" thin circles. Cook on hot griddle, turning often until lightly brown. Stack between wax paper and freeze in zipper freezer bags or use in recipes. Makes 35

to 45 tortillas. Or form 30 to 40 balls an place on cookie sheet lined with wax paper, freeze, and then bag. To use, defrost by microwaving for one minute before rolling out. Or defrost at room temperature as needed.

Crackers: Add 2 tablespoons sugar and ⅓ cup sesame seeds to flour. Roll into very thin rectangles to fit cookie sheets. Cut into squares with pizza cutter. Bake at 350° for 7 to 8 minutes or until crisp. They will crispen as they cool.

## Flour Tortillas II

3 cups flour
¼ to ⅓ cup oil
1 scant teaspoon salt (I use ½ teaspoon)
½ teaspoon baking powder
⅔ to 1 cup water (can add more if too dry)

Mix dry ingredients. Add water and oil, then knead well until blended. Form into 10 to 12

balls and cover with damp cloth or plastic wrap. Let sit for 10 minutes. Roll each out very thin to a 7" diameter circle on floured cloth. Bake on hot ungreased pan, turning to cook both sides (30 seconds on each side). Use immediately or freeze in plastic bag. The baking powder is omitted in some traditional recipes.

# Navajo Fried Bread

4 cups flour
1 teaspoon salt
4 teaspoons baking powder
1 ½ to 1 ¾ cups milk or water

*These are great topped with hot chili and condiments, such as cheese, tomatoes, onions, and shredded lettuce.

Mix dry ingredients and add enough liquid to make soft dough. Knead until smooth. Place in a bowl, cover, and let set 30 minutes. Divide into golf ball-sized balls. Roll ¼ to ½" thick circles on a floured surface. Fry until golden in a hot skillet with ¼" oil. Serve with honey, sugar, cinnamon, or powdered sugar.

# Pita Bread

1 tablespoon yeast
2 cups warm water
2 teaspoons salt
2 teaspoons honey or sugar
2 tablespoons oil (optional)
4 ½ to 5 ½ cups flour (whole wheat or white)

Dissolve yeast in warm water with honey or sugar. Stir in salt, oil, and 3 cups flour. Beat well (3 minutes). Work in enough flour (1 ½ to 2 more cups) to make a soft dough. Knead on a floured or oiled surface for 8 to 10 minutes. Place in oiled bowl, cover with plastic wrap or

towel, and let rise until doubled. Punch down and knead lightly. Divide into 8 to 10 pieces and shape into balls. Let sit on floured or oiled surface for 20 to 25 minutes. Make sure they do not touch. Roll out each ball into a circle ⅛" thick. Let circles sit for 20 minutes. Preheat oven 450° to 500°. Dust baking sheets with cornmeal and carefully place pitas on sheets. Bake on lowest oven rack for about 5 minutes. Bread should be very puffy and barely starting to brown. Let cool and store in plastic bags. Fill to make pita sandwiches or use as a base for little pizzas.

# Rye Bread
## Delicious and hearty!!

1 teaspoon sugar or 1 teaspoon molasses
2 tablespoons dry yeast
2 ½ cups warm water
¼ cup molasses
2 tablespoons oil or butter
2 ½ cups rye flour
1 tablespoon caraway seeds
5 ½ cups flour
dry corn-meal or farina to coat pans

In large bowl, place water, yeast, 3 cups white flour, and the sugar. Mix well and let set 10 minutes. Add rye flour, salt, seeds, oil, and molasses and stir well. Add remaining 2 ½ cups

flour and knead for 10 minutes. Up to ½ cup more flour may be added if too sticky. Cover and let rise until doubled, 1 to 1 ½ hours. Punch down and divide dough in half. Let sit while greasing a cookie sheet or 2 loaf pans with oil. Sprinkle sheet or pans with cornmeal. Shape dough into 2 balls and place on cookie sheet 4 inches apart or shape into 2 loaves for pans. Slit tops with sharp knife. Cover and let rise for 45 minutes to 1 hour or until doubled. Rub tops gently with water and bake 30 to 40 minutes at 400°.
*2 tablespoons cocoa may be added with seeds.

## Wheat Skinnies (Crackers)

3 cups flour (half white, half whole wheat)
¼ teaspoon salt
2 tablespoons brown sugar
2 tablespoons sugar
⅔-1 cup milk or water
4 tablespoons vegetable oil

Mix ingredients together until well blended. If sticky, add more flour. Knead 3 minutes on a floured towel or oiled surface. Divide into 4 pieces. Roll 1 out at a time into a 12 x 16" rectangle 1/16" thick. Place on cookie sheet. With pizza cutter or knife, cut into 2" squares or diamonds by cutting on the diagonal. Sprinkle lightly with salt. Bake 12-15 minutes at 350° or until golden brown. Cool and break apart. May freeze. Sesame or poppy seeds may be added to dough.

## Wheat Wafers

2 cups whole wheat flour
1 teaspoon salt
½ cup sesame seeds
¼ cup raw wheat germ
¼ cup oil
½ cup plus 1 tablespoon cold water

Mix dry ingredients. Add oil and water and knead for 10 minutes. Let rest for 10 minutes and roll in small batches as thin as possible. Cut into 1 ½" squares with pizza cutter. Bake on ungreased sheets at 375° for 8 minutes. Ovens vary. I bake mine at 350° for 9 to 10 minutes. Watch closely as they brown quickly toward the end.
Add sugar or honey for a sweeter cracker.

## Delicate Yam Biscuits
## Be sure to double!

1 cup mashed cooked yams
2/3 cup milk or water
4 teaspoons melted butter
2 cups flour
3 ½ teaspoons baking powder
2 tablespoons sugar
½ teaspoon salt

Blend yams, milk, and butter. Add remaining ingredients and make a soft dough. Place on well floured cloth and gently knead (12 times) until smooth, adding flour as needed. Roll to ½" thickness and cut into squares or circles. Bake at 400° for 12 to 15 minutes.

## Deb's 50/50 Wheat Bread

In large mixer or bowl, mix:
4 ½ cups warm water
3 tablespoons plain dry yeast
4 tablespoons sugar
2 tablespoons honey
1¼ cups applesauce (unsweetened)
½ teaspoon pure vitamin C crystals (health food stores)

Add and knead for 1 minute:
7 cups organic whole wheat flour
2 eggs
4 tablespoons soft butter or oil
1 tablespoon salt

Add 6 cups white flour, adding more if too sticky. Knead for 8 to 10 minutes. Let rise once if desired. Form into 4 loaves and place in pans, cover, and let double. Bake at 375° for 25 minutes. All white flour may be used. Mashed potatoes may be substituted for applesauce.

## Fried Scones
### (A great treat.)

Break chunks from any favorite bread dough. Pat into 4" circles, ½" thick. Drop into ½" hot oil in pan and fry until golden on both sides (medium high heat). Drain on paper towels. Top with butter and honey or jam.

## Graham Crackers

1 cup whole wheat flour
⅓ cup plus 1 tablespoon sugar
⅓ cup butter or oil
1 to 2 tablespoons milk or rice milk
½ cup oat flour (or process oatmeal in blender)
½ teaspoon soda
1 tablespoon honey
pinch of salt (optional)

Mix together dry ingredients. Heat butter, honey, and milk until melted. Pour into dry ingredients and mix until smooth. Chill for 30 minutes. Roll out dough right onto ungreased cookie sheet, ¼" thick or less. Bake at 350° for about 7 to 10 minutes. Watch so it doesn't burn. Prick with fork as it comes out of the oven and quickly cut with pizza cutter into desired sized rectangles.

Variation: May be crumbled and used as cereal. Sugar amount may be decreased. If you decide to decrease butter or oil amount, add corresponding amount of water or applesauce.

# BREAKFAST
(Water, rice milk, or fruit juice may be substituted for milk in most pancake and muffin recipes.)

### Cornmeal Pancakes

1 cup cornmeal or farina
1 teaspoon salt
1 cup boiling water
2 tablespoons oil
1 egg
1 cup soured milk (1 tablespoon cider vinegar or lemon juice plus milk to make 1 cup)
¾ cup flour
½ teaspoon baking powder
¼ teaspoon baking soda

In bowl, combine cornmeal and salt. Stir in the boiling water and add oil. Let sit for 10 minutes, covered. In smaller bowl, beat egg and add the sour milk. Blend into cornmeal mix with whisk or blender. Mix flour, soda, and baking powder together and add to the cornmeal mixture. Up to ½ cup water may be added if batter is too thick. Fry in hot oil. Flip when bubbles form. Serve with syrup or honey and butter.

### Feather Light Flapjacks

Mix together:
1 ½ cups flour
1 teaspoon sugar
1 teaspoon baking soda
pinch of salt

Add and mix well:

1 teaspoon oil or applesauce
1 cup homemade yogurt or soured milk
2 eggs
½ cup water or milk

If batter is too thick, add a little more liquid. Fry on hot skillet.

### Fluffy Wheat Pancakes

In 2 cups of water, soak ¾ cup whole wheat berries overnight. In the morning, drain and place in blender with ¾ cup milk. Blend 3 minutes, then add 3 egg yolks, 2 tablespoons oil, 1 tablespoon honey, and ¾ teaspoon salt. Blend another 3 minutes. Beat egg whites until stiff and fold into wheat mixture. Fry on griddle or pan. Serves six.

## German Apple Pancakes

1 cup milk
1 cup flour
6 eggs
¼ cup butter
1 lemon
2 teaspoons sugar
dash salt
5 to 7 apples

In large oven proof pan, melt butter. Core and slice apples and fry in butter until tender. Beat together milk, flour, eggs, sugar, and salt. Pour batter over apples. Bake in 475° oven for 10 to 20 minutes or until pancake puffs. Remove from oven. Sprinkle with lots of cinnamon sugar. Return to oven to brown. Just before serving, sprinkle with juice of 1 lemon. Serves 8.

## Oatmeal Pancakes

2 cups rolled oats
2 cups sour milk (2 tablespoons vinegar added to milk to make 2 cups)
1 cup flour (may be part whole wheat)
2 teaspoons sugar
1 ½ teaspoons baking powder
1 ½ teaspoons baking soda
1 teaspoon salt (may decrease to ½ teaspoon)
2 eggs
2 tablespoons oil

Night before:
Mix the oatmeal and sour milk. Cover and let sit (refrigerate if kitchen is hot).

Next morning:
Mix together flour, sugar, baking powder, baking soda, and salt. In large bowl, beat eggs and add oil. Add the oatmeal mixture and blend in the flour. If too thick, add water or milk. Fry on oiled pan. Spread out a bit. These pancakes are hearty and make a good meal anytime.

## Ginnie's Pancakes/Waffles

2 cups milk
2 tablespoons vinegar or lemon juice
2 tablespoons oil
1 egg
1 teaspoon sugar
½ teaspoon salt
1 teaspoon baking soda
2 teaspoons baking powder
up to 2 cups flour ( ½ whole wheat, ½ white is good too)

Mix milk with vinegar. Wait three minutes to sour. Add remaining ingredients except baking powder. Mix, then stir in baking powder. Let sit 1 minute. Cook on greased grill or waffle iron.

These are exceptionally light.

*⅓ cup applesauce may be substituted for oil.

## Wheat Pancakes

1 cup milk
1 cup uncooked whole wheat
2 eggs
2 tablespoons oil
2 teaspoons baking powder
1 to 2 tablespoons honey
½ teaspoon salt

Place wheat and milk in blender. Blend on high speed 4 to 5 minutes until smooth. Add the remaining ingredients and blend on low. Bake on hot griddle.

*Wheat may be soaked in the milk overnight in the refrigerator. Add more liquid if too thick.

## Easy Hash Browned Potatoes and Eggs
### (Good any time)

Scrub 1 large russet or 2 medium potatoes. Grate and place in drainer. Press out juices (starch) with knuckles real hard (can drain over a bowl and empty as it forms). Get a pan very hot with 2 tablespoons oil. Put grated potatoes into pan and pat down firmly and square up into a patty ½" thick or form into a circle. Keep pressing down on it as it crisps up and cooks. Turn when bottom is brown (about 5 minutes). Cook until golden and crisp, then sprinkle with salt and pepper (add onion or garlic powder if desired). Slide on plate and fry eggs in same pan. Good and satisfying. Great with fresh salsa or fruit if you like.

## Harvest Hash
### (by Krista Jensen)

1 apple chopped finely
2 medium potatoes chopped finely
¼ cup onion diced
¼ to ½ cup cooked MSG free breakfast sausage
(in bulk) (see Country Sausage in the Meat, Poultry and Seafood section)
salt and pepper
oil or butter

Melt 1 tablespoon butter in large saute pan. Add potatoes and cook 2 minutes on medium high, stirring. Add onions and continue cooking until they begin to turn golden. Add salt, pepper, and 1 more tablespoon of butter. Stir gently. Add apples and sausage and cook until potatoes brown on edges and apples are just soft, not mushy. Great served with eggs, canned fruit, and hot cocoa.

*Make your own breakfast sausage by processing pork butt with sage, thyme, sugar, salt, pepper, and paprika.

## Krista's Apples and Sausage
### Use homemade or non-MSG sausage.

7 cooking apples
1 lb. non-MSG pork sausage (bulk or link)
⅓ to ½ cup sugar
cinnamon

Shape sausage into patties and brown. Slice apples into ¼" pieces. Place apples in a large baking dish and sprinkle with sugar and a little cinnamon. Place sausage over apples and bake at 350° until apples are tender. Great served with biscuits or muffins. Sugar amount varies depending on tartness of apples used.

## Swiss Muesli

3 cups rolled oats (not quick)
2 cups rolled barley
2 cups rolled wheat
1 cup chopped dried fruit (unsulfured, any kind)
1 cup oat bran
½ cup wheat germ

¼ cup brown sugar (optional)

Mix ingredients and store in a tight container. Serve with milk and fresh fruit. It's best to let it sit in the milk for a few minutes before eating. Offer more sugar or honey.

## Apple Granola
### I mix and bake this in a very large stainless steel bowl.

Mix:
20 cups rolled oats
1½ cups brown sugar
½ teaspoon salt

Mix the following and pour over the oatmeal:
3 cups unsweetened applesauce
⅔ cup oil
1 teaspoon pure vanilla

Toss mixture well with 2 large spoons. Bake at 300° up to 1 hour, stirring often until dry and toasted. Add 2 cups any kind chopped nuts, ½ cup sunflower seeds, and ¼ cup sesame seeds the last 10 minutes of roasting. Store in tight container. Dried unsulfured fruit may be added after baking.

Eat with milk and fruit for breakfast. Use in cookies or to make granola bars.

## Christmas Granola

Mix:
14 cups rolled oats
2 cups wheat germ
2 cups bran wheat
½ cup whole wheat flour
1 cup sunflower seeds
⅓ cup sesame seeds

In bowl, mix:
2 cups oil
2 cups honey
½ cup plus 2 tablespoons brown sugar
2 tablespoons vanilla
1 teaspoon almond extract

Pour second mixture over first mixture and mix well. Spread in several pans. Bake for 1 hour at 250°, stirring every 15 minutes. Remove from oven and add 4 cups almonds and 4 cups dried fruits (unsulphured). Dried cranberries are good for color, but avoid ones containing dextrose or other additives. Chop larger fruit in processor with ½ cup whole wheat flour.

*Oil may be decreased to 1 cup plus 1 cup applesauce or juice.

We make this and pack it in pretty tins for gifts.

## Cooked Wheat Berries

Method I
1 cup wheat berries
6 cups water

Soak whole wheat in 2 cups water overnight. Add berries to 4 cups water in a pot. Cover and bring to a boil. Lower heat and simmer until tender. Drain and freeze or refrigerate and use within one week. Serve with whole milk and honey or sugar for breakfast (hot). Also good hot with butter and honey. Mash and add to meat loaf. Add to salads and soups. Substitute for rice or beans in casseroles. Substitute for mashed potatoes or noodles and eat with gravy or butter.

Method II
Bring 1 cup wheat, 4 cups water, and dash of salt to a boil in a sauce pan. Cover and take off heat. Let sit overnight. Heat and serve in morning.

## Refried Cornmeal Mush

Pour cooked cornmeal (or farina) into a buttered bread pan and refrigerate until firm (overnight is best). Slice ½" thick, and fry until light gold and crisp outside. Serve with butter and honey or syrup and fried eggs.

# CONDIMENTS, SAUCES, AND MARINADES

## Caribbean Salsa

Chop the following and place in medium bowl:

2 tomatoes
2 avocados
1 orange peeled and diced (may use mango or papaya instead)
¼ cup sweet or red onion
2 tablespoon chopped parsley or cilantro or 1 teaspoon dried
½ red pepper, chopped
½ yellow pepper, chopped

Toss lightly and add:
Juice of 1 lemon or lime
1 ½ teaspoon sugar
1 teaspoon chili powder

½ teaspoon cumin
Salt and pepper to taste

Toss again and serve with chicken, fish, or pork. There are never any leftovers at our table. We always eat this with chicken breasts that I have pounded thin, dredged in bread crumbs, and sauteed. We add a diced mango to original recipe. To prepare mango, hold vertically on cutting board, with dimple or "nose" tip facing you. Slice downward on either side of flat seed. Hold a section, skin side in palm of hand and with knife, cut to skin, ½" vertically and then ½" horizontally. Then pop back skin to form what resembles a "porcupine" of mango cubes. Simply slice off cubes. Repeat with other half.

## Guacamole I

6 avocados
¼ cup lemon juice (1 small lemon)
1 - 4 oz. can green chilies - rinse, seed, chop (fresh are better)
1 small onion (sweet) chopped
2 tablespoons MSG free mayonnaise or 2 tablespoons whole sour cream (optional)
salt and pepper

Dash cayenne
2 tomatoes - seed and dice

Mash avocados and stir in rest of ingredients.

Can freeze if you omit tomatoes. Add later. Thaw and drain any excess liquid after thawing.

## Guacamole II

1 or 2 chopped jalapeno peppers
2 tablespoons fresh cilantro, chopped
1 teaspoon salt
2 avocados, diced
2 tablespoons finely chopped onions
1 to 2 tomatoes, diced (may use canned)

Mash together jalapenos, cilantro, and salt until juice starts to form. Add tomatoes, avocados, and onions and serve with tortilla chips or warm flour tortillas.

## Salsa

2 cups fresh chopped tomatoes
¼ to ⅓ cup cilantro, chopped
⅓ to ½ cup sweet onion, chopped
2 cups finely chopped cabbage
Dash garlic powder or 1 small clove, minced
1 teaspoon sugar
3 tablespoons mild or hot peppers, chopped or small can green chilies

salt and pepper to taste
a squeeze of lime juice

Mix ingredients and chill.

Chopped avocado or mangos may be added.
Cabbage may be omitted for traditional salsa.

## Mexican Red Sauce

Process together in blender:
2 cups fresh chopped tomatoes
3 tablespoons flour

Pour into sauce pan and add:
1 cup water
1 teaspoon salt
1 tablespoon chili powder
¼ teaspoon cumin
½ teaspoon cilantro
2 teaspoons sugar

1/8 teaspoon garlic powder
Dash pepper
3 tablespoons minced onion

Stir constantly and simmer until thick. For a hotter sauce, add dash cayenne pepper or red pepper flakes. Thin to desired thickness with water.
Use for enchiladas, in burritos, or as a sauce for Mexican meatloaf or Mexican pizza.

## Oriental Orange Sauce
### (For chicken or pork)

Mix together:
½ cup fresh orange juice (not concentrated)
2 tablespoons brown sugar
1 slice ginger or ¼ teaspoon powdered ginger
1 tablespoon fresh lemon juice
2 tablespoons water

Pre-cook 4 pork chops or 4 chicken breasts by braising on range or baking in the oven. Do not microwave the chicken. It will not always kill salmonella bacteria. Pour above mixture over meat and simmer 5 minutes. Remove meat to platter. Blend 1 tablespoon cornstarch or 2 tablespoons flour with ⅓ cup water. Add to sauce in pan and cook until thick. Pour over meat and serve with rice.

## Oriental Marinade

Up to 2 pounds of sliced chicken, beef, or pork.
2 tablespoons water
½ teaspoon sesame seed oil
1 teaspoon soy sauce (omit if severely sensitive to MSG)

Juice of 1 lemon or ¼ cup vinegar
¼ cup oil
1 clove garlic minced
½ teaspoon ginger
Dash pepper

1 teaspoon salt
¼ teaspoon red pepper flakes
1 teaspoon or more sugar to taste
½ teaspoon Chinese Five Spice (optional)

Marinate 1-4 hours in refrigerator. Drain and grill or stirfry.

Variation:
For making hot Mongolian style beef, mix with ⅓ cup sugar, ½ teaspoon hot red pepper flakes, and 1 teaspoon 5 spice powder. Omit water, and use only 1 tablespoon lemon juice or vinegar and 2 tablespoons oil. Marinate briefly. Sauté meat, adding some reserved marinade if it becomes too dry.

Marinating in any acid may release glutamate. Use variation method if hypersensitive.

## Sweet and Sour Sauce

2 tablespoons vinegar
¼ cup honey
2 tablespoons lemon juice

1 teaspoon paprika

Heat and serve over batter fried chicken or fish.

## Herbal Vinegars

General Instructions

Wash several glass bottles. We use old vinegar and beverage bottles with plastic or cork lids. Canning bottles may be used but plastic wrap or small plastic bag must be placed between vinegar and lid. Wash and dry any favorite herbs. Place at least 4 sprigs inside bottle along with any of the following: peppercorns, peeled garlic, hot peppers, small onions, chives, etc.. Pour real apple cider vinegar into bottle and cap. Let them steep for several weeks. Attractive bottles make wonderful gifts. Tie with raffia and label. (I used what I thought was pure apple cider vinegar, but had a MSG reaction. I read the label and in small writing it said it contained carmel flavors, natural flavor, and distilled vinegar, not apple cider vinegar.

Suggested herbs: thyme, lemon thyme, tarragon, oregano, basil, rosemary, lemon balm, lemon verbena, cilantro, fennel, violets, nasturtiums, borage blossoms.

Fruit Vinegar:
Place 1 to 2 cups clean, dry fruit in each bottle. Follow directions as for herbal vinegars.
Suggested fruits: berries, lemon peel, grapes, and currants.

Vinegars may be strained after steeping. Then sprig of herb or piece of fresh fruit may be added to bottle for decoration if desired. Vinegar may also be brought to a boil before adding to bottle.

### Deb's Catsup
(Not recommended for highly sensitive individuals as the long cooking time of tomatoes plus vinegar will release free glutamate)

1 teaspoon cloves, ground
1 ½ teaspoon cinnamon
½ teaspoon hot pepper flakes or powder
2 teaspoons dry mustard
2 tablespoons salt
3 cups pure apple cider vinegar
3 cups sugar
1 - 6 lb. can tomatoes or tomato puree (Muir Glen)
2 - 14 oz. cans tomatoes or tomato puree
2 large or 3 medium onions
1 Anaheim pepper, chopped (optional)
1 bell pepper

1. If using tomatoes, puree first. Then puree the peppers and onions with 1 to 2 cups of the tomatoes.
2. Place tomatoes and remaining ingredients in a large roasting pan and bake at 300° until desired thickness, at least 3 hours. Stir occasionally. Freeze, leaving 1" headspace or process in pint jars for 15 to 20 minutes and 20 to 25 minutes for quart jars (hot water bath), leaving ¼" headspace.

Variation:
10 to 12 lbs. fresh pureed tomatoes may be substituted. To reduce cooking time, puree, then drain tomatoes in a cloth lined strainer over a bowl in the refrigerator overnight.

### Instant No-Cook Catsup
(Our favorite)

Blend in bowl:
1 - 28 oz. can Glen Muir tomato puree
⅔ cup sugar
⅓ cup + 1 teaspoon pure cider vinegar
½ teaspoon dry mustard
dash hot red pepper (powdered)
scant ½ teaspoon cinnamon
½ teaspoon dry onion granules

2 teaspoons salt
⅛ teaspoon black pepper
⅛ teaspoon cloves (optional)
dash garlic powder

Store in freezer in ½ pint freezer containers (3 to 4). Try seasoning with other spices such as nutmeg, allspice, or celery seeds.

### Homemade Sweet Mustard

In sauce pan whisk together until smooth:
½ cup water
¼ cup flour
⅓ cup sugar (may add more to taste)
¼ teaspoon salt

⅓ cup plus 1 tablespoon dry mustard
¾ cup vinegar

Cook over medium heat, stirring constantly until thickened. Store covered in refrigerator.

### Uncooked Homemade Mustard
(Made from mustard powder)

½ cup flour
¼ cup sugar
½ cup dry mustard

⅔ cup vinegar

Blend and store in glass container. Let stand for 4 days. Keep in refrigerator. If too thick, add more vinegar. Salt may also be added.

## Chinese Mustard Sauce
### Use as you would cocktail sauce.

¾ cup homemade ketchup
¼ cup water
1 to 2 teaspoons dry mustard (to taste)
½ teaspoon salt

sugar to taste

Blend and chill. Serve with shrimp, fried fish, or spareribs.

## Cranberry Sauce

2 - 12 oz. packages cleaned and sorted cranberries (fresh or frozen)
2 cups water
2 cups sugar

Combine all ingredients and bring to boil over medium heat, stirring constantly. Boil until skins

pop, about 8 to 10 minutes. Sauce will thicken as it cools. May be served warm or cold with fish or poultry.

Variation: Add 1 ⅓ cups raspberry jam, ½ teaspoon powdered ginger, and 1 teaspoon cinnamon.

## Fresh Cranberry Orange sauce for Poultry
### (A must every Thanksgiving)

In blender or processor, puree the following:
1 bag sorted and cleaned cranberries
1 ½ cups sugar
1 red or green apple quartered and cored
Zest and fruit (or sections) of 1 medium orange - Remove white pith and add orange pieces

## Marinade for Chicken, Pork, or Fish

¼ cup apple cider vinegar (or fresh lemon juice)
3 tablespoons oil
1 clove garlic minced
dash cayenne pepper (optional)
3 tablespoons water
½ teaspoon salt
¼ teaspoon pepper
2 teaspoons sugar (optional)

Combine ingredients and place in zipper bag with meat. Marinate in refrigerator, turning occasionally. Marinate at least ½ hour. Enough for 1 to 2 pounds of meat. Grill or stir fry.

* Any favorite herbs may be added to marinade.

## Onion Gravy

Saute 3 large chopped onions in 3 tablespoons oil until rich brown. Blend in processor with 1 cup water and 3 tablespoons flour until smooth. Return to pan and add salt, pepper, and 1 cup water or milk. Bring to a boil and simmer for 3 minutes.

## Vegetarian Gravy

2 cups water
½ cup cashews (raw)
2 teaspoons onion powder
1 teaspoon salt
⅛ teaspoon pepper

3 teaspoons flour

Blend in processor or blender until smooth. Bring to a boil.

## Basic Cream or White Sauce
### Use as a substitute for canned cream style soups.

2 tablespoons butter
2 tablespoons flour
1 cup milk
salt and pepper to season

Melt butter and add flour, cook, stirring on low heat for 1 minute. Add milk and whisk smooth . Cook, stirring until thickened.

Variations:
1.  Add ½ teaspoon dry mustard, 1 additional cup milk and 2 cups cheese for cheese sauce for vegetables or macaroni and cheese.

2.  Add parsely, minced onion and add to sliced potatoes for scalloped potatoes.
3.  Beat 1 or 2 eggs with 1 cup milk and add to cream sauce, then cook until thickened. Add to top of casseroles, pasta dishes, cooked vegetables, stuffed peppers, or eggplant. It's a tasty substitute for cheese. A teaspoon of parmesan cheese or nutmeg is a good addition.
4.  Add curry, paprika, garlic powder, and any favorite herbs.
5.  Add 4 large chopped mushrooms to the butter, then saute for 2 minutes before adding the flour. Thin with water to desired consistency for mushroom soup.

## Instant White Sauce Base

Blend equal parts butter and flour with mixer. Line cookie sheet with waxed paper. Place 1/4 cup scoops of mixture evenly on sheet and freeze. When solid, place in freezer bags and store in freezer.

To make sauce, place one piece in sauce pan with one cup milk. Stir and cook over medium heat until thickened. Season with salt and pepper to taste.

# DESSERTS

## Chocolate Substitutes

| | | |
|---|---|---|
| 3 tablespoons cocoa<br>1 tablespoon oil or butter | Equals | 1 square or 1 oz. of baking chocolate |
| 3 tablespoons cocoa<br>1 tablespoon oil | Equals | 1 oz. pre-melted unsweetened chocolate |
| 6 tablespoons cocoa<br>7 tablespoons sugar<br>¼ cup butter or oil | Equals | 6 oz. package semi-sweet chocolate chips or 6 squares (1 oz. each) of semi-sweet chocolate. |
| 4 tablespoons cocoa<br>4 ⅔ tablespoons sugar<br>2 ⅔ tablespoons butter | Equals | one 4 oz. bar sweet cooking chocolate bar. |

Fresh lemon juice may be used to sour milk instead of cider vinegar. When cider vinegar is used, be sure it contains no preservatives and is unpasteurized such as Hain Apple Cider Vinegar (health food stores).

Honey may be substituted for molasses in most recipes. If using stevia, use as replacement for half the sugar for best results.

## Apple Cake

2 eggs
4 cups apples, chopped with skins on
2 cups sugar
½ cup chopped nuts or raisins or both
2 teaspoons cinnamon
½ cup oil
2 cups flour
1 teaspoon salt (decrease if desired)
2 teaspoons baking soda
1 teaspoon vanilla

Mix together oil, sugar, and eggs. Add apples and nuts. Mix together dry ingredients and add to apple mixture. Stir in vanilla and pour into a greased 9" x 13" pan. Bake at 350° for 45 minutes or at 325° for 1 hour. Frost with brown sugar or white frosting. Or sprinkle ½ cup sugar mixed with 1 teaspoon cinnamon on top before baking.

May also be topped with a nutmeg sauce.

## Applesauce Spice Cake
### I get more requests for this cake recipe than any other.

Mix:
2 cups sugar
3 cups flour
2 ¼ teaspoons baking soda
½ teaspoon baking powder
1 teaspoon ginger
½ teaspoon cloves
½ to 1 teaspoon allspice
2 teaspoons cinnamon
½ teaspoon nutmeg

1 teaspoon salt

Make 3 indentations. In one, put ¼ cup molasses and ½ cup oil. In another, put 2 tablespoons vinegar. In the third, put 1 cup applesauce. Pour 1 cup water over all and whisk to blend. Add 1 to 2 cups raisins if desired. Bake in 10" x 15" pan or 9" x 13" pan at 350° for 40 to 45 minutes. Top with a brown sugar frosting or eat plain.

## Best Banana Bread

5 large ripe bananas, mashed
4 eggs
1 cup oil or butter
2 cups sugar
3 ½ cups flour
2 teaspoons baking soda
1 teaspoon salt
1 cup broken walnuts (optional)

In mixer, beat sugar and oil or butter together. Add mashed bananas and beat until well mixed. Add eggs and beat well. Add dry ingredients and mix. Fold in nuts. Pour into 2 greased loaf pans and bake at 325° for 1 hour or until center is firm to touch. Cinnamon sugar may be sprinkled on top before baking. Low fat version ingredients: 5 bananas, 4 eggs, ⅓ cup oil, 1 cup applesauce, 2 cups sugar, 4 cups flour, 3 teaspoons soda, 1 teaspoon salt.

I put batter in muffin tins and bake. Wrap and freeze individually, then place in one large freezer bag. Great for work, school, or traveling. Don't bake as long as for regular bread.

## Carrot Cake

2 cups flour
2 teaspoons baking powder
1 ½ teaspoons baking soda
1 teaspoon salt
2 teaspoons cinnamon
½ teaspoon nutmeg
2 cups sugar
1 ½ cups oil
4 eggs
2 cups grated carrots

8½ oz drained crushed pineapple or ½ cup plus 2 tablespoons applesauce
1½ cups walnuts
½ cup raisins (optional)

Mix dry ingredients. Add sugar, oil, eggs, and mix well. Add soda to pineapple and stir into batter with carrots and nuts. Fill 2 greased and floured 9" pans or one 9" x 13" pan. Bake at 350° for approximately 40 minutes. Frost with butter cream frosting.

## Delicious Pumpkin Bars

Beat together:
2 cups pumpkin puree
4 eggs
¼ cup molasses (unsulphured) or honey
¾ cup oil or ½ cup applesauce plus ¼ cup oil
¾ cup brown sugar
½ cup white sugar

Stir together and add to above mixture:
2 cups flour

2 teaspoons baking powder
1 teaspoon soda
½ teaspoon salt
½ teaspoon each, nutmeg, cloves, ginger
2 teaspoons cinnamon

Mix well. Spread batter in floured 12" x 18" pan. Bake at 350° for 25 to 30 minutes. Cool. Frost.

# Chocolate Fudge Dessert

**Batter:**
1 tablespoon butter
½ cup sugar
½ cup whole milk
1 teaspoon vanilla
1 cup flour
1 teaspoon baking powder
¼ teaspoon salt
1 ½ tablespoons cocoa

**Sauce:**
¼ cup cocoa
½ cup brown sugar
½ cup sugar

½ cup nuts
1 ¼ cups boiling water

Cream sugar and butter, then add the milk and vanilla. Blend in dry ingredients and place in an 8" greased pan.

Mix together the sauce ingredients, pour over batter, and bake for 35 minutes at 350°.

A cake-like topping will form at the top over a thick sauce.

# Fast Yellow Cake

Mix in a bowl with whisk:
2 ¼ cups flour (white or whole wheat pastry flour)
1 tablespoon baking powder
1 teaspoon salt
1 ¼ cups sugar

In another bowl, beat together:
½ cup oil (or melted butter)
½ cup whole milk
½ cup water
2 eggs

2 teaspoons vanilla or 1 teaspoon almond extract

Blend wet and dry ingredients together and pour into an ungreased 9" x 13" pan, a tube pan, or two 8" circles. Bake for 30 to 35 minutes at 350° or until inserted toothpick comes out clean. Tube pan may take longer.

Make a lemon cake by adding 2 teaspoons lemon rind or the juice of one lemon and enough water to substitute for the ½ cup milk.

# Gramma Graesser's Roman Apple Cake
## (One of my favorites as a child)

1 cup butter
1 ½ cups sugar
¼ cup brown sugar
2 ½ cups flour
2 eggs, beaten
1 teaspoon vanilla
1 teaspoon baking powder
1 teaspoon baking soda
1 cup sour milk or sour cream
2 cups diced apples (any baking type, such as Macintosh. Grannysmith, and Rome)

Topping

½ cup sugar
1 teaspoon cinnamon
½ cup nuts, chopped (optional)

1. Cream butter and sugar.
2. Add eggs and vanilla.
3. Mix dry ingredients and add alternately with sour milk.
4. Add apples and pour into a 9" x 13" pan. Sprinkle topping over mixture.
5. Bake for 45 minutes at 350°.

To sour the milk: Place 1 tablespoon cider vinegar or lemon juice in a measuring cup and add milk to make 1cup. Stir and let set a couple of minutes.

## Great Grandma's Sponge Cake
### (No shortening)

4 eggs
1 cup sugar
¼ teaspoon salt
1 cup flour
1 ½ teaspoons baking powder
⅓ cup boiling water
1 teaspoon vanilla

Beat eggs well and add sugar gradually, then beat until frothy and pale. Sift or stir together the remaining dry ingredients. Add gradually to the egg mixture. Pour in the boiling water and vanilla while stirring and mix until blended. Pour into two 8" pans or one tube pan and bake at 350° until toothpick comes out clean.

Fill layers with whipped cream or softened ice cream and top with sweetened fruit. Also good filled with cold vanilla pudding or stirred custard.

## "Hummingbird Grandpa" Cake

Named in honor of my dad who, many years ago affixed a long paper cone to his nose and flapped his hands near our humming bird feeder to the delight of our little ones watching at the window.

3 cups flour
2 cups sugar
1 teaspoon baking soda
1 teaspoon ground nutmeg
½ teaspoon salt
½ teaspoon ground cloves or allspice
¾ cup butter or oil
3 eggs
2 cups mashed banana
1 - 8 oz. can crushed Dole pineapple, undrained (or use applesauce)
2 teaspoons vanilla
¾ finely chopped walnuts or pecans (optional)

Mix together dry ingredients, except sugar. In large mixing bowl, beat sugar and butter. Then add eggs, banana, pineapple, and vanilla. Beat well. Add flour mixture and blend well. Add nuts. Mix 30 seconds. Spread in a greased and floured bundt pan or 9" X 13" pan. Bake at 325° for 1 hour 10 minutes or until inserted toothpick comes out clean. If baked in bundt pan, cool 10 minutes then remove from pan. Cool completely.

Lemon glaze:
3 cups confectioners sugar
juice of 1 lemon
2 tablespoons softened butter

Beat together and add enough water so that glaze can be drizzled over cake.

### Strawberry Variation

Substitute 1 cup pureed strawberries for the pineapple. Add 1 teaspoon baking powder, 1 tablespoon vinegar, omit the nutmeg, and add ¼ teaspoon cinnamon and ¼ teaspoon cloves instead of ½ teaspoon cloves. 1 teaspoon of almond extract may be substituted for 1 teaspoon of vanilla extract.
For the glaze: Blend ⅓ to ½ cup strawberry puree with enough confectioners sugar to make a creamy glaze to drizzle over the cake. A little softened butter may be added.

*Start with ⅓ cup puree and 3 cups sugar, then add more puree to desired consistency. To serve, spoon 1 cup sweetened sliced strawberries on bottom of each plate. Place slice of cake on top of berries.

## Lemon Meringue Pie

1. In large sauce pan mix together: 1 cup sugar, ½ cup flour, ⅛ teaspoon salt.
2. Whisk in 4 egg yolks, 1 ¾ cup water, and ½ cup flour until smooth. Cook over medium heat, stirring until it comes to a boil. Simmer for 2 minutes, stirring constantly.
3. Remove pot from heat and stir in: ½ cup fresh lemon juice (2 lemons or 1 each lemon and lime), 3 tablespoons butter, and 1 teaspoon grated lemon zest (optional).
4. Beat egg whites with ¼ teaspoon cream of tartar until frothy and gradually add ½ cup sugar, beating until stiff and shiny.
5. Pour filling into a 9" baked pie crust and spread with meringue. Bake for 10 minutes at 375° or until golden. Chill before serving.

Variation: Spread filling over a baked nut crumb crust in a 9" x 13" pan for bars. Spread with meringue and bake as above.
Nut crumb crust:
Mix together 1 cup finely chopped nuts (almonds, pecans, walnuts), ⅓ cup quick oats or wheat germ, 1 ¾ cups flour, ¾ cup sugar, ¾ teaspoon baking powder and ¼ teaspoon salt. Add 7 tablespoons melted butter and mix well. Pat in a 9" x 13" pan and bake for 10 minutes at 375°.

## Lemon Poppy Seed Cake
### (Eggless and butterless)

Mix together in large bowl:
3 cups flour
2 cups sugar
2 teaspoons baking soda
1 teaspoon baking powder
1 teaspoon salt
1 tablespoon poppy seeds (optional)

Add the following and stir:

½ cup oil
¼ cup applesauce

½ teaspoon almond extract
juice of 1 lemon plus enough water to make 2 cups of liquid

Pour into greased 9" x 13" pan and bake at 350° for 40 to 50 minutes.

Glaze:
Combine the juice of 1 lemon with enough confectioners sugar to make a thick, creamy glaze. 2 tablespoons of softened butter may be added if desired. Spread over warm cake.

## Chocolate Magic Cake

Eggless and butterless, this cake is moist and fool proof. Good without frosting, too.

Mix together in large bowl:
3 cups flour
2 cups sugar
6 tablespoons cocoa
2 teaspoons baking soda
1 teaspoon salt

Form 3 holes in dry mixture. Place one of the following ingredients in each hole: ⅔ cup oil, 2 tablespoons vinegar, and 2 teaspoons vanilla. Pour 2 cups cold water over all and whisk together until blended. Pour into ungreased 9" x 13" pan. Bake at 350° for 30 to 40 minutes to an hour or until toothpick inserted in center comes out clean. Cool and frost. Variation: For low fat version, substitute ¼ cup oil and ½ cup applesauce for the 2/3 cup oil..

## Chocolate Cake
### (Low sugar and low fat)

⅔ cup sugar
½ teaspoon white powdered stevia
2 teaspoons baking soda
3 cups flour
6 tablespoons cocoa

Stir in:

2 cups water
⅓ cup honey
½ cup applesauce
¼ cup oil
2 tablespoons fresh lemon juice or cider vinegar

Put in ungreased 9" x 13" pan. Bake at 350° for 25 to 35 minutes.

Cooked Chocolate Frosting

In sauce pan, mix 6 tablespoons cocoa, 1 cup sugar, 4 tablespoons flour, and pinch of salt. Add 1 cup hot water and 2 tablespoons butter or oil. Bring to boil, stirring. Cook until thickened. Remove from heat and beat in 1 tablespoon butter. Spread on cake. Stevia may be used for part of sugar (¼ teaspoon stevia plus ½ cup sugar).

## Apple Zucchini Pie
I invented this when I didn't have enough apples.

1 medium or 3 small zucchinis (3 cups peeled and thinly sliced)
3 baking apples, peeled, cored, and sliced (Macintosh work well)
Juice of 1 lemon
⅓ cup flour
⅔ cup sugar
½ teaspoon cinnamon
Pastry for 1 double crusted pie

Toss apples and zucchini with lemon juice. Mix the flour, sugar, and cinnamon before adding to the apples and zucchini. Fill pastry lined pie tin. Dot with 1 tablespoon butter (optional). Top with remaining pastry. Slit top. Bake at 425° for 25 minutes. Reduce heat to 400° for 15 to 20 minutes longer or until bubbly and golden.

## Chess Pie
### (Single pastry for 8 inch pie)

Mix together:
1 cup brown sugar
1 teaspoon flour

Beat in:
2 eggs
2 tablespoons milk or sour cream

1 teaspoon vanilla
½ cup melted butter

Fold in:
1 cup pecans or walnuts

Pour into shell and bake at 375° for 40 minutes.

## Fast Fruit Pies

10 flour tortillas
4 cups fruit
½ cup sugar (or more to taste)
⅓ cup flour

Suggested fruit:
berries
apricots
peaches
apples

Mix sugar and flour in small bowl. In sauce pan, simmer any fruit (fresh or frozen) until tender. Add the sugar and flour mix and stir, cooking until thick. Taste for sweetness and adjust as necessary. Fruit may be seasoned with cinnamon or other spices.

Divide fruit among tortillas and spread to ¼" of edges. Roll gently (not tightly). Secure with a toothpick where tortilla edge overlaps. Insert at an angle, to avoid puncturing bottom of tortilla. Oil a cookie sheet or large pan. Place pies on sheet, toothpick on top. Rub a little oil on tops. Bake at 375° until golden and crisp. Sprinkle with sugar or cinnamon sugar and serve. Remove toothpicks.

Variation:
Divide 1 ½ cups jam among tortillas instead of fruit. Great for snacks, school lunches, or breakfast.

## Fudge Pie

1 cup sugar
3 to 4 tablespoons cocoa
½ cup flour
½ cup butter, softened
1 teaspoon vanilla
2 eggs

Blend ingredients together and pour into glass pie plate. Microwave on medium for 15 to 17 minutes. Cut into slices while hot and top with ice cream.

## Instant Pumpkin Pie

1 cup sugar
½ cup flour
⅔ cup whole milk or half water and half cream
4 eggs
½ cup melted butter (may reduce)
¼ teaspoon salt
2 cups pumpkin
2 teaspoons cinnamon

1 teaspoon nutmeg
½ teaspoon clove
½ teaspoon ginger

Blend all ingredients in blender and pour into 9" pie pan. Bake at 350° for 60 minutes. Forms its own crust.

## Pecan Pie
### (Popular with my family)

½ cup melted butter
1 cup pecans

1 cup light brown sugar
½ cup sugar (may decrease)

1 tablespoon plus 1 teaspoon flour
2 eggs
3 tablespoons milk
1 unbaked 8" pie crust shell

Place pecans in shell. Combine ingredients and pour into shell. Bake at 375° for 15 minutes. then at 275° to 300° for 25 to 35 minutes or until center jiggles slightly when shaken.

## Rhubarb Custard Pie

Years ago I ate a piece of pie at a Nebraska cafe. This was my attempt at recreating it and it's pretty close.

5 to 6 cups chopped rhubarb (small pieces)
3 ½ cups sugar
6 eggs
½ cup + 2 teaspoons flour
dash nutmeg
1 ½ teaspoons vanilla
2 ½ cups milk
½ cup cream (may use milk instead)

Beat all but rhubarb together well. Divide rhubarb between 2 unbaked pie crusts. Pour egg mixture over both evenly. Bake at 400° for 15 minutes, then at 325° for 30 to 40 minutes or until center still jiggles when shaken. Best served slightly warm or chilled. This recipe will convert most people to rhubarb!

## Baked Peaches or Peach Tart

Peel and pit 4 peaches. Place in a dish, cut sides up, and sprinkle with brown sugar (1 to 2 tablespoons each half). Dot with butter (may omit). Bake at 350° for 10 minutes or until bubbly and hot. Serve topped with cold heavy cream or homemade sauce or pudding. A peach or apricot tart may be made by combining ⅔ cup sugar and 3 tablespoons flour. Roll pastry into a 16" circle and center in a pie plate. Sprinkle half the sugar mix on bottom. Line with 8 peach or 12 to 14 apricot halves. Sprinkle with rest of sugar and dot with butter. Fold edges of excess pastry up over fruit and bake at 375° for 25 minutes or until golden.

## Baked Peaches Over Ice Cream

Halve and pit 1 peach per person. Place in a baking dish cut side up. Sprinkle each half with 2 tablespoons brown sugar and dot with butter. Bake at 350° at least 1 hour, basting often with juices. Place 2 halves on each plate. Top with ice cream or custard sauce and drizzle juices on top.

Variation:

Try other fruit such as apples, nectarines, pineapples, apricots, and plums.

## Berry Crisp
### Topping has a wonderful chewy crisp texture.

1 cup flour
1 cup sugar
1 teaspoon baking powder
1 egg, beaten
⅓ cup melted butter

4 to 5 cups berries or favorite fruit
2 tablespoons flour
¾ cup sugar

Blend together 1 cup flour and 1 cup sugar with baking powder. Add egg and mix well. This works well in processor. Mix remaining flour and sugar and add to berries. Place berries in a large casserole dish (9" or 10") or large pie plate. Spoon topping over fruit and drizzle with butter. Bake at 375° for 45 minutes or until golden and bubbly.

## Fruit Crunch Dessert

¾ cup light or dark brown sugar
¾ cup oat meal
1 cup butter
¾ cup flour

6 to 8 cups fresh fruit cleaned and cut up (apples, berries, etc.)
¼ to ½ cup sugar depending on tartness of fruit used
½ teaspoon cinnamon

1. Mix dry ingredients and cut in butter.

2. Mix together fruit, sugar, and cinnamon. Place fruit in large dish. Sprinkle topping over all and bake at 350° for 35 minutes or until fruit is tender.

## Fruit Cobbler

1 cup sugar
1 cup flour
2 teaspoons baking powder
¾ cup milk
½ cup melted butter
1 quart bottled or canned fruit (drain and reserve juice. Use any fruit.)

1. Melt butter in 9" x 9" pan.
2. Mix dry ingredients and then whisk in milk.
3. Pour batter onto butter in pan and lay fruit on batter.
4. Pour juice over fruit and sprinkle with a little sugar (1 tablespoon). Cinnamon may be sprinkled on too, if desired.
5. Bake at 350° for 45 to 50 minutes.

## Rhubarb Crisp

2 lbs. (10 cups) fresh rhubarb cut in ½" pieces or 2 bags 16-20 oz. frozen rhubarb
1 cup sugar
2 tablespoons flour

Topping

½ cup butter
½ cup brown sugar (packed)
3 tablespoons granulated sugar
1 ½ cups flour
1/8 teaspoon cinnamon

½ cup walnuts or pecans, chopped, toasted
    (Toast in pan at 350° for 10-12 minutes.)

Mix flour and sugar and combine with rhubarb. Put in 10" deep dish pie plate or casserole dish. Beat butter and sugar. Stir in flour and cinnamon. Add walnuts. Crumble over rhubarb. Bake 35-40 minutes at 375° until bubbly and golden brown. Place foil under pan for drips.

## Brown Sugar Frosting

Boil together for 1 minute:
2 to 3 tablespoons butter
½ cup brown sugar
dash salt
¼ cup water

Let cool for 5 minutes. Beat in 2 to 3 cups confectioners sugar. Add more until desired consistency. Will thicken more as it cools. Thin with milk or water if too thick.

## Brown Sugar Pudding Dessert
### (Low fat)

1 cup brown sugar, firmly packed
3 cups water
½ tablespoon butter
½ cup sugar
1 cup flour
2 teaspoons baking powder
½ teaspoon salt
½ cup nuts, chopped

½ cup water or whole milk

In sauce pan, boil together the brown sugar, 3 cups water, and butter for 8 minutes. Pour into an 8" pan. Mix remaining ingredients and drop by spoonfuls onto hot syrup. Bake at 350° for 25 minutes. ½ cup dates or raisins may be added to batter.

## Chocolate Creme Pudding

⅔ cup semi-sweet chocolate chips
1 tablespoon sugar
1 cup milk
1 cup cream
½ teaspoon vanilla
3 egg yolks
1 cup whipped cream

In a heavy bottomed pot, mix together sugar, yolks, milk, and cream. Add chips and cook over medium heat, stirring constantly until mixture thickens. Add vanilla and pour into

bowl or custard cups. Chill and garnish with whipped cream (optional).

*Milk may be substituted for the cream in this recipe. Cocoa and butter may be substituted for chips, using the chocolate substitute chart.

This may be used as a pie filling. Three egg whites may be beaten with ½ cup sugar and spread on top. Bake meringue for 8 to 10 minutes at 425°. Watch closely to prevent burning. Chill.

## Christmas Apple, Orange, Rum, Bread Pudding

Pudding:
Break into pieces in large casserole (9" x 13") 7 pieces of bread. Drizzle ½ cube (4 tablespoons) melted butter over bread and toss lightly. Grate 2 medium apples (may keep skins on) and stir into bread along with ⅓ cup raisins. In bowl, beat 7 eggs and 3 ½ cups whole milk with ½ cup brown sugar, ½ teaspoon cinnamon, and ¼ teaspoon nutmeg. Pour over bread and put in 350° oven for 40 to 60 minutes or until knife comes out clean.

Sauce:
In saucepan, mix 4 tablespoons flour with ½ cup brown sugar. Add 2 cups water, ¼ cup butter, ¼ teaspoon or more grated orange rind, ¼ teaspoon salt, and ¼ teaspoon nutmeg. Stir and bring to boil. Take off heat and add ¼ teaspoon rum flavoring (optional) and 1 teaspoon vanilla. If too thick, add more water. Add more sugar to taste. Serve over pudding.

*Butter amount in both pudding and sauce may be decreased.

## European Clotted Cream

1.  Mix equal parts whipping cream and sour cream in glass or ceramic bowl. Cover with plastic wrap and let stand at room temperature 4 hours then chill.

2.  May flavor with some marmalade or jam and serve over fruit, scones, or short cake.

## Corn Starch Pudding
If cornstarch bothers you, use suggested flour substitution..

In medium sauce pan combine the following:
⅓ cup sugar
¼ cup corn starch
⅛ teaspoon salt

Gradually stir in 2 ¾ cups milk. Whisk until smooth. Bring to boil over medium heat, stirring constantly. Boil 1 to 2 minutes. Remove from heat and stir in 1 to 2 tablespoons butter and 1

teaspoon vanilla. Cover and refrigerate. Thickens more as it cools.

Variation:

Add 3 tablespoons cocoa to dry ingredients and increase sugar to taste.

Substitution: ⅓ cup + 1 tablespoon flour instead of corn starch.

## Mexican Rice Pudding
(For hypersensitive individuals, cooking the milk may release glutamate. It would be preferable to make a pudding first and fold it into cooked rice instead.)

1.  In large sauce pan, put 2 cups raw rice, 4 cups water, and 1 stick cinnamon. Cover and cook 30 minutes on low heat.

2.  Stir in 6 cups milk and 2 cups sugar. Cook another 20 to 30 minutes on lowest heat until about half of milk is absorbed, stirring often.

3.  Remove from heat. Add ½ stick butter and 2 teaspoons vanilla. Sprinkle with cinnamon before serving. Raisins may be added at beginning.

## Quick Fruit Rice Pudding

2 ½ cups cooked rice
½ cup water

1 pint cream, whipped
⅓ cup sugar

1 teaspoon vanilla
½ cup seedless raspberry jam

Fold all together and serve chilled. Try other fruit jams for variety.

## Fast Strawberry Mousse

3 cups sliced strawberries
¾ cup sugar
1 teaspoon vanilla extract
½ cup sour cream

In blender or food processor, combine the ingredients. Put in pan, cover with plastic wrap, and freeze. Let sit at room temperature 10 minutes before serving. Try with other berries.

## Mock Whipped Cream Frosting

1 cup butter
1 cup granulated sugar
6 tablespoons flour
1 teaspoon vanilla
½ cup milk

Beat all but vanilla and milk with mixer at highest speed for 5 minutes. Add vanilla and milk and beat 5 more minutes.

Variation:
3 tablespoons cocoa may be beaten in last 3 minutes.

## Grandma Graesser's "Maple" Frosting (Very old recipe)
(Frosts two 9" cakes)

2 egg whites beaten stiff
1 cup light brown sugar (packed)
⅓ cup water

Mix sugar and water in small pot. Cook on medium low until it threads off of spoon (8 to 10 minutes). With mixer on, slowly pour liquid into egg whites, beating until thick. A little vanilla may be added.

## Almond Puff Pastry
(Rich and tender)

1. Cut together: ½ cup butter and 1 cup flour.
2. Sprinkle with 2 tablespoons water and stir gently with fork.
3. Divide in half and pat each piece into a 12" x 3" strip, 3" apart, on an ungreased cookie sheet.
4. In a small sauce pan, heat to boiling: 1 cup water and ½ cup butter.
5. Remove from heat and quickly stir in 1 teaspoon almond extract and 1 cup flour. Stir while cooking on low heat for about 1 minute and a ball forms.
6. Remove from heat and beat in 3 eggs until smooth.
7. Divide in half and spread on strips, covering well.
8. Bake at 350° for 50 to 60 minutes or until top is crisp and brown. Cool.

9. Make a glaze of 1 ½ cups confectioners sugar, 2 tablespoons soft butter, 1 to 1 ½ teaspoons almond extract, and 1 to 2 tablespoons warm water.
10. Spread pastries with glaze and sprinkle with chopped nuts if desired.

Variation:
⅓ cup jam may be spread on bottom layer before egg mixture.

## Crepe Dessert

Beat together:
3 eggs
¾ cup whole milk
1 tablespoon oil
¾ cup flour
2 teaspoons sugar

Pour ¼ cup mixture in a hot skillet and quickly roll pan around to cover bottom. Flip and cook each side a minute or so, just until light gold.

Stack between layers of wax paper (may be frozen).

Fill with sweetened sliced fruit, jam, or ice cream. We eat these for breakfast with butter spread on first, then we add jam or cinnamon-sugar and roll up.
Batter should have a creamy consistency. Thin with water or milk if too thick.

## Grandma Suzanne Gifford's Crepes
### (or Crepe Suzies as we call them)

4 eggs
3 cups milk
3 cups flour
1 teaspoon sugar (optional)
½ teaspoon baking powder
dash salt (optional)
2 teaspoons oil (optional)

Blend or whisk together well. Pour ⅓ cup for each crepe into hot oiled saute pan and swirl to coat bottom of pan. On medium-high heat, saute about 30 seconds or until light gold. Flip with spatula and cook other side. Slide onto plate and repeat, stacking with wax paper or plastic wrap between crepes. Crepes may be filled and eaten, baked until heated through, or stored in plastic freezer bags in freezer until ready to use.

Filling I:
1 pint cottage cheese
1 teaspoon vanilla
3 tablespoons sugar
Top with sugar, sour cream, yogurt, jams, or fruit.
Most commercial cottage cheeses contain MSG. We can no longer use it. It's hard to find a better substitute. This was Grandma's main filling.

Filling II:
Spread with butter and jam or sprinkle cinnamon sugar on butter, then roll.

Filling III:
Creamed vegetables or any meat filling. Top with grated cheese or sour cream.

## Best Brownies

5 to 6 tablespoons cocoa
2 cups sugar

⅔ cup + 1 tablespoon butter
4 eggs

1 tablespoon vanilla
1 ¼ cups flour
1 teaspoon baking powder
1 teaspoon salt
2 teaspoons sour cream (optional)
1 cup nuts (optional)

In large sauce pan, melt butter. Add cocoa and remove from heat. Beat in sugar, then eggs, vanilla, and rest of ingredients. Pour into greased and floured 9" x 13" pan and bake at 350° for 20 to 30 minutes.

My daughter makes a lower fat version:

Melt together 7 tablespoons butter and 6 tablespoons unsweetened applesauce. Add 6 to 7 tablespoons cocoa and stir. Remove from heat and add 2 cups sugar, 3 eggs, 1 teaspoon vanilla and 1 teaspoon vinegar. Add 1 ¼ cups flour, ½ teaspoon salt, and 1 teaspoon baking powder. Pour in a greased and floured 9" x 13" pan. Bake at 350° for 15 minutes and check every 5 minutes until toothpick comes out clean. For a less chewy brownie, add more flour.

## Decadent Chocolate Sandwich Cookies
### You've got to try these!

2 cups sugar
½ cup butter
2 eggs
1 cup hot water
1 cup sour milk (1 tablespoon vinegar plus enough milk to make 1 cup)
1 teaspoon vanilla
4 cups flour
½ teaspoon baking powder
½ cup cocoa plus 3 tablespoons
2 teaspoons baking soda

Mix butter and sugar, then add eggs. Beat until creamy. Add water, milk, and vanilla, then mix. In separate bowl, mix flour, baking powder, cocoa, and soda. Add flour mixture to egg mixture and mix until blended. Drop by heaping tablespoons on greased cookie sheets about 2" apart. Bake for 12 to 15 minutes at 325°. Let cool and make filling.

Filling:
5 heaping tablespoons flour
1 cup milk
1 cup butter
1 teaspoon vanilla
1 cup sugar

Mix flour and milk with whisk in a sauce pan. Cook over medium heat, stirring quickly or beating with portable mixer as it cooks and thickens, to prevent lumps. Cook until very thick. Let cool, covered. In separate bowl, beat remaining ingredients together. Beat flour mixture again and add to other ingredients. Mix until fluffy and sugar is dissolved. Spread filling generously on a cookie and press another cookie on that to make sandwiches. Smaller cookies may be made to make more. These freeze well. Wrap individually or freeze in plastic containers to store. These are a cross between a filled cupcake and a sandwich cookie. Makes lots!

## Fruit Bars

These are moist and can be made with any canned fruit, such as cherries, peaches, pumpkin, or apple sauce. If using diced fruit, gently fold in last. I've also used fresh fruit and grated zucchini in this recipe.

Mix together with whisk:
1 cup oil

2 cups sugar
4 eggs

1 teaspoon vanilla
1 teaspoon baking soda
2 teaspoons cinnamon
1 teaspoon salt
2 ¼ cups flour
½ teaspoon almond extract (optional)
2 cups canned fruit, diced

Spread in a greased 17 x 11" baking sheet. Bake 25 minutes at 350°. Spread with very soft butter cream frosting while still warm.

For frosting, beat together:
 3 cups confectioners sugar
⅓ cup butter
1 teaspoon vanilla
2 to 6 tablespoons milk

Variation: Lower fat glaze - Beat together 3 cups confectioners sugar, 1 ½ teaspoons vanilla, dash salt, and enough water or milk for a soft glaze. A tablespoon of soft butter may be added if desired.

## Chewy Ginger Cookies
My kids loved these, now the grandkids do.

2 cups sugar
½ cup butter
2 eggs
½ cup unsulphured molasses or honey
4 cups flour
2 teaspoons cinnamon
1 teaspoon cloves
1 teaspoon ginger
½ teaspoon salt

4 teaspoons baking soda
1 teaspoon vanilla
1 tablespoon water

Mix sugar and butter, add eggs, water, vanilla, and molasses. Mix dry ingredients and add to egg mixture. Chill in refrigerator. Roll into balls the size of walnuts and roll in sugar. Bake at 350° for 10-12 minutes.

## Granny's Sugar Cookies

1 cup sour milk, sour cream or yogurt
1 teaspoon baking soda
1 cup oil
1 ½ cups sugar
2 eggs
1 teaspoon salt
¼ teaspoon nutmeg or cinnamon
2 teaspoons vanilla extract
3 cups flour
3 teaspoons baking powder

To sour milk, mix 1 tablespoon vinegar and enough milk to make 1 cup. Let sit for 3

minutes. Mix sour milk, cream, or yogurt and soda in small bowl and set aside. In a large bowl or mixer, blend oil, sugar, and eggs. Add the sour milk and soda and mix well. Add flour, salt, nutmeg, vanilla and baking powder, then mix well. Cover and refrigerate overnight. Next morning, preheat oven to 400°. Best cooked on non-stick cookie sheets. Drop by large tablespoons. Sprinkle tops with sugar. Bake for 5 minutes or until they are still white, not golden. Let sit on hot cookie sheet for 3 minutes and then remove to cool. (I have made these without refrigerating first and they bake up well.)

## Grandma Graesser's "Chew" Bread
The correct name for this is "Jew" bread, but Grandma mispronounced it.

3 eggs

2 tablespoons milk

1 cup sugar
7 tablespoons flour
1 teaspoon baking powder
1 cup walnuts
2 cups dates

Beat eggs until light in color and thick. Add milk and sugar and beat well. Cut up dates and nuts. Sprinkle them with flour and separate them with fingers. Add dates, nuts, and flour mixture to egg mixture and fold together gently. Pour in greased 9" pan. Bake at 350° for 25 minutes. A wonderful chewy confection.

## Lemon Squares

1.  Blend together 1 cup flour, ½ cup butter, and ¼ cup confectioners sugar. Press into a 9" square pan. Bake at 350° for 15 minutes.

2.  Beat together 2 eggs, ¼ teaspoon salt, ½ teaspoon baking powder, 1 cup sugar, and 2 tablespoons fresh lemon juice. Lemon zest may be added.

3.  Pour mixture over crust and bake 15 to 20 more minutes. Cool and cut into bars.

## Oatmeal Cookies

1 cup butter
1 cup brown sugar
1 cup white sugar
2 eggs
1¾ cups flour
1½ teaspoon baking soda
1 teaspoon salt
3 cups oatmeal (quick or rolled)
1 teaspoon vanilla
1 tablespoon water

Cream together the butter and sugars and beat in the eggs.
Add the remaining ingredients, mix, and drop by tablespoons on a cookie sheet. Flatten with a fork dipped in cold water. Bake at 375° for 10 - 12 minutes. Raisins or nuts may be added.

Variation: Instead of 1 cup butter, use ½ butter and ½ oil or applesauce. All white sugar may be substituted or 1 cup sugar plus ½ teaspoon stevia.

## Oatmeal Honey Cookies
### (Mix in the pot)

1 ¼ cups flour
1 teaspoon baking soda
½ teaspoon salt
¾ cup butter
⅔ cup sugar
⅓ cup honey
1 egg
1 teaspoon vanilla

2 cups oatmeal
1 cup nuts

Melt butter in pot. Add sugar, honey, egg, and vanilla. Then stir in flour and remaining ingredients. Drop by spoonfuls on greased pan. Bake at 350° for 10 to 12 minutes.

## Old Fashioned Oatmeal Refrigerator Cookies

1 cup butter
1 cup brown sugar
1 cup sugar
2 eggs
1 teaspoon vanilla
1 ½ cups flour
1 teaspoon salt

1 teaspoon baking soda
3 cups oatmeal
1 cup nuts, chopped

Mix ingredients and roll into logs. Chill and slice thin. Bake at 350° for 8 minutes.

## Wonderful Peanut Butter Cookies
### (Makes lots for freezing)

2 cups butter or shortening
2 cups peanut butter
2 cups sugar
2 cups brown sugar
4 eggs
5 cups flour
2 teaspoons baking powder
1 tablespoon baking soda
1 teaspoon salt

1. Cream butter, sugar, and peanut butter.
2. Add eggs and mix well.
3. Add dry ingredients and mix.
4. Roll in large balls (1 ¼") and place on ungreased cookie sheet (12 per large pan). May flatten with a fork dipped in sugar.
5. Bake at 375° for 10- 12 minutes.

## Raisin or Pecan Tarts
### (Makes 24 small tarts)

Crust:
1 cup flour
¼ cup confectioners sugar
½ cup butter, softened

Mix until crumbly and press in small (tiny) tins.

Filling:
1 egg

¾ cup brown sugar
1 teaspoon vanilla
dash salt
½ cup chopped pecans

Put a scant teaspoon in each shell. Bake for 20 minutes at 350°.
*May use bottom of muffin tins for a larger tart. Add more filling.

## Stove Top Quickie Cookies

1 cup sugar
2 tablespoons cocoa
¼ cup (½ stick) butter
¼ cup whole milk
½ teaspoon vanilla
¼ cup (4 tablespoons) peanut butter
1 ½ cups oatmeal, uncooked

½ cup toasted wheat germ or nuts, or omit and use 2 cups oatmeal total

Combine sugar, cocoa, butter, and milk in a sauce pan. Boil over medium heat for 1 minute. Stirring constantly , fold in remaining ingredients. Drop by teaspoonfuls on wax paper and let harden.  Work quickly .  Store in air tight container.

For less saturated fat, substitute 3 tablespoons applesauce for 2 tablespoons of the butter.  Add 1 tablespoon more cocoa and boil for 2 minutes.

## Favorite Old Fashioned Soft Sugar Cookies
### (Almost as good as Grandma's)

1 cup butter (may use oil)
1 ½ cups sugar
3 eggs
1 cup sour cream or yogurt (sour milk may be used - not as rich a cookie)
1 tablespoon vanilla
¼ teaspoon almond extract (optional)
zest of 1 lemon (optional)
1 teaspoon salt
1 teaspoon baking soda
2 teaspoons baking powder
6 cups flour

Cream butter and sugar and add eggs, vanilla, sour cream, almond extract, and zest. Mix in dry ingredients. Roll ¼" thick. Cut into circles or shapes. Bake at 350° for 8 to 10 minutes on lightly greased cookie sheet. Frost with butter cream frosting after cooling, if desired.

Variation I: Roll into ¼" thick rectangle.  Brush with milk and sprinkle with sugar and/or cinnamon.  With knife or pizza cutter, cut into 2" squares and bake as above.

Variation II: Roll into logs, chill and slice.

## Microwave Jam Bars
### (May be baked in oven)

¾ cup butter (half may be oil)
1 ½ cups flour
1 cup brown sugar
1 teaspoon baking powder
½ teaspoon salt
1 ½ cups quick oats
1 cup finely chopped pecans or walnuts
12 oz. jam (about 1 ¼ cups) raspberry, strawberry, or blackberry (cooked dates or apricots may be substituted for jam)

Place butter in a 9" x 13" glass pan.  Cover and melt in microwave.  Mix dry ingredients and toss with butter in pan.  Remove half of the mixture. Pat remaining crumbs in pan evenly.  Microwave on medium high for 6 minutes, turning pan once. Cover crumbs with jam and sprinkle on remaining crumbs.  Pat down gently.  Microwave on medium high for 8 to 10 minutes, turning pan once. Variation:  Bars may be assembled all at once and baked at 350° for 18 to 20 minutes.

## Italian Lemon Ice

3 cups water
2 cups sugar
1 ½ cups fresh lemon juice
1 teaspoon lemon zest
1 teaspoon vanilla (optional)

Mix ingredients together until sugar is dissolved. Use ice cream maker or freeze in a bowl, stirring every 35 minutes until firm enough to scoop.

## Pasta Fruit Salad
Use as dessert or salad.

1 - 6 oz. box cooked and rinsed tiny egg pastina pasta (looks like tapioca).
4 cups fruit cocktail, homemade or use fresh cut up fruit such as grapes, bananas, berries, apples, pineapple
1 pint whipping cream (whipped)

In sauce pan, beat 2 egg yolks, 1 cup sugar, pinch salt, and juice from drained fruit cocktail plus water to measure 1 cup (or 1 cup water if using fresh fruit) and 3 tablespoons flour. Bring to a boil and stir, cooking untill thickened (2 minutes). Stir in the juice of ½ lemon. Stir egg mixture into the fruit and then gently fold in the whipped cream. Serve chilled.

## Non-fat Meringues

Line 2 cookie sheets with brown paper (grocery bags work, print side down). Beat 4 egg whites until very stiff. Beat in ¾ cup sugar a little at a time until meringue holds its shape well. Beat in 2 teaspoons vanilla and then gently fold in 4 more tablespoons sugar. Drop by spoonfuls onto brown paper or use a pastry tube. Bake at 250° for 50 to 60 minutes or until dry. Cool and store in a tight container. These store well for weeks. If they stick to paper, rub back of paper with a damp cloth. May be eaten plain or topped with fruit and/or French cream sauce (found in Dessert Sauces and Syrups section).

# DESSERT SAUCES AND SYRUPS

(Remember, cooking milk may release free glutamate. The ultra-sensitive should watch for any reactions as a result.)

## Chocolate Sauce

In sauce pan, combine:
½ cup whole milk
½ cup cream or milk
½ cup sugar
¼ cup cocoa
3 tablespoons butter or oil (or half of each)
dash salt (optional)

Whisk and cook over low heat until mixture just comes to a simmer. Remove from heat and add vanilla. Good over cake, ice cream, or berries.

## Chocolate Syrup

For use in drinks, sodas, and ice cream.

1⅓ cups cocoa powder (may use less)
2¼ cups granulated sugar
¼ teaspoon salt
1⅓ cups hot water
1½ teaspoons vanilla

Mix dry ingredients in heavy sauce pan. Add water and boil for 10 minutes. Stir in vanilla. Store in refrigerator 10 to 12 weeks.

For hot fudge sauce, combine 1 ½ cups syrup with 6 tablespoons butter and cook over low heat for 5 minutes or until smooth and shiny.

## French Cream Sauce
### (For fresh fruit and cake)

6 egg yolks
2 cups whole milk
½ cup sugar
1 teaspoon vanilla
½ teaspoon grated lemon rind (optional)

Mix together ingredients, except vanilla, and cook in double boiler until thickened and coats back of spoon. Add vanilla. Chill and serve over berries or other fruit.

## Gram's Nutmeg Sauce

1 cup white or brown sugar
2 ½ cups water
¼ cup flour
dash salt
2 tablespoons butter

1 teaspoon vanilla
¼ teaspoon nutmeg (may add more)

Mix salt, flour, sugar, and nutmeg together well in a sauce pan. Add water and bring to a boil.

Boil for 2 minutes, adding more water if too thick. Remove from heat and add butter and vanilla. Serve over apple dumplings, cobblers, pies, bread pudding, or cakes such as apple cake.

## Hot Fudge Sauce

In a sauce pan, put ⅓ cup sugar, dash salt, 5 to 6 tablespoons cocoa, and 2 tablespoons flour, then stir to blend. Add ½ cup water and ⅔ cup milk. Bring to boil stirring constantly for 1 to 2 minutes. Remove from heat and add 1 teaspoon vanilla and 1 tablespoon butter (optional). Serve on ice cream or cake. Add more sugar for a sweeter sauce.

Less milk and more water may be used for a darker sauce.

## Pancake Syrup

Boil together 2 cups brown sugar, 2 cups white sugar, ¼ teaspoon salt, and 2 cups water until sugar dissolves. Add 2 teaspoons vanilla (optional). Bottle and refrigerate.

# DRESSINGS

A word about oil and vinegar. Not all are created equally. I have reacted to some oils that contain sulfites or other additives. Also many individuals react to vinegars. Experiment with fresh citrus juices or plain rice vinegar.

## Boiled Salad Dressing

Combine in heavy sauce pan:
2 teaspoons sugar
1 teaspoon salt
1 teaspoon mustard
2 tablespoons flour
Dash cayenne pepper

Add 1 beaten egg and mix well. Add 2 tablespoons butter or oil, ¼ cup vinegar or fresh lemon juice, and ¾ cup water. Cook over low heat, stirring constantly until thickened. Refrigerate.

For sweeter salad dressing add more sugar (or honey).

## Cooked Mayonnaise

2 large egg yolks
2 tablespoons cider vinegar or fresh lemon juice
2 tablespoons water
1 ½ teaspoons sugar (may reduce)
¼ teaspoon dry mustard or ½ teaspoon prepared
¼ teaspoon salt
¼ teaspoon pepper
¼ cup vegetable oil

In small pot, whisk together all ingredients but oil. Over low heat, bring to just boiling, stirring constantly. Remove from heat and let cool completely. Place mixture in a blender or processor and blend at highest speed. Gradually add oil until mixture is thick and smooth. Refrigerate. Use within three days.

## Pioneer Mayonnaise
Great to use in potato, macaroni, chicken, and sea food salads.

¼ cup plus 1 teaspoon sugar
2 tablespoons flour
3 eggs
⅛ teaspoon dry mustard or ½ teaspoon prepared
¼ cup oil
½ teaspoon salt
½ cup vinegar
1 ½ cups water

dash cayenne pepper
dash black pepper

Mix all ingredients in sauce pan with whisk. Bring to boil and cook for 1 to 2 minutes, stirring until thickened. Store in quart glass jar in refrigerator.

*Use 3 tablespoons flour for thicker mayonnaise.

138

## Cooked Salad Dressing

1 egg
2 tablespoons sugar
1 ½ teaspoons salt
¾ teaspoon dry mustard
¼ teaspoon paprika
¼ cup vinegar
¾ cup oil
1 cup water
⅓ cup flour or ¼ cup cornstarch

Put egg, sugar, seasonings, vinegar, and oil in mixing bowl. Do not stir. Blend flour or cornstarch and ½ cup cold water in a sauce pan. Add remaining water and cook over low heat, stirring until thick and bubbly. Add hot mixture to remaining ingredients and whisk briskly. Mixture may be returned to heat and just brought to boil to ensure egg is cooked.

## Banana Dressing for Fruit Salad

2 ripe bananas
2 tablespoons sugar
2 tablespoons brown sugar
1/4 cup honey
2 tablespoons lemon or lime juice
1 cup whipping cream (optional)

Blend together in blender or food processor the above ingredients except for cream.
Whip cream stiffly and add to other ingredients. If desired, sour cream may be substituted. If omitting cream, dilute ingredients with a little water.

## Strawberry Vinegar Dressing
### (Lovely color and delicate flavor)

Steep 2 cups of halved strawberries in 4 cups of cider vinegar for 2 weeks. Strain into a clean bottle.

To make dressing, mix:
1 cup strawberry vinegar
1 ½ cups oil
¼ to ⅓ cup honey
½ teaspoon salt

Blend or shake in jar and serve over tossed greens or fruited salad. This dressing may be made sweeter to taste with more honey or sugar or made milder by adding a little water.

## Citrus Dressings

I.
¾ cup orange juice - fresh
¼ cup olive or vegetable oil
2 tablespoons lemon juice
2 teaspoons honey or sugar
1 teaspoon prepared mustard
¼ teaspoon salt
⅛ teaspoon pepper
Blend and refrigerate.

II.
½ cup vegetable oil
¼ cup vinegar
2 tablespoons honey
¼ teaspoon dry mustard
¼ teaspoon salt
¼ cup orange or grapefruit juice
Blend and refrigerate.

## Craig's Favorite Dressing

My son likes this so much, that I double and store it in two plastic salad dressing bottles in refrigerator.

1 cup oil
½ cup plain apple cider vinegar
1 teaspoon dry mustard
½ teaspoon garlic granules or 1 clove garlic peeled
1 teaspoon paprika (Hungarian style)
4 tablespoons fresh lime or lemon juice
6 tablespoons honey or sugar
½ teaspoon salt

dash pepper

Whisk together. If using fresh garlic, cut in half and place a piece in each bottle. Lasts for weeks in refrigerator (if not consumed before that).

P.S. Makes a delicious dressing for pasta or taco salad. May decrease sugar if desired.

## Creamy Vinaigrette
### (Enough for 1 salad)

2 tablespoons vinegar
4 tablespoons olive oil
2 tablespoons sour cream or yogurt
salt and pepper to taste

Mix and toss with salad.

Variations:

Add garlic powder.
Add ½ teaspoon mustard.
Use herb or fruit vinegars. Raspberry is very good.
May sweeten with sugar or honey.

## Cucumber Salad Dressing

1 cup whole milk + 1 tablespoon vinegar or fresh lemon juice - set aside, or 1 cup whole sour cream
1 medium cucumber, peeled, sliced, minced, or processed smooth
1 clove garlic, minced
2 teaspoons fresh dill (or 1 teaspoon dried)
¼ teaspoon salt
Dash pepper
Dash cayenne pepper - optional

1 teaspoon vinegar
sugar to taste (optional)

Mix together. More vinegar may be added if more tartness is desired.
Good on mixed greens or potato salad.

Tip: Sprinkle garlic clove on cutting board with 1 tablespoon water, then mince. Garlic won't stick to knife.

## Dill Salad Dressing
### (A lot like ranch-style dressing)

1 cup plain yogurt or 1 cup sour cream
⅛ teaspoon garlic powder
⅛ teaspoon onion powder
½ teaspoon dry parsley
½ teaspoon dry dill
¼ teaspoon thyme
Dash cayenne pepper

salt and pepper to taste
1 teaspoon oil
½ teaspoon vinegar
Dash of sugar or to taste

Blend ingredients and use on tossed salads, as dip, or on fish.

## French Dressing I

Mix together:
½ cup oil
¼ cup vinegar or lemon juice
¼ teaspoon salt
½ teaspoon paprika

2 teaspoons sugar
Dash cayenne
1 tablespoon homemade catsup (optonal)
1 teaspoon prepared mustard (optional)

## French Dressing II

½ cup sugar
½ cup oil
½ cup vinegar
⅓ cup homemade catsup
1 teaspoon paprika

½ teaspoon dry mustard or 1 teaspoon prepared mustard
¼ teaspoon garlic powder or 1 clove cut in half
½ teaspoon salt
1 to 2 teaspoons lemon juice (optional)

Mix and store in jar in refrigerator.

## French Vinaigrette

2 tablespoons vinegar
1 tablespoon water
¼ teaspoon dry mustard
½ teaspoon salt
dash pepper

Whisk ingredients together. Then, just before tossing, whisk in 3 tablespoons oil. Toss with salad just before serving. Makes enough for one salad.
Variations: Use flavored vinegars, different oils, minced garlic, herbs, homemade catsup, sugar or honey, or anchovy paste.

## Grandma's Celery Seed Dressing

½ cup sugar
2 tablespoons lemon juice

1 teaspoon dry mustard
1 teaspoon salt

dash pepper
2 tablespoons minced onion
⅓ cup apple cider vinegar
1 cup oil
1 teaspoon celery seed

Blend sugar, juice, mustard, salt, pepper, onion, and half the vinegar. While whisking, add the oil and remaining vinegar. Stir in the seeds. Sometimes, she would add 1 teaspoon paprika for color.

## My Green Goddess Dressing
### (Makes 2 cups)

Place in blender or processor:
1 avocado cut into chunks
juice of ½ lemon
1 clove garlic
¼ teaspoon salt
pepper
½ cup olive oil

¼ teaspoon thyme, dry
½ teaspoon dill, dry
½ to 1 teaspoon sugar

Process until smooth. While processing, add ⅓ cup milk. More may be added if too thick. Add more salt to taste.

## Mustard Cream Dressing
### (Old Recipe)

⅔ cup sour cream
¼ teaspoon salt
Juice of ½ lemon
1 teaspoon mustard

2 teaspoons sugar

Blend together and serve on vegetables or salads.

## Old Fashioned Salad Dressing

½ cup whipping cream or sour cream
⅓ cup vinegar
1 ½ teaspoons sugar
1 teaspoon salt

1/8 teaspoon black pepper

Combine and use in tossed green salads, potato salads, or pasta salads. Add more sugar to taste.

## Poppy Seed Dressing
### (Great with fruit and tossed salads)

1 cup honey
1 cup vinegar
1 cup vegetable oil
1 tablespoon poppy seeds

Mix together and pour ¼ to ½ cup over 1 head torn lettuce or spinach, 3 tablespoons diced sweet onion and any of the following ingredients: Sliced cucumbers, grapes, orange slices, mushrooms, cubed cheese, or avocados. Store rest in refrigerator.

## Red Pepper Vinaigrette

1 cup oil
½ cup vinegar
3 tablespoons of any blend of ground peppers such as paprika, ancho, cayenne, and chili powder

1 teaspoon salt
1 teaspoon sugar

Blend together. Good on salads, baked fish, or as a marinade.

## Basic Vinaigrette

This dressing is rather tart, so use it sparingly. Leave the garlic whole if you prefer a more subtle flavor. Substitute cider vinegar and plain prepared or dry mustard (1 teaspoon) if sulfite sensitive. Dijon style mustard and balsamic vinegar contain wine, which contains sulfites.

⅔ cup olive oil
⅔ cup canola oil
⅔ cup balsamic vinegar
2 teaspoons Dijon style mustard
1 clove garlic peeled and halved
Salt and freshly ground black pepper to taste

Put all ingredients in a glass jar. Cover tightly and shake until well blended. Store in refrigerator. Shake before using. Sweeten if desired.
Makes 2 cups.

## Herb Vinaigrette

Prepare Basic Vinaigrette, adding ¼ cup tightly packed minced fresh herb leaves such as parsley, basil, dill, cilantro or mint or a combination. Or add 1 teaspoon dried tarragon, oregano or basil.

## Onion Vinaigrette

Prepare Basic Vinaigrette, adding 2-3 tablespoons each thinly sliced scallions and snipped chives.

# FREEZER OR CANNED GOODS

Since tomatoes are naturally high in glutamate, the longer the cooking process used with them, the more likely free glutamate will be formed. Tomatoes can be pureed and strained in a cloth lined strainer over a bowl overnight in the refrigerator. This will thicken them without the long cooking required otherwise. Boil the other vegetables until tender before adding the pureed tomatoes. Be sure to use apple cider vinegar that contains no preservatives and is unpasteurized such as Hain Apple Cider Vinegar. Some highly sensitive individuals should avoid all fermented products which includes all vinegars. Substitute fresh lemon juice.

## Rhubarb Relish

8 cups chopped rhubarb
8 cups chopped onions
4 cups vinegar
6 cups sugar (brown is good in this recipe)
2 teaspoons each of cinnamon, cloves, allspice, and ginger.

1 ½ teaspoons black pepper
2 tablespoons salt

Place ingredients in pot and simmer until thick. Ladle into pint jars leaving ¼ inch head space. Process 10 minutes in hot water bath.

## General Directions for Cooked No Pectin Jam
### Usually 3 cups sugar to 4 cups fruit is a good measurement.

1. Grind, chop, or puree 12 cups fruit and place in large pot (heavily bottomed).
2. Bring to a boil.
3. Heat 9 to 12 cups sugar (depending on tartness) in microwave in a bowl and then add to boiling fruit. Microwave step may be skipped but will take longer to boil.
4. Boil for 20 minutes or until thickened. Stir occasionally to prevent sticking (medium heat). Skim foam. ( Adding ¼ teaspoon butter to batch will cut down on foam.)
5. Pour to within ¼" of jar top, wipe edges, and seal.
6. Process quarts 20 to 30 minutes in hot water bath (10 to 15 minutes for pints). (Can invert for 5 minutes, then place right side up and omit water bath. Check seals after 1 hour.) For low pectin or too ripe fruit, process a couple of under-ripe apples with skins on to a puree, then add to fruit. Lemon juice may also be added.

## No Cook, No Pectin Freezer Jam

In mixer, blend equal parts fruit and sugar. Use juice of half a lemon for every 6 cups of fruit. Mix until sugar is dissolved. Leave 1" head space in freezer containers and store in freezer. More sugar than fruit may be used with very tart fruit.

## Grape Jam

3 lbs. grapes, washed and stemmed
3 lbs. sugar
½ cup water

Boil ingredients for 30 minutes. Put through strainer and pour into clean jars. Seal and process for 10 minutes for half pints or pints.

Concord grapes are most flavorful.

## Canned Fruit Cocktail

Peel and cube:
6 peaches
6 pears (or Asian pears)
1 ripe cantaloupe
2 cups fresh or canned pineapple in chunks and drained

Place in a bowl and add 1 lb. seedless grapes, washed and stemmed, and 2 cups pitted cherries if available. For every 4 cups of fruit, add ½ cup of sugar and mix. Refrigerate 6 hours or over night. Pack into sterile pint jars. Leave ¼ inch head space and process in hot water bath for 20 minutes.

*I have made this reducing sugar to 1 tablespoon sugar per 4 cups fruit.

*Can also be packed into quart freezer bags and frozen. Juice of 1 lemon may be added for flavor and color retention.

## Crockpot or Oven Apple Butter

7 cups homemade or unsweetened applesauce
2 cups pure apple cider
1 ½ cups honey or sugar
1 teaspoon cinnamon
1 teaspoon ground cloves (may use ½ teaspoon allspice plus ½ teaspoon cloves)
1 teaspoon cider vinegar

Mix ingredients in a crockpot or roasting pan. Cover and set on low for crockpot and cook about 12 to 14 hours. Or roast for 6 to 8 hours uncovered in oven at 250° to 300°, stirring occasionally. Butter should be thick and brown. Place in hot pint jars and process for 10 minutes in hot water bath or freeze, leaving 1" head space. Double, and give as holiday gifts, along with plates of muffins.

Variation:
1. Spices may be omitted.
2. Omit cider and use 8 cups applesauce plus 1 cup water.

## Flash Frozen Fruit

Clean whole berries, cherries, and other small fruit. Pit and halve apricots or cut larger fruit into quarters. Line cookie sheets with wax paper and place fruit on pan in single layer. Deeper pans may be used and fruit may be layered between sheets of wax paper. Place in freezer and when solid, peel from paper and place in gallon or quart size freezer bags. Label. This is wonderful when only a small amount of fruit is needed since individual pieces remain separate in bag. Whole tomatoes may be frozen the same way.

## Dill Pickles
### (6 quarts)
### (These are so good, you'll want to double recipe)

6 cups real cider vinegar
6 cups water (not softened water)
½ cup salt (pickling)
½ to 1 cup sugar

6 large cloves garlic (use 9 if small)
mustard seeds
6 lbs. pickling cucumbers (3" to 4" long)
whole pepper corns

fresh dill, 6 heads divided into it's flowerets

In stainless steel pot, bring vinegar, sugar, water, and salt to a boil then reduce to lowest heat. Slice garlic cloves in half lengthwise and place 2 halves, along with 2 flowerets of dill, 1 teaspoon mustard seeds, and 2 pepper corns into each of 6 clean wide mouth quart jars. Place cleaned cucumbers (may be sliced in half lengthwise) firmly into jars. A little of the stem may remain

on the cucumber. Top with another dill floweret and pour hot vinegar mixture over cucumbers leaving ½" headspace. Release air bubbles by running narrow plastic spatula between cucumbers and jar sides. Wipe rim, seal with lid and band, and process in water bath for 15 minutes. Begin timing when water comes to a continuous, slow, steady boil.
Variation: Spicy dill. Add 1 to 2 whole dry or fresh cayenne or other small pepper to each jar.

## End of Summer Garden Relish
### (Great for using up the last of the garden's bounty)

18 cups of finely chopped vegetables
Suggested vegetables:
Green and/or ripe tomatoes, bell peppers, chilies, onions, cucumbers, zucchini, cabbage.

Place in a large pot with:
3 cups vinegar
½ teaspoon celery seed
1 teaspoon mustard seed
1 teaspoon cinnamon
½ teaspoon cloves
¼ teaspoon nutmeg
½ teaspoon ginger
2 teaspoons salt
¼ teaspoon pepper

Simmer 15 minutes or until slightly thickened. Add 2 to 4 cups sugar to taste. Simmer 20 to 30

more minutes until thick, stirring often. Ladle into pint bottles with ⅛" head space and water bath process for 20 minutes or cool and ladle into freezer containers and freeze leaving 1" headspace. If freezing, vinegar amount can be decreased by half.

Remember, if tomatoes are overripe or are cooked for long periods of time, free glutamate can be created.

*To make corn relish from this recipe, divide finished batch in half. To one half the relish, add 2 cans drained corn, 3 stalks chopped celery, 1 chopped bell pepper, ½ cup more vinegar, ½ teaspoon curry powder, ½ teaspoon tumeric, 1 teaspoon more mustard seed. Simmer together 7 minutes longer and process as for above relish.

## Freezer Tomato Sauce

4 large onions, chopped
4 cloves garlic, minced or 2 teaspoons powder
24 ripe tomatoes (10 lbs.)
2 bell peppers, seeded and chopped
1 tablespoon salt
1 teaspoon pepper
5 to 6 stalks celery, chopped (optional)
1 teaspoon paprika
2 teaspoons dry basil

1 teaspoon dry oregano
1 cup sugar

Bring to boil. Simmer until desired thickness and freeze in 2 cup portions. Tomatoes may be pureed and strained in cloth lined strainer over bowl in refrigerator overnight to thicken and reduce boiling time.

# Homemade Tomato Soup Base
## (Can or freeze)

17 lbs. tomatoes
2 medium onions
2 small anaheim peppers or 1 bell pepper
(optional)
5 stalks celery
½ cup fresh parsley
½ cup coarse salt (pickling or Kosher)
1 cup sugar
1 cup flour
½ teaspoon allspice
½ teaspoon cinnamon
½ teaspoon cloves
¼ teaspoon black pepper
½ cup butter or oil

*For a more bland soup base like commercial canned soup, omit all vegetables (except tomatoes), parsley, and spices. Season with salt and pepper. A pinch of cinnamon and allspice is good, though.

Core tomatoes and cut into eighths. Chop onions, peppers, celery, and parsley. Place vegetables in a large heavy stock pot or 2 pots, dividing all ingredients equally between them. Add salt and bring to a boil. Simmer on low for 1 hour. Puree vegetables. I use a hand held Braun blender and process in pots. Place the puree in a large kettle. Mix the sugar and flour and whisk into the hot mixture. Add spices, seasonings, and butter and whisk smooth. Bring to boil and simmer on low heat for 3 to 4 minutes. Freeze or pour into 12 pint jars, leaving ½ inch head space. Process for 15 minutes in hot water bath.

To serve, add approximately 1 cup water or milk to each pint of soup base. Use as a base for chili or vegetable soup or casseroles.

Variation:
Spices may be increased or omitted. Again, to cut down on boiling time, strain the tomatoes first. Cook the other vegetables in enough water to cover until tender, then puree. Add the tomatoes with the sugar and flour and continue as recipe directs.

# Nada's Sweet Relish

4 cups chopped onions
4 cups chopped cabbage
2 cups chopped bell peppers (red and green)
8 cups chopped cucumbers
8 cups green tomatoes
4 cups vinegar
3 cups sugar
3 tablespoons salt
1 tablespoon tumeric

Grind or process all vegetables. Place in large bowl. Cover with water and add salt. Let stand 4 hours or over night at room temperature. Drain. Place in a large pot with vinegar, tumeric and sugar. Cook until thick and place in pint jars with ¼ inch head space. Seal and process 12 minutes.

# Spaghetti Sauce for Freezing

2 - 6 lb. 10 oz. cans tomato puree or diced tomatoes (or use 40 fresh tomatoes, diced or pureed)
2 onions, chopped
2 green peppers, chopped

1 Anaheim pepper, chopped (optional)
4-5 cloves garlic, minced
⅓ cup sugar (may add more or less to taste)
1 tablespoon salt
½ teaspoon red pepper flakes (optional)

2 teaspoons chili powder
3 tablespoons dry parsley
3 tablespoons dry basil
1 ½ teaspoons dry oregano

Saute onions, peppers, and garlic in ¼ cup olive oil. Place in large pot with tomatoes, herbs, and spices. Simmer 20 minutes. Taste and adjust seasonings (I add a little sugar). Ladle into freezer containers or jars, leaving 2" head space in jars, 1" in plastic. Freeze up to 6 months.

Freezing fresh ground beef:

Divide fresh ground beef into desired portions and place back in a freezer bag. Remove air and seal. Then spread and press meat until it is ½" thick or less. Meat will stack well in freezer and defrost quickly.

Freezing cooked ground beef:

To have cooked beef on hand for quick meals, fry up several pounds and place in a single layer on cookie sheets. Freeze and then place in freezer bags. Fat will solidify and can be left behind before bagging.

## MAIN DISHES

### Best Bean Burritos

1. Process fresh tomatoes to make 2 cups liquid.
2. Put the tomatoes in small pot. Add 3 1/2 tablespoons of flour, 1 teaspoon salt, 1/4 teaspoons oregano, 2 teaspoons chili powder, 1/4 teaspoons cumin, 1/8 teaspoons garlic powder, dash onion powder, 1 1/2 teaspoons sugar, dash pepper.
3. Beat with whisk. Can add more chili powder if needed, to taste.
4. Bring to a boil, stirring all the time until thickened.
5. Spread this on a warm tortilla, top with warm refried beans and cheese. Serve with salsa, sour cream and fruit.

### Calzones

Use Favorite French bread recipe.

Roll dough into 2 to 3 inch balls and flatten into 7 inch circles. Fill with ⅔ cup filling on ½ of circle. Rub edge with water. Fold in half and pinch shut. Let rise 20 minutes. Bake at 375° for 18 to 20 minutes. Serve spaghetti sauce on side or over calzones.

Filling

1 lb. Italian sausage (recipe in meat section). Ground beef may be used. To season, add ½ teaspoon fennel, dash of cayenne pepper, salt, and pepper.
½ cup chopped onion
3 cloves garlic, minced
1 small box frozen spinach, thawed and drained well (or use 7 cups fresh, chopped)
1 cup shredded mozzarella or thick cream sauce
½ teaspoon oregano
½ teaspoon basil
1 chopped tomato drained
salt and pepper to taste

Fry together the sausage, onion, and garlic until cooked well. Drain. Add spinach, seasonings, and tomato. Simmer together 5 minutes. Remove from heat and add cheese, tossing lightly. 1 medium chopped zucchini may be added to saute.

## Chicago Pizza
### (A family standard)

Use ½ Favorite French bread recipe for 2 large pizza crusts. Roll out to fit two 16" rounds. Oil pans and sprinkle with cornmeal. I use entire bread recipe and make 3 pizzas, freezing extra for later use.

Divide between and layer on crusts in the following order:

1. Broken up chunks of cheddar mozzarella cheese. About 1 to 1 ½ lbs.
2. Meat of choice or omit (I use Italian sausage recipe. Sprinkle cooked sausage evenly over pizzas.)
3. 4 to 6 cups fresh chopped tomatoes, drained.
4. Sprinkle with the following seasonings: salt, pepper, oregano, basil. Chopped fresh herbs are especially good.
5. Drizzle lightly with olive oil and bake 20 minutes at 425°.
6. Can sprinkle lightly with imported romano cheese.
7. Red pepper flakes can be sprinkled on sparingly.

*Note: Pizzas will appear sparsely covered but toppings will cook and spread. Also, any favorite toppings may be added after tomatoes have been sprinkled on pizza. But try without any meat. It's still exceptional.

## Chili Relleno Casserole I

2 - 7 oz. cans whole green chilies, rinsed and seeded (or use 1 lb. fresh Anaheim chilies, seeded)
1 lb. Monterey jack or cheddar cheese grated
4 eggs, beaten slightly
½ cup milk
1 teaspoon salt
¼ teaspoon dry mustard
¼ teaspoon black pepper

Line a greased dish with ½ of the chilies spread open. Spread ½ cheese over chilies. Top with remaining chilies and cheese. Combine eggs, milk, and seasonings and pour over top. Bake 30 to 35 minutes at 350°. Cool 5 minutes before serving.

We plant lots of Anaheim pepper plants each year and freeze the whole pepper for year-round use. Leave whole but microwave for 5 minutes in a pan containing ¼ cup water. Plunge in ice water, drain, and freeze. Seeds and stems may be removed first, but are easy to remove later while partially frozen.

## Authentic Chili Relleno
### Be sure to double this recipe!

2 eggs separated
2 tablespoons flour
4 whole green chilies, fresh, seeds removed
Flour for dusting
Pinch of salt
4 strips of jack cheese
oil for frying

1. Beat egg whites until stiff. Fold in flour. Beat egg yolks and fold into whites.
2. Stuff each chili with cheese slice. Roll in flour, dip in egg batter and drop into hot oil, ¼" deep in fry pan. Brown on both sides. Drain on towels. Serve with salsa.

## Egg Burritos

In fry pan, melt 3 tablespoons butter. Add 1 chopped onion, 2 fresh Anaheim peppers, chopped. Simmer 6 minutes. Beat 8 eggs with ⅓ cup whole milk or water. Add salt, pepper, and ⅛ teaspoon cumin and 1 teaspoon chili powder. Cook, stirring gently. When almost done, sprinkle 1 cup shredded cheese on top. Don't stir. Heat tortillas in microwave to soften, fill, and serve with salsa. May omit the cheese.

## Pasties

Welsh miner's lunch. With a name like Anglesey, we had to include this recipe.
My husband eats these cold for lunch the next day.

1 lb. lean ground beef
5 potatoes, grated or chopped
6 carrots, grated or chopped
2 stalks celery, chopped
3 onions, minced
pastry dough (equivalent of 2 double crusted pies)
1 ½ teaspoons salt (may decrease)
¼ teaspoon pepper
½ cup water

Mix the raw ground beef, vegetables, water, and seasonings. Divide pastry into 8 balls and roll into circles. Place about ⅔ to 1 cup of vegetable and meat mixture on half of dough circle. Wet edges of dough with water and fold dough over to cover filling and pinch edges shut. Place on a cookie sheet and bake for 1 hour at 350°.
For less fat, use a biscuit dough, covering pasties if they get too brown. Or use an oil pastry dough recipe for less cholesterol.

Variation:
Line 2 pie plates with pastry and divide filling between them. Cover with pastry tops, slit tops and bake for 1 to 1 ½ hours at 350°. I add ½ cup water for more moist pies.

## Jackie's Quick Quiche
### (Forms its own crust)

2 cups whole milk
½ cup plus 2 tablespoons flour
5 eggs
½ teaspoon baking powder
½ teaspoon salt
¼ teaspoon pepper
1 tablespoon romano cheese (optional)

Blend ingredients in blender and pour over sauteed or steamed vegetables topped with any shredded or sliced cheese in a large pie plate or 10" x 10" pan..

Bake at 400° for 40 to 60 minutes. If pie begins to brown too much, can reduce heat after 25 minutes to 350°. Non-MSG bacon or sausage may be fried and added to vegetables. Saute with onions or peppers if desired.

Suggested vegetables: asparagus, broccoli, Swiss chard, spinach, onions, peppers, mushrooms, etc. Cheeses: Swiss, provolone, mild cheddar, mozzarella.

A good combination is sauteed onions and garlic with cut up steamed asparagus. Favorite herbs may also be added.

Cheese may be omitted.

## Quick Quiche II

Beat together:

6 eggs
1 cup milk
½ teaspoon salt
dash pepper

Add 2 cups filling in any combination.
Pour into a 9" pie shell and bake at 350° for 40 to 50 minutes.

Suggested fillings:
Grated mild cheese
Chopped fresh green onions or herbs.
Cooked, chopped spinach, Swiss chard, summer squash, green beans, mushrooms, onions, asparagus, green peppers, cooked salmon.

Variation: Mexican quiche
Use drained corn, chopped tomatoes, green onions, cilantro, oregano, chili powder, and jack cheese. Cooked ground beef may be added.

## Speedy Burritos

1 - 16 oz. can beans, rinsed and drained (such as black or pinto)
1 cup fresh or frozen corn
2 cups fresh, diced tomatoes
¼ teaspoon cumin
¼ teaspoon oregano
2 teaspoons chili powder
1 teaspoon sugar
¼ teaspoon salt or to taste

1 cup shredded jack or cheddar cheese
8 flour tortillas

Mix ingredients except tortillas. Spoon mixture evenly onto tortillas. Fold into burritos. Place into baking dish and bake at 400° for 7 to 10 minutes or microwave until hot. Serve with salad and salsa.

## Veggie Egg Foo Yung

Beat 7 eggs with ⅓ cup plus 1 tablespoon flour, ½ teaspoon salt, and ¼ teaspoon pepper. Add the following and mix: 7 large chopped mushrooms, 1 medium minced onion, 1 chopped bell pepper, and 2 small zucchini, chopped fine. Drop by spoonfuls into ⅛" hot oil in skillet. Sauté until golden.

## Swiss Chard Casserole

1 ½ lbs. Swiss chard
1 onion, chopped
5 eggs
1 cup milk
⅓ cup flour
dash cayenne pepper
½ teaspoon salt
2 to 3 cups mild cheese, shredded

Cut Swiss chard into pieces and simmer in water for 5 minutes (add stalks 1 minute before leaves). Drain. Saute onions in 2 tablespoons oil or butter. Add chard and cook for 5 minutes. In 9" x 13" pan, place a third of the cheese, half the chard, then one third more cheese, the rest of the chard, and then the remaining cheese on top. Beat eggs, milk, flour, and seasonings and pour over casserole. Bake at 350° for 30 minutes. Good served with salsa. Cheese may be omitted and a white sauce may be served over it instead.

## Shelli's Favorite Tamale Pie

1 large onion chopped
2 cloves garlic minced
¼ cup oil
2 cups fresh or frozen corn
2 cups fresh, diced tomatoes
1 cup sliced black olives
2 eggs
1 cup milk
1 cup water
1¼ cups corn meal
1 tablespoon chili powder
1 teaspoon salt

¼ teaspoon pepper

Saute onion and garlic until tender. Mix remaining ingredients together and place in a 9x13" casserole pan. Bake at 350° for 30 to 40 minutes.

Variation: Ground beef, chopped peppers, or zucchini may be added to sauté. If sensitive to corn, omit and add different vegetables if desired.

## Tostados

Bake 10 corn tortillas on two cookie sheets at 350° for 15 to 20 minutes or until crisp. Heat 3 cups refried beans and spread evenly on tortillas. Top with other toppings: Shredded lettuce, shredded cheese, chopped onion. chopped tomatoes, chopped cilantro, avocados or guacamole, or salsa.

Variation:
Saute ½ lb. ground beef and sprinkle on top of beans. I like to season my beans with cumin, chili powder, garlic powder, and oregano.

## Veggie Pizzas

Brush bread slices, flour tortillas, or pita bread (preferably homemade) with olive oil. Spread with your own spaghetti sauce or sprinkle with fresh sliced tomatoes. Add cheese slices, chopped black olives, mushrooms, semi-cooked broccoli pieces, chopped onion, and bell pepper. Sprinkle a little grated romano cheese (optional) on top and bake at 450° for 10 minutes or until light brown and cheese is melted.

## Busy Day Casserole

1 lb. ground beef or leftover meat
1 onion, chopped
1 carrot, chopped
2 cups fresh tomatoes, diced
2 cups water
1 clove garlic, minced or ¼ teaspoon powder
2 cups uncooked egg noodles
1 tablespoon chili powder
1 teaspoon salt
dash pepper
1 - 8 oz. can corn, drained (or 1 cup fresh kernals)
½ can sliced olives

1 cup mozzarella or cheddar cheese

Brown beef in skillet, add onion, and cook until brown. Add water, noodles, and seasonings. Cover and simmer for 20 to 30 minutes or until noodles are tender adding more water as needed. Add corn, tomatoes, and olives. Heat through. Sprinkle with cheese (optional), take off heat, and cover until cheese melts, then serve.

Sliced mushrooms may be substituted for olives and added with noodles. Sour cream may be substituted for cheese. Serve as a condiment.

## Busy Day Supper

1 large head cabbage
2 cups chopped tomatoes
1 lb. ground beef
salt and pepper
2 teaspoons sugar

Chop cabbage coarsely and place in a large casserole dish or roasting pan. Scatter ½" to 1" pieces of raw meat over cabbage. Sprinkle with sugar, salt and pepper. Cover and bake at 350° for 1 ½ hours or until tender. Uncover, stir, add tomatoes, and cook 10 more minutes. Add water if too dry. Tomatoes may be omitted.

Variations:
1.  Add chopped onion, corn, or carrots.
2.  Add favorite herbs
3.  Add ½ teaspoon caraway seeds.
4.  ½ cup sour cream may be stirred in just before serving.
5.  2 chopped tart apples may be substituted for the tomatoes. Add ½ cup water.

## Chicken and Green Chili Burritos

1½ lbs. chicken breasts
1 large onion sliced
2 cloves garlic chopped
3 green chilies seeded and chopped (We prefer Anaheims)

Simmer chicken in enough water to cover for 20 to 25 minutes. Cut into ½" to 1" pieces. Or cut up raw chicken and saute with onions first.
Add remaining ingredients and saute until golden and add the following: 1 teaspoon cumin, 1 teaspoon dry cilantro, ½ teaspoon salt, 2 teaspoons chili powder, 1 teaspoon sugar. Simmer 5 minutes and stir in ½ cup sour cream or yogurt. Sprinkle 1 cup grated jack or cheddar cheese on top and let simmer and melt. Serve on soft warm flour tortillas. Garnish with lime wedges and salsa.
*Note: chopped tomatoes may be added the last two minutes of cooking.

## Chicken Enchilada Casserole
### (by Krista Jensen)

1 batch Mexican Red Sauce (Sauce chapter)
12 corn or 8 flour tortillas
2 to 4 chicken breasts skinned and boned
1 lime
1 green pepper, chopped (optional)
½ onion chopped
1 clove garlic, minced
2 fresh Anaheims, chopped
½ lb. Jack cheese, grated
2 tablespoons fresh chopped cilantro (or 1 teaspoon dry)
2 cups cooked rice
½ to 1 cup water

Saute chicken breasts in oil for 6 minutes on each side. Remove to cutting board and cube. In same pan, saute onion, garlic, and peppers until tender. Add chicken, water, red sauce, and seasonings. Salt and pepper to taste. Add rice. In a large greased casserole, place half of the tortillas, half of the chicken mixture, and half of the cheese. Repeat layers, ending with cheese on top. Bake at 350° for 25 minutes. Serve with sour cream and salsa and lime wedges. May substitute 2 cups or 1 can drained beans for chicken.

*Tortillas may be filled individually with chicken mixture, grated cheese, and sprigs of cilantro.

*Corn may be substituted for rice.
*Ground beef may be substituted for chicken.

## Chelsea's Chicken Tetrazzini

1 cup sliced mushrooms (optional)
½ onion, sliced thinly
1 to 2 carrots, julienned or chopped thinly
¼ cup butter
¼ cup flour
1 ¾ cups water or stock
1 cup whole milk
1 tablespoon parsley fresh, less if dried
½ teaspoon salt
⅛ teaspoon nutmeg or allspice
¼ teaspoon pepper
3 cups cubed cooked chicken
8 oz. spaghetti
¼ cup shredded mozzarella cheese

¼ cup parmesan, may omit if too sensitive or use just 1 or 2 tablespoons

Cook spaghetti (first break noodles in thirds). In skillet, cook vegetables in butter until tender. Stir in flour, gradually add chicken broth or water and milk while stirring. Cook, stirring constantly until sauce boils. Remove from heat. Stir in parsley and seasonings. Fold in chicken and spaghetti. Turn into lightly greased pan or casserole dish. Sprinkle with mozzarella cheese, then parmesan. Bake uncovered at 350° for 30 minutes.

## Chicken Tamale Casserole

1 onion chopped
1 green pepper chopped
2 tablespoons oil or butter
2 cups diced tomatoes
3 cups cooked, boned, diced chicken
1½ cup corn or black beans
1 can black olives, drained and halved
1 clove garlic minced or ¼ teaspoon dry
1 teaspoon salt
3 teaspoons chili powder
⅛ teaspoon cayenne pepper
1 ½ cups grated cheddar or jack cheese

In a sauce pan, combine the following: ¾ cup corn meal, 2 cups cold water, ½ teaspoon salt, and 2 tablespoons butter (optional). Cook over medium heat until thick. Set aside.

Saute onions and green pepper in oil. Add chicken, corn, olives, garlic, and seasonings. Simmer 10 minutes. Stir in cheese and pour into shallow casserole dish or 9" x 13" pan. Spoon corn meal topping over casserole. Bake at 350° for 40 minutes.
*Ground beef may be substituted. Saute with vegetables. White cream sauce may be substituted for the cheese.

## Creole Casserole

A wonderful dish for left-over vegetables, beans, rice, and pasta.

Process into small pieces or chop the following:
1 large onion
3 cloves garlic
1 green pepper
1 medium zucchini
2 stalks of celery diced
½ small head of cabbage (optional)

Saute the above in 3 tablespoons of oil. Add 2 teaspoons ground pasilla pepper or 2 teaspoons chili powder, a dash of cayenne pepper, 1 teaspoon salt, 2 teaspoons sugar, ½ teaspoon dry basil, and dash of pepper. Stir and cook until tender. Add 1 cup cooked rice, 2 cups cooked pasta, and 1 cup cooked beans. One cup cooked leftover meat (chicken or sulfite free shrimp are good) may be added. Add 2 cups of water and simmer 15 minutes on low heat. Add 2 cups diced tomatoes. Taste and season. Simmer 1 minute longer. Just before serving pour 1 cup heavy cream into Creole. Stir gently and serve. For lower calorie version, omit cream and add milk. Add more cayenne pepper, if desired.

## Fast Enchilada Casserole

2 lbs. lean ground beef
1 onion, chopped
3 tablespoons chili powder
1 teaspoon sugar
1 teaspoon cumin
¼ teaspoon oregano
½ teaspoon salt
dash pepper
12 - 5" corn tortillas
1 can (15 oz.) chili or kidney beans (drained and rinsed)

1 cup grated cheese
3½ cups diced tomatoes

Oil a 9" x 13" pan. Saute beef and onion until brown. Add chili powder, cumin, sugar, salt, and pepper. Remove from heat and stir in beans. Overlap 6 tortillas in pan. Spoon beef mixture over evenly. Cover with 6 tortillas and sprinkle with cheese evenly. Pour tomatoes over all and bake at 350° until bubbly.

## Brandon's Garden Chicken

1 medium zucchini, sliced in circles (½" thick)
2 medium yellow crookneck squash, sliced in circles (½" thick)
1 large onion, sliced in rings and separated (¼" thick)
butter
4 chicken breasts or other parts
salt and pepper
garlic powder
Italian spices, such as oregano, basil

Place ½ onion on bottom of medium casserole dish. Layer ½ of squash. Place rinsed chicken on squash. Salt and pepper well. Sprinkle with garlic powder and spices. Turn chicken over and season. Place remaining squash over chicken, then remaining onion. Dot with butter. Salt and pepper.
Cover and bake at 350° for 40 minutes. Serve over egg noodles. May sprinkle lightly with mozzarella cheese.
Makes 3 servings.

## German Pork Casserole

Since sauerkraut contains sulfites, this recipe is a good substitute for those who love sauerkraut but are sensitive. A lot of pork is being treated with hydrolyzed proteins today and some products are being treated with phosphates to prevent e-coli. People report reactions. Unfortunately, with various products, experimenting or using a knowledgeable butcher may be the only way to find a safe product.

1 head cabbage chopped in 2" chunks
2 apples cored and diced
1 onion chopped

4 to 6 pork chops or pork steaks
¼ cup vinegar or fresh lemon juice
⅓ cup brown sugar or white

2 teaspoons caraway seeds
1 teaspoon salt
¼ teaspoon pepper
1 cup water

Sear pork chops quickly on both sides in hot oil. Set aside. Mix remaining ingredients and spoon half into large casserole. Place pork chops evenly on top and cover with remaining cabbage mixture. Bake at 350° for 45 minutes to 1 hour or until cabbage and meat are tender. May cover for half the roasting time Hamburger may be substituted for the pork. Roll hamburger into meat balls and add to casserole before baking.

## Rachel's Hot Tamale Pie
(Not really hot, just spicy)

1 lb. lean ground beef
1 large onion, chopped
1 bell pepper, chopped
2 cups fresh tomatoes
1½ cups corn or black beans
1 chopped Anaheim pepper
½ can sliced black olives (optional)
1 tablespoon chili powder
1 teaspoon dry cilantro (optional)
⅓ cup water

Topping:
¾ cup cornmeal
1 tablespoon flour

2 teaspoon sugar
1 ½ teaspoons baking powder
⅔ cup whole milk
1 tablespoon oil

Brown meat, onions, and bell pepper. Add tomatoes, water, corn, chilies, olives, and seasonings. Simmer covered for 10 minutes. Place in a 9" x 13" pan or large casserole dish. Spread topping evenly and bake for 30 to 35 minutes at 375°.

For topping, combine cornmeal, flour, sugar, and baking powder. Stir in milk and oil.

## Inca Rice Casserole
This recipe is pure gold, creamy and nutritious.

Cook 2 cups brown rice according to package directions (yields 4 to 5 cups)

In a large bowl, mix:
4 cups fresh, diced tomatoes
1 teaspoon salt
1 teaspoon cilantro
½ teaspoon cumin
¼ teaspoon oregano
3 cloves garlic, minced
4 to 6 anaheim peppers, chopped (may use large can green chilies or 2 - 7 oz. cans, chopped)

1 medium onion, chopped fine
1 medium zucchini, chopped
1 teaspoon sugar
dash pepper
1 to 2 tablespoons chili powder
2 cups diced mild cheese (jack or mozzarella)

Add all but 1 cup rice and stir well. Add more rice if mixture is not too dry or reserve and freeze. Pour into a 9" x 13" pan. Bake covered for 1 hour at 350°, then uncovered for 10 to 15 minutes. Serve with refried beans and fruit for a meatless, hearty meal.

## Creamy Mexicali Bake
### (A family favorite)

2 to 4 cups cooked, diced chicken or beef
12 corn tortillas
1 tablespoon dry cilantro
2 teaspoons chili powder
1 teaspoon cumin
2 to 4 cups grated cheese
1 large onion, chopped
1 cup broth or water
5 tablespoons butter or oil
1 bell pepper, chopped
2 anaheim peppers, chopped or 1 small can diced
6 tablespoons flour
4 cups milk
2 cloves garlic, chopped
2 to 3 tomatoes, diced

This is a good dish to use up leftovers such as beans, corn, mushrooms, etc. May be made meatless.

Grease large casserole dish or 9" x 13" pan. Saute peppers and onions in oil for 5 minutes. Add garlic and saute until tender. Add flour and stir until blended. Add milk, broth, or water, stirring and cooking over medium heat. Add seasonings and salt and pepper to taste. Add tomatoes and meat. Let simmer just until it begins to thicken. If too thick, add more liquid. Place 6 tortillas evenly over bottom of pan and spoon half of mixture on them. Sprinkle ⅔ of cheese on top and place 6 more tortillas over cheese. Spoon remaining mixture on tortillas. Cover and bake at 375° for 40 minutes. Remove from oven. Top with remaining cheese and chopped green onions if desired (optional). May garnish with black olives, chopped tomatoes, and avocados if desired.

## Quinoa and Beef Stuffed Peppers

3 to 4 large red or green bell peppers, cut in half lengthwise and seeded
3 cups cooked quinoa
½ to 1 lb. ground beef
3 cloves garlic, minced
1 large onion, chopped
1 egg (may omit)
1 teaspoon salt
dash pepper
1 teaspoon marjoram or thyme (dry)
4 cups fresh pureed tomatoes (or 2½ cups tomato puree) seasoned with salt, pepper, ½ teaspoon basil, ¼ teaspoon oregano, and 1 teaspoon sugar (or use 1 quart homemade spaghetti sauce)

1. Strain the pureed tomatoes in a cloth lined strainer over a bowl for several hours before preparation or use Muir Glen pureed tomatoes.
2. Sauté meat, vegetables, spices, salt, and pepper until tender. Mix with quinoa.
3. Season tomatoes with salt and pepper, ½ teaspoon dry basil, ¼ teaspoon dry oregano, and 1 teaspoon sugar.
4. Mix ½ cup of the puree with the meat and quinoa.
5. Place peppers in bowl and microwave, covered for 5 minutes or bake at 350° for 15 minutes. Drain any liquid.
6. Spread half of remaining puree on bottom of a 9" x 13" pan. Place peppers on top, cut sides up and fill evenly with the meat and quinoa mixture. Spoon remaining sauce over tops and bake uncovered at 375° for 30 to 40 minutes or until hot throughout.

Variations:
1. May substitute 1" thick circles of eggplant for peppers. Microwave for 6 minutes first and drain. Lay in pan and mound filling on each circle.
2. Substitute quinoa with cooked brown rice, couscous, barley, or bulgur wheat.
3. May be made meatless by increasing quinoa by 1 cup.

## Jacob's Speedy Chicken Rice Casserole

1 fryer, cut up and skinned (or 6 breasts)
4 stalks celery, chopped (include leaves)
1 large onion, chopped
4 carrots, cut in ½" circles or 2 cups baby carrots
2 cups raw brown rice
2 teaspoons salt
½ teaspoon thyme (dry)

¼ teaspoon each : ground sage, dry marjarom,
dry parsley, and dry garlic granules
4 cups water

Mix all but chicken in a large roasting pan.
Spread evenly in pan. Place chicken, meatiest
side down on rice. Bake covered for 1 hour at
375° or until rice is tender and chicken
thoroughly done.

## Spicy Mexican Casserole
### (Or Italian)

1 - 8 oz. package of egg noodles
1 ½ to 2 lbs. ground beef
1 large or 2 medium onions chopped
1 medium green pepper chopped
2 tablespoons flour
3 cups chopped tomatoes
2 tablespoons chili powder
1 teaspoon salt
¼ teaspoon black pepper
2 cups shredded jack or mild cheddar cheese
½ to 1 cup water (to moisten)

Cook noodles and drain. Saute beef, onion, and
pepper. Drain fat. Sprinkle flour over meat. Stir
and cook one minute. Add tomatoes, water, and
seasonings. Combine with noodles and put in
9" x 13" pan. Top with cheese. Bake at 350°
for 35 minutes. May garnish with black olives
and fresh cilantro.

For Italian version, substitute ½ teaspoon garlic
powder, 1½ teaspoons basil, and 1 teaspoon
oregano for chili powder.

## Speedy Tomato Pasta Bake

1 lb. pasta (any kind), cooked, rinsed, drained
½ lb. mild grated cheese
4 large or 6 small tomatoes
butter
salt and pepper
flour
garlic powder
sugar (optional)
4 cups milk
bread

Slice tomatoes in ¼" circles and place half in
bottom of a 9" x 13" pan. Place half the pasta
over the tomatoes and all the cheese (amount of
cheese can be reduced if desired). Sprinkle with,

salt, pepper, and a little sugar. With a sifter or
small strainer, sprinkle evenly with 2 tablespoons
flour. Dot with butter. Place remaining pasta
over this and remaining tomatoes over that.
Season again and dot with butter again. Sift with
2 more tablespoons flour and pour 4 cups milk
over all. Bake at 400° for 20 to 35 minutes or
until bubbly.

Butter 3 pieces of bread. Sprinkle with garlic
powder. Stack and cut into ½" cubes. Sprinkle
on casserole last 5 minutes of cooking to toast
(optional step).

Variation:

Substitute tomatoes with partially cooked summer squash, asparagus, or a medley of vegetables. Substitute thick white cream sauce or ricotta cheese substitute for cheese (Substitute Chart).

## Spaghetti in Garlic and Herb Oil

1 lb. cooked spaghetti
6 tablespoons olive oil
1 onion, chopped
5 cloves garlic, finely chopped
3 tablespoons fresh chopped parsley or 1 tablespoon dry
1 teaspoon dry basil
salt and pepper
dash red pepper flakes

Start water to boil for spaghetti. Heat oil in pan and add onions and cook until almost golden and add the garlic. Turn to low heat and saute for 1 to 2 minutes longer. Add the herbs and seasonings. Drain cooked pasta and transfer to a large dish. Add the oil mixture and season with more salt and pepper if desired. Toss and serve immediately. Add more oil or some water if too dry. Try different pasta shapes. Cheese may be offered as topping. 2 cups diced tomatoes may be stirred into hot oil just before tossing with pasta.

## Macaroni and Cheese
### (General directions)

1. Boil 1 lb. elbow macaroni.
2. Make 4 cups thick cream sauce and add 2 extra cups milk to thin. Add ½ teaspoon dry mustard and more salt and pepper to taste.
3. Place half the macaroni in a large buttered casserole and pour half the sauce over it.
4. Sprinkle 2 cups grated mild cheese over sauce and cover with remaining macaroni.
5. Pour rest of sauce over macaroni.
6. Bake at 350° for 30 minutes or until bubbly.
7. Buttered bread cubes or plain dry bread crumbs may be sprinkled on last 5 minutes of baking.

Variations:
1. Cheese may be added to cream sauce and blended before pouring over macaroni. May be served immediately this way without baking.
2. Thin sliced tomatoes may be layered over casserole before cheese is added.
3. More cheese may be used.
4. For scalloped potatoes, layer sauce with thinly sliced potatoes (omit cheese and bread crumbs). Bake until potatoes are tender. Cover first 30 minutes of baking. Parsley and onion powder may be used to season sauce.
5. Speedy version. Grate 3 cups cheese. Add to hot, drained macaroni along with ½ teaspoon dry mustard, 4 tablespoons butter, and ½ cup milk. Stir to blend over low heat. Season and serve.

## Gourmet Baked Potatoes
### With a salad, potatoes can become a meal.

4 large potatoes
1 cup sour cream
1 tablespoon parsley flakes
¼ teaspoon garlic powder
salt and pepper to taste
⅓ cup milk or water

Mix sour cream, seasonings, and milk. Bake potatoes, split, and butter (optional). Top each with some of sour cream mixture and any of the following: Fresh chopped tomatoes, green peppers, sweet onions, grated cheese, sauted mushrooms and/or onions, steamed chopped broccoli, or other favorite steamed vegetables. Be creative!

Variations:
1.  White cream sauce may be used instead of sour cream mixture.
2.  Top with chili and condiments.

## Baked Beans

4 cups cooked beans (white, navy, or pinto)
1 large onion, chopped (2 medium)
2 cloves garlic, minced
½ cup homemade catsup or tomato puree (optional)
1 teaspoon salt
½ cup brown sugar packed (or white)
¼ cup cider vinegar

1 tablespoon mustard
1 cup water
2 tablespoons unsulfered molasses or honey
¼ teaspoon red pepper flakes

Combine and place in casserole dish. Cover and bake at 325° for 1 hour. If too dry, add more water.

## Braeden's Chuckwagon Beans

1 lb. ground beef
1 onion chopped
3 cloves garlic chopped

1 tablespoon prepared mustard (or 1 teaspoon dry)
3 cups fresh diced tomatoes
3 tablespoons chili powder
2 tablespoons unsulphured molasses
⅓ cup brown or white sugar
2 tablespoons vinegar
1 ½ teaspoons salt
¼ teaspoon red pepper flakes
2 cups water

Wash and soak 3 cups pinto or navy beans over night in water. Drain. Return to large pot and add water to 4 inches above beans. Simmer slowly on medium low heat until tender but not mushy. Test often.

In fry pan, saute ground beef, onion, and garlic.

Drain beans and add the sauted beef and vegetables with the remaining ingredients.

Simmer in pot on low heat, 20 to 30 minutes, partially covered, stirring often. Or bake in oven, covered, at 350° for 35 to 40 minutes. Add water if beans become dry. Add tomatoes last 5 minutes of cooking.

# Tanner's Cowboy Bake

4 carrots sliced
1 onion sliced
5 medium potatoes sliced
milk (start with 2 cups)
¼ cup butter
¼ teaspoon each of sage, thyme, and garlic powder
1 lb. ground beef
2 tablespoons flour

Place carrots in bottom of large casserole dish. Add half of the sliced onions. Sprinkle with salt and dot with half of the butter. Top with layer of potatoes. Sprinkle with salt and pepper. Top with onions and dot with remaining butter.

Break up beef with hands into small pieces and sprinkle over casserole. Sprinkle with salt. Mix seasonings and flour with milk and pour into casserole until it can be seen just below potatoes. Bake 1 hour at 350°. Test vegetables for tenderness.

*Note: May be made meatless.
*Some people may react to free glutamate created from cooking the milk so long. Potatoes and carrots may be steamed or microwaved first. Hamburger and onions may be sauted separately and then assembled as above. Pour 4 cups prepared white sauce over casserole and bake until heated through.

# Chili Relleno Casserole II

Highly sensitive people should avoid this recipe as cooking the milk may contribute to glutamate formation. They may find that the cheese causes problems also.

6 eggs
4 cups milk
2 - 7 oz. cans chopped green chilies (or 14 oz. fresh Anaheim chilies, chopped)
3 cups grated cheddar, jack, or Mozzarella cheese (may increase or decrease amount)
½ teaspoon chili powder
1 teaspoon salt
¼ teaspoon black pepper

6 slices bread
butter

Butter 9" x 13" pan. Butter bread on one side. Place bread butter side up in pan. Sprinkle cheese over bread. Distribute drained chilies over cheese. Beat together eggs, milk, and seasonings and pour over cheese. Bake at 350° for 30 to 40 minutes or until eggs are set.

# Easy Fruited Chicken Curry

2 cups uncooked brown or wild rice (may use white)
8 prunes, chopped
½ cup raisins or currants
2 cups boiling water
3 cooked chicken breasts, cut in chunks
2 onions, sliced
2 tablespoons oil
2 cloves garlic, minced
1 teaspoon salt
¼ teaspoon tumeric
1 ½ teaspoons dry cilantro
½ teaspoon powdered ginger

½ teaspoon cumin
dash of cayenne pepper
dash cloves
½ teaspoon cinnamon
dash black pepper

Cook rice according to package directions. Pour boiling water over fruit to soften and let stand for 10 minutes. In large fry pan, saute onions in oil until soft. Add garlic, salt, pepper, and spices. Simmer for 2 minutes. Add fruit plus soaking water and chicken. Turn to lowest heat and let simmer for 5 minutes. Add 3 cups cooked rice to chicken. If too moist, more rice can be added. Garnish with chopped peanuts, almonds, or walnuts.

*2 teaspoons curry powder may be substituted for the dry spices.

*Other dry fruits may be substituted, such as apricots, cranberries or pears.

## Chicken and Red Pepper With Pasta

Saute 1 sliced (¼" thick) chicken breast with 1 chopped clove garlic and 2 sliced red peppers in hot oil. Whisk 1½ cups homemade chicken stock, milk, or water with 2 tablespoons flour. Add to chicken and stir. Add 1 cup snow peas or fresh peas and simmer just until sauce thickens. Season to taste. Pour over pasta of choice and serve. Variation: substitute sliced mushrooms for peas.

## Eggplant Tomato Sauce with Pasta
### (May substitute zucchini for eggplant)

2 bell peppers, chopped
1 large onion, chopped
1 small eggplant, chopped
2 cups tomatoes, chopped
2 cloves garlic, minced
½ to 1 teaspoon salt
½ teaspoon oregano (dry)
1 teaspoon basil (dry)
1 to 2 teaspoons parsley (dry)
1 cup fresh mushrooms, sliced

grated mozzarella

Simmer all vegetables and seasonings until tender. Taste and add more seasonings if desired. Serve over hot pasta and offer mozzarella to sprinkle on top.

*To minimize free glutamate formation, add mushrooms to sauté last 5 minutes.

## Fast Fried Rice

4 cups cooked rice
1 lb. package frozen mixed vegetables (we use Stahlbush preservative free brand, sif@stahlbush.com)
1 large onion, chopped
2 cloves garlic, minced
3 beaten eggs
3 tablespoons oil
½ teaspoon Chinese Five Spice
dash of cayenne pepper
salt and pepper to taste

Microwave frozen vegetables until tender crisp. In oil in large skillet or wok, stir fry the onion until golden. Add garlic and the vegetables and stir fry for 3 minutes. Push vegetables to one side and pour eggs onto clear area of pan. Stir gently until cooked through. Add rice and seasonings and stir mixture until mixed and heated.

*Leftover meat such as chicken, pork, or beef may be added to vegetables. Any fresh or frozen left over vegetables may be added or substituted.

163

## Fast Refried Bean Dinner
### (or snack)

1.  Spread 2 cups refried beans on a plate and microwave to heat.
2.  Spread 1 cup grated mild cheese on top and let melt or return to microwave to melt.
3.  Spoon on salsa and any of the following garnishes and serve with tortilla chips or spoon on warm flour tortillas.

Garnishes: sour cream, chopped onion, chopped avocados, sliced black olives, and chopped jalapenos.

## Hurry Up Hash (Beef or Chicken)
### (A family favorite)

1 lb. ground beef or leftover chicken, chopped
2 onions sliced in rings
5 stalks celery, chopped
3½ cups diced tomatoes
1⅔ cups raw rice
1½ teaspoons salt
3 tablespoons chili powder
1 to 2 tablespoons sugar
2 cloves garlic, minced (optional)
⅛ teaspoon pepper
1 cup water

In large fry pan, cook meat, onion, garlic, and celery until tender. Drain fat. Stir in remaining ingredients and pour into 2 quart casserole or 9" x 13" pan. Bake for 1 hour at 350° or until rice is tender. Add more water if dry and more seasonings to taste. Green pepper is good in this, too.

For highly sensitive individuals, reserve adding tomatoes until last few minutes of baking. Add 4 cups water (total) to rice mixture before baking and decrease tomatoes to 3 cups.

## Haystacks

Crispy corn chips (look for ones without lime or sprouted corn)
Pinto beans seasoned with chili powder, salt, pepper, garlic powder, cumin, and cilantro and heated.
Diced tomatoes
Shredded mild cheese (optional)
Chopped lettuce
Chopped green onion

Chopped black olives
Sour Cream and/or guacamole (optional)

Place each ingredient, in same order as listed, on each person's plate, forming a stack.

Variation: May use refried beans or seasoned, cooked lentils or wheat berries.

## Hungarian Cabbage and Noodles

1.  Boil 1 lb. noodles until tender, drain, rinse, and keep warm.
2.  Chop 1 head cabbage and 2 onions coarsely.
3.  In some oil, saute, over medium heat, the cabbage and onions with ½ teaspoon salt and 1 teaspoon sugar until limp and golden, adding oil or water to prevent sticking.
4.  Toss with noodles and serve.

Suggestions:
This is good served with spiced applesauce (sugar, nutmeg, and cinnamon) and green beans. My grandmother made this often for lunch. 3 to 4 cups rice may be substituted.

## Fresh Pasta Sauce
### (Uncooked)

6 to 8 tomatoes, chopped
2 tablespoons dry basil or ⅓ cup fresh
¼ teaspoon dry oregano
3 large cloves garlic
dash red pepper flakes
2 teaspoons sugar
½ teaspoon salt
¼ teaspoon black pepper
4 tablespoons oil (olive or canola)
1 cup grated mozzarella (optional)

Process half or the tomatoes with basil (if fresh) and garlic and mix with remaining ingredients. Or if processor is not available, finely mince the garlic and chop the basil. Then add to ingredients. Let set at room temperature for 2 hours. Boil 1 lb. rigatoni or penne pasta. Do not rinse. Drain and toss with sauce and cheese. Sauce may be heated slightly but not cooked and then added to pasta if desired.

## Sicilian Style Spaghetti Sauce

Saute together until meat is brown:
2-3 onions chopped
4 cloves garlic
2 grated carrots
2 lbs. hamburger
2 tablespoons olive oil

Add:
6 lbs. pureed or crushed tomatoes
4 cups water
3 tablespoons dry basil

1 teaspoon to 1 tablespoon dry oregano (optional)
1 tablespoon chili powder (optional)
2 tablespoons parsley (dry)
1 tablespoon salt (add more to taste)
½ teaspoon black pepper
¼ teaspoon red pepper flakes

Simmer 20 minutes on low heat, stirring often. Add 3-6 tablespoons sugar to taste. 1 bay leaf may be added. Simmer 10 more minutes. Remove bay leaf. Taste and add more seasonings if desired. Freeze leftovers.

## Uncooked Pasta Sauce II
### (A family favorite and so easy)

10 to 14 plum tomatoes chopped
½ cup chopped fresh basil
1 clove garlic minced
⅓ lb. mozzarella cheese grated or ½" cubes (optional)
2 tablespoons olive oil
1½ teaspoons sugar
dash red pepper flakes

Mix all ingredients and let stand at room temperature covered for 3-6 hours. Cook and drain a 10 oz. or 1 lb. package of corkscrew pasta or any favorite shape. Add sauce to hot pasta and mix well. Add salt and pepper to taste. Serve with salad and bread. I have turned leftovers into a salad the next day by adding chopped green peppers, onions, and celery, then adding oil and cider vinegar or lemon juice to taste.

## Japanese Pork and Noodles

1 small head cabbage, shredded
2 large carrots, grated
3 stalks celery, diced thinly
1 large onion, sliced thin
1 lb. lean pork, diced or ground (any meat works)
7 mushrooms, sliced
4 eggs, scrambled
1 lb. package of any kind noodles, cooked (rice strands or spaghetti works well)
salt and pepper

½ teaspoon Chinese Five Spice
1 teaspoon sugar
1 teaspoon cider vinegar or lemon juice

Brown pork in a little oil in a large frying pan or wok. Add the vegetables except for the mushrooms. Stir fry until almost cooked, about 5 minutes. Add the mushrooms and seasonings, vinegar, and sugar. In a separate pan, fry the eggs and add with noodles to the vegetables. Stir and fry for 2 minutes and serve. May use rice.

## Lentil Roast

2 cups cooked lentils (or mashed beans)
2 cups shredded-style wheat cereal
1 cup unseasoned nuts, chopped fine (any favorite)
2 cups milk or water
3 eggs
½ teaspoon sage
1 teaspoon thyme
1 teaspoon marjoram
2 onions, chopped

½ cup oil (may decrease)
1 teaspoon salt
⅛ teaspoon pepper

Mix shredded wheat and milk and let sit until softened. Add eggs and beat well. Add remaining ingredients. Pour into large bread pan or 9" x 13" pan and bake at 350° for 45 to 60 minutes. Serve with onion gravy. I have also added 1 large grated carrot to this recipe.

## Hamburger and Vegetable Meat Balls

1 lb. hamburger
2 medium potatoes grated
2 medium carrots grated
1 onion chopped
½ cup bread crumbs dry (unseasoned)
1 egg
1 teaspoon salt
dash pepper
1 tablespoon dry parsley

¼ teaspoon powdered garlic

Mix all ingredients and form into balls. Brown in pan with hot oil. Remove from pan to a 9" x 13" pan or 2 quart casserole. Drain all but 3 tablespoons fat in pan and stir in 3 tablespoons flour. Add 1 ½ cups milk and stir until thickened. Season with salt and pepper. Pour over meat balls. Bake 1 hour at 350°.

## Trevor's Brazilian Rice and Beans
### (Deceptively simple, the taste is incredibly good!)

1. Wash 1 lb. pinto beans. Put in water 4 times as deep as the beans. Cook for 1¼ hours in pressure cooker.

2. In large pan or Dutch oven, sauté 1 minced onion and 3 to 4 cloves minced garlic in ¼ cup oil for 5 minutes. Add 3 cups raw rice and sauté for 3 minutes. Add 5 cups water, cover, reduce heat, and simmer for 25 minutes.

3. In small pan, sauté 1 small onion, chopped and 3 to 4 cloves minced garlic in some oil for 5 minutes. Add to the beans. Simmer a few minutes to reduce liquid if desired. Season to taste. Mixture should still be somewhat runny. Serve by spooning some rice into bowls and ladling beans on top. Offer salt. Good with fruit salad.

Variation: Beans may be soaked overnight. Drain water and add fresh water to cover along with the garlic and onion. Simmer until tender.

## Mushroom and Rice Patties

2 cups minced mushrooms
1 onion, chopped
2 cloves garlic, minced
1 ½ cups raw brown rice
3 cups water
½ teaspoon salt
dash pepper
1 teaspoon dry basil or thyme
½ cup finely chopped walnuts or almonds
2 tablespoons oil
2 eggs

In oil, brown onions, mushrooms, and garlic. Add the rice and saute until it begins to brown, stirring constantly. Add water and seasonings and bring to a boil. Cover and reduce heat and simmer until rice is tender and mixture thickens (approximately 45 minutes). Add water if mixture becomes too dry while cooking. Remove from heat. Let mixture cool a little and beat in eggs and nuts. In a non-stick fry pan, spray or add some oil. Scoop out ½ cup spoonfuls and fry in hot oil. Flatten into 3" patties, ½" thick. Fry for 5 minutes on each side or until golden. Flip carefully. Serve with fruit, salad, and rolls.

Cooking the mushrooms for 45 minutes may release free glutamate, so adding them with the nuts may be preferable.

Variation:
A grated carrot is a colorful addition. Try zucchini, also. Mashed beans, oatmeal, or wheat germ may be added.

This may be flattened into 1 large patty in the skillet. Cook 8 to 10 minutes. Invert on a plate. No need to cook both sides (will break if flipped). Cover for last 2 minutes of cooking.

## Meatless Stuffed Peppers

Mix together:
2 teaspoons oil
¼ teaspoon dry ginger
½ teaspoon curry powder or cumin powder
3 cloves garlic, minced
½ cup chopped onion

½ cup cubed mozzarella cheese (optional)
salt and pepper to taste
½ cup whole milk
2 cups cooked rice (brown)
1 egg

Place 4 to 5 large bell peppers on a greased pan and roast at 375° until browned. Place in brown or plastic bag and let steam for 10 minutes. Peel skin.

Remove seeds and stem, then stuff with rice mixture. Place in 9" x 13" pan and bake at 350° for 20 to 25 minutes.

Instead of roasting peppers, I often remove stems, seeds, and microwave covered for about 5 to 6 minutes or until partially cooked. No need to skin. Stuff and bake as above. May serve with cream sauce or tomato sauce.

## Multigrain Roast

4 cups mixture of any cooked grains (millet, quinoa, cracked wheat, brown rice)
2 cups diced fresh tomatoes (diced zucchini, or tart applesauce may be substituted)
2 onions, chopped
4 tablespoons sesame seeds or sesame butter (ground seed)
½ cup finely chopped nuts (any kind)
1 teaspoon salt
¼ teaspoon sage
½ teaspoon thyme
pepper
2 eggs
1 cup finely chopped mushrooms (optional but a tasty addition, although they may contain free glutamate from cooking)

Mix ingredients and spoon into greased casserole. Bake at 350° for 35 minutes.

## No Meat Chili

3 tablespoons oil
1 large onion, chopped
2 bell peppers, diced
1 large carrot, sliced
2 tablespoons garlic, minced
3 tablespoons chili powder
1 tablespoon pasilla powder (optional)
2 teaspoons ground cumin
1 teaspoon salt
4 cups chopped tomatoes
2 cans beans (pinto, black, or kidney), rinsed and drained or 4 cups cooked beans or lentils
1 zucchini, chopped

1 cup chopped tomatillos or green chilies (optional)
2 cups water

In a large pot add oil and saute the onion, bell peppers, and carrots for 3 minutes. Add the garlic and cook for 1 minute longer. Add the remaining ingredients and simmer on low for 20 minutes. Good served over brown rice. Garnish with chopped avocado, grated jack cheese and sour cream if desired. Tomatoes may be added last few minutes of cooking, if preferred.

## Garden Vegetable Omelet

In a little butter or oil, saute ½ chopped onion, ½ chopped green pepper, 1 small sliced zucchini for 1 minute. Add 4 green onions, sliced in circles and ½ lb. sliced mushrooms. Saute 2 more minutes. Remove to a plate and keep warm.

Beat together 9 eggs, ½ cup milk or water, ½ teaspoon salt, dash of pepper, and any favorite herbs. Pour into same pan vegetables were cooked in and cover with lid. Cook on lowest heat until almost set. Sprinkle vegetables evenly on top. Sprinkle 1 to 2 cups grated cheddar, jack, or mozzarella cheese over all. Cover and heat until cheese melts. Cut into 6ths like a pie. Garnish with sliced tomatoes and serve with bread and fruit. Makes a good egg sandwich, too. Cheese is optional.

## "Oyster"-Style Beef and Noodles
### (Without the Oriental oyster sauce)

1 ½ lbs. ground beef (may use thin sliced beef)
2 onions, sliced, not chopped
3 large cloves garlic, chopped
¼ teaspoon red pepper flakes
⅓ cup brown or white sugar, packed
1 teaspoon salt
dash pepper
2 tablespoons cider vinegar or fresh lemon juice
½ teaspoon fresh grated or dry ginger
¾ teaspoon Chinese Five Spice

Boil 1 lb. fettucine or spaghetti noodles until cooked (firm, not mushy).
On medium-high heat, saute onions in a little oil in a wok or large fry pan until they begin to

brown. Add beef, garlic, and red pepper flakes, then saute until beef is no longer pink. Add vinegar, sugar, and seasonings. Stir well and add 1 package of organic frozen peas and cook until heated through.
Toss hot noodles into beef and serve.

Variations:
1. May add ½ lb. sliced mushrooms.
2. Peas may be omitted.
3. Substitute peas with zucchini or asparagus.
4. If using beef, partially freeze before slicing (tri-tip steaks work well).
5. 2 bunches of green onions sliced in 2" pieces may be substituted for onions.

## Polenta Tuscany

Long cooking of cornmeal may create free glutamate. It may be soaked for 1 hour first to reduce cooking time. Farina may be substituted.

Buy polenta in most health food or grocery stores. It is coarse ground corn meal. To cook,
mix together in bowl: 3 cups cold water and 2 cups polenta.
Bring 5 cups water and ½ teaspoon salt to boil in a large pot. Slowly add the polenta and water stirring rapidly. Simmer on low, stirring often. Italians say it is done when the wooden spoon stands up in it. Top with a saute of favorite vegetables moistened with fresh diced tomatoes and seasoned with your favorite herbs and spices. Garnish with grated cheese if desired.

Suggested vegetables: onions, mushrooms, zucchini, broccoli, egg plant, green pepper.

Variation: Drizzle polenta with a little olive oil or melted butter and some grated cheese. Offer chopped tomatoes and black pepper.

Variation: Saute mushrooms, garlic, and onions together and spoon over polenta. Offer shredded cheese or sour cream to top.

## Vegetarian Bean Croquettes

1 ½ cups cooked beans
2 ½ cups cooked brown rice
2 slices fresh bread crumbs (fine)
¼ cup milk or water
2 tablespoons natural peanut butter
½ cup pecans or walnuts, chopped fine
4 tablespoons finely chopped onion
2 tablespoons olive oil
¼ teaspoon thyme
¼ teaspoon marjoram
dash sage
½ teaspoon salt
pepper

fine dry bread crumbs, corn meal, or flour for dredging
oil for baking

Puree the beans and add all the ingredients except dry crumbs and oil for cooking. Form mixture into mounds using ⅓ cup mixture. Spray or sprinkle each with oil and roll in dry bread crumbs. Place on oiled cookie sheet and bake at 375° for 25 to 03 minutes.

May form into ½" thick patties and saute in a little oil for 5 minutes on each side on medium-low heat.

## Vegetable and Grain Roll-ups

1 cup dry lentils, barley, or brown rice
2 large or 3 small carrots, chopped finely or shredded coarsely
½ sweet onion
1 bell pepper, diced
¼ teaspoon cumin
¼ cup fresh cilantro or basil, chopped
1 large clove garlic, minced
1 stalk celery, diced
½ cucumber, diced
⅓ cup mild cheese, shredded (optional)
⅓ cup olive oil
6 flour tortillas
dash red pepper flakes
4 tablespoons cider vinegar or lemon juice
⅓ cup oil
2 teaspoons sugar

1. Rinse and cover choice of grain with 3 cups water in pot and simmer until tender. Drain any remaining water. If using rice, simmer covered in 2 cups water.
2. Add carrots to pot of hot grain. Stir to cover and let steam while preparing remaining recipe.
3. Whisk the oil and vinegar in a large bowl. Add sugar, cilantro or basil, garlic, red pepper flakes, cumin, chopped pepper, celery, cucumber, onion, and mix. Stir in the cooked grain with carrots until thoroughly mixed. Fill tortillas, adding grated cheese or sour cream if desired. Roll and eat.

# MEATS, POULTRY, AND SEAFOOD

## Apricot Glazed Chicken

In 9" x 13" pan, combine:
1 cup apricot jam (no pectin)
⅓ cup apple cider vinegar or fresh lemon juice
1 teaspoon ginger (powdered)
¼ teaspoon pepper
Dash cayenne pepper (optional)
1 teaspoon salt

Skin and soak to clean 2-3 lbs. cut up chicken. Add to pan turning to coat with mixture. Bake uncovered 15 minutes at 375°. Turn and bake 30 to 40 minutes, turning chicken every 10 minutes until done. Serve with rice.

Plum or currant jam may be substituted.

## Crispy Baked Chicken

In plastic bag, place:
½ cup dried bread crumbs or flour, unseasoned
3 tablespoons cornmeal
1 cup flour
2 teaspoons salt
dash pepper
1 teaspoon garlic powder
1 teaspoon dry parsley (optional)
¾ teaspoon cayenne pepper

Coat a 9" x 13" pan with oil. Dip 2-3 lbs chicken pieces in mixture of ⅔ cup milk, water, yogurt, or sour cream and 1 egg. Shake 2 pieces at a time in bag to coat. Bake uncovered at 375° for 45 minutes to 1 hour until golden brown.

Variation: Honey Mustard Chicken

Add 1 more teaspoon garlic powder to flour mixture and dip chicken in mixture of ¼ cup honey, ¼ cup mustard, and 4 tablespoons water before dipping in flour mixture.

## Buffalo Wings
### (My home town)

3 or 4 lbs. chicken wings, tips removed

Wash well. Grease 2 baking pans and place chicken in single layer in the 2 pans. Bake at 375° for 45-60 minutes or until nicely browned and crispy.

In a large pot on range place the following
(double for a thicker coating):

4 tablespoons butter or oil
½ teaspoon salt
⅛ teaspoon pepper
¼ teaspoon garlic powder
½ teaspoon cayenne pepper
3 tablespoons cider vinegar or lemon juice
5 tablespoons catsup (homemade)
¼ cup water

1 tablespoon mustard (or 1 teaspoon dry)
1 teaspoon sugar

Melt together and mix well. Turn off heat. Drain chicken and with tongs, place in pot. Cover with lid and shake pot several times to coat chicken. Serve with celery sticks and dip in sour cream seasoned with salt and pepper instead of typically served blue cheese dressing which is high in MSG. Delicious plain. Increase or

171

decrease cayenne pepper to desired heat. Traditionally, chicken wings are hot.

Variations:

1. Use skinned chicken legs instead of wings. May take longer to brown.
2. Use applesauce instead of catsup.

## Chicken Paprika (Paprikash)

One of my favorite, nastalgic dishes from my Austrian Grandmother Suzanne Gifford. She was a gifted cook.

1. Melt 2 tablespoons butter or use 2 tablespoons oil in large skillet. Add 1 cut up chicken, chicken breasts, or thighs (you may skin) and 3 large sliced onions. Cook until onions are soft and chicken is cooked. Add more oil or water if too dry.
2. Mix together 1 cup sour cream and 3 tablespoons flour. Beat with whisk or fork until smooth. Beat in 1 cup water.
3. Remove chicken to a plate and pour sour cream mixture into pan with onions and drippings. Stir constantly until thicker. Add 2 teaspoons Hungarian style paprika. Salt and pepper to taste.
4. Put chicken back in pan and simmer 5 to 10 minutes on lowest heat. Add water if dry or too thick.
5. Meanwhile, boil up noodles or rice on which to ladle gravy and meat.

## Chicken and Chile Verde Casserole

2 cups sliced onions
3 to 4 chicken breasts
¼ cup water
¼ cup oil
4 Anaheim chilies, chopped
1 cup fresh tomatillos, peeled and chopped fine
1 teaspoon salt
2 tablespoons lemon or lime juice
1 cup sour cream
1½ cups grated mozzarella cheese
1½ cups grated jack cheese
Corn tortillas or tortilla chips

1. Coat a 9" x 13" pan with cooking spray or oil.
2. Saute sliced onion with chicken breasts in 1 tablespoon oil for 10 minutes. Remove chicken and cut into small pieces.
3. Return to pan and add green chilies, tomatillos, fresh oil, cilantro, salt, lemon or lime juice. Simmer for 5 minutes and remove from heat.
4. Stir in sour cream (or substitute 1 cup white cream sauce).
5. Pat a layer of corn tortillas in bottom of pan. Spoon half the chicken mixture on top and sprinkle half the cheese on the chicken.
6. Cover with more corn tortillas and then the rest of meat mixture and cheese.
7. Bake in 375° oven for 45 minutes.

Can substitute pork or beef for the chicken. Leftover cooked meat may be used or saute uncooked meat in onions until cooked.
Cheese amount may be decreased or omitted.

## Chicken Fingers
### We love these!

1. Cut 4 chicken breasts in 1" strips and marinate in 1 cup plain yogurt or whole milk (rice milk or water may be used instead of milk) over night (or dip in mixture of 1 beaten egg and ⅔ cup milk just before frying).
2. Mix 1 cup cornmeal, 1 teaspoon garlic powder, 1 teaspoon paprika, and ½ teaspoon salt in a plastic bag. Fine, dry bread crumbs may be used as coating or mixed with cornmeal, half and half.
3. Shake strips in cornmeal and fry in a little oil.
4. Dip in a mixture of ½ cup fruit preserves or honey and 2 tablespoons prepared mustard or 1 teaspoon dry mustard. Good jams to use are: plum, currant, and apricot.

## Chicken With Chinese Plum Sauce

4 chicken breasts, cut into ¼" strips
oil
1 cup peanuts or toasted almonds, chopped finely

For Plum Sauce, blend together:
1 cup plum, apricot, or currant jam
1 teaspoon dry mustard, Chinese style is best
½ teaspoon dry ginger
½ teaspoon salt
2 teaspoons fresh lemon juice
few dashes of cayenne pepper

In a large skillet or wok, saute chicken in the oil for 5 minutes or until a little golden and no longer pink. Place nuts in one bowl and sauce in another.

Chicken is eaten by dipping first in plum sauce, then in nuts.
Toasting nuts may release free glutamate. Use raw, if preferred.

## Chicken in Plum Sauce
### (Or apricot sauce)

6 to 8 boneless, skinless chicken breast halves
1 cup plum or apricot jam
1 cup water
3 tablespoons flour
½ teaspoon ginger
⅓ cup sugar, to taste
⅓ cup cider vinegar or fresh lemon juice
½ teaspoon salt
dash garlic powder
½ teaspoon Chinese 5 spice powder

Wash and drain chicken. Place on cutting board and sprinkle with salt and a dusting of flour on both sides. Heat large pan with 3 tablespoons of oil and place chicken in pan. Saute on both sides on medium heat until done (20 minutes). Keep warm in uncovered pan. Beat together the flour and water in a pot. Add remaining ingredients and bring to a boil. Serve on the side or over chicken with rice.

## Kristi's Chicken Parmesan

My daughter, also MSG sensitive, has developed some wonderful recipes. I'm proud to say, both our daughters are great cooks and we love their dinner invitations.

Mix in shallow bowl:
1 teaspoon lime juice

1 egg yolk
1 tablespoon water

1 minced garlic clove

In large bag, mix:
1 ¼ cups flour
1 tablespoon parmesan cheese (omit if very sensitive to MSG)
½ teaspoon salt and ¼ teaspoon pepper
½ teaspoon each of oregano and basil

Dip 4-6 chicken breasts in lime mixture, then shake in flour bag. Place in baking dish that has 3 tablespoons melted butter in it. Bake 20 minutes at 350°. Turn with spatula. Bake 15 to 20 more minutes or until chicken is done. Can do the same thing with zucchini rounds and bake along with chicken. Remove chicken from oven. Spoon 3 tablespoons of homemade spaghetti sauce over each chicken piece. Top with slice of mozzarella cheese. Place back in oven and turn off heat. Boil cork screw pasta to serve on side with more spaghetti sauce. Remove chicken when heated through and cheese is melted and "ooey gooey" as Kris says. I have used uncooked pasta sauce heated slightly with this, and used a thick cream sauce instead of the cheese.

## Jamaican Chicken Wings

1 bay leaf crushed
1 ½ teaspoons dry thyme
2 teaspoons dry mustard
2 cloves garlic, peeled
2 medium or hot green peppers (Anaheim or jalapeno), minced
2 tablespoons lime, lemon, or grapefruit juice
2 teaspoons sugar
1 teaspoon salt
¼ teaspoon black pepper

1 teaspoon cinnamon
5 teaspoons allspice

Place ingredients in large plastic zipper bag and shake well. Add 2 lbs. rinsed chicken wings to bag and shake. Bake at 400° for 35 to 40 minutes or until golden.

Chicken legs or thighs may be substituted.

## Crispy Honey Mustard Baked Chicken

Place in plastic bag:
½ cup bread crumbs or flour
3 tablespoons cornmeal
3 tablespoons flour
2 teaspoons salt (may reduce)
¼ teaspoon black pepper
1 ½ teaspoons garlic powder
1 teaspoon dry parsley (optional)
¼ - ½ teaspoon cayenne pepper

In a large bowl, combine:
2 tablespoons mustard
2 tablespoons honey
¼ cup water

Place 2 ½ lbs. chicken pieces in honey mixture and stir to coat (best to use hands). Shake 3 pieces of chicken at a time in bag of crumbs. Place on oiled 9" x 13" pan. Bake at 375° in oven for 45-50 minutes.

## Chicken in Mushroom Gravy

3 boneless, skinless chicken breasts sliced in 2" pieces, 1/8" thick

1 sliced onion

½ lb. fresh mushrooms sliced (or 2 small cans, drained)
1 large clove garlic
paprika
⅓ cup sour cream (optional)
½ cup milk, rice milk, or water
⅓ cup flour
3 cups water

In pan, saute onions in 2 tablespoons oil plus 2 tablespoons butter for 5 minutes. Add chicken and saute until pink in meat is gone. Add garlic and saute for 1 minute. Sprinkle flour over chicken and stir and cook 1 minute on medium heat. Add milk, sour cream and water. Simmer 10 minutes. Add mushrooms and cook for 2 more minutes. Add salt and pepper to taste. Sprinkle with paprika and serve over rice, mashed potatoes, or pasta. Sour cream may be omitted. Use more milk or water.

## Lemon Chicken, Oriental Style
### (One of my son Michael's favorite dishes)

1. Cut 2 large lemons in half. Squeeze 3 halves and set aside juice. Slice the remaining half in circles, paper thin.
2. In sauce pan, blend 2 cups water, ⅓ to ½ cup sugar, 5 tablespoons flour, pinch of ginger, and ⅛ teaspoon salt. Bring to a boil, stirring until thick. Stir in lemon juice. Set aside.
3. Soak and drain 6 chicken breasts.
4. Place 1 breast at a time in a plastic gallon zipper bag and leave open while pounding to ½" thickness or less with bottom of a heavy glass. Place in bowl. I sprinkle in a tablespoon of the lemon juice, stir, and let stand for 10 minutes.
5. Dredge each breast in plain flour. An easy way to flour breasts is to sprinkle flour on with a small strainer. Fry for 5 to 6 minutes on each side in 3 tablespoons oil. Sprinkle with salt and pepper while frying.
6. Reheat sauce and slip lemon slices into sauce and simmer for 5 minutes. Can thin sauce with water if necessary. Keep breasts hot in 250° oven while frying in batches or while heating sauce.
7. Arrange on platter. Pour sauce on top and arrange lemon circles on top. Great with rice and steamed vegetables.
8. For a sweeter sauce, add more sugar.

## Garden Chicken
### Delicious!

¼ cup butter or oil
1 cup chopped celery
1 cup chopped onion
1 cup chopped carrots
¼ cup flour
1 ½ cup stock (saved from boiling chicken or use water or milk)
1 cup whole milk
4 cups dry bread crumbs (cubes)
½ teaspoon salt
½ teaspoon thyme
¼ teaspoon sage
½ teaspoon marjoram

1 teaspoon parsley
2 cups cooked cubed chicken or turkey
1 cup shredded cheese (optional)

In large pan, saute the vegetables in the oil until almost tender. Add the flour and stir, cooking 1 minute. Add the stock and milk and stir until it thickens. Add chicken, bread cubes, and seasonings. Toss gently to coat. Add more liquid if very dry. Spoon into 9" x 13" pan and bake at 350° for 30 to 40 minutes. Sprinkle with cheese and let melt before serving.

## Kristi's Kung Pow Chicken
### (Serves 2 to 4)

1 lb. boneless chicken breast, cut in small cubes
1 clove garlic, minced
⅛ teaspoon red pepper flakes
1 ½ teaspoons sugar
¼ teaspoon salt
⅛ teaspoon pepper
⅛ teaspoon ginger
½ teaspoon soy sauce (may omit)

1. Mix all ingredients and let chicken marinate while chopping the following:
    2 medium carrots, finely diced
    3 to 4 stalks celery, diced
    ½ small onion, finely diced
    1 clove garlic, minced
    1 large red bell pepper, diced

2. Heat 1 tablespoon oil in large skillet or wok on medium-high. Add chicken and stir fry until caramel colored.
3. Start rice. Cook enough to make 2 cups.
4. Add vegetables to chicken and stir fry until tender crisp. Add ⅓ to ½ cup peanuts (no salt added). Reduce to low heat.
5. Mix sauce: In small bowl, combine 1 cup homemade chicken stock. If stock is frozen in ice cube trays, use 4 cubes. Add 1 ½ cup water, 2 teaspoons cornstarch, ⅛ teaspoon ginger, 1 teaspoon salt, 1 teaspoon sugar, dash pepper, dash celery seed (optional). Turn up heat in skillet and add sauce, stirring gently until bubbly and thick. Taste and add more salt and sugar to taste. May stir in rice and serve or spoon over rice to serve
*Water or vegetable stock may be substituted for stock.

## New York Style Marinated Chicken
### (For grill or broiler)

½ cup oil
1 cup cider vinegar or fresh lemon or orange juice
2 tablespoons salt
1 egg
1 teaspoon thyme
¼ teaspoon sage
¼ teaspoon marjoram

¼ teaspoon pepper

Beat egg. Add oil and beat again. Add remaining ingredients and mix. Marinate 2 cutup chickens for 2 hours or overnight in refrigerator. Broil or barbeque chicken. Experiment with different herbs.

## Oven Fried Chicken

1 chicken, cleaned, skinned, and cut up
½ cup oil, can be part melted butter
¼ teaspoon garlic powder
¼ teaspoon paprika
¼ teaspoon thyme
1 teaspoon salt
1 ½ cups fine dry bread crumbs
½ cup flour

Dip chicken in oil and shake in a bag of crumbs mixed with seasonings. Place on lightly greased baking dish and bake for 50 minutes to 1 hour at 350°. I have used 1½ cups flour with ½ cup cornmeal or farina instead of crumbs and increased garlic powder to 1 teaspoon. Can be baked at 375° for approximately 45 minutes.

## Peachy Chicken

3 chicken breasts (6 halves) (bone-in)
½ cup flour
salt and pepper
2 tablespoons butter
2 tablespoons oil
1 ½ cups orange juice
2 tablespoons cider vinegar
2 tablespoons brown or white sugar
1 teaspoon basil (optional)
½ teaspoon nutmeg or ginger
3 fresh peaches or 6 fresh apricots, pitted and halved

Shake chicken pieces in bag with flour, salt, and pepper. Brown in butter and oil. Place browned chicken in greased, 3 quart casserole dish. Combine orange juice with vinegar, sugar, basil, nutmeg, and pour mixture over chicken. Cover and bake at 375° for 1 hour or until tender. Baste often. Then place peach or apricot halves between chicken pieces. Baste well and bake uncovered for 15 minutes longer. Serves 6.

If using boneless chicken, bake only 1 hour total time.

Variation:
½ teaspoon dry mint leaves may be substituted for the basil.

## Crackly Roast Chicken

2 small chickens or 1 large (4 to 6 lbs.)
kosher salt or sea salt
3 cloves garlic halved
Juice of 1 large lemon or 2 small limes
Black pepper

Pre-heat oven to 425°. Wash chickens well and pat dry. Sprinkle each chicken liberally with the coarse salt. Rub 3 garlic halves cut side down over each chicken and place inside chickens. Sprinkle lemon juice evenly over chickens. Sprinkle with a little more salt and the pepper. For a spicier flavor, sprinkle each with ½ teaspoon chili powder. Roast in oven for 1 hour and 15 minutes. Do not open oven. Chicken is done when juices run clear when pierced with knife.

## Baked Crumb Top Fish

1 lb. cod or sole fillets, (can use any favorite fish)
1 cup fine bread crumbs
1 teaspoon dry dill or thyme
3 tablespoons olive or other oil
½ teaspoon salt
dash pepper

Mix all ingredients but fish in a bowl. Grease a baking dish and place fish in dish and sprinkle crumbs over top. Bake at 450° for 12 to 15 minutes or until thickest part of fish is opaque and flakes. Be sure to buy fish not treated with sulfites.

## Perfect Blackened Salmon

In a shallow pan, mix together:
3 tablespoons chili powder
2 tablespoons pasilla powder
1 teaspoon salt
¼ teaspoon black pepper
dash cayenne pepper

Dip one side of salmon steak or filet (not skin side) into seasoning. Place coated side down in hot oil and fry 3 to 4 minutes or until dark and crisp on the bottom. Flip over and place pan in 400° oven for 7 minutes or until fish is done. Great served with fruit salsa. Covers 4 salmon steaks. Works for most fish steaks or fillets also.

.*Use oven safe fry pan or transfer to another pan.

## Herb Fish Bake

1 lb. fresh fish fillets
1 lemon, sliced thin or a small orange
1 tomato, sliced thin (optional)
¼ teaspoon thyme, dry
¼ teaspoon dill, dry
¼ teaspoon basil, dry

Place fish in baking dish. Sprinkle with herbs, then layer with lemon slices and tomato slices. Drizzle with 1 tablespoon olive oil. Bake at 425° for 10 minutes or until fish is white and flakes. Season with salt and pepper and serve.

## Oven Baked Fish

In 2 qt. casserole, melt ¼ cup butter. Add ⅓ cup minced onion and the juice of ½ lemon or lime. Place 1 ½ - 2 lbs. fish fillets or steaks in casserole, turning once to coat. Salt and pepper lightly. Sprinkle ¼ lb. fresh sliced mushrooms over fish (optional). Bake at 350° for 15 - 25 minutes or until fish flakes. Remove from oven and sprinkle with ½ cup grated cheese (optional). Turn off oven and place casserole back in oven until cheese melts. This is great served with fresh tomatoes, baked potatoes and green beans. Suggested fish: sole, halibut, salmon, red snapper, cod. Mushrooms may be added for last 10 minutes of baking if preferred.

## Crab or Salmon Cakes

Even kids love these crispy patties. We make them often with canned salmon, using milk instead of mayonaise.

1 cup fresh bread crumbs
2 eggs
2 tablespoons mayonnaise (sour cream, milk or water may be substituted)
1 tablespoon minced onion
2 tablespoons minced celery
1 clove garlic minced
1 tablespoon fresh chopped parsley (1 teaspoon dry)
¼ teaspoon dry mustard

¼ teaspoon cayenne pepper
½ teaspoon salt
1 lb. crab meat (or cooked or canned salmon)
flour for dredging
2 tablespoons olive oil

Combine all but last 2 ingredients. Shape into patties and dredge in flour. Fry in oil 5 minutes on each side. Serve with lemon wedges, salad, and baked potato.

## Salmon Patties

1 - 16 oz. can salmon, drain and mash
1 carrot, grated
1 onion, finely chopped
½ cup fine plain bread crumbs, oat bran, or oatmeal
1 egg
salt and pepper
1 teaspoon parsley

¼ teaspoon dill (optional)
dash cayenne pepper

Mix well together and form into patties. Brown in a little oil for 6 minutes on each side.

Grated potato or zucchini may be substituted for carrot.

## Spinach Stuffed Sole
### (Serves 2)

Sauce:
3 tablespoons butter or olive oil
4 mushrooms, sliced
3 tablespoons flour
1 ½ cups whole milk (or half cream and half water)

Melt butter in sauce pan and add mushrooms. Saute and then sprinkle with flour. Stir and cook for 1 minute. Add milk and stir until bubbly and thickened. Salt and pepper to taste. Remove from heat.

Filling:

1 - 10 oz. package frozen chopped spinach, thawed and drained or 6 to 8 cups chopped fresh
1 egg, beaten
½ onion, chopped fine
1 tablespoon oil

*Fresh spinach will reduce in size when cooked.

Saute onion in oil until tender. Take off heat and add spinach. If using fresh, saute for 2 minutes. Add the egg when mixture cools a bit. Sprinkle with salt and pepper. Place filling on each of 4 large pieces of sole or perch filets and roll up. Put in a greased pan and bake at 375° for 20 minutes or until fish is done. Reheat sauce and serve over fish on plates.

## Speedy Shrimp Creole

2 cups cooked medium unsulphured shrimp (defrost if frozen)
5 cups cooked rice (hot)
1 teaspoon dry chives or ¼ teaspoon powdered onion
¼ teaspoon celery seeds
1 teaspoon parsley
½ teaspoon thyme
dash cayenne pepper or more
salt and pepper to taste

2 teaspoons sugar
4 cups chopped tomatoes
1 cup sour cream or heavy cream

Mix all ingredients except cream in a glass casserole and microwave until hot for 8 to 10 minutes or bake for 20 minutes at 350° until heated through. Just before serving, stir in cream.

## Barbecued Pork Chops
### (These are very easy and very tasty)

Place or spread on top of each pork chop in the following order: 1 tablespoon homemade catsup, 1 tablespoon chopped onion, 1 tablespoon brown sugar, 2 teaspoons vinegar or fresh lemon juice, 1 more tablespoon homemade catsup, salt, and pepper. Bake in pan at 350° for 45 minutes to 1 hour or until brown and tender. Applesauce may be substituted for catsup.

## Krista's Braised Pork Chops with Pears

2 to 4 pork loin chops (1" cut is good)
flour
salt
pepper
2 to 4 fresh pears
butter:
   2 tablespoons for 2 chops
   4 tablespoons for 4 chops

Peel, halve, and poach pears gently in water to cover with 1 tablespoon sugar per pear for 10 to 15 minutes.

Lightly dust chops with flour. Shake off excess. Sprinkle both sides with salt and pepper. Melt butter in large skillet, add 2 tablespoons pear juice and swirl to mix. Brown chops over medium-high, for 1 ½ minutes on each side. Gently arrange pears around chops in skillet. Pour remaining juice over all. Cover and cook over medium heat for 30 minutes. Great served with green beans and baked potatoes, or sweet potatoes. Chicken breasts may be substituted.

## Country Sausage

2 lbs. lean ground pork (ask butcher to grind some pork butt for you or process your own)
5 tablespoons minced onion
1 tablespoon fresh minced parsley or 1 teaspoon dry
2 teaspoons salt
1 teaspoon ground sage
1 teaspoon dry basil
1 teaspoon marjoram or thyme
1 teaspoon chili powder
1 teaspoon pepper
½ teaspoon ground red pepper (optional)
1 teaspoon sugar

Combine ingredients in a bowl. Shape into 2 logs, 6" or 7" long. Wrap in plastic wrap and let flavors blend overnight. Slice into ½" rounds and fry on medium heat for 3 to 4 minutes on each side. Logs may be frozen and used later. Wrap foil over plastic wrap.

Variation:
Sausage may be rolled into balls (1" to 1 ½") and frozen on cookie sheets, then stored in freezer bags. To serve, bake frozen in pans for 25 to 30 minutes at 350°. Makes good hors d' oeuvres served with a honey mustard mixture, or jam heated with mustard and a little vinegar. May be sauteed and added to bean soup or other stews.

## Italian Sausage

Raised in Buffalo, N.Y., we were able to buy the best Italian sausage in the world! I sure miss it but try to make a close second. If parmesan cheese doesn't bother you, add a little for variety.

2 lbs. ground pork
2 teaspoons salt
½ teaspoon black pepper
1 tablespoon fennel seed
¼ teaspoon red pepper flakes
¼ teaspoon garlic powder or 1 clove garlic minced (optional)
1 teaspoon dry parsley (optional)

Mix well. Best to refrigerate 1 hour to blend flavors, but this is optional. Shape into patties or hotdog shapes and saute or grill until well done. Serve on buns with favorite condiments. May be frozen in patty shapes on cookie sheet, then packaged in freezer bags.

## Italian Sausage II
### Spicier

2 lbs. ground lean pork (butt is good)
1 tablespoon fennel seed
1 crushed bay leaf
1 teaspoon dry basil
½ teaspoon dry oregano
1 tablespoon dry parsley
2-3 cloves garlic minced

½ teaspoon hot pepper flakes
2 teaspoons salt
½ teaspoon pepper
4 tablespoons water

Mix and shape into patties or fry up to put on pizza.

## Polish Sausage

2 lbs. ground pork
½ teaspoon pepper
½ teaspoon marjoram
1 tablespoon salt
1 clove garlic, minced

Mix together well with hands. Shape into patties and saute or grill until well done. Serve on buns with mustard and onions or plain.

## Pork Chops and Gravy (Easy and Fast)
### My husband loves this.

1.  Wash and pat dry 4 pork chops.
2.  In pan place 2 tablespoons oil.
3.  Get pan very hot (starts to smoke) on high.
4.  Place chops in pan and let sear for 1 minute on each side.
5.  Turn heat down to med-low. Sprinkle some chopped onion in pan (½ cup). Sprinkle salt, pepper, and a little garlic powder on chops.
6.  Add ¼ cup water and cover pan. Turn to low and simmer 15 min.
7.  Turn over, cover, and simmer 15 more minutes. Add water if dry.
8.  Remove meat to a plate.
9.  Put 1 cup water in a small bowl. Add 3 tablespoons flour and beat until lumps are gone with whisk or fork.
10. Pour into pan drippings and stir, cooking until gravy thickens.
11. Add chops to pan, simmer, and reheat chops. You can do this with chicken breast, beef steak, or hamburger patties.
12. Meanwhile, microwave potatoes to eat with gravy. Rice or cooked noodles are also good with this.

## Pork Chili Verde
### One of my favorite Mexican dishes.

2 to 3 pounds pork shoulder roast, boneless
1 - 14 oz. can tomatillos rinsed and drained (or use 2 cups fresh chopped)
1 - 7 oz. can diced green chilies or 3 fresh Anaheim peppers, diced
2 to 3 cloves garlic
1 onion, diced
1 teaspoon salt
dash pepper
1 tablespoon sugar
2 teaspoons chili powder (optional)
1 teaspoon dry cilantro
½ teaspoon cumin

Blend or process tomatillos or chop finely. Put in a medium bowl. Add the rest of the ingredients. Cut up pork shoulder by slicing in ½" x 2" pieces. Place all ingredients in roasting pan, stir, and cover. Bake at 375° for 45 minutes to 1 hour. If too dry, add some water. Reduce heat to 325° and bake until fork tender. Meat may be cut into smaller chunks with 2 forks. Serve with or place in warm tortillas and serve with condiments such as grated cheese, sour cream, and avocados, if desired.

## Mexican Burrito Beef Filling

4 dry pasilla peppers
3 dry New Mexico chilies (HOT), or may use all pasilla peppers if mild sauce is desired
1 small onion
4 cups fresh, chopped tomatoes
3 cloves garlic
1 cup water
1 teaspoon salt
½ teaspoon cumin
¼ teaspoon black pepper

3 lbs. beef (chuck or round)
2 tablespoons sugar (optional)

*The meat may be left whole and roasted and unshredded. Cut into serving portions and serve with soft heated flour tortillas or rice.

Wash and soak peppers in 2 cups hot water to soften. Drain all but ½ cup of the liquid. Put softened peppers (stems and seeds removed), tomatoes, garlic, and quartered onions in processor or blender and process until smooth. Add with the reserved chili liquid to roasting pan with water, salt, and spices. Cut beef into chunks and stir into sauce. Bake uncovered at 375° for 45 minutes. Reduce heat to 325° and roast until fork tender. If too dry, add more

water. Shred or cube meat with knife and fork. Use to fill tortillas or as a topping for polenta. If preferred, leave out the tomatoes when roasting beef, adding more water if needed. Add the tomatoes the last 15 minutes of cooking.

*2 to 3 tablespoons ground pasilla peppers or chili powder plus ¼ teaspoon cayenne pepper may be substituted for the dry chili peppers.

## Ground Beef Patties

Mix:
1 lb. ground beef
1 onion, chopped
½ chopped bell pepper
1 egg
½ cup oatmeal or oat bran
½ cup milk
2 tablespoons catsup (optional)
salt and pepper to taste
*Favorite seasonings

Form patties, dip in flour, and brown well on both sides. Remove from pan and stir 3 tablespoons flour into drippings. Add 2 cups water or milk and stir well while it thickens on medium heat. Return patties to gravy and let simmer, adding more liquid if needed. Meanwhile, cook rice, noodles, or potatoes to serve with patties and gravy.

*Our son, Mike, likes to add all kinds of herbs and spices, changing the flavor of the meat all the time.

## Dorothy's Meatloaf (Mom's)

2 lbs. ground beef
3 eggs
⅓ cup oatmeal (optional. May use an extra slice of bread instead)
1 chopped onion
3 slices bread, cubed
½ cup milk
1 tablespoon mustard
1 teaspoon salt
¼ teaspoon pepper
¼ teaspoon garlic
¼ teaspoon sage
¼ teaspoon thyme

½ cup raisins (optional)

Place bread and milk in a large bowl and let soak for 2 minutes. Add remaining ingredients and mix well. Shape into 2 loaves and place into bread pans or one 9" x 13" pan. Homemade catsup may be drizzled on top during last 5 minutes of baking. Bake 45 minutes to 1 hour at 350°.

*Try the raisins! They plump up and flavor the meat wonderfully. If bread bothers you, use a total of 1 cup oatmeal instead.

## Mexi-Meatloaf

2 lbs. ground beef
5 cups tortilla chips crushed to 1 1/4 cups (look for ones without lime)
1 can black, kidney, or pinto beans (10 ½ oz.)
1 cup corn
½ cup chopped onion
1 egg
1 tablespoon chili powder
2 teaspoons salt

1 teaspoon cumin or 2 teaspoons cilantro
1/4 cup salsa (optional)

Mix all ingredients (mashing some beans). Shape into 2 small or 1 large loaf and bake in loaf pans or casserole dishes. (May shape into patties and fry in 1 tablespoon oil until cooked throughout over medium heat.

## Mom's Swiss Steak

6 carrots, cleaned and cut in 2" chunks
2 onions sliced
2 cups fresh green beans, cleaned (optional)
1 large or 2 medium zucchini
1 large round steak
2 cloves garlic chopped
salt and pepper
thyme or marjoram
4 stalks celery

*Various vegetables may be added or substituted such as green pepper, Anaheim chilies, potatoes, cabbage, etc..

Slice zucchini in half inch thick circles and place in single layer on bottom of roaster pan. Sprinkle with half of the garlic, onion, and celery. Lightly season with salt, pepper, and herbs. Distribute beans evenly on top. Place steak over vegetables. Sprinkle remaining garlic, onion, and celery on top. Sprinkle with salt and pepper. Place carrots and any remaining squash on top of steak. Sprinkle again with salt, pepper, and herbs. Cover and roast at 350° to 375° for 2 hours. Serve with juices. Chicken, fish, and pork can be cooked this way. Fish will take less time so roast until vegetables are tender. Add water after 1 hour if too dry.

## Lamb Chops

Marinade:
1 clove garlic, minced
½ teaspoon rosemary, dry or 1 teaspoon fresh
⅓ cup oil
¼ teaspoon pepper

Marinade 6 to 8 lamb chops in plastic bag or shallow dish for 3 to 6 hours. Fry in hot oil for 2 to 3 minutes on each side. Lightly season with salt before serving.

# MIXES

## Biscuit Mix

8 cups flour
5 tablespoons baking powder
1 teaspoon baking soda
3 teaspoons salt
1 ½ cups butter or plain shortening

Mix dry ingredients and cut in butter or shortening. Store in canister in refrigerator if using butter. To make biscuits, mix 2 ½ cups with ¾ cup milk. Drop by tablespoons full on greased cookie sheet. Bake for 10 minutes at 425°. For rolled biscuits, roll out on well floured towel. Cut into squares or circles before baking.

## Cocoa Mix

Mix 2 parts sugar to 1 part cocoa and store in container. Mix 2 tablespoons mix with hot or cold milk. For cold milk, mix first with a little very hot water. Then add cold milk or rice milk.

Variation: Spiced cocoa mix
1 cup sugar

½ cup cocoa
2 teaspoons pumpkin pie spice

*2 parts mixture with 1 part hot water to dissolve makes a good syrup for ice cream and sodas.

## Pancake Mix

12 cups flour
2 tablespoons salt
⅔ cup baking powder
⅔ cup sugar

Mix ingredients with whisk and store in air tight container. No refrigeration required. To use, combine 1 egg, 1 ⅓ cup milk, 2 tablespoons oil, and 1 ½ cups pancake mix. Add water if thinner batter is desired. Serves 4. For less puffy pancakes use, 14 cups flour. For more puffy pancakes, use ¾ cup baking powder.

## Ginny's Pie Crust Mix

8 cups flour
1 tablespoon salt
3 cups unflavored, uncolored shortening or unsalted butter

Mix flour and salt. Cut in shortening with pastry cutter. If using shortening, store on pantry shelf in air tight container. If using butter, store in refrigerator or freezer. For a double crust pie, mix 3 cups mixture with 5 tablespoons ice water.

## Pudding Mix

3 cups sugar
2 cups cornstarch or 2 ½ cups flour
½ teaspoon salt

Mix together and store in cool place
Variation: Use 3 ¼ cups packed brown sugar for butterscotch flavor.

## Vanilla Pudding

1 egg yolk
½ cup pudding mix
2 cups milk or 1 cup cream and 1 cup water
1 tablespoon butter
2 teaspoons vanilla extract

Stir egg yolk and set aside.
In medium sauce pan mix milk and pudding mix. Stir over medium heat until thick and bubbly. Stirring quickly, add half of hot mixture to yolk. Return egg mixture to sauce pan and cook, stirring for 1 minute. Remove from heat and stir in butter and vanilla. Cover with plastic wrap.

Add 2 to 3 tablespoons cocoa to dry ingredients for chocolate pudding.

## Shake It and Bake It
### (Chicken or pork coating)

4 ½ cups dried bread crumbs, finely crushed
½ cup plus 2 tablespoons flour
6 tablespoons paprika
2 tablespoons plus 2 teaspoons salt
4 tablespoons sugar
2 tablespoons onion powder
2 teaspoons oregano flakes or powder
2 teaspoons thyme flakes or powder
2 teaspoons cayenne pepper powder (may decrease)

1 teaspoon sage powder
½ to 1 teaspoon garlic powder
½ teaspoon black pepper

Mix well and store in covered glass container.
To use:
Dip meat in oil, then into 1 to 2 cups of the dry mixture placed in a plastic bag. Bake skin side down at 375° for 1 hour. Turn when half done. May use on skinless chicken also.

## Homemade Baking Powder
### (Cornstarch contains MSG residue and is usually found in commercial brands)

2 tablespoons baking soda
4 tablespoons cream of tartar
4 tablespoons powdered arrowroot or tapioca

Large batch
¼ cup baking soda
½ cup cream of tartar
½ cup powdered arrowroot or tapioca

Place in jar, cover and shake.
Measure as for regular baking powder

# SALADS

### Barley Salad

½ cup pearl barley
1 bunch fresh kale, collard greens, or spinach washed and chopped (or some of each)
3 tablespoons olive oil
4 tablespoons lime or lemon juice
2 tablespoons cider vinegar or fresh lemon juice
3 tablespoons cilantro or parsley chopped (use less if dry)
2 cloves garlic minced
1 teaspoon cumin
salt and pepper to taste
1 package frozen corn or peas thawed (organic is preferred)
1 - 15 oz. can black beans drained and rinsed
1 bell pepper chopped
sugar or honey (optional)

Bring 2 cups water to boil. Stir in barley. Cover and simmer 45 minutes. When tender, add the kale or spinach and cook 5 minutes longer. In large bowl, mix together the oil, juice, vinegar, garlic, herbs, and spices. Add the barley mixture, corn, beans and pepper. Mix well and serve chilled.

*This is an easy recipe to experiment with different grains and vegetables. Dressing may be sweetened if desired with sugar or honey. Try substituting cooked rice, wheat berries, or quinoa instead of barley and try adding chopped cucumbers, zucchini, or sweet onion. Nuts, raisins, and currants would be nutritious additions.

### Old-Fashioned Cabbage Salad

Mix the following ingredients:
2 cups sugar (may decrease)
½ cup cider vinegar or fresh lemon juice
1 teaspoon salt
1 teaspoon celery seed
½ teaspoon dry mustard
1 large head cabbage, shredded
1 green pepper, chopped
1 cup celery, chopped
½ cup sweet onion, chopped (optional)

Mix vegetables with dressing in large bowl. Cover and refrigerate over night or use at least 20 minutes after mixing. Keeps 7 to 10 days in refrigerator. This is good in veggie sandwiches or on hamburgers instead of catsup or pickles.

### Overnight Cole Slaw
Our teenager loves this even though its "healthy" food.

12 cups shredded cabbage (1 large head)
1 green pepper chopped
1 medium red onion chopped (any sweet variety)
2 carrots shredded

1 cup sugar

Dressing:

2 teaspoons sugar
1 teaspoon dry mustard
1 teaspoon celery seed
1 teaspoon salt
1 cup vinegar
¾ cup vegetable oil

In a large bowl, combine first 4 ingredients. Sprinkle with sugar, stir, and set aside.

In a sauce pan, combine dressing ingredients and bring to a boil. (I usually omit this step -- just mix in a bowl). Remove from the heat and pour over vegetables, stirring to cover evenly. Cover and refrigerate overnight or serve at least 20 minutes after making.

Stir well before serving. A processor saves time chopping. We've made this without cooking the dressing. Just whisk together and pour over salad. We make this often and use it to top sandwiches or hamburgers. It's even a good condiment with fried eggs.

Variation:
Use ½ teaspoon celery seed and just before serving, add 1 can rinsed kidney beans or 2 cups other cooked beans and 1 cup toasted chopped or whole almonds or walnuts. Toast nuts in oven for 10 minutes at 350°. This is a meal in a salad!!

## Chicken Salad

2 ½ cups cooked diced chicken
1 ½ cups seedless grapes, halved
2 teaspoons dried parsley
1 ½ cups chopped celery
½ cup slivered almonds
1 teaspoon salt
1 cup sour cream or homemade yogurt
1 tablespoon cider vinegar or fresh lemon juice
1 tablespoon oil

2 teaspoons sugar
dash pepper
dash cayenne pepper

Combine and serve on lettuce. Sprinkle with paprika. Most of the dressing recipes may be substituted for the sour cream, vinegar, oil, and seasonings.

## Chicken Salad II

5 to 6 cups cubed cooked chicken
2 cups seedless grapes
¾ cup halved or sliced almonds (toast for 6 to 8 minutes at 350°)
1 cup sour cream
1 teaspoon vinegar

2 tablespoons honey or currant jelly
dash salt and pepper

May substitute 1 cup homemade mayonnaise or whipped cream for sour cream and omit honey.

## Deli Salad

2 cloves garlic minced
2 tablespoons onion minced
½ teaspoon dry mustard

1 tablespoon honey or sugar
2 tablespoons vinegar or fresh lemon juice

½ cup fresh dill chopped (or 1to 2 tablespoons dry)
⅔ cup oil

Mix ingredients and pour over 2 cups cooked shrimp or cooked cubed chicken. Let chill in refrigerator. Mix together 2 sliced tomatoes, 1 sliced cucumber, and mixed greens. Divide among plates and top with meat and drizzle with marinade. Garnish with black olives.

*If sulfite sensitive, do not use small cocktail shrimp. They are usually sprayed with sulfites on the fishing boat to prevent "Black Spot" infestation.

## Shelli's Fruit Salad with Lemon Dressing

3 oranges, peeled, sectioned, and sliced
3 bananas, sliced
2 medium apples, chopped (unpeeled)
1 - 20 oz. can pineapple tidbits or 2 cups fresh diced

Dressing:
½ cup sour cream or homemade yogurt
2 tablespoons honey

1 teaspoon vanilla
2 tablespoons fresh lemon juice
⅛ teaspoon nutmeg
dash cinnamon

Mix and combine with fruit. Chill before serving. For a low calorie version, omit sour cream.

## Fruit Salad with Cooked Fruit Sauce

Sauce ingredients:
1 egg
1 tablespoon fresh lime juice or water
¼ cup fresh lemon juice
½ cup fresh orange juice
1 cup sugar

Beat egg in a small pot and blend in remaining ingredients. Bring to boil and cook for 1 minute. Let cool.

Peel, clean, and cut up the following fruit:
1 large cantaloupe or honeydew melon

1 pineapple
2 grapefruit
2 oranges
1 red apple (keep skin on)
1 banana
2 cups blueberries, strawberries, or raspberries

Gently mix all the fruit (except berries) in a bowl. Pour sauce over all. Chill for 2 hours, stir once, and sprinkle berries on top just before serving. I have made the sauce with all orange juice and it's very tasty, too.

## Fruit Salad
### (Our kids don't notice the cabbage)

½ cup orange pieces or 1 can drained Mandarin oranges (may contain sulfites)
½ cup pineapple chunks
½ cup apple cubes
4 cups shredded cabbage
2 tablespoons pineapple juice (or orange juice)
½ cup sour cream (optional)

2 tablespoons vinegar or fresh lemon juice
2 tablespoons sugar or honey
¼ teaspoon nutmeg
dash salt

Mix ingredients. Chill and serve.

## Melon Pecan Salad

1 large cantaloupe or honeydew melon peeled and diced in 1" chunks.
1 cup diced red bell pepper
1 cup chopped celery
2 tablespoons fresh parsley or mint, chopped
1 cup broken pecans or walnuts, toasted at 350° for 10 minutes or 3 minutes in microwave oven if desired

Dressing:
¼ cup lime or lemon juice (or vinegar)

2 tablespoons honey
½ cup oil (may decrease)
salt and pepper to taste

Mix salad with dressing and sprinkle nuts on top just before serving.

Variation:
Diced, cooked chicken or cooked shrimp may be added.

## Grilled Herb Chicken or Shrimp Salad

Mix together for marinade:
⅓ cup oil
3 tablespoons lemon juice
1 tablespoon of your favorite fresh herb or mixture of herbs.
½ teaspoon salt
dash pepper
2 large or 3 small cloves garlic, minced
1 teaspoon sugar or honey

Suggested herbs are oregano, thyme, rosemary, basil, sage, or tarragon.

Large shrimp may be substituted for the chicken.

Marinade 4 chicken breasts in large plastic zipper bag for at least ½ hour before cooking. Grill chicken breasts 6 to 7 minutes on each side. Slice on the diagonal and serve over fresh greens (romaine tossed with fresh basil leaves is good). Garnish with tomatoes and olives. Can fill 4 to 6 individual salad plates or can be arranged on one large platter to serve.

Top with vinaigrette of:
½ cup olive oil
¼ cup fresh lemon juice
1 teaspoon salt
pepper
1 teaspoon same herbs used in marinade.
½ teaspoon sugar

## Green Salad and Poppy Seed Dressing

1 head lettuce torn
1 small cucumber sliced
¼ red onion sliced

Dressing:
1 cup honey

1 cup vinegar or fresh lemon juice
1 cup vegetable oil
1 tablespoon poppy seeds
2 slices red onion finely diced (optional)

Pour ½ cup dressing over salad just before serving. Refrigerate remaining dressing.

## Honey Almond Fruit Salad

1 - 20 oz. can pineapple chunks or use fresh
½ teaspoon almond extract
2 large oranges
2 cups strawberries, hulled and halved
2 cups seedless grapes
1 grapefruit
2 bananas
3 tablespoons honey

Drain pineapple chunks, reserving 1 cup juice. Mix honey, almond extract, and reserved juice. Peel and section oranges and grapefruit and cut into bite size chunks. Toss with remaining fruit and honey dressing. Refrigerate and chill before serving. Apples and other fruits may be added, including berries.

## Ice Box Vegetable Bean Salad

Combine following ingredients in a bowl:
1 can (16 oz.) cut green beans
1 can (17 oz.) tiny peas
1 can (16 oz.) corn
1 cup celery finely chopped
1 medium sweet onion finely chopped
1 medium green pepper chopped
1 can kidney beans rinsed and drained (optional)

Dressing:
1 cup sugar (may decrease)
½ cup oil

1 teaspoon salt
½ teaspoon pepper
Juice of 1 large lemon

In a sauce pan, combine the above ingredients and bring just to boil. Cool slightly and pour over vegetables. Cover and refrigerate overnight. Store up to 1 week. I use organic defrosted mixed vegetables in this recipe to avoid preservatives or MSG, often found in canned vegetables.

## New England Salad

1 head lettuce, torn
2 cups spinach, torn
5 bacon strips, cooked and crumbled (MSG free)
1 tomato, sliced
Any of the following: grapes, avocado, orange slices, sweet onion, mushrooms

Dressing:
1 teaspoon fresh lime juice
¼ cup minced onion
2 tablespoons catsup (omit or use homemade)
½ teaspoon salt
¼ teaspoon pepper
½ cup oil
¾ cup sugar
¼ cup vinegar

In large bowl, combine salad ingredients, except bacon, and chill.
Just before serving, pour dressing over salad and toss. Toss in bacon just before serving. Toasted nuts can be substituted for bacon. Most sensitive individuals react to it or can't find it MSG or nitrate free.

Variation:
Decrease sugar to ⅓ cup. Omit onion and lime juice. Toss with spinach, sweet onions, chopped hard boiled eggs, 1 can kidney or garbanzo beans, and cubed cheese. Served with bread, it's a meal. Look for brands without smoke or natural flavoring.
*Canned garbanzo beans usually contain sulfites.

## Krista's Marinated Zucchini Salad

½ cup vinegar or lemon juice
¼ cup oil
2 teaspoons sugar
¼ teaspoon salt
1 teaspoon dry basil
1 clove minced garlic
2 small zucchini, halved lengthwise and sliced
¼" thick
1 cup kidney beans, rinsed and drained
¼ cup sliced black olives
2 tomatoes, cut in wedges
2 tablespoons green or sweet onions, sliced

Marinade:
Combine and mix well the first six ingredients. In another bowl, mix zucchini, beans, and olives. Pour marinade over mixture to coat. Cover and refrigerate 3 hours or over night. To serve, drain, reserving marinade. Spoon salad on lettuce or spinach leaves. Top with onion and tomato. Drizzle with remaining marinade. Salt and pepper to taste.

Variations:
Leftover cooked chicken or shrimp may be added just before serving. Cucumber may be substituted for zucchini. Green pepper may be added.

## Krista's Summer Chicken salad

Spinach leaves or lettuce
1 to 2 cooked chicken breasts, cut into chunks
2 cups cut up fruit (oranges, strawberries, nectarines, grapes)
½ cup celery, chopped
2 tablespoons sliced almonds
2 tablespoons sliced green onions

On salad plates, arrange spinach, chicken, fruit, celery, almonds, and onion.

Drizzle with following dressing:
4 tablespoons sour cream (optional)
3 tablespoons orange juice
2 tablespoons honey
pinch of salt

Garnish with orange and strawberry slices.

Variation:
Use any favorite sweet dressing.

## Layered Mexican Bean Salad

For salad, mix together:
1 - 1 lb. 10 oz. can or 2 small cans (14 oz.) kidney, black, or pinto beans rinsed and drained
2 tablespoons chopped sweet onion
½ green pepper, chopped (optional)
1 can corn rinsed and drained (fresh kernels or frozen organic are best)
1 teaspoon sugar
1 teaspoon chili powder
¼ cup fresh chopped cilantro or 1 tablespoon dry
Salt and pepper to taste
2 dashes cayenne
½ chopped Anaheim pepper (optional)

1 teaspoon apple cider vinegar or fresh lemon juice

Bake 6 flour tortillas (check to find them without sulfites or L-cysteine or make those found in this book) in 350° oven for 10 minutes or until crisp. Tortillas may be fried in a tiny amount of oil in skillet on both sides until crisp.
Layer on plates in this order:
    bean salad
    grated cheddar cheese
    sour cream
    chopped tomatoes

chopped avocado
chopped black olives (optional)
Omit any toppings that give you problems.

Break up tortillas and dip and eat with salad.

## Penne Pasta Salad
### A standard recipe at our house. A must try!
This is a summer perennial with our garden tomatoes and bell peppers. Rice vinegar is especially good in this recipe.

1 lb. penne pasta
3 large or 4 medium diced tomatoes
2 teaspoons dry or ¼ cup fresh basil
1 to 2 large cloves garlic, minced
3 tablespoons vinegar
4 tablespoons olive oil
2 teaspoons sugar
dash cayenne pepper
1 teaspoon salt
dash black pepper
bell peppers, onion, and black olives (optional)

Puree all but pasta, bell peppers, onion, and olives in blender or processor. Set aside. Cook pasta according to directions. Drain and plunge in cold water. Drain and toss with puree. Add fresh, chopped green pepper, sweet onion, and black olives if desired.

Variation: Soak and wash 4 chicken breasts. Simmer 35 minutes in water. Drain, cool, de-bone, and chop. Add to pasta.

## Peanut Broccoli Slaw

16 oz. package broccoli slaw, cole slaw, or chop 5 lbs. Fresh broccoli or cabbage
2 apples cubed
½ cup raisins, currants, or dried cranberries
½ cup dry roasted peanuts (unsalted, unseasoned)

Dressing:
⅔ cup sour cream or yogurt
4 teaspoons sugar

2 tablespoons vinegar or fresh lime juice
1 teaspoon salt
1 teaspoon celery seed

Rinse slaw. Combine all but nuts. Cover and refrigerate at least 2 hours. Top with nuts just before serving. Other dressings may be substituted. For lower calorie salad dressisng, omit sour cream.

## Salad for Dinner
### (Lots of protein without meat)

3 hard-boiled eggs, chopped
4 cups fresh or frozen peas (organic)
2 cups cooked beans, any kind
3 tablespoons chopped fresh cilantro, basil, parsley, mint, or combination
½ teaspoon salt
2 large tomatoes, chopped

½ sweet onion, chopped
3 tablespoons cider vinegar or lemon juice
¼ cup olive oil
dash pepper
1 teaspoon sugar (optional)

Toss all ingredients and serve on lettuce.

## Strawberry Spinach Salad

1 lb. fresh cleaned spinach with stems removed and leaves torn
3 hard-cooked eggs cut in wedges
½ sweet white or red onion sliced thinly
½ cup slivered almonds
1 cup sliced strawberries or any fresh fruit in season

Toss with a sweet oil and vinegar dressing such as Craig's Favorite Dressing found in this book.

Our favorite: 2 tablespoons lemon juice, strawberry, or raspberry vinegar, 2 tablespoons sugar or honey, 4 tablespoons water, and 3 tablespoons oil. Salt and pepper to taste.

## Picnic Potato Salad
### (no mayonnaise)

6 to 8 large potatoes
6 hard boiled eggs, chopped
½ cup chopped sweet onion
4 stalks celery, diced
1 ½ to 2 teaspoons dry mustard or 1 ½ tablespoons prepared
2 teaspoons salt
6 tablespoons sugar
4 eggs
6 tablespoons melted butter
1 cup hot cider vinegar or fresh lemon juice
2 cups heavy cream, whipped

Cook potatoes until tender but not mushy. Cool and dice into ½" bite size pieces. Add chopped eggs, onion, celery, then salt and pepper to taste.

Dressing:

In double boiler, mix together mustard, salt, and sugar. Beat in the eggs, melted butter and hot vinegar. Cook over boiling water until thickened. Chill. Mix whipped cream with above mixture. Toss salad with enough of the dressing to achieve desired moistness. Refrigerate rest. Makes 12 to 14 servings.

*Oil may be substituted for butter.

Variation: Mix together potatoes, eggs, and vegetables. Add ½ cup cider vinegar, 1½ teaspoons dry mustard, 6 tablespoons sugar, ½ to ⅔ cup oil, salt, and pepper to taste. Stir well. Thin with water or cream, if needed. Taste and adjust seasonings.

## Taco Salad

1 head lettuce
4 tomatoes, chopped
1 cup grated cheese (optional)
1 can drained kidney beans
1 - 6 oz. bag plain tortilla chips
½ cup Craig's favorite dressing
½ lb. ground beef
1 tablespoon chili powder

1 onion, chopped
1 avocado, chopped

Mix first five ingredients as you would a salad. Brown beef, onion, and chili powder for 10 minutes. Add avocado, dressing, and hamburger, while still hot, to salad and serve immediately.

## Fresh Tomato and Mozzarella Salad

¼ cup olive oil
2 tablespoons vinegar or fresh lime juice
1 to 2 tablespoons fresh basil chopped or 1
teaspoon dry
¼ teaspoon black pepper
¼ teaspoon salt
3 large ripe tomatoes sliced
8 oz. thinly sliced Mozzarella cheese
½ sliced sweet onion (optional)

Mix all but tomatoes, cheese, and onions.
Arrange tomatoes and cheese alternately on large
serving plate. Drizzle dressing over all. Garnish
with onions and fresh basil leaves if desired.
Serve with garlic bread.

*Cooked garbanzo or kidney beans may be
added for more protein.

If you are using canned beans and are sulfite
sensitive, rinse well or use a dark canned bean.
Many light colored beans are treated with
sulfites.

## Tuna Macaroni Salad

Mix together:
1 lb. cooked elbow macaroni, rinsed with cold
water.
5 chopped celery stalks
3 chopped green onions or ½ cup sweet chopped
onion
1 can black olives, chopped coarsely
5 chopped hard boiled eggs
3 cans tuna, rinsed and drained (unsalted, no
broth added)
1 chopped bell pepper (optional)
Blend and toss into salad:

⅔ to 1 cup canola oil
4 tablespoons fresh lemon juice or cider vinegar
½ avocado, mashed
2 teaspoons sugar (optional)
½ teaspoon dry mustard
salt and pepper to taste

Variation:
Cooked couscous or brown rice may be
substituted for macaroni.

## Wheat Berry Salad

1½ cups cooked wheat berries (Bring 1 cup
wheat to boil with 3 cups water and let stand
overnight. Drain.)
1½ cups fresh or frozen peas (organic)
1 cup diced celery
½ sweet onion, chopped
1 cup cashews or almonds toasted at 350° for 10
minutes and chopped.

Dressing:
½ cup sour cream
2 tablespoons oil

1 tablespoon cider vinegar
½ teaspoon salt
dash pepper
½ teaspoon sugar

Mix dressing with all ingredients. Chill and
serve.

Variation:
Pioneer mayonnaise or other dressing may be
substituted.

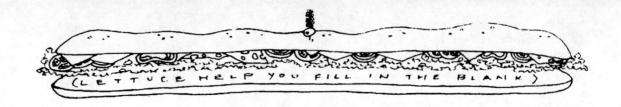

## SANDWICHES

### Grilled Cheese Sandwiches
(with optional fillings)

mild cheese
favorite bread slices
butter

Butter bread slices. Place half of the slices in pan butter side down. Top with thin cheese slices and any other filling. Place other slices on top, butter side up. Grill on medium-low heat until golden. Flip and grill other side.
Suggested fillings: sliced tomato, pineapple slice, thin apple slices, or sliced pickle.
*Severely sensitive people cannot tolerate most cheeses and other dairy products.

### Vegetable Egg Sandwiches

3 bell peppers, chopped
1 onion, sliced thin
1 clove garlic, minced
1 large tomato, chopped fine
4 to 6 eggs
salt and pepper
hot pepper flakes

Saute onions, peppers, and garlic in oil until golden. Add tomato and saute for 30 seconds. Add seasonings. Add beaten eggs and stir into the vegetable mixture. Cook until eggs are set, stirring constantly. Add hot pepper flakes, if desired. Cut into wedges and serve on bread for sandwiches or as main entre with fruit and rolls. This is a good cold picnic sandwich, too.

### Egg Salad Sandwich Filling
(no mayonnaise)

Mix together:
4 to 6 hard boiled eggs, chopped
1 to 2 tablespoons oil
1 ½ teaspoons vinegar or fresh lemon juice
½ teaspoon prepared mustard
pinch of sugar

salt and pepper to taste

May be moistened further with sour cream, milk, or water. Chopped black olives or onion may be added. Make deviled eggs by adding ingredients to yolks only.

## Hot Beef Sandwiches
### These are better than deli-style sandwiches!

1. Freeze 1 ½ lbs. top round or sirloin. Defrost slightly and slice paper thin across grain.
2. Heat 2 tablespoons oil in skillet. Add meat with 2 cloves of minced garlic and ¼ teaspoon black pepper. Saute over medium heat until pink is gone. Remove from heat.
3. Grate 3 carrots and cut 2 celery stalks in thin slices (diagonal slices).
4. Split a large loaf of French bread lengthwise and spread bottom half with soft butter and mustard.
5. Spoon hot beef onto bread. May spoon into pita bread or flour tortillas.
6. In hot drippings, place carrots, celery, ¼ teaspoon oregano, ½ teaspoon salt, 1 tablespoon vinegar or fresh lime juice, dash sugar, and stir over high heat until just heated through (still crisp).
7. Spoon vegetables on top of meat and top with ⅓ cup fresh basil or oregano leaves, or a mixture of favorite herbs (2 teaspoons dried herbs may be substituted).
8. Drizzle with oil and vinegar if desired.
9. Put top half on and cut in slices and serve.

## Open Faced Hot Italian Sandwiches

6 to 8 small flour tortillas, pita breads, or sliced french bread pieces
1 ½ to 2 cups shredded mild cheese, mozzarella or jack
1 tablespoon olive oil
4 tomatoes, diced or chopped
⅓ cup chopped fresh basil leaves (2 tablespoons dry)
¼ cup chopped sweet onion (optional)
1 clove garlic, minced
½ teaspoon dry or 2 teaspoons fresh chopped oregano
salt and pepper to taste
dash sugar (optional)

Mix all but the cheese and tortillas and let sit at room temperature at least 3 hours or overnight in refrigerator.

Sprinkle cheese evenly over tortillas or bread on cookie sheet. Bake for 10 to 12 minutes at 400° until cheese is bubbly. Place on plates and spoon tomato mixture on each to serve. Garnish with fresh basil and pass cracked pepper and hot pepper flakes.

Variation:
1. Place cheese on tortillas or bread and spoon tomato mixture evenly over cheese. Bake at 425° for 12 to 15 minutes or until bubbly and hot.
2. Goat cheese may be substituted for other cheese, but use a little less as it is stronger flavored.
3. Make a hot Mexican sandwich by substituting Mexican herbs and spices, such as cilantro, chili powder, and cumin.
4. If you are too sensitive to most cheeses, omit and brush bread with olive oil or butter and bake.

## Party Sandwiches

12 hard cooked eggs, chopped well
½ cup black olives, chopped
4 tablespoons fresh parsley, chopped
4 tablespoons mayonnaise or homemade salad dressing
4 teaspoons prepared mustard
1 teaspoon cider vinegar
¼ teaspoon tarragon
2 teaspoons grated onion

1 teaspoon salt
2 loaves bread, sliced thin
1 cup butter

Garnishes:
radishes, pickles, sliced olives, green onion circles, tomatoes, cucumber or fresh herbs such as watercress, basil, oregano, and parsley.

Combine first nine ingredients. Remove crusts from bread and spread with butter. Top with egg mixture and cut into fourths. Cover with plastic wrap and damp towel. Chill well before serving. Garnish with different toppings just before serving.

## Pocket Bread or Flour Tortilla Fillings

1. Mashed or diced avocado with 1 teaspoon lemon juice, ½ cup diced tomatoes, ½ cup chopped celery, ¼ cup sweet onion, ½ cup alfalfa sprouts, salt, pepper, and fresh herbs.
2. Peanut butter and sliced bananas or apples, drizzled with some honey.
3. 1 sliced tomato, 1 tablespoon chopped sweet onion, ¼ cup sunflower seeds or chopped peanuts, ½ cup grated cheese. This may be heated before eating.
4. Marinated, grilled, or fresh vegetables.
5. Chopped red peppers, cooked beans, chopped sweet onion, chopped tomato, lettuce, and a favorite salad dressing to moisten.

## Spanish Tomato Sandwich

1 loaf french bread
6 cloves garlic
6 medium ripe tomatoes, halved crosswise
4 to 5 tablespoons olive oil
2 tablespoons vinegar
¼ cup mustard, preferably herb flavored
1 sweet onion or bunch of scallions, thinly sliced

Mix together olive oil, mustard, and vinegar.

Cut bread lengthwise and broil bread 5 inches from heat. Keep warm in 150° oven after toasting. Peel and cut garlic cloves in half, lengthwise and arrange on plate with tomatoes.

To serve, place warm bread, bowl of mustard sauce, and bowl of onions by tomato plate. Place a garlic half on each plate. Each person starts by rubbing garlic half cut side down over a piece of bread. Then ½ tomato, cut side down is rubbed onto bread, pressing so that juice, seeds, and pulp are spread on bread. Drizzle with the vinegar/mustard mixture and eat with fork.

Suggestion: Blend dry or fresh herbs (oregano, basil, thyme) with mustard if herb mustard is unavailable. Sour dough bread is good, too. We did this with yeast free bread and it was good (see the bread section).

## Meatloaf Sandwiches
### (great for the cooler for traveling or for picnics)

General directions:

Slice cold meatloaf and place on buttered bread. Offer catsup, mustard, sliced tomatoes, and lettuce, if desired.

Variation:
When making meat loaf, pat half of meat mixture in a bread pan. Place a line of peeled hard-boiled eggs the length of loaf. Press remaining mixture over eggs to cover and seal. Bake as usual. Slice for a surprise sandwich filling.

## Fish Sandwiches

Make salmon or tuna patties or cakes and serve on a bun with mustard, homemade mayonnaise or other dressing, lettuce, and tomato.

# SOUPS

### Ground Beef and Mushroom Stew

2 lbs. lean ground beef, partially frozen
5 carrots, cut in half inch rounds
½ lb. mushrooms, cut in fourths
3 onions, cut in half inch chunks
4 large potatoes, diced in 1" pieces
4 ribs celery, cut in half inch chunks
2 teaspoons sugar
⅔ cup flour
2 qts. water
1 teaspoon thyme
2 teaspoons salt
¼ teaspoon pepper
1 tablespoon dry parsley
1 bay leaf
5 rosemary leaves
dash cayenne pepper
¼ teaspoon garlic powder or 2 cloves garlic, minced

Cut ground beef in 1 inch cubes and brown in a little oil until just cooked through. Remove from pan and set aside. In same pan, sauté celery, onion, and garlic until golden. Add to a large pot along with seasonings, water, carrots, and potatoes. Simmer until almost tender. Add the mushrooms and meat and remove bay leaf. Simmer 5 minutes. In a quart jar, shake 1½ cups water and the flour until blended. Add to the stew and simmer until it thickens, stirring gently. Add water and more seasoning to taste.

### General Meat Stock

Remember, many people will react to any stock since the meat and bone proteins can be hydrolyzed by long cooking in a liquid. Vegetable stock will have less free glutamate. Roast onions, carrots, celery, peppers, and seasonings until brown. Add water and boil until flavorful as for meat stock.

1. Use any inexpensive cuts of bone-in meat (2 to 4 lbs.) or chicken pieces.
2. Place in large roasting pan with cut up carrots (2), celery (2 stalks), and onion (2). Sprinkle with salt and pepper and roast at 400° for ½ hour or until browned.
3. Add water to cover, pepper corns, favorite herbs such as bay leaf, parsley, thyme, marjoram, and roast for 3 hours at 350°.
4. Let cool and strain. Meat can be eaten or frozen for casseroles or soup. Vegetables may be pureed, frozen, and later added to soups or gravy.
5. Pour stock in freezer containers and freeze. May be poured into ice-cube trays, frozen, removed from trays, and stored in freezer bags.
6. Add to soups, pilaf, or use for flavoring vegetables and stir fries.

TIP: After roasting and carving turkey or chicken, place carcass (keep a little meat on) in large pot of water with onion, celery, and herbs and simmer at least 2 hours. (May be roasted in oven also. Strain and store as above.)

## Homemade Chicken Soup

1 chicken (no additives or preservatives)
2 onions chopped
5 stalks celery cut into chunks
4 carrots cut into chunks
2 tablespoons dry parsley
salt and pepper to taste (start with at least 2 teaspoons salt)
1 teaspoon sugar
water

Wash chicken and place in large pot with water just to cover. Add onion, celery, and seasonings. Bring to boil and reduce heat. Simmer on low heat until meat begins to fall from bone (1 to 1½ hours). Remove chicken to a plate and let cool slightly. Add carrots to broth and simmer while removing meat from bones. Return meat to pot. Increase heat to medium and add spaetzels or 1 to 2 cups uncooked noodles if desired. Simmer until tender.

For spaetzels or German dumplings, beat 3 eggs with 3 tablespoons milk or water and ¼ teaspoon salt. Add 1 tablespoon melted butter or oil and enough flour, approximately 1 to 1 ½ cups, to make a sticky batter. Beat well, until smooth and glossy. Drop by rounded teaspoons, pushing batter off of edge of spoon into simmering soup with a finger. Simmer 10 minutes, half of the time covered.

*To help minimize glutamate formation, roast chicken in pot without water for 45 minutes to 1 hour. Remove from oven, add vegetables and seasonings which have been simmering in another pot along with the water. Simmer for a few more minutes to deglaze. Remove and debone chicken and return to pot. Add more water and seasonings if needed.

## Chili Con Carne

1 to 2 lbs. ground beef
4 cups cooked kidney or pinto beans or 2 to 4 cans rinsed and drained
4 cups Muir Glen tomato puree or 5 cups pureed fresh tomatoes
1 large onion, chopped
2 cloves garlic, chopped
2 stalks celery, chopped (optional)
2 tablespoons chili powder
1 tablespoon sugar
1 teaspoon cumin
½ teaspoon oregano
¼ teaspoon red pepper flakes (optional)
salt and pepper to taste
4 to 5 cups water

Brown meat and set aside. To pan drippings, add and brown onions, celery, and garlic. Add remaining ingredients except beans and simmer on low heat for 15 minutes, adding more water if necessary. Add meat and beans and heat through. Taste and adjust seasonings.

Variations: Cincinnati Chili. Add ½ teaspoon cinnamon. Serve over cooked spaghetti with the following condiments: Sour cream, chopped onion, tomatoes, and grated cheese.

We add 1 teaspoon cocoa powder to the simmering chili. You might want to add some pasilla chili powder also (find at the Mexican food section).

## Chicken and Pumpkin Soup
Your family will be surprised where the leftover pumpkin went.

4 to 5 chicken breasts
2 qts. water

2 cups canned pumpkin or ½" chunks of fresh
2 onions, chopped

2 cloves garlic, chopped
3 tablespoons oil
¼ teaspoon black pepper
1 teaspoon chili powder
½ teaspoon cinnamon
2 teaspoons dry cilantro
2 teaspoons dry parsley
½ teaspoon thyme or marjoram
2 teaspoons salt
2 teaspoons sugar (optional)
1 can corn, drained (1½ cups organic frozen is preferable)
3 cups water

1 cup cream (optional)

Simmer chicken in 2 qts. water for 40 minutes or until well cooked. De-bone and chop. Set aside broth and chicken. Saute onion and garlic in oil until tender. In pot, place water, onion, garlic, herbs, spices, and pumpkin, then simmer for 10 minutes. Add chicken, broth, and corn, then reheat. Cream may be stirred in just before serving.

Variation: If desired, 1 cup cooked rice or pasta may be added with cooked chicken.

## French Onion Soup
### (wonderful peasant food for pennies)

3 or 4 large yellow onions, thinly sliced
olive oil
salt and pepper
french bread (or any kind)
Swiss, provolone, or mozzarella cheese

Place onions in a large Dutch oven. Drizzle with a little oil and toss to cover. Place in a 400° oven and roast until well browned, stirring occasionally. Watch closely to avoid burning. The French often stir in a little sugar to promote

carmelization. Remove from oven. Add 2 quarts of beef stock or water. Salt and pepper to taste. Add ½ teaspoon dry thyme and pinch of tarragon. Simmer on range for 20 minutes. Ladle into oven proof bowls. Place a piece of toasted french bread on each bowl of soup and then a piece of cheese. Place under broiler until cheese is bubbly and starts to brown. Serve immediately. May be enjoyed without the cheese or French bread.
Variation: Cooked beans or lentils may be added.

## Hamburger Soup

In large pot, brown:
1½ lbs. hamburger (May be sauteed separately and set aside. Add to soup last 5 to 10 minutes to avoid hydrolysis)
2 onions, chopped
2 tablespoons green pepper, chopped (optional)
2 stalks celery, chopped

Add:
6 cups water
½ cup pearl barley or rice (uncooked)
2 carrots, diced
1½ cups corn (may add last few minutes of cooking as corn is high in natural glutamate)
3 tablespoons dry parsley
2 teaspoons sugar

1 large bay leaf (remove after 15 minutes)
2 teaspoons salt
¼ teaspoon black pepper

Simmer 30 minutes and add ½ cabbage, cut into one inch chunks, and 2 cups cubed potatoes. Simmer on lowest heat for 30 minutes longer or until vegetables are tender. Season to taste.

Variation:
3 to 4 cups chopped tomatoes may be added the last 5 minutes of cooking to heat through. Over-cooking tomatoes will release free glutamate. In fact, I cook hamburger and only add to soup or sauces the last few minutes for the same reason.

Tuscan style - Add ½ teaspoon oregano, 1 teaspoon basil, ¼ teaspoon rosemary, and 1 tablespoon sugar. Omit barley and add 3 cups cooked white beans. Omit corn and add 1 cup green beans. During last 10 minutes of cooking add 4 slices of cubed bread to the top of the soup. Let simmer. Just before serving, whisk bread into the top of the soup only. Then stir entire pot to thicken and blend. Delicious sprinkled with mozzarella or provolone cheese.

## Italian Onion Soup

3 tablespoons butter
3 onions, sliced thin
3 eggs
1 tablespoon imported parmesan cheese (optional)
2 cloves garlic, minced
¼ teaspoon oregano
¼ salt and dash pepper

Saute onions and garlic in butter until golden brown. Add with oregano to 2 quarts of water in pot and simmer for 30 minutes. Beat eggs with salt, pepper, and cheese. Pour in boiling soup but do not stir for 2 minutes. Stir to form clusters. Season to taste. Add more water if desired. Serve with buttered toast.

Variation:
Substitute ½ cup grated mozzarella cheese for parmesan.

## Lentil or Barley Soup

1 ⅔ cups lentils, rinsed
1 ½ quarts water or stock
3 stalks celery, chopped
3 carrots, chopped
1 tablespoon dry parsley
1 onion, chopped
1 tablespoon oil
4 tomatoes, chopped
1 bay leaf
¼ teaspoon thyme

2 to 3 cups chopped Swiss chard, spinach, or kale
salt and pepper to taste

Simmer altogether in large pot until lentils are tender. During last 10 minutes of cooking, add 1 cup uncooked shell or elbow macaroni (optional). Add more water if too thick.

*You may reserve adding tomatoes until the last 5 to 10 minutes of cooking to avoid free glutamate formation.

## Potato Soup

4 potatoes cubed
2 slices non-MSG bacon or ½ lb. sausage, fried and crumbled (optional)
3 carrots, cubed
3 stalks celery, chopped
1 onion, chopped
1 can corn (1 to 2 cups organic frozen or fresh are preferable)

1 summer squash, chopped (optional)
2 cups milk
¼ cup flour
thyme, sage, rosemary
salt and pepper

Place vegetables in large pot and cover with water. Bring to boil and simmer until potatoes are just tender. Mix 1 cup milk with flour and add to simmering soup. Stir and let thicken, gradually adding remaining milk. Add herbs, salt, and pepper to taste. Stir in bacon or sprinkle on top and serve.

Variation:
Add 2 small cans of non-MSG clams with juice to make clam chowder.

## Mushroom Soup

1. Sauté 1 large onion in 4 tablespoons butter or oil until golden. Add 1 lb. sliced or chopped mushrooms and sauté just to wilt.
2. Add 2 quarts water and bring to a simmer.
3. Beat 4 egg yolks with 2 cups cream.
4. Beat some of the hot soup into the egg mixture, a ladle or so at a time and then add the mixture back into the soup, stirring constantly.
5. Reheat just to simmer point. Remove from heat and add salt and pepper to taste.

## Soup on a Plate
### (Italian peasant food using Swiss chard)

3 garlic cloves, minced
1 chopped onion
6 cups tomatoes, chopped
2 cups Swiss chard or spinach, cooked
2 teaspoons dry basil
4 rosemary leaves
1 teaspoon sugar (optional)
salt and pepper to taste
water
oil

mozzarella or imported Parmesan cheese
1 loaf French bread

Saute garlic and onions in oil. Add tomatoes, Swiss chard, herbs, salt , sugar and simmer 10 to 15 minutes. Slice French bread into 1 inch thick pieces and lay side by side on serving dish. Spoon vegetables over bread. Sprinkle with shredded mozzarella or imported Parmesan cheese. Eat this soup with a fork!

## Tortilla Soup

2 cups cooked and shredded chicken, sliced beef, or ground beef
1 onion chopped
1 clove garlic chopped
1 teaspoon oil
1 can diced green chilies (6 oz.)
4 cups diced tomatoes
¼ cup fresh snipped cilantro or 1 tablespoon dry
1 teaspoon dry oregano
½ teaspoon cumin
1 can black, pinto, or kidney beans rinsed and drained
1 tablespoon chili powder
1 tablespoon cocoa powder
1 ½ teaspoons peanut butter (optional)

4 cups water
1 lime
grated mild cheese

Saute onion and garlic in oil in large pot until tender. If uncooked, meat may also be sauted at this time. Add remaining ingredients and simmer 15 to 20 minutes on low. Salt and pepper to taste. Cut lime in wedges and squeeze juice of 1 wedge into soup. To serve, gently crush tortilla chips into bowls. Ladle soup over chips, top with cheese, and serve with lime wedges.

This may be made without the meat.

## Tortilla Soup II
It's a good idea to double this one.

Saute in 4 tablespoons oil until tender:
1 onion, chopped
2 cloves garlic, sliced

Add:
2 cups water
6 tomatoes, diced

Simmer 10 minutes and process until smooth.
Season with dash pepper, cayenne pepper, ½
teaspoon cumin, and 1 teaspoon chili powder.

Offer the following garnishes to put in soup:

Tortilla chips
Flour or corn tortillas - cut into 1" strips and
deep fry in hot oil for 10 to 15 minutes. Drain on
paper towel.
Chopped avocados
Shredded cheese
Chopped fresh cilantro
Chopped scallions
Chopped black olives
Sour cream

## Fresh Tomato Soup

8 large tomatoes (not too ripe) peeled and
chopped
1 onion, chopped
2 stalks celery, chopped

Sauté onion and celery in 3 tablespoons oil until
tender.
Add:
tomatoes
1 to 2 tablespoons sugar or honey (optional)
2 tablespoons fresh, chopped parsley (or 1
teaspoon dry)

1 tablespoon fresh, chopped basil (or ½ teaspoon
dry)
2 to 4 cups water (depending on desired
thickness)
salt and pepper to taste

Simmer just until heated through. After
removing from heat and placed in bowls, cream
or sour cream may be swirled in each bowl.
Good served with garlic bread, May be used as a
pizza or pasta sauce if water is omitted.

# TREATS AND CANDY

Many highly sensitive individuals react to the lecithin in most chocolate. Instead, refer to the cocoa/chocolate substitution chart at the beginning of the recipe section.

## Almond Crunch Candy
(A lot like my favorite candy bar)

1 cup butter
1 ¼ cups sugar
2 tablespoons water
2 tablespoons honey
2 dashes salt
1 cup chopped almonds
½ to 1 cup semi-sweet chocolate chips

1. Line a 10" x 15" pan with foil.
2. In heavy 2 quart pot, combine first 5 ingredients and bring to boil on medium heat, stirring constantly until it reaches the *hard crack stage (approximately 7 to 8 minutes). Should be a rich golden color.
3. Stir in almonds and pour into center of pan and quickly spread to edges with spoon.
4. Sprinkle chips all over top. Let set until they melt, then spread with a spatula. This candy is good even without chocolate.
5. Cool completely, peel off foil, and break into small pieces. Store in a canister. Also freezes well. Makes about 2 pounds of candy. Great for gift giving.

Variation:
For caramels, boil only to firm ball stage, about 5 minutes, and pour into 8" x 8" pan. Cut into 1" squares or scoop out and wrap each piece in wax paper or plastic wrap. Omit chocolate chips. Can make without nuts, also.

*To test, let a drop of the hot mixture fall into a glass of cold water. Spoon it out and see if it is brittle and cracks easily.

## Almond or Pecan Toffee

⅔ cup butter, melted
½ cup brown sugar
1 cup sugar or use 1 ½ cups all brown sugar
⅓ cup water
¼ teaspoon salt
1 cup almonds or pecans
¼ teaspoon baking soda
⅓ cup chopped almonds or pecans
1 - 12 oz. bag semi-sweet chocolate chips (without whey or milk solids) (optional)

Butter a cookie sheet and sprinkle ⅓ cup chopped nuts over pan. In heavy bottom pot, melt first five ingredients over low heat, stirring until it comes to a boil. Let boil undisturbed until it reaches soft ball stage (230°). Add 1 cup whole almonds or pecans when it reaches 290° and add soda, stirring constantly. Remove from heat and pour immediately onto cookie sheet. Sprinkle with chips if desired. Let melt for 1 to 2 minutes, then spread chocolate evenly. Cool and break into pieces.

## Butter Cream Eggs

½ cup butter
2 cups confectioners sugar
2 tablespoons cream or milk
2 teaspoons vanilla (pure)
semi-sweet chocolate chips without whey or milk solids, melted

Cream butter, sugar, cream, and vanilla until very well blended. Chill if necessary. Form into desired shape (eggs, hearts). Don't make too big, about 1 ½". Place on waxed paper on a cookie sheet. Chill thoroughly. Cover bottom, let harden, then cover top with the chocolate. Keep chocolate on a pan of hot water to keep thin. Add a little more butter if too thick. Eggs may be dipped in chocolate or use a brush to "paint" on chocolate. Do tops first, re-chill, then do bottoms.

Try different flavors, almond for a cherry flavor or add orange peel. If confectioner's sugar bothers you (cornstarch), it can be made by pulsing regular sugar in the blender.

## Candied Nuts (Brittle)

⅔ cup sugar
¼ teaspoon salt
1 cup pecans
1 cup whole almonds

Mix ingredients in a skillet and stir over low heat until sugar melts and nuts are coated (about 20 to 25 minutes). Put nuts on waxed paper or oiled pan to cool. Break apart when hard.

Variations:
Try adding spices such as cinnamon, cayenne pepper, or cloves.

## Chocolate Popcorn clusters

Melt 1 cup semi-sweet chocolate chips. Add 1 cup popped corn or puffed cereal (plain rice or wheat), 1 cup nuts, and drop by spoonfuls on wax paper. Raisins may be used also. Let set up.

## Fruit Leather

Puree 2 cups of any fruit. Add ½ cup sugar. Spread thinly (¼ ") on 2 cookie sheets lined with plastic wrap. Bake at 150° for 2 hours or until not sticky to touch. Leave oven door ajar. When cool, roll up with plastic and cut into 2 inch lengths if desired. Store in plastic bag.

*Commercial dehydrators have special trays for making fruit leather.

## Frozen Bananas

Cut each banana in half and push a popsicle stick in lengthwise for a handle. Wrap in plastic wrap and freeze. To eat, dip in honey or mixture of peanut butter and honey. May dip in chopped nuts or coconut (unsulfited) and serve. Also may melt semi-sweet chocolate chips and dip frozen banana in to coat.

## Fast Granola Bars I

Beat 1 egg, add 2 ¼ cups granola or muesli, ⅓ cup honey and dash salt. Mix well and press into an 8" x 8" greased pan. Bake for 20 minutes at 325°. Cool for 10 minutes. Cut into bars.

## Fast Granola Bars II

2 cups granola
2 eggs
½ teaspoon vanilla
1 tablespoon flour

Beat eggs and vanilla. Mix into granola with flour. Bake in a greased 10" pan at 350° for 20 minutes. May spread with peanut butter. Honey or peanut butter may be added with the granola for variety.

## Fast Fridge Fudge

½ cup honey
½ cup peanut butter or other nut butter
½ cup cocoa
2 cups nuts, chopped, any kind or combination
½ cup raisins or other dried fruit
½ to 1 cup coconut, unsulphured (optional)

Heat honey and peanut butter. Add cocoa and stir to blend. Remove from heat and add remaining ingredients and pour into greased 9" pan. Refrigerate until firm and cut. Store in refrigerator.

## Trail Mix

Raisins
dark chocolate chips
nuts
dried fruit

puffed rice or wheat

Mix together and store in plastic bags.

## Granola Bars III

¾ cup melted butter or oil
⅓ cup brown sugar
1 teaspoon vanilla
dash salt
3 eggs (or use 4 egg whites)
5 to 6 cups granola

Blend brown sugar and butter. Beat in vanilla and eggs. Add granola and mix well. Bake in greased 9" x 13" pan at 375° for 15 to 20 minutes. Cool before cutting. For lower fat version, use egg whites and half butter and half applesauce.

## Granola Bars IV

Mix together in large bowl:
5 cups rolled oats
3 cups quick oats
½ cup raisins
½ cup dates cut up
½ cup chopped almonds
½ cup walnuts or pecans
½ teaspoon cinnamon

In another bowl, mix together:
1 cup unsweetened applesauce or 100% fruit juice
½ cup peanut or almond butter
½ cup oil (may decrease for lower calorie recipe, increasing applesauce if needed)
½ teaspoon salt
2 egg whites
2 teaspoons vanilla
⅔ cup brown sugar
¼ cup honey

Pour liquid ingredients over dry ingredients, mixing well. Pat into a large greased jelly roll pan or 2 smaller baking pans. Bake at 325° for 35 minutes or until golden. For crispier bars, turn oven off and allow to remain in oven until desired dryness. Cut while warm into 2 inch bars. To store, bag and place in freezer.

Variations:

The following ingredients may be added (be creative):sesame seeds, sunflower seeds, flax seeds, any dried fruit (sulfite free), bran, wheat flakes, coconut (sulfite free).

Any fruit juice may be substituted for the applesauce if desired. Increase oil to ⅔ cup and omit peanut or almond butter. Mix as above and pour into 2 pans. Bake at 300° stirring occasionally until toasted and dry.

* For a lower fat version, extra fruit juice or apple sauce may be substituted for all the oil.

## Honey Munch Mix

6 cups plain puffed wheat cereal
½ cup pecans
¼ cup raisins
¼ cup butter
¼ cup honey
¼ teaspoon vanilla

Mix cereal, nuts, and raisins in a greased 9" x 13" pan. Melt butter. Stir in honey and vanilla.

Pour over cereal mix and stir until coated. Bake, stirring occasionally, 30 minutes or until dry at 300°. Store tightly covered.

*May be eaten with milk like sweetened cereal

Variation:
Try other favorite unsweetened cereals, nuts, and dry fruit.

## Sweet Popcorn

Add some sugar to the melted butter and dissolve before pouring over popcorn. A teaspoon of fresh lemon juice may also be added for variety.

## Honey Popcorn

½ cup honey
¼ cup butter
6 cups popped corn
1 cup shelled peanuts

Mix popcorn and peanuts in large bowl. Heat honey and butter in sauce pan and stir until blended. Pour over popcorn, stirring to coat well. Spread in large pan and bake for 5 to 10 minutes at 350° or until crisp.

*2 tablespoons of unsulfured molasses may be substituted for 2 tablespoons of the honey.

## Honey Taffy

3 cups sugar
1 cup honey
⅔ cup water
3 tablespoons vinegar
3 tablespoons butter
¼ teaspoon salt

Combine all ingredients in pot and cook, stirring often to a medium ball stage, about 265°. Pour into a buttered dish and let cool enough to handle. Stretch and pull until light gold, then cut into 1" pieces. Wrap in wax paper or plastic wrap.

## Mints

4 cups confectioners sugar
4 tablespoons butter (¼ cup)
3 tablespoons water
mint oil
food color if desired

Mix sugar, butter, and water, then knead well. Can add more water but mixture should be stiff and smooth. Add flavoring , starting with ½ teaspoon. Taste and add more as desired.

Add color if desired. Pale shades are better. Roll into little balls and flatten slightly and allow to dry on wax paper overnight. You may press balls in rubber molds made for mints found at specialty stores. When using molds, roll ball in sugar before pressing, for an easy release of candy. Candies, once outer shell is firm, can be stored in containers and kept frozen for months. Best to store in glass jars to protect mint flavor.

## Mike's Favorite Trail Mix
### (great for the busy student for a quick snack)

Mix in any amount desired:
whole almonds (may be toasted 10 minutes in 350° oven.
Raisins
sunflower seeds
Ghiradelli semi-sweet chocolate chips (best to go easy on these)

any unsulfured dried fruits (We use pear and peach halves, papaya, and dates)

Divide into small zipper plastic bags. Place small bags in a larger container or plastic bag for storage.

## No Fuss Caramel Corn

3 quarts popped corn
1 ½ cups peanuts
1 cup packed brown sugar
½ cup butter
4 tablespoons honey
½ teaspoon salt
½ teaspoon baking soda

Place popped corn and peanuts in large brown paper bag. Set aside.

Combine brown sugar, butter, honey, and salt in 2 quart glass bowl or casserole.
Microwave on high setting for 2 to 4 minutes, stirring after each minute, until mixture comes to a boil. Microwave for 2 minutes more. Stir in baking soda.
Pour syrup mixture over popped corn and peanuts in bag. Microwave on high setting for 1 ½ minutes more. Shake bag and pour caramelized corn in large roasting pan. Cool and eat or store.

## Nut Brittle

2 cups nuts (pecans, walnuts, macadamia)
4 cups sugar

Toast nuts in pan at 350° for 8 to 10 minutes. Lightly grease aluminum foil and set on baking sheet or heat proof cutting board. In a large sauce pan, heat sugar slowly until melted and golden. Stir in nuts and cook for 1 minute. Pour onto foil and spread. Let stand until hard. Break or cut into pieces.

## Ohio Buckeye Candy

1 cup butter
1 lb. peanut butter (natural)
1 lb. confectioners sugar
1 - 12 oz. bag chocolate chips without whey or milk solids, melted

Knead first 3 ingredients until smooth and form into 1" balls. With a toothpick, dip each ball into the chocolate and place on waxed paper. If chocolate gets too thick, place over hot pan of water while dipping or add a tiny bit of butter.

## Old Time Maple Candy

Boil 1 cup real maple syrup to soft ball stage, 230° to 240°. Drizzle over clean snow that is spread evenly in a pan. When cool, twirl on a fork to eat.

## Fruity Popsicles

Mix 1 can 100% juice, reconstituted and 3 tablespoons sugar or honey. Pour into molds and freeze. Fresh citrus juice may be used if diluted and sweetened to taste. Best to avoid juice sweetened with corn syrup. Also, most juices contain preservatives such as sulfites which affect many individuals. Even those labeled "no preservatives" can contain minute amounts by law.

## Creamsicles

Whip 1 cup cream until creamy, not thick. Add 2 to 3 cups pureed fruit (bananas, berries, peaches) and sweeten to taste. Pour into molds and freeze (can use yogurt or milk). This can also be used as a drink base. Place some in a glass and add seltzer water.

## Praline Covered Nuts
### (Almonds, pecans,or walnuts)

Spread 3 cups nuts in a shallow pan and roast for 10 to 12 minutes at 350°. In large fry pan, melt ¼ cup butter. Add ½ teaspoon salt and 1 ½ cups brown sugar. Melt together. Should be like very thick cream and smooth. Boil on low heat for 2 minutes. Add nuts to pan and stir to coat. Pour on greased plate and let cool. Break up to eat.

## Spiced Almonds

1 lb. whole almonds
4 tablespoons sugar
1 tablespoon cinnamon
¼ teaspoon paprika
2 tablespoons honey
cayenne pepper to taste

Place almonds in a single layer on a cookie sheet or shallow pan and bake at 350° for 10 minutes. Let cool. Mix sugar and spices together and set aside. Drizzle honey over nuts in a bowl and toss well. Sprinkle with sugar mixture. Return to pan and bake at 350° for 5 to 10 minutes more until nuts are glazed. Cool.

Variation:
1. Use pecans or walnuts.
2. Decrease cinnamon to ½ teaspoon and add 1 teaspoon chili powder and omit paprika.

## Very Old Fashioned Candy
### (original "sugar plums")

1 lb. raisins
1 lb. nut meats
1 lb. dates, unsulphured
1 lb. figs, unsulphured
3 cups sugar
1 cup whole milk or half cream, half milk
½ cup butter

Any dry fruit may be substituted. Up to 1 more lb. fruit can be added to this recipe.

Grind or process until fine the first 4 ingredients. Boil together the last 3 ingredients until the soft ball stage (230°). Pour over the fruit and nut mixture and blend. With greased hands, roll in a long roll. Wrap in a wet cloth and refrigerate to chill. Unwrap and slice to serve.

For sugar plums, do not form a roll. Chill mixture, then form into balls (plums) and roll each in granulated sugar. Store in container with waxed paper between layers. Can roll twice in sugar.

## Date Fingers

Insert an almond in each date and serve.

# VEGETABLES, BEANS, AND GRAINS

## Boston Baked Beans

1 lb. pea beans (any small white beans will do)
¼ teaspoon baking soda
3 pieces salt pork (fresh) or ½ lb. homemade
sausage, cooked and crumbled
1 large onion, chopped
½ teaspoon dry mustard or 1 tablespoon
prepared
½ teaspoon salt
¼ teaspoon pepper
½ cup unsulphured molasses or ½ cup brown
sugar, packed

Soak beans overnight in water to cover. The
next day , bring to boil and add soda. Reduce
heat, skim off foam, and simmer partially
covered for 20 minutes or until skins will peel
back when pressed or blown on. More water
may be added if beans become too dry.

Drain, reserving liquids. Place in a large bowl.
Place half the salt pork on bottom of a bean pot
or deep 2 quart ceramic or glass casserole. To
beans, add onion, brown sugar, mustard, salt,
pepper, molasses, and mix. Pour beans over the
pork in pot. Pour enough liquid in to just cover
beans. Place rest of pork on top. Cover and
bake for 8 hours at 300°. Check often and add
more liquid as needed. Top beans should never
dry out. **Do not stir.** This is a meal served with
fruit and bread or a side dish served with
barbecued meat.

Variation:
I add a dash of cayenne pepper and have also
made this without the salt pork. Also, I have
fried 1 lb. ground beef with the onions and
stirred that into the beans, omitting the salt pork
Beans cooked this way may contain free
glutamate, so be cautious if you are highly
sensitive..

## Citrus Herb Pilaf
### Can use couscous, rice, barley, lentils, or wheat berries.

3 cups water or homemade stock
2 tablespoons oil
2 carrots, diced
1 large onion, chopped
⅓ cup chopped or sliced almonds (toast 7 to 10
minutes at 350°)
2 cloves garlic, minced
1 medium chopped summer squash (optional)
1 teaspoon salt
3 tablespoons fresh lemon juice
2 tablespoons fresh parsley or 1 tablespoon dry
(1 teaspoon cilantro may be substituted)
½ teaspoon marjoram
½ teaspoon dry thyme
¼ teaspoon dry dill
dash pepper
rice or other grain
1 teaspoon sugar (optional)

In large skillet saute the vegetables, except
garlic, for 4 to 6 minutes until almost tender.
Add garlic, water, salt, and herbs and bring to a

simmer. Add either 1 ½ cups raw rice, 2 cups
uncooked couscous, 1 ½ cups uncooked barley,
1 ½ cups uncooked lentils or 3 ½ cups wheat
berries that have soaked overnight. Cover and
cook on lowest heat for 20 to 40 minutes or until
the grain is tender. Most of the liquid should be
absorbed. Couscous will take only 5 to 6
minutes, so simmer garlic and herbs 5 minutes
before adding couscous. Add couscous, bring to
a boil, cover, remove from heat, and let sit for 5
to 6 minutes.
Stir in lemon juice and season to taste. ¼ cup
orange juice may be added also. Serve with
nuts sprinkled on top.

Variation:
1. Add ⅓ cup raisins or currants plus 1
teaspoon curry powder with water.
2. 1 cup peas may be added last 5 minutes of
cooking.
3. 2 cups diced cooked chicken or shrimp may
be added last 5 minutes of cooking.

# Fried Squash Blossoms

½ cup flour
2 tablespoons corn meal
¼ teaspoon garlic powder
1 egg
½ cup milk or water
2 teaspoons oil
12 squash blossoms, freshly picked

*Pick early in morning and soak in cold water until ready to use. Summer or winter variety may be used. Squash blossoms are also good in salads as are nasturtiums and pansies (organic).

Combine dry ingredients. Mix together egg, milk, and oil and blend into dry ingredients. Oil in pan should be at least 1 inch deep. Dip blossoms, one at a time, in batter. Fry in hot oil until golden. Drain and serve immediately. Goat cheese may be blended with fresh herbs and stuffed inside blossom (1 teaspoon), then dipped in batter and fried.

Batter is also good for fresh vegetables and seafood.

# Onion Fritters

¾ cup flour
2 tablespoons corn meal
1 tablespoon sugar
2 teaspoons baking powder
1 teaspoon salt
1 teaspoon dry parsley (optional)
dash cayenne pepper
¾ cup whole milk or water
2 ½ cups chopped onion (½" pieces)
vegetable oil for frying

Combine first 7 ingredients. Add the milk and blend. Stir in the onions. Drop by little spoonfuls in hot oil and flatten slightly. Fry until golden brown (2 minutes) and flip and fry 2 more minutes. Drain on paper towels. Keep warm in oven as they are made. Great served with applesauce and corn on the cob for a garden feast! These disappear so fast, that you may want to double the recipe.

Variation:
Try half onion and half chopped zucchini or eggplant.

# Zucchini Fritters

3 medium zucchini shredded
½ teaspoon salt

Mix and place in colander for ½ hour. Squeeze out as much liquid as possible with hands. Chop 1 small onion finely and add to zucchini. Stir in the following:
2 eggs

¼ cup flour
¼ teaspoon salt
dash pepper

Add 2 to 4 tablespoons oil to a saute pan. Drop batter by spoonfuls into hot oil. Flatten slightly. Saute until brown. Turn and cook until both sides are brown.

# Garden Rice

1 large chopped onion
2 small chopped zucchini

1 tablespoon oil

1 can corn, drained or 1 cup fresh kernals (optional)
2 cups tomatoes, chopped
3 cups cooked rice
1 teaspoon salt (can add more to taste)
¼ teaspoon pepper
¼ teaspoon cumin or 1 teaspoon cilantro

¼ teaspoon oregano

Saute onions and squash in oil until tender. Add remaining ingredients and simmer for 10 to 15 minutes. Can add 1 cup cooked beans for added protein.

## Gramma Gifford's French-style Green Beans
### (In her own words)

"You use a little butter. Chop a little onion and brown it a little. Take a big teaspoonful of flour and brown it in the butter. Take some of the juice from the cooked beans and pour it in the browned flour and stir it and pour over the beans."

## Herbed Rice

1 tablespoon fresh or 1 teaspoon dry parsley
4 green onions cut into circles
dash sage
⅛ teaspoon dry marjoram (may use more)
¼ teaspoon dry thyme (may use more)
dash black pepper
1 ½ teaspoon salt
1 ½ cups rice
3 cups boiling water
2 tablespoons butter

In a two quart casserole, place rice, water, salt, butter, herbs and seasonings. Stir until butter melts. Cover tightly and bake at 375° for 45 to 60 minutes or until rice is cooked.

Experiment with favorite herbs and different rices. I've added grated carrots, celery leaves, and even fresh cilantro.
If using white rice, rinse well before using. Often it is coated with corn starch or other MSG containing substance.

## Mashed Root Vegetables

Boil any favorite root vegetables until tender, such as carrots, potatoes, rutabagas, turnips, sweet potatoes, and parsnips, (remove pithy centers first). Mix in any combination and mash, adding milk to moisten. Add pepper, salt, and butter to taste.

Especially good are the following:
Carrots with parsnips (add 1 to 2 tablespoons brown sugar).
White potatoes with carrots (add some sauted onions or garlic).
Turnips or rutabagas with sweet potatoes (add brown sugar or honey).
3 to 4 cloves of garlic added to white potatoes while boiling. Mash together (or add garlic powder to mashed potatoes when in a hurry).
Favorite herbs can spice up flavors, too. Try mint, scallions, chervil, tarragon, and fresh fennel leaves.

## Roasted Onion Mushroom Bake

4 large onions, peeled and quartered
1 lb. mushrooms
2 tablespoons melted butter or oil
1 teaspoon thyme
¼ teaspoon rosemary

black pepper
salt

Melt butter in pan with seasonings in 325° oven. Add onions, coating gently with butter.

Roast for 35 to 45 minutes. Remove from oven and add mushrooms, stirring gently. Return to oven and bake for 15 to 20 minutes or until mushrooms are hot and tender.

*Overcooking mushrooms may create free glutamate. Also, be sure mushrooms have not been sprayed with preservatives.

## Roasted Onions and Potatoes
### (A rustic French method)

My great-grandmother was from Alsace-Lorraine. My grandmother said her meals were simple and always made from fresh ingredients. The best way to eat.

4 large onions
4 large potatoes
3 tablespoons oil
1 tablespoon butter
salt and pepper to taste

Melt butter and oil in large pan and stir to blend. Sprinkle pan liberally with salt and pepper. Wash potatoes and onions without peeling. Slice onions in half so that rings show. Slice potatoes lengthwise. Pour some oil in hands and rub skins of onions and potatoes lightly with oil. Place cut sides down in pan. Roast in 375° oven for 1 hour or until tender and golden.

Variation: Herbs such as thyme and rosemary may be sprinkled on pan with salt and pepper if desired. Most vegetables can be cooked this way.

## Potato Bake
### (Avoid if highly sensitive to MSG or dairy products)

2 lb. package frozen hash browns (defrosted) or grate 5 or 6 large potatoes (make sure hash browns are not treated with MSG, sulfites or phosphates)
5 green onions, chopped or ⅓ cup minced onion
2 cups grated cheddar cheese
1 pint sour cream (optional)
⅔ cup milk
salt and pepper to taste
2 cups cream sauce*

*Cream Sauce:
Melt 4 tablespoons butter and add 4 tablespoons flour. Stir and cook 1 minute. Whisk in 2 cups milk and stir until thickened. If not using sour cream, add a bit more milk.

Mix all ingredients and bake at 350° for 45 minutes or until tender.

Variation: Vegetable Bean Bake
Substitute 2 lbs. of favorite vegetables such as green beans.

To minimize free glutamate formation in the dairy products, vegetables may be pre-cooked before combining with rest of ingredients. Reduce the baking time to 15 to 20 minutes.

## Potato Treats

I.  JOJOs: Slice potatoes lengthwise into ½" thick pieces. Turn and slice again lengthwise making large french fry type pieces. Place in large bowl. Drizzle with oil to coat lightly. Toss with hands. Spread in baking pan and sprinkle liberally with salt, pepper, and favorite herbs and spices such as garlic powder, cayenne pepper, chili powder, oregano, and basil flakes. Bake in 450° oven for 20 to 30 minutes or until light brown and crispy on edges. Sweet potatoes may be prepared same way. Spices may be omitted.

II. Wash and bake some potatoes. Cut in half. Mash lightly in shell. Sprinkle each half with 2 tablespoons milk. Sprinkle with salt and pepper. Top with grated cheese and/or some chopped onion. Place under broiler until cheese is melted.

III. Bake yams or sweet potatoes until tender. One way to keep them moist while cooking in microwave oven is to add a little water to dish and cover potatoes. Split and top with any of the following: Brown sugar, butter, honey, cinnamon, or nutmeg. I eat this often for lunch. Sweet potatoes can be eaten raw or even deep fried like french fries. We spread a raw slice with peanut butter , top with a few raisins and then add another slice of sweet potato for an unusual but tasty "sandwich".

IV. Never underestimate the satisfying and simple baked or steamed potato with butter, salt, and pepper when you've "got the hungries"!

V. Microwave 5 cleaned potatoes (do not peel) covered in casserole dish with 1 cup water for 20 minutes or until very tender. Or boil potatoes quartered in water until soft. Beat with mixer adding milk, butter, salt, and pepper.

## Refried Beans and Chilpotle Peppers

5 cups cooked pinto beans
1 tablespoon chilpotle pepper (pasilla or chili powder may be substituted)
¼ cup oil
1 clove garlic
⅓ cup water
½ teaspoon cumin
salt and pepper to taste

Whip or process together until smooth. Add more water if needed. Heat in pan or bake in oven or microwave until hot.

Chilpotles in 7 oz. cans can be found in the Mexican section of your grocery store. Since some contain tomato sauce, paste, or citric acid, some MSG may be present. But used very sparingly , you may be able to enjoy these smoked, spicy chilies. They add so much flavor, it's worth a try. I divide and put 1 tablespoon each in a separate packet of plastic wrap and freeze in a quart freezer bag.

## Refried Beans
### (We use these in lots of Mexican dishes)

2 to 3 cups cooked beans
1 cup diced tomatoes
2 cloves garlic
½ teaspoon cumin
½ teaspoon oregano
1 onion chopped
½ to 1 teaspoon salt to taste
2 tablespoons oil

Try pinto, pink kidney, black, or any favorite beans.
Blend or process all ingredients. Or mash beans with fork. May moisten with water. Mince garlic and add with rest of ingredients to beans. Place in casserole dish and bake at 350° or microwave until bubbly. May cook on top of stove, stirring constantly. Serve with tortilla chips or soft warm tortillas and grated cheese.

## Roasted Summer Veggies

2 medium zucchini
1 medium eggplant

2 yellow squash
3 onion

3 bell peppers (any color)
1 lb. mushrooms, wash, leave whole
3 to 4 tablespoons olive oil (may decrease amount)
1 tablespoon fresh herbs, such as rosemary, dill, oregano, basil, tarragon, or mixture of these
1 teaspoon salt
dash pepper
1 lemon cut in wedges as garnish

Quarter zucchini and squash lengthwise and cut into 3" lengths. Peel and quarter the onions or cut in ½" circles. Slice eggplant into ½" pieces.

Mix oil, herbs, juice from 1 lemon section, and seasonings in bowl. Add vegetables and toss to coat. Roast at 400° for 20 to 25 minutes or until tender. Serve lemon on each plate to squeeze over vegetables. Vegetables may be grilled over coals.

Variation:
These vegetables are also great steamed together. Try adding quartered potatoes and corn on the cob cut into 2" pieces for a steamed vegetable meal.

## Scalloped Potatoes (Mom's Style)

5 to 6 medium or 4 large potatoes, sliced ⅛" thick (can leave unpeeled)
2 tablespoons flour
salt and pepper
2 teaspoons dry parsley (use more if fresh)
4 tablespoons (½ stick) butter (may use olive oil instead)
2 cups whole milk
paprika

Oil a casserole dish or pan. Make 2 or more layers of the following in this order: potato slices, a light sprinkling of flour, salt, pepper, and parsley. (A small strainer works well for sprinkling flour.)

Heat together the milk and butter and pour over casserole. Sprinkle with paprika. Cover with foil or lid and bake at 350° until potatoes are golden and tender, about 1 hour.

Variation:
1.  A dash of nutmeg or garlic powder may be added to the milk. My Mom sometimes added finely sliced onions in the layers.
2.  Potatoes may be pre-baked or boiled to decrease the cooking time, reducing the chance for free glutamic acid to be created in the milk. Bake just until casserole is bubbly.
3.  Hot white cream sauce may be stirred into hot sliced cooked potatoes and served immediately to avoid long cooking of milk.

## Spicy Broccoli Saute

1.  Clean 1 large bunch of broccoli.
2.  Peel stem if tough.
3.  Slice stem into ¼" circles and rest into 1" flowerets.
4.  In 2 tablespoons oil in skillet, saute the broccoli with ½ cup unseasoned peanuts and ¼ teaspoon hot pepper flakes.
5.  Saute for 2 minutes, stirring constantly. Add 2 cloves of thinly sliced garlic, dash of salt, and ½ teaspoon sugar. Continue stir frying until almost tender. This is a family favorite. I have added a dash of ginger or Chinese 5-spice. Pistachios are high in magnesium and can be substituted for peanuts.

## Summer Garden Vegetable Bake

This is a great way to use that extra zucchini. Be creative and try other vegetables.

6 to 8 cups zucchini, ¼" thick slices (10 small or 5 medium)
4 tomatoes, chopped
1 large onion, sliced
2 cloves garlic, chopped
½ teaspoon basil
1 teaspoon salt
6 slices fresh bread, cubed
¼ teaspoon pepper
1 to 2 cups grated mild cheese (optional)
½ cup melted butter or olive oil (may decrease)

Toss vegetables, seasonings, bread, and cheese together. Pour oil or butter over all and toss again (hands work well). Pour into large buttered casserole dish and bake at 350° for 35 to 45 minutes or until vegetables are tender and top is golden. Leftover cooked meat may be mixed with vegetables.

* 2 tablespoons grated Parmesan cheese is great on this. Omit if sensitive to it.

Experiment with various herbs such as thyme or marjoram.
Omit tomatoes if they bother you when cooked, or add them during the last 7 minutes of baking to just heat through.

## Crispy Coated Roasted Vegetables

Beat together in a large bowl:
2 eggs
2 tablespoons oil

Lightly season with salt and pepper.

In 1 gallon plastic zipper bag, combine:
⅔ cup flour
½ cup corn meal
½ teaspoon garlic powder
dash cayenne pepper
½ teaspoon salt
dash pepper
½ teaspoon sugar (optional)
1 teaspoon any favorite herbs (optional)

Slice up 6 to 8 cups of favorite fresh garden vegetables such as: green tomatoes (½ inch thick), onion circles (½ inch thick), zucchini or yellow squash (½ inch thick circles), hot or mild peppers in chunks. Place in egg mixture, using hands to coat well. If too dry, add more oil and egg. Shake pieces of vegetables a few at a time in flour mixture. Coat bottom of large pan with oil. Place coated vegetables in single layer in pan and bake in 425° oven until golden (about 25 minutes). If desired, turn vegetables with spatula half way through cooking time. Add whole wheat bread, cheese, and fruit to make a meal. Small peppers may be stuffed with mild cheese before dipping in egg mixture.

## Wheat Berry Pilaf

5 cups water
1 ¼ cups wheat berries
¼ cup orzo (rice shaped pasta) any small pasta will work
2 cups sliced mushrooms (optional)
2 medium carrots, coarsely grated or chopped
2 cups diced tomatoes
1 large onion, chopped
1 clove garlic, minced

½ teaspoon thyme, dry dill, or any favorite herbs
dash red pepper flakes (may add up to ¼ teaspoon)

Boil water and add wheat. Reduce heat and simmer 60 minutes, covered. Add orzo and cook uncovered 10 more minutes. Drain and keep warm.

Sauce:
In large pan, saute mushrooms, onions, carrots, and garlic in 3 tablespoons olive or vegetable oil until tender. Stir in undrained tomatoes, ½ cup water, and seasonings. Bring to simmer. Salt and pepper to taste. Stir gently into wheat berries and serve.

Variations:
Try herbs like fennel or basil.
4 cups cooked rice, couscous, or polenta may be substituted for wheat berries. Omit orzo.

## Zucchini and Rice Casserole

1 cup rice, lentils, quinoa, or couscous
1 medium onion, diced
1 small bell pepper, diced
½ lb. mushrooms, sliced
1 tablespoon oil
4 cups chopped tomatoes
1 lb. zucchini, sliced
½ cup cashews
1 teaspoon oregano
1 teaspoon parsley
2 to 3 cups grated mozzarella cheese

Cook rice in 2 cups water and 1 teaspoon salt. Cover and simmer for 20 minutes. In a skillet, saute onions, bell pepper, and in oil. Blend in remaining ingredients except cheese. Mix in rice, place in a greased casserole dish and bake at 350° for 20 minutes or until hot throughout. Can wait to put cheese on until last 10 minutes of cooking.

## Sweet Potato With Praline Topping
### (A Thanksgiving hit)

1.  Mash together: 7 to 8 cooked sweet potatoes (boil or bake), ½ cup butter, salt and pepper to taste.
2.  Spread in a 9" X 13" pan and keep warm.
3.  Simmer together for 3 minutes: ½ cup butter, 1 ½ cups brown sugar (add enough to make a soft thick paste), and ⅛ teaspoon salt. Unsweetened applesauce may be substituted for part of the butter.
4.  Add 1 ½ cups pecans to the praline mixture and spoon onto the sweet potatoes (pecans may be toasted first at 350° for 8 minutes). Serve.

# MISCELLANEOUS

## Italian Herbs

Mix well and store in bottle:
6 tablespoons oregano
2 tablespoons thyme
8 tablespoons basil
5 tablespoons marjoram
5 tablespoons savory
1 tablespoon sage
3 tablespoons rosemary

Use to season salad dressings, marinades, sauces, and meatballs.

Suggestion:
Mix 1 tablespoon herbs, 2 tablespoons salt, and ¼ teaspoon pepper and use as a rub on steaks, roasts, and fish before cooking.

## My Seasoning Salt

1 cup salt
2 teaspoons black pepper (may increase)
1 tablespoon garlic granules or powder
2 teaspoons onion granules or powder
1 tablespoon sweet paprika
1 teaspoon cayenne pepper
½ teaspoon thyme

1 teaspoon pasilla pepper powder or chili powder
½ teaspoon lemon peel granules (optional)

Mix and add to meat, soup, stews, hamburgers, salad dressings, and marinades. I triple this recipe and store in a large shaker bottle.

## Spaetzels
### (Little German dumplings)

2 eggs
1 ½ cups flour
¼ cup whole milk
2 tablespoons oil or melted butter
¼ teaspoon baking powder (optional)
dash salt and pepper

Combine all ingredients and mix well, adding more milk if too stiff. Mixture should be thick and glossy. Drop by teaspoonfuls into boiling water or soup. Or push through a colander into the soup. Simmer a few minutes.

My grandmother always put these in her chicken soup. For Lent, she would fry up onions and add the cooked, drained spaetzels to the pan and sprinkle some caraway seeds or buttered bread crumbs on top. She always served it with spiced applesauce or stewed prunes. Sometimes, she omitted the baking powder, which she said wasn't traditionally used.

Variation: Omit milk and baking powder. Use 4 eggs. Add more flour if too runny.

## Homemade Yogurt
### (Mild and thick)

This is simple and no special equipment is needed.

Heat 4 cups whole milk just to a boil or microwave (to a boil) in same bowl it will set up in.
Pour into glass or ceramic container and cool to warm temperature.
Add 2 tablespoons commercial plain or vanilla yogurt and mix well. Use a kind without gelatin.
Cover bowl with plastic wrap and then wrap entire bowl with a bath towel.
Place in warmest place in house such as top of refrigerator during colder months. I fill a large pot with hot water and place a pizza pan on top, setting the wrapped bowl on the pizza pan. Don't look at or touch it for 24 hours.
Refrigerate and save some for next batch.
Eat with jam, fruit, or use as a topping. Or use in baking and cooking instead of sour cream or buttermilk. I've also found yogurt makers in thrift stores to make 8 oz. size containers of yogurt for lunch or trips. Add sugar, vanilla, or fruit jam before pouring into containers if flavored yogurt is desired.

## Barbecue Sauce
### (for chicken, pork, and beef)

1 cup catsup (homemade)
1 to 2 tablespoons prepared mustard (or 1 to 2 teaspoons dry)
¼ cup brown sugar or molasses (or more to taste)
½ teaspoon garlic granules
¼ to ½ cup cider vinegar or fresh lemon juice (depending on desired tartness)
salt and pepper to taste
cayenne pepper to taste (optional)

When meat is almost done on the grill, baste with sauce on both sides. Using the oven, sauce may be basted midway through cooking time. Drain any accumulated drippings first, then spoon sauce onto meat.

Variation:
3 cups pureed tomatoes may be simmered until thickened (about 12 minutes) and used in place of catsup. Extra spices or sugar may be added. To avoid cooking the tomatoes and freeing glutamate, tomatoes may be cut in half and squeezed to remove liquid before they are pureed.

## Beef Jerky

Semi-freeze 1 lb. very lean round or flank steak. Trim away any fat and slice into 3/8" to 1/4" strips (cut with grain, jerky will be chewy; cut across grain, it will break more easily).

Mix the following.

2 tablespoons water
½ teaspoon dry mustard or 1 teaspoon regular mustard
2 tablespoons tomato puree (optional)
2 tablespoons fresh lemon or lime juice (may decrease)
¼ teaspoon Chinese Fivespice (optional)
¼ to ½ teaspoon black pepper
⅛ to ¼ teaspoon cayenne pepper (may be increased or omitted)
¼ to ½ teaspoon garlic powder
¼ to ½ teaspoon onion powder
2 tablespoons sea salt

2 tablespoons brown or white sugar (may vary amount)

With hands, mix and coat all sides of meat. Marinate for 1 hour in refrigerator.

Follow the directions for the dehydrator. Do not overlap meat slices on trays. Turn meat at least once (145° F for 8 hours).

## Uses for Old Dry Bread

When bread begins to stale, cut each slice into fourths and put in a pan, then air dry or toast until dry in a warm oven. Serve warm to spread with peanut butter sweetened with a little honey, jam, or any other spreads. Also, may be soaked over night in egg and milk mixture and fried up as french toast the next day. Or break old bread into cubes and after they are dry, bag up in zipper bags to use later for stuffing, bread pudding, and as breading. To make breading, process until fine or mash in plastic bag with rolling pin.

## Leftovers

Our family size is dwindling, but instead of cooking smaller dinners, we continue to cook for six, packaging leftovers for next day snacking or for freezing. This saves time and energy. I often have a baking day and make bread, rolls, and cookies to freeze. I also freeze quart size bags of cookie dough labeled with the name, date, and baking directions. Just defrost to use. I do the same with spaghetti sauce, chili, soups, and stews. It takes the same amount of energy to cook a huge pot of soup as it does to cook a small one. On busy days, it's convenient to be able to grab a bottle or bag of chili from the freezer.

## Pesto

Place enough fresh basil leaves in cup of processor to fill without packing too hard. Add 3 to 4 cloves of garlic, ⅓ cup olive oil, ½ cup nuts, ½ teaspoon salt (or less), dash pepper, and pepper flakes. Puree until smooth. If not thick enough, add more nuts. If too thick, add more oil.

Place tablespoon size dollops on a cookie sheet lined with plastic wrap and freeze. When firm, place in quart size freezer bags and label. Use to toss into hot pasta as an addition to sour cream for dips and as a tasty spread on sandwiches or to flavor dressings.

Suggested nuts: walnuts, almonds, pecans, or pine nuts.

A little parmesan cheese can be added to pesto if desired, unless you cannot tolerate aged cheese. We tolerate foreign parmesian cheese better than domestic, but use it sparingly.

Remember, tomatoes can be frozen whole and stored in freezer bags. As they defrost, the skin will slip off quite easily.

## Homemade Egg Noodles

Knead together until smooth: 2 cups white flour or 1½ cups whole wheat flour or 1 cup white flour plus ¾ cup whole wheat flour, 2 eggs, ¾ cup water, ½ teaspoon salt. Roll out until desired thickness on flour cloth. Let almost dry on towel, then cut in strips with pizza cutter. Let dry thoroughly. Freeze in bags or boil until tender. May use pasta machine first on #6, then #4, then #2.

Recommended Cook Books

There are so many wonderful new ones out there. But these are just a few of my favorites.

Moosewood Cookbook by Molly Katzen. Any of the Moosewood cookbooks are excellent. A new low fat one has been published. You will hardly realize you are eating vegetarian. Easy to adapt recipes. TEN SPEED Press, PO Box 7123, Berkeley, CA 94707.

The Fannie Farmer Cookbook. Published since 1896, this is a "must have" for all the cooking basics. The older versions use fewer processed products, so watch for copies in flea markets and antique stores.

Betty Crocker's Cookbook. Old or new, it is an American standard. Many adaptable recipes are reliable and good.

For Bees and Me and other fun cookbook/idea books from Gooseberry Patch. Delightful reading and innovative ideas for meals, entertaining, gardening crafts, and gift giving. Gooseberry Patch, 27 N. Union St., PO Box 190, Dept GAR, Delaware, Ohio 43015, (800) 854-6673.

Make-A-Mix Cookery by Karina Eliason, Nevada Harward, and Madeline Westover. One of several Make-A-Mix cookbooks. Excellent recipes for busy people. Just avoid dry milk in some mixes and reconstitute with milk instead of water. Includes salad dressing mixes (More Make-A-Mix Cookery), and bagel mixes.

Sunset Cookbooks by the editors of Sunset Books and Sunset Magazine, Jane Publishing Co., Menlo Park, California. A huge variety of books and recipes, offering recipes for holidays, specialty cooking, and dishes from various regions and countries.

Set for Life by Jane P. Merrill and Karen M. Sanderland, Sunrise Publishers. Low cholesterol, fat, sugar, and sodium recipes that are terrific. We make many of their recipes often, adapting some to avoid MSG with easy substitutes. The bread, rolls, and muffins chapter is my favorite. Directions are excellent. I make their muffin recipes up and bake in the huge muffin tins, freeze, and have handy for a quick snack or breakfast.

I am always scanning book stores, garage sales, and antique stores for good cookbooks. The library is filled with cookbooks and magazines, too.

## Our Wish List

1. That all factory made flavor enhancers, along with a lot of other lab-created additives, be outlawed!
2. That people take more charge of their own health with positive life style changes.
3. That an institute for the study of MSG and other excitotoxins be established with unbiased, dedicated doctors and researchers running it, or that a university decides to do research on MSG.
4. That clinics be created where people, parents, and children with possible MSG sensitivity can go to be properly tested for it and be educated about neurotoxin avoidance.
5. That doctors and other care givers become knowledgeable about MSG and other neurotoxic sensitivity and consider it when making a diagnosis.
6. That dietitians, nurses, staff at hospitals, juvenile institutes, jails, nursing homes, colleges, public schools, and even summer camps reconsider the food they are serving their charges.
7. That people in the food industry create a line of pure unadulterated whole convenience foods like grandma used to make.
8. That parents make sure that they not only provide healthy meals and snacks for their families, but that they see to it that their sons and daughters know basic cooking skills and that food doesn't just come out of a box, frozen package, or can.
9. That this book will inspire you to re-examine what you are consuming and how it may be causing you needless suffering now or in the future.
10. That you help battle the "MSG/Aspartame" myth by sharing with others what you know.

## Index of Recipes

# Index of Recipes

RECIPES . . . . . . . . . . . . . . . . . . . . . . . . . . . . . . . . . . . . . . . . . . . . . . . . . . . . 83
    SUBSTITUTIONS . . . . . . . . . . . . . . . . . . . . . . . . . . . . . . . . . . . . . . . . . 83
    COOKING AND STORING BEANS, GRAINS, AND PASTA . . . . . . . . . . . . . . . . 88
    APPETIZERS, SNACKS, AND DIPS . . . . . . . . . . . . . . . . . . . . . . . . . . . . . . . 89
        Baked Tortilla Chips . . . . . . . . . . . . . . . . . . . . . . . . . . . . . . . . . 91
        Chicken Paté . . . . . . . . . . . . . . . . . . . . . . . . . . . . . . . . . . . . . 89
        French Onion Dip for Chips and Crackers . . . . . . . . . . . . . . . . . . . . 89
        Fritters . . . . . . . . . . . . . . . . . . . . . . . . . . . . . . . . . . . . . . . . . 89
        Grilled Vegetables . . . . . . . . . . . . . . . . . . . . . . . . . . . . . . . . . . 91
        Olive Spread . . . . . . . . . . . . . . . . . . . . . . . . . . . . . . . . . . . . . 90
        Quesadillas . . . . . . . . . . . . . . . . . . . . . . . . . . . . . . . . . . . . . . 90
        Roasted Onion and Garlic Spread . . . . . . . . . . . . . . . . . . . . . . . . . 91
        Steam Buns . . . . . . . . . . . . . . . . . . . . . . . . . . . . . . . . . . . . . . 90
        Steamed Vegetables . . . . . . . . . . . . . . . . . . . . . . . . . . . . . . . . . 91
        Stuffed Baked Green Chilies . . . . . . . . . . . . . . . . . . . . . . . . . . . . 90
        Stuffed Mushrooms . . . . . . . . . . . . . . . . . . . . . . . . . . . . . . . . . 92
    BEVERAGES . . . . . . . . . . . . . . . . . . . . . . . . . . . . . . . . . . . . . . . . . . . 93
        Banana Smoothy . . . . . . . . . . . . . . . . . . . . . . . . . . . . . . . . . . . 93
        Boston Cooler . . . . . . . . . . . . . . . . . . . . . . . . . . . . . . . . . . . . 93
        Breakfast Shake . . . . . . . . . . . . . . . . . . . . . . . . . . . . . . . . . . . 93
        Chocolate Frappe . . . . . . . . . . . . . . . . . . . . . . . . . . . . . . . . . . 93
        Cooked Egg Nog for a Crowd . . . . . . . . . . . . . . . . . . . . . . . . . . . 94
        Cooked Egg Nog . . . . . . . . . . . . . . . . . . . . . . . . . . . . . . . . . . 94
        Easy Grape Juice . . . . . . . . . . . . . . . . . . . . . . . . . . . . . . . . . . 95
        Fruit Blitz . . . . . . . . . . . . . . . . . . . . . . . . . . . . . . . . . . . . . . 95
        Gazepacho . . . . . . . . . . . . . . . . . . . . . . . . . . . . . . . . . . . . . . 95
        German Switchel . . . . . . . . . . . . . . . . . . . . . . . . . . . . . . . . . . 95
        Hot Winter Punch . . . . . . . . . . . . . . . . . . . . . . . . . . . . . . . . . . 96
        Mulled Cider . . . . . . . . . . . . . . . . . . . . . . . . . . . . . . . . . . . . 96
        Orange Smoothie . . . . . . . . . . . . . . . . . . . . . . . . . . . . . . . . . . 96
        Protein Fruit Drink . . . . . . . . . . . . . . . . . . . . . . . . . . . . . . . . . 94
        Punch for a Crowd . . . . . . . . . . . . . . . . . . . . . . . . . . . . . . . . . 93
        Slush . . . . . . . . . . . . . . . . . . . . . . . . . . . . . . . . . . . . . . . . . 96
        Sun Tea . . . . . . . . . . . . . . . . . . . . . . . . . . . . . . . . . . . . . . . 96
    BREADS AND BAKED GOODS . . . . . . . . . . . . . . . . . . . . . . . . . . . . . . . 97
        50/50 Wheat Bread . . . . . . . . . . . . . . . . . . . . . . . . . . . . . . . . 104
        Barb's Best Biscuits . . . . . . . . . . . . . . . . . . . . . . . . . . . . . . . . 101
        Bran Muffins . . . . . . . . . . . . . . . . . . . . . . . . . . . . . . . . . . . . 98
        Bread for a Week . . . . . . . . . . . . . . . . . . . . . . . . . . . . . . . . . 102
        Corn Bread . . . . . . . . . . . . . . . . . . . . . . . . . . . . . . . . . . . . . 98
        Crescent Rolls . . . . . . . . . . . . . . . . . . . . . . . . . . . . . . . . . . . 99
        Date and Nut Bread . . . . . . . . . . . . . . . . . . . . . . . . . . . . . . . . 101
        Delicate Yam Biscuits . . . . . . . . . . . . . . . . . . . . . . . . . . . . . . . 104
        Favorite French Bread . . . . . . . . . . . . . . . . . . . . . . . . . . . . . . . 97
        Flour Tortillas I . . . . . . . . . . . . . . . . . . . . . . . . . . . . . . . . . . 102
        Flour Tortillas II . . . . . . . . . . . . . . . . . . . . . . . . . . . . . . . . . . 102
        Fried Scones . . . . . . . . . . . . . . . . . . . . . . . . . . . . . . . . . . . . 105
        Graham Crackers . . . . . . . . . . . . . . . . . . . . . . . . . . . . . . . . . . 105

Johnny Cake (sweet corn bread) . . . . . . . . . . . . . . . . . . . . . . . . . . . . . . . . . . . . . . . . . 98
Large Batch Muffins for Freezing  . . . . . . . . . . . . . . . . . . . . . . . . . . . . . . . . . . . . . . . 99
Multi-grain Bread with Flax Seed . . . . . . . . . . . . . . . . . . . . . . . . . . . . . . . . . . . . . . . . 97
Navajo Fried Bread . . . . . . . . . . . . . . . . . . . . . . . . . . . . . . . . . . . . . . . . . . . . . . . . . . . 103
Pita Bread . . . . . . . . . . . . . . . . . . . . . . . . . . . . . . . . . . . . . . . . . . . . . . . . . . . . . . . . . . 103
Pumpkin Bread . . . . . . . . . . . . . . . . . . . . . . . . . . . . . . . . . . . . . . . . . . . . . . . . . . . . . . 101
Rye Bread . . . . . . . . . . . . . . . . . . . . . . . . . . . . . . . . . . . . . . . . . . . . . . . . . . . . . . . . . . 103
Soft Whole Wheat Rolls . . . . . . . . . . . . . . . . . . . . . . . . . . . . . . . . . . . . . . . . . . . . . . . 99
Sticky Pecan Rolls and Cinnamon Rolls . . . . . . . . . . . . . . . . . . . . . . . . . . . . . . . . . . 100
Wheat Skinnies (Crackers) . . . . . . . . . . . . . . . . . . . . . . . . . . . . . . . . . . . . . . . . . . . . . 104
Wheat Wafers . . . . . . . . . . . . . . . . . . . . . . . . . . . . . . . . . . . . . . . . . . . . . . . . . . . . . . . 104
Whole Wheat Bread . . . . . . . . . . . . . . . . . . . . . . . . . . . . . . . . . . . . . . . . . . . . . . . . . . 100
Yeast Free Bread . . . . . . . . . . . . . . . . . . . . . . . . . . . . . . . . . . . . . . . . . . . . . . . . . . . . 100
BREAKFAST . . . . . . . . . . . . . . . . . . . . . . . . . . . . . . . . . . . . . . . . . . . . . . . . . . . . . . . . . 106
Apple Granola . . . . . . . . . . . . . . . . . . . . . . . . . . . . . . . . . . . . . . . . . . . . . . . . . . . . . . 109
Christmas Granola . . . . . . . . . . . . . . . . . . . . . . . . . . . . . . . . . . . . . . . . . . . . . . . . . . . 109
Cooked Wheat Berries . . . . . . . . . . . . . . . . . . . . . . . . . . . . . . . . . . . . . . . . . . . . . . . . 110
Cornmeal Pancakes . . . . . . . . . . . . . . . . . . . . . . . . . . . . . . . . . . . . . . . . . . . . . . . . . . 106
Easy Hash Browned Potatoes and Eggs . . . . . . . . . . . . . . . . . . . . . . . . . . . . . . . . . . 108
Feather Light Flapjacks . . . . . . . . . . . . . . . . . . . . . . . . . . . . . . . . . . . . . . . . . . . . . . . 106
Fluffy Wheat Pancakes . . . . . . . . . . . . . . . . . . . . . . . . . . . . . . . . . . . . . . . . . . . . . . . 106
Fried Cornmeal Mush . . . . . . . . . . . . . . . . . . . . . . . . . . . . . . . . . . . . . . . . . . . . . . . . 110
German Apple Pancakes . . . . . . . . . . . . . . . . . . . . . . . . . . . . . . . . . . . . . . . . . . . . . . 107
Harvest Hash . . . . . . . . . . . . . . . . . . . . . . . . . . . . . . . . . . . . . . . . . . . . . . . . . . . . . . . 108
Apples and Sausage (Krista's) . . . . . . . . . . . . . . . . . . . . . . . . . . . . . . . . . . . . . . . . . . 108
Oatmeal Pancakes . . . . . . . . . . . . . . . . . . . . . . . . . . . . . . . . . . . . . . . . . . . . . . . . . . . 107
Pancakes/Waffles (Ginnie's) . . . . . . . . . . . . . . . . . . . . . . . . . . . . . . . . . . . . . . . . . . . 107
Swiss Muesli . . . . . . . . . . . . . . . . . . . . . . . . . . . . . . . . . . . . . . . . . . . . . . . . . . . . . . . . 109
Wheat Pancakes . . . . . . . . . . . . . . . . . . . . . . . . . . . . . . . . . . . . . . . . . . . . . . . . . . . . . 108
CONDIMENTS, SAUCES, AND MARINADES . . . . . . . . . . . . . . . . . . . . . . . . . . . . 111
Basic Cream or White Sauce . . . . . . . . . . . . . . . . . . . . . . . . . . . . . . . . . . . . . . . . . . . 116
Caribbean Salsa . . . . . . . . . . . . . . . . . . . . . . . . . . . . . . . . . . . . . . . . . . . . . . . . . . . . . 111
Catsup (Deb's) . . . . . . . . . . . . . . . . . . . . . . . . . . . . . . . . . . . . . . . . . . . . . . . . . . . . . . 114
Chinese Mustard Sauce . . . . . . . . . . . . . . . . . . . . . . . . . . . . . . . . . . . . . . . . . . . . . . . 115
Cranberry Sauce . . . . . . . . . . . . . . . . . . . . . . . . . . . . . . . . . . . . . . . . . . . . . . . . . . . . . 115
Fresh Cranberry Orange sauce for Poultry . . . . . . . . . . . . . . . . . . . . . . . . . . . . . . . . 115
Guacamole II . . . . . . . . . . . . . . . . . . . . . . . . . . . . . . . . . . . . . . . . . . . . . . . . . . . . . . . 111
Guacamole I . . . . . . . . . . . . . . . . . . . . . . . . . . . . . . . . . . . . . . . . . . . . . . . . . . . . . . . . 111
Herbal Vinegars . . . . . . . . . . . . . . . . . . . . . . . . . . . . . . . . . . . . . . . . . . . . . . . . . . . . . 113
Homemade Sweet Mustard . . . . . . . . . . . . . . . . . . . . . . . . . . . . . . . . . . . . . . . . . . . . 114
Instand No-cook Catsup . . . . . . . . . . . . . . . . . . . . . . . . . . . . . . . . . . . . . . . . . . . . . . 114
Instant White Sauce Base . . . . . . . . . . . . . . . . . . . . . . . . . . . . . . . . . . . . . . . . . . . . . 116
Marinade for Chicken, Pork, or Fish . . . . . . . . . . . . . . . . . . . . . . . . . . . . . . . . . . . . 115
Mexican Red Sauce . . . . . . . . . . . . . . . . . . . . . . . . . . . . . . . . . . . . . . . . . . . . . . . . . . 112
Onion Gravy . . . . . . . . . . . . . . . . . . . . . . . . . . . . . . . . . . . . . . . . . . . . . . . . . . . . . . . . 116
Oriental Marinade . . . . . . . . . . . . . . . . . . . . . . . . . . . . . . . . . . . . . . . . . . . . . . . . . . . 112
Oriental Orange Sauce . . . . . . . . . . . . . . . . . . . . . . . . . . . . . . . . . . . . . . . . . . . . . . . . 112
Salsa . . . . . . . . . . . . . . . . . . . . . . . . . . . . . . . . . . . . . . . . . . . . . . . . . . . . . . . . . . . . . . . 112
Sweet and Sour Sauce . . . . . . . . . . . . . . . . . . . . . . . . . . . . . . . . . . . . . . . . . . . . . . . . 113
Uncooked Homemade Mustard . . . . . . . . . . . . . . . . . . . . . . . . . . . . . . . . . . . . . . . . 114
Vegetarian Gravy . . . . . . . . . . . . . . . . . . . . . . . . . . . . . . . . . . . . . . . . . . . . . . . . . . . . 116

DESSERTS ............................................................................ 117
    Almond Puff Pastry ............................................................ 128
    Apple Cake .................................................................... 117
    Apple Zucchini Pie ............................................................ 122
    Applesauce Spice Cake ........................................................ 117
    Baked Peaches or Peach Tart .................................................. 124
    Baked Peaches Over Ice Cream ................................................ 124
    Berry Crisp ................................................................... 124
    Best Banana Bread ............................................................ 118
    Best Brownies ................................................................. 129
    Brown Sugar Frosting ......................................................... 126
    Brown Sugar Pudding Dessert ................................................. 126
    Carrot Cake ................................................................... 118
    Chess Pie ..................................................................... 122
    "Chew" Bread (Grandma Graesser's) ........................................ 131
    Chewy Ginger Cookies ........................................................ 131
    Chocolate Cake ............................................................... 122
    Chocolate Creme Pudding ..................................................... 126
    Chocolate Fudge Dessert ...................................................... 119
    Chocolate Magic Cake ........................................................ 121
    Chocolate Substitutes ......................................................... 117
    Christmas Apple, Orange, Rum, Bread Pudding .............................. 126
    Corn Starch Pudding .......................................................... 127
    Crepe Dessert ................................................................. 129
    Crepes (Grandma Susan Gifford's) ........................................... 129
    Decadent Chocolate Sandwich Cookies ....................................... 130
    Delicious Pumpkin Bars ....................................................... 118
    European Clotted Cream ...................................................... 127
    Fast Fruit Pies ................................................................ 123
    Fast Strawberry Mousse ....................................................... 128
    Fast Yellow Cake ............................................................. 119
    Fruit Bars .................................................................... 130
    Fruit Cobbler ................................................................. 125
    Fruit Crunch Dessert ......................................................... 125
    Fudge Pie .................................................................... 123
    Granny's Sugar Cookies ...................................................... 131
    Great Grandma's Sponge Cake ............................................... 120
    "Hummingbird Grandpa" Cake .............................................. 120
    Instant Pumpkin Pie .......................................................... 123
    Italian Lemon Ice ............................................................. 134
    Lemon Meringue Pie .......................................................... 121
    Lemon Poppy Seed Cake ...................................................... 121
    Lemon Squares ............................................................... 132
    "Maple" Frosting (Grandma Graesser's) ..................................... 128
    Mexican Rice Pudding ........................................................ 127
    Microwave Jam Bars .......................................................... 134
    Mock Whipped Cream Frosting ............................................... 128
    Non-fat Meringues ............................................................ 135
    Oatmeal Cookies .............................................................. 132
    Oatmeal Honey Cookies ....................................................... 132
    Old Fashioned Oatmeal Refrigerator Cookies ................................ 133

Old Fashioned Soft Sugar Cookies . . . . . . . . . . . . . . . . . . . . . . . . . . . . . . . . . . . . . . . . . 134
Pasta Fruit Salad . . . . . . . . . . . . . . . . . . . . . . . . . . . . . . . . . . . . . . . . . . . . . . . . . . . . . . 135
Peanut Butter Cookies . . . . . . . . . . . . . . . . . . . . . . . . . . . . . . . . . . . . . . . . . . . . . . . . . . 133
Pecan Pie . . . . . . . . . . . . . . . . . . . . . . . . . . . . . . . . . . . . . . . . . . . . . . . . . . . . . . . . . . . . 123
Quick Fruit Rice Pudding . . . . . . . . . . . . . . . . . . . . . . . . . . . . . . . . . . . . . . . . . . . . . . . . 127
Raisin or Pecan Tarts . . . . . . . . . . . . . . . . . . . . . . . . . . . . . . . . . . . . . . . . . . . . . . . . . . . 133
Rhubarb Custard Pie . . . . . . . . . . . . . . . . . . . . . . . . . . . . . . . . . . . . . . . . . . . . . . . . . . . 124
Rhubarb Crisp . . . . . . . . . . . . . . . . . . . . . . . . . . . . . . . . . . . . . . . . . . . . . . . . . . . . . . . . 125
Roman Apple Cake (Grandma Graesser's) . . . . . . . . . . . . . . . . . . . . . . . . . . . . . . . . . . 119
Stove Top Quickie Cookies . . . . . . . . . . . . . . . . . . . . . . . . . . . . . . . . . . . . . . . . . . . . . . 133

DESSERT SAUCES AND SYRUPS . . . . . . . . . . . . . . . . . . . . . . . . . . . . . . . . . . . . . . . . . . . . 136
Chocolate Sauce . . . . . . . . . . . . . . . . . . . . . . . . . . . . . . . . . . . . . . . . . . . . . . . . . . . . . . 136
Chocolate Syrup . . . . . . . . . . . . . . . . . . . . . . . . . . . . . . . . . . . . . . . . . . . . . . . . . . . . . . 136
French Cream Sauce . . . . . . . . . . . . . . . . . . . . . . . . . . . . . . . . . . . . . . . . . . . . . . . . . . . 136
Gram's Nutmeg Sauce . . . . . . . . . . . . . . . . . . . . . . . . . . . . . . . . . . . . . . . . . . . . . . . . . 136
Hot Fudge Sauce . . . . . . . . . . . . . . . . . . . . . . . . . . . . . . . . . . . . . . . . . . . . . . . . . . . . . . 137
Pancake Syrup . . . . . . . . . . . . . . . . . . . . . . . . . . . . . . . . . . . . . . . . . . . . . . . . . . . . . . . 137

DRESSINGS . . . . . . . . . . . . . . . . . . . . . . . . . . . . . . . . . . . . . . . . . . . . . . . . . . . . . . . . . . . . 138
Banana Dressing for Fruit Salad . . . . . . . . . . . . . . . . . . . . . . . . . . . . . . . . . . . . . . . . . . 139
Basic Vinaigrette . . . . . . . . . . . . . . . . . . . . . . . . . . . . . . . . . . . . . . . . . . . . . . . . . . . . . . 143
Boiled Salad Dressing . . . . . . . . . . . . . . . . . . . . . . . . . . . . . . . . . . . . . . . . . . . . . . . . . . 138
Citrus Dressings . . . . . . . . . . . . . . . . . . . . . . . . . . . . . . . . . . . . . . . . . . . . . . . . . . . . . . . 139
Cooked Mayonnaise . . . . . . . . . . . . . . . . . . . . . . . . . . . . . . . . . . . . . . . . . . . . . . . . . . . 138
Cooked Salad Dressing . . . . . . . . . . . . . . . . . . . . . . . . . . . . . . . . . . . . . . . . . . . . . . . . . 139
Creamy Vinaigrette . . . . . . . . . . . . . . . . . . . . . . . . . . . . . . . . . . . . . . . . . . . . . . . . . . . . 140
Cucumber Salad Dressing . . . . . . . . . . . . . . . . . . . . . . . . . . . . . . . . . . . . . . . . . . . . . . . 140
Dill Salad Dressing . . . . . . . . . . . . . . . . . . . . . . . . . . . . . . . . . . . . . . . . . . . . . . . . . . . . 141
Favorite Dressing (Craig's) . . . . . . . . . . . . . . . . . . . . . . . . . . . . . . . . . . . . . . . . . . . . . . 140
French Dressing I . . . . . . . . . . . . . . . . . . . . . . . . . . . . . . . . . . . . . . . . . . . . . . . . . . . . . . 141
French Dressing II . . . . . . . . . . . . . . . . . . . . . . . . . . . . . . . . . . . . . . . . . . . . . . . . . . . . . 141
French Vinaigrette . . . . . . . . . . . . . . . . . . . . . . . . . . . . . . . . . . . . . . . . . . . . . . . . . . . . . 141
Grandma's Celery Seed Dressing . . . . . . . . . . . . . . . . . . . . . . . . . . . . . . . . . . . . . . . . . 141
Herb Vinaigrette . . . . . . . . . . . . . . . . . . . . . . . . . . . . . . . . . . . . . . . . . . . . . . . . . . . . . . 143
Mustard Cream Dressing . . . . . . . . . . . . . . . . . . . . . . . . . . . . . . . . . . . . . . . . . . . . . . . . 142
My Green Goddess Dressing . . . . . . . . . . . . . . . . . . . . . . . . . . . . . . . . . . . . . . . . . . . . . 142
Old Fashioned Salad Dressing . . . . . . . . . . . . . . . . . . . . . . . . . . . . . . . . . . . . . . . . . . . . 142
Onion Vinaigrette . . . . . . . . . . . . . . . . . . . . . . . . . . . . . . . . . . . . . . . . . . . . . . . . . . . . . 143
Pioneer Mayonnaise . . . . . . . . . . . . . . . . . . . . . . . . . . . . . . . . . . . . . . . . . . . . . . . . . . . 138
Poppy Seed Dressing . . . . . . . . . . . . . . . . . . . . . . . . . . . . . . . . . . . . . . . . . . . . . . . . . . 142
Red Pepper Vinaigrette . . . . . . . . . . . . . . . . . . . . . . . . . . . . . . . . . . . . . . . . . . . . . . . . . 143
Strawberry Vinegar Dressing . . . . . . . . . . . . . . . . . . . . . . . . . . . . . . . . . . . . . . . . . . . . 139

FREEZER OR CANNED GOODS . . . . . . . . . . . . . . . . . . . . . . . . . . . . . . . . . . . . . . . . . . . . . 144
Canned Fruit Cocktail . . . . . . . . . . . . . . . . . . . . . . . . . . . . . . . . . . . . . . . . . . . . . . . . . . 145
Crockpot or Oven Apple Butter . . . . . . . . . . . . . . . . . . . . . . . . . . . . . . . . . . . . . . . . . . 145
Dill Pickles . . . . . . . . . . . . . . . . . . . . . . . . . . . . . . . . . . . . . . . . . . . . . . . . . . . . . . . . . . 145
End of Summer Garden Relish . . . . . . . . . . . . . . . . . . . . . . . . . . . . . . . . . . . . . . . . . . . 146
Flash Frozen Fruit . . . . . . . . . . . . . . . . . . . . . . . . . . . . . . . . . . . . . . . . . . . . . . . . . . . . . 145
Freezer Tomato Sauce . . . . . . . . . . . . . . . . . . . . . . . . . . . . . . . . . . . . . . . . . . . . . . . . . 146
Freezing cooked ground beef . . . . . . . . . . . . . . . . . . . . . . . . . . . . . . . . . . . . . . . . . . . . 148
Freezing fresh ground beef . . . . . . . . . . . . . . . . . . . . . . . . . . . . . . . . . . . . . . . . . . . . . . 148
General Directions for Cooked No Pectin Jam . . . . . . . . . . . . . . . . . . . . . . . . . . . . . . . 144

Grape Jam .................................................. 144
Homemade Tomato Soup Base ............................. 147
No Cook, No Pectin Freezer Jam .......................... 144
Rhubarb Relish ........................................... 144
Spaghetti Sauce for Canning or Freezing .................. 147
Sweet Relish (Nada's) .................................... 147

MAIN DISHES .................................................. 149
Authentic Chili Relleno .................................. 150
Baked Beans .............................................. 161
Best Bean Burritos ....................................... 149
Brazilian Rice and Beans (Trevor's) ...................... 167
Busy Day Casserole ....................................... 153
Busy Day Supper .......................................... 154
Calzones ................................................. 149
Chicago Pizza ............................................ 150
Chicken and Green Chili Burritos ......................... 154
Chicken and Red Pepper With Pasta ........................ 163
Chicken Enchilada Casserole .............................. 154
Chicken Tamale Casserole ................................. 155
Chicken Tetrazzini (Chelsea's) ........................... 155
Chili Relleno Casserole I ................................ 150
Chili Relleno Casserole II ............................... 162
Chuckwagon Beans (Braeden's) ............................. 161
Cowboy Bake (Tanner's) ................................... 162
Creamy Mexicali Bake ..................................... 158
Creole Casserole ......................................... 155
Easy Fruited Chicken Curry ............................... 162
Egg Burritos ............................................. 151
Eggplant Tomato Sauce with Pasta ......................... 163
Fast Enchilada Casserole ................................. 156
Fast Fried Rice .......................................... 163
Fast Refried Bean Dinner ................................. 164
Fresh Pasta Sauce ........................................ 165
Garden Chicken (Brandon's) ............................... 156
Garden Vegetable Omelet .................................. 169
German Pork Casserole .................................... 156
Gourmet Baked Potatoes ................................... 161
Hamburger and Vegetable Meat Balls ....................... 166
Haystacks ................................................ 164
Hot Tamale Pie (Rachel's) ................................ 157
Hungarian Cabbage and Noodles ............................ 164
Hurry Up Hash (Beef or Chicken) .......................... 164
Inca Rice Casserole ...................................... 157
Japanese Pork and Noodles ................................ 166
Lentil Roast ............................................. 166
Macaroni and Cheese ...................................... 160
Meatless Stuffed Peppers ................................. 167
Multigrain Roast ......................................... 168
Mushroom and Rice Patties ................................ 167
No Meat Chili ............................................ 168
"Oyster"-Style Beef and Noodles .......................... 169

Pasties . . . . . . . . . . . . . . . . . . . . . . . . . . . . . . . . . . . . . . . . . . . . . . 151
Polenta Tuscany . . . . . . . . . . . . . . . . . . . . . . . . . . . . . . . . . . . . . . . 169
Quick Quiche (Jackie's) . . . . . . . . . . . . . . . . . . . . . . . . . . . . . . . . . . 151
Quick Quiche II . . . . . . . . . . . . . . . . . . . . . . . . . . . . . . . . . . . . . . . . 152
Quinoa and Beef Stuffed Peppers . . . . . . . . . . . . . . . . . . . . . . . . . . 158
Sicilian Style Spaghetti Sauce . . . . . . . . . . . . . . . . . . . . . . . . . . . . . 165
Spaghetti in Garlic and Herb Oil . . . . . . . . . . . . . . . . . . . . . . . . . . . 160
Speedy Chicken Rice Casserole (Jacob's) . . . . . . . . . . . . . . . . . . . . 159
Speedy Tomato Pasta Bake . . . . . . . . . . . . . . . . . . . . . . . . . . . . . . 159
Speedy Burritos . . . . . . . . . . . . . . . . . . . . . . . . . . . . . . . . . . . . . . . 152
Spicy Mexican Casserole . . . . . . . . . . . . . . . . . . . . . . . . . . . . . . . . 159
Swiss Chard Casserole . . . . . . . . . . . . . . . . . . . . . . . . . . . . . . . . . . 152
Tamale Pie (Shelli's Favorite) . . . . . . . . . . . . . . . . . . . . . . . . . . . . 153
Tostados . . . . . . . . . . . . . . . . . . . . . . . . . . . . . . . . . . . . . . . . . . . . 153
Uncooked Pasta Sauce II . . . . . . . . . . . . . . . . . . . . . . . . . . . . . . . . 165
Vegetable and Grain Roll-ups . . . . . . . . . . . . . . . . . . . . . . . . . . . . 170
Vegetarian Bean Croquettes . . . . . . . . . . . . . . . . . . . . . . . . . . . . . 170
Veggie Egg Foo Yung . . . . . . . . . . . . . . . . . . . . . . . . . . . . . . . . . . 152
Veggie Pizzas . . . . . . . . . . . . . . . . . . . . . . . . . . . . . . . . . . . . . . . . 153
MEATS, POULTRY, AND SEAFOOD . . . . . . . . . . . . . . . . . . . . . . . . . . 171
Apricot Glazed Chicken . . . . . . . . . . . . . . . . . . . . . . . . . . . . . . . . . 171
Baked Crumb Top Fish . . . . . . . . . . . . . . . . . . . . . . . . . . . . . . . . . 177
Barbecued Pork Chops . . . . . . . . . . . . . . . . . . . . . . . . . . . . . . . . . 180
Braised Pork Chops with Pears (Krista's) . . . . . . . . . . . . . . . . . . . . 180
Buffalo Wings . . . . . . . . . . . . . . . . . . . . . . . . . . . . . . . . . . . . . . . . 171
Chicken and Chile Verde Casserole . . . . . . . . . . . . . . . . . . . . . . . . 172
Chicken Fingers . . . . . . . . . . . . . . . . . . . . . . . . . . . . . . . . . . . . . . 173
Chicken in Mushroom Gravy . . . . . . . . . . . . . . . . . . . . . . . . . . . . . 174
Chicken in Plum Sauce . . . . . . . . . . . . . . . . . . . . . . . . . . . . . . . . . 173
Chicken Paprika . . . . . . . . . . . . . . . . . . . . . . . . . . . . . . . . . . . . . . 172
Chicken Parmesan (Kristi's) . . . . . . . . . . . . . . . . . . . . . . . . . . . . . 173
Chicken With Chinese Plum Sauce . . . . . . . . . . . . . . . . . . . . . . . . 173
Country Sausage . . . . . . . . . . . . . . . . . . . . . . . . . . . . . . . . . . . . . 180
Crab or Salmon Cakes . . . . . . . . . . . . . . . . . . . . . . . . . . . . . . . . . 178
Crackly Roast Chicken . . . . . . . . . . . . . . . . . . . . . . . . . . . . . . . . . 177
Crispy Baked Chicken . . . . . . . . . . . . . . . . . . . . . . . . . . . . . . . . . 171
Crispy Honey Mustard Baked Chicken . . . . . . . . . . . . . . . . . . . . . 174
Garden Chicken . . . . . . . . . . . . . . . . . . . . . . . . . . . . . . . . . . . . . . 175
Ground Beef Patties . . . . . . . . . . . . . . . . . . . . . . . . . . . . . . . . . . . 183
Herb Fish Bake . . . . . . . . . . . . . . . . . . . . . . . . . . . . . . . . . . . . . . 178
Italian Sausage . . . . . . . . . . . . . . . . . . . . . . . . . . . . . . . . . . . . . . 181
Italian Sausage II . . . . . . . . . . . . . . . . . . . . . . . . . . . . . . . . . . . . . 181
Jamaican Chicken Wings . . . . . . . . . . . . . . . . . . . . . . . . . . . . . . . 174
Kung Pow Chicken (Kristi's) . . . . . . . . . . . . . . . . . . . . . . . . . . . . . 176
Lamb Chops . . . . . . . . . . . . . . . . . . . . . . . . . . . . . . . . . . . . . . . . 184
Lemon Chicken, Oriental Style . . . . . . . . . . . . . . . . . . . . . . . . . . . 175
Mexi-Meatloaf . . . . . . . . . . . . . . . . . . . . . . . . . . . . . . . . . . . . . . 184
Mexican Burrito Beef Filling . . . . . . . . . . . . . . . . . . . . . . . . . . . . . 182
Mom's Meatloaf . . . . . . . . . . . . . . . . . . . . . . . . . . . . . . . . . . . . . 183
Mom's Swiss Steak . . . . . . . . . . . . . . . . . . . . . . . . . . . . . . . . . . . 184
New York Style Marinated Chicken . . . . . . . . . . . . . . . . . . . . . . . . 176

Oven Baked Fish . . . . . . . . . . . . . . . . . . . . . . . . . . . . . . . . . . . . . . . . . . . . . . . . . . 178
Oven Fried Chicken . . . . . . . . . . . . . . . . . . . . . . . . . . . . . . . . . . . . . . . . . . . . . . . . 176
Peachy Chicken . . . . . . . . . . . . . . . . . . . . . . . . . . . . . . . . . . . . . . . . . . . . . . . . . . . . 177
Perfect Blackened Salmon . . . . . . . . . . . . . . . . . . . . . . . . . . . . . . . . . . . . . . . . . . . 178
Polish Sausage . . . . . . . . . . . . . . . . . . . . . . . . . . . . . . . . . . . . . . . . . . . . . . . . . . . . 181
Pork Chili Verde . . . . . . . . . . . . . . . . . . . . . . . . . . . . . . . . . . . . . . . . . . . . . . . . . . . 182
Pork Chops and Gravy . . . . . . . . . . . . . . . . . . . . . . . . . . . . . . . . . . . . . . . . . . . . . . 182
Salmon Patties . . . . . . . . . . . . . . . . . . . . . . . . . . . . . . . . . . . . . . . . . . . . . . . . . . . . 179
Speedy Shrimp Creole . . . . . . . . . . . . . . . . . . . . . . . . . . . . . . . . . . . . . . . . . . . . . . 179
Spinach Stuffed Sole . . . . . . . . . . . . . . . . . . . . . . . . . . . . . . . . . . . . . . . . . . . . . . . 179

MIXES . . : . . . . . . . . . . . . . . . . . . . . . . . . . . . . . . . . . . . . . . . . . . . . . . . . . . . . . . . . 185
Biscuit Mix . . . . . . . . . . . . . . . . . . . . . . . . . . . . . . . . . . . . . . . . . . . . . . . . . . . . . . 185
Cocoa Mix . . . . . . . . . . . . . . . . . . . . . . . . . . . . . . . . . . . . . . . . . . . . . . . . . . . . . . . 185
Homemade Baking Powder . . . . . . . . . . . . . . . . . . . . . . . . . . . . . . . . . . . . . . . . . 186
Pancake Mix . . . . . . . . . . . . . . . . . . . . . . . . . . . . . . . . . . . . . . . . . . . . . . . . . . . . . 185
Pie Crust Mix (Ginnie's) . . . . . . . . . . . . . . . . . . . . . . . . . . . . . . . . . . . . . . . . . . . 185
Pudding Mix . . . . . . . . . . . . . . . . . . . . . . . . . . . . . . . . . . . . . . . . . . . . . . . . . . . . . 185
Shake It and Bake It . . . . . . . . . . . . . . . . . . . . . . . . . . . . . . . . . . . . . . . . . . . . . . . 186
Vanilla Pudding . . . . . . . . . . . . . . . . . . . . . . . . . . . . . . . . . . . . . . . . . . . . . . . . . . 186

SALADS . . . . . . . . . . . . . . . . . . . . . . . . . . . . . . . . . . . . . . . . . . . . . . . . . . . . . . . . . 187
Barley Salad . . . . . . . . . . . . . . . . . . . . . . . . . . . . . . . . . . . . . . . . . . . . . . . . . . . . . 187
Chicken Salad . . . . . . . . . . . . . . . . . . . . . . . . . . . . . . . . . . . . . . . . . . . . . . . . . . . . 188
Chicken Salad II . . . . . . . . . . . . . . . . . . . . . . . . . . . . . . . . . . . . . . . . . . . . . . . . . . 188
Deli Salad . . . . . . . . . . . . . . . . . . . . . . . . . . . . . . . . . . . . . . . . . . . . . . . . . . . . . . . 188
Fresh Tomato and Mozzarella Salad . . . . . . . . . . . . . . . . . . . . . . . . . . . . . . . . . . 195
Fruit Salad with Cooked Fruit Sauce . . . . . . . . . . . . . . . . . . . . . . . . . . . . . . . . . . 189
Fruit Salad with Lemon Dressing (Shelli's) . . . . . . . . . . . . . . . . . . . . . . . . . . . . . 189
Fruit Salad . . . . . . . . . . . . . . . . . . . . . . . . . . . . . . . . . . . . . . . . . . . . . . . . . . . . . . 189
Green Salad and Poppy Seed Dressing . . . . . . . . . . . . . . . . . . . . . . . . . . . . . . . . 190
Grilled Herb Chicken or Shrimp Salad . . . . . . . . . . . . . . . . . . . . . . . . . . . . . . . . 190
Honey Almond Fruit Salad . . . . . . . . . . . . . . . . . . . . . . . . . . . . . . . . . . . . . . . . . 191
Ice Box Vegetable Bean Salad . . . . . . . . . . . . . . . . . . . . . . . . . . . . . . . . . . . . . . 191
Layered Mexican Bean Salad . . . . . . . . . . . . . . . . . . . . . . . . . . . . . . . . . . . . . . . 192
Marinated Zucchini (Krista's) . . . . . . . . . . . . . . . . . . . . . . . . . . . . . . . . . . . . . . . 192
Melon Pecan Salad . . . . . . . . . . . . . . . . . . . . . . . . . . . . . . . . . . . . . . . . . . . . . . . 190
New England Salad . . . . . . . . . . . . . . . . . . . . . . . . . . . . . . . . . . . . . . . . . . . . . . . 191
Old-Fashioned Cabbage Salad . . . . . . . . . . . . . . . . . . . . . . . . . . . . . . . . . . . . . . 187
Overnight Cole Slaw . . . . . . . . . . . . . . . . . . . . . . . . . . . . . . . . . . . . . . . . . . . . . . 188
Peanut Broccoli Slaw . . . . . . . . . . . . . . . . . . . . . . . . . . . . . . . . . . . . . . . . . . . . . 193
Penne Pasta Salad . . . . . . . . . . . . . . . . . . . . . . . . . . . . . . . . . . . . . . . . . . . . . . . 193
Picnic Potato Salad . . . . . . . . . . . . . . . . . . . . . . . . . . . . . . . . . . . . . . . . . . . . . . . 194
Salad for Dinner . . . . . . . . . . . . . . . . . . . . . . . . . . . . . . . . . . . . . . . . . . . . . . . . . 193
Strawberry Spinach Salad . . . . . . . . . . . . . . . . . . . . . . . . . . . . . . . . . . . . . . . . . . 194
Summer Chicken salad (Krista's) . . . . . . . . . . . . . . . . . . . . . . . . . . . . . . . . . . . . 192
Taco Salad . . . . . . . . . . . . . . . . . . . . . . . . . . . . . . . . . . . . . . . . . . . . . . . . . . . . . . 194
Tuna Macaroni Salad . . . . . . . . . . . . . . . . . . . . . . . . . . . . . . . . . . . . . . . . . . . . . 195
Wheat Berry Salad . . . . . . . . . . . . . . . . . . . . . . . . . . . . . . . . . . . . . . . . . . . . . . . 195

SANDWICHES . . . . . . . . . . . . . . . . . . . . . . . . . . . . . . . . . . . . . . . . . . . . . . . . . . . 196
Egg Salad Sandwich Filling . . . . . . . . . . . . . . . . . . . . . . . . . . . . . . . . . . . . . . . . 196
Fish Sandwiches . . . . . . . . . . . . . . . . . . . . . . . . . . . . . . . . . . . . . . . . . . . . . . . . . 198
Grilled Cheese Sandwiches . . . . . . . . . . . . . . . . . . . . . . . . . . . . . . . . . . . . . . . . . 196

Hot Beef Sandwiches . . . . . . . . . . . . . . . . . . . . . . . . . . . . . . . . . . . 197
Meatloaf Sandwiches . . . . . . . . . . . . . . . . . . . . . . . . . . . . . . . . . . . . 198
Open Faced Hot Italian Sandwiches . . . . . . . . . . . . . . . . . . . . . . . . 197
Party Sandwiches . . . . . . . . . . . . . . . . . . . . . . . . . . . . . . . . . . . . . . 197
Pocket Bread or Flour Tortilla Fillings . . . . . . . . . . . . . . . . . . . . . . 198
Spanish Tomato Sandwich . . . . . . . . . . . . . . . . . . . . . . . . . . . . . . . 198
Vegetable Egg Sandwiches . . . . . . . . . . . . . . . . . . . . . . . . . . . . . . . 196
SOUPS . . . . . . . . . . . . . . . . . . . . . . . . . . . . . . . . . . . . . . . . . . . . . . . . . . 199
Chicken and Pumpkin Soup . . . . . . . . . . . . . . . . . . . . . . . . . . . . . 200
Chili Con Carne . . . . . . . . . . . . . . . . . . . . . . . . . . . . . . . . . . . . . . 200
French Onion Soup . . . . . . . . . . . . . . . . . . . . . . . . . . . . . . . . . . . 201
Fresh Tomato Soup . . . . . . . . . . . . . . . . . . . . . . . . . . . . . . . . . . . 204
General Meat Stock . . . . . . . . . . . . . . . . . . . . . . . . . . . . . . . . . . . 199
Ground Beef and Mushroom Stew . . . . . . . . . . . . . . . . . . . . . . . . 199
Hamburger Soup . . . . . . . . . . . . . . . . . . . . . . . . . . . . . . . . . . . . . 201
Homemade Chicken Soup . . . . . . . . . . . . . . . . . . . . . . . . . . . . . . 200
Italian Onion Soup . . . . . . . . . . . . . . . . . . . . . . . . . . . . . . . . . . . 202
Lentil or Barley Soup . . . . . . . . . . . . . . . . . . . . . . . . . . . . . . . . . 202
Mushroom Soup . . . . . . . . . . . . . . . . . . . . . . . . . . . . . . . . . . . . . 203
Potato Soup . . . . . . . . . . . . . . . . . . . . . . . . . . . . . . . . . . . . . . . . 202
Soup on a Plate . . . . . . . . . . . . . . . . . . . . . . . . . . . . . . . . . . . . . 203
Tortilla Soup . . . . . . . . . . . . . . . . . . . . . . . . . . . . . . . . . . . . . . . 203
Tortilla Soup II . . . . . . . . . . . . . . . . . . . . . . . . . . . . . . . . . . . . . . 204
TREATS AND CANDY . . . . . . . . . . . . . . . . . . . . . . . . . . . . . . . . . . . . 205
Almond Crunch Candy . . . . . . . . . . . . . . . . . . . . . . . . . . . . . . . . 205
Almond or Pecan Toffee . . . . . . . . . . . . . . . . . . . . . . . . . . . . . . . 205
Butter Cream Eggs . . . . . . . . . . . . . . . . . . . . . . . . . . . . . . . . . . . 206
Candied Nuts (Brittle) . . . . . . . . . . . . . . . . . . . . . . . . . . . . . . . . . 206
Chocolate Popcorn clusters . . . . . . . . . . . . . . . . . . . . . . . . . . . . . 206
Creamsicles . . . . . . . . . . . . . . . . . . . . . . . . . . . . . . . . . . . . . . . . 211
Date Fingers . . . . . . . . . . . . . . . . . . . . . . . . . . . . . . . . . . . . . . . . 211
Fast Fridge Fudge . . . . . . . . . . . . . . . . . . . . . . . . . . . . . . . . . . . . 207
Fast Granola Bars I . . . . . . . . . . . . . . . . . . . . . . . . . . . . . . . . . . . 207
Fast Granola Bars II . . . . . . . . . . . . . . . . . . . . . . . . . . . . . . . . . . 207
Favorite Trail Mix (Mike's) . . . . . . . . . . . . . . . . . . . . . . . . . . . . . 209
Frozen Bananas . . . . . . . . . . . . . . . . . . . . . . . . . . . . . . . . . . . . . 206
Fruit Leather . . . . . . . . . . . . . . . . . . . . . . . . . . . . . . . . . . . . . . . 206
Fruity Popsicles . . . . . . . . . . . . . . . . . . . . . . . . . . . . . . . . . . . . . 210
Granola Bars III . . . . . . . . . . . . . . . . . . . . . . . . . . . . . . . . . . . . . 207
Granola Bars IV . . . . . . . . . . . . . . . . . . . . . . . . . . . . . . . . . . . . . 208
Honey Munch Mix . . . . . . . . . . . . . . . . . . . . . . . . . . . . . . . . . . . 208
Honey Popcorn . . . . . . . . . . . . . . . . . . . . . . . . . . . . . . . . . . . . . 209
Honey Taffy . . . . . . . . . . . . . . . . . . . . . . . . . . . . . . . . . . . . . . . . 209
Mints . . . . . . . . . . . . . . . . . . . . . . . . . . . . . . . . . . . . . . . . . . . . . 209
No Fuss Caramel Corn . . . . . . . . . . . . . . . . . . . . . . . . . . . . . . . . 210
Nut Brittle . . . . . . . . . . . . . . . . . . . . . . . . . . . . . . . . . . . . . . . . . 210
Ohio Buckeye Candy . . . . . . . . . . . . . . . . . . . . . . . . . . . . . . . . . 210
Old Time Maple Candy . . . . . . . . . . . . . . . . . . . . . . . . . . . . . . . 210
Praline Covered Nuts . . . . . . . . . . . . . . . . . . . . . . . . . . . . . . . . . 211
Spiced Almonds . . . . . . . . . . . . . . . . . . . . . . . . . . . . . . . . . . . . . 211
Sweet Popcorn . . . . . . . . . . . . . . . . . . . . . . . . . . . . . . . . . . . . . . 208

Trail Mix . . . . . . . . . . . . . . . . . . . . . . . . . . . . . . . . . . . . . . . . 207
Very Old Fashioned Candy . . . . . . . . . . . . . . . . . . . . . . . . . . 211
VEGETABLES, BEANS, AND GRAINS . . . . . . . . . . . . . . . . . . . . 212
Boston Baked Beans . . . . . . . . . . . . . . . . . . . . . . . . . . . . . . 212
Citrus Herb Pilaf . . . . . . . . . . . . . . . . . . . . . . . . . . . . . . . . 212
Crispy Coated Roasted Vegetables . . . . . . . . . . . . . . . . . . . 218
French-style Green Beans . . . . . . . . . . . . . . . . . . . . . . . . . 214
Fried Squash Blossoms . . . . . . . . . . . . . . . . . . . . . . . . . . . 213
Garden Rice . . . . . . . . . . . . . . . . . . . . . . . . . . . . . . . . . . . 213
Herbed Rice . . . . . . . . . . . . . . . . . . . . . . . . . . . . . . . . . . . 214
Mashed Root Vegetables . . . . . . . . . . . . . . . . . . . . . . . . . . 214
Onion Fritters . . . . . . . . . . . . . . . . . . . . . . . . . . . . . . . . . 213
Potato Bake . . . . . . . . . . . . . . . . . . . . . . . . . . . . . . . . . . . 215
Potato Treats . . . . . . . . . . . . . . . . . . . . . . . . . . . . . . . . . . 215
Refried Beans . . . . . . . . . . . . . . . . . . . . . . . . . . . . . . . . . 216
Refried Beans and Chilpotle Peppers . . . . . . . . . . . . . . . . . 216
Roasted Onions and Potatoes . . . . . . . . . . . . . . . . . . . . . . 215
Roasted Onion Mushroom Bake . . . . . . . . . . . . . . . . . . . . 214
Roasted Summer Veggies . . . . . . . . . . . . . . . . . . . . . . . . . 216
Scalloped Potatoes (Mom's Style) . . . . . . . . . . . . . . . . . . . 217
Spicy Broccoli Saute . . . . . . . . . . . . . . . . . . . . . . . . . . . . . 217
Summer Garden Vegetable Bake . . . . . . . . . . . . . . . . . . . . 218
Sweet Potato With Praline Topping . . . . . . . . . . . . . . . . . . 219
Wheat Berry Pilaf . . . . . . . . . . . . . . . . . . . . . . . . . . . . . . . 218
Zucchini and Rice Casserole . . . . . . . . . . . . . . . . . . . . . . . 219
Zucchini Fritters . . . . . . . . . . . . . . . . . . . . . . . . . . . . . . . 213
MISCELLANEOUS . . . . . . . . . . . . . . . . . . . . . . . . . . . . . . . . . 220
Barbecue Sauce . . . . . . . . . . . . . . . . . . . . . . . . . . . . . . . . 221
Beef Jerky . . . . . . . . . . . . . . . . . . . . . . . . . . . . . . . . . . . . 221
Homemade Egg Noodles . . . . . . . . . . . . . . . . . . . . . . . . . 222
Homemade Yogurt . . . . . . . . . . . . . . . . . . . . . . . . . . . . . . 221
Italian Herbs . . . . . . . . . . . . . . . . . . . . . . . . . . . . . . . . . . 220
Leftovers . . . . . . . . . . . . . . . . . . . . . . . . . . . . . . . . . . . . . 222
Pesto . . . . . . . . . . . . . . . . . . . . . . . . . . . . . . . . . . . . . . . . 222
Seasoning Salt . . . . . . . . . . . . . . . . . . . . . . . . . . . . . . . . . 220
Spaetzels . . . . . . . . . . . . . . . . . . . . . . . . . . . . . . . . . . . . . 220
Uses for Old Dry Bread . . . . . . . . . . . . . . . . . . . . . . . . . . 222
Recommended Cook Books . . . . . . . . . . . . . . . . . . . . . . . . . . . . . 223
Our Wish List . . . . . . . . . . . . . . . . . . . . . . . . . . . . . . . . . . . . . . 224